D1784645

Research and Practice in Applied Linguistics

General Editors: **Christopher N. Candlin**, Linguistics Department, Macquarie University, Australia; **David R. Hall**, Linguistics Department, Macquarie University, Australia; **Jonathan Crichton**, Research Centre for Languages and Cultures, University of South Australia

All books in this series are written by leading researchers and teachers in Applied Linguistics, with broad international experience. They are designed for the MA or PhD student in Applied Linguistics, TESOL or similar subject areas and for the language professional keen to extend their research experience.

Titles include:

Dick Allwright and Judith Hanks
THE DEVELOPING LANGUAGE LEARNER
An Introduction to Exploratory Practice

Francesca Bargiela-Chiappini, Catherine Nickerson and Brigitte Planken
BUSINESS DISCOURSE

Christopher N. Candlin and Stephen H. Moore
EXPLORING DISCOURSE IN CONTEXT AND ACTION

David Cassels Johnson
LANGUAGE POLICY

Francesca Bargiela-Chiappini, Catherine Nickerson and Brigitte Planken
BUSINESS DISCOURSE, SECOND EDITION

Helen de Silva Joyce and Susan Feez
EXPLORING LITERACIES
Theory, Research and Practice

Alison Ferguson and Elizabeth Armstrong
RESEARCHING COMMUNICATION DISORDERS

Lynne Flowerdew
CORPORA AND LANGUAGE EDUCATION

Sandra Gollin-Kies, David R. Hall and Stephen H. Moore
LANGUAGE FOR SPECIFIC PURPOSES

Sandra Beatriz Hale
COMMUNITY INTERPRETING

Geoff Hall
LITERATURE IN LANGUAGE EDUCATION

Richard Kiely and Pauline Rea-Dickins
PROGRAM EVALUATION IN LANGUAGE EDUCATION

Marie-Noëlle Lamy and Regine Hampel
ONLINE COMMUNICATION IN LANGUAGE LEARNING AND TEACHING

Annamaria Pinter
CHILDREN LEARNING SECOND LANGUAGES

Virginia Samuda and Martin Bygate
TASKS IN SECOND LANGUAGE LEARNING

Norbert Schmitt
RESEARCHING VOCABULARY
A Vocabulary Research Manual

Helen Spencer-Oatey and Peter Franklin
INTERCULTURAL INTERACTION
A Multidisciplinary Approach to Intercultural Communication

Cyril J. Weir
LANGUAGE TESTING AND VALIDATION

Tony Wright
CLASSROOM MANAGEMENT IN LANGUAGE EDUCATION

Research and Practice in Applied Linguistics
Series Standing Order ISBN 978–1–403–91184–1 hardcover
978–1–403–91185–8 paperback
(*outside North America only*)

You can receive future titles in this series as they are published by placing a standing order. Please contact your bookseller or, in case of difficulty, write to us at the address below with your name and address, the title of the series and the ISBN quoted above.

Customer Services Department, Macmillan Distribution Ltd, Houndmills, Basingstoke, Hampshire RG21 6XS, England

---

Exploring Literacies
Theory, Research and Practice

Helen de Silva Joyce
University of New England, Australia

and

Susan Feez
University of New England, Australia

First published 2016 by
PALGRAVE MACMILLAN

Palgrave Macmillan in the UK is an imprint of Macmillan Publishers Limited, registered in England, company number 785998, of Houndmills, Basingstoke, Hampshire RG21 6XS.

Palgrave Macmillan in the US is a division of St Martin's Press LLC, 175 Fifth Avenue, New York, NY 10010.

Palgrave Macmillan is the global academic imprint of the above companies and has companies and representatives throughout the world.

Palgrave® and Macmillan® are registered trademarks in the United States, the United Kingdom, Europe and other countries.

ISBN 978-0-230-54540-3   ISBN 978-1-137-31903-6 (eBook)
DOI 10.1057/9781137319036

This book is printed on paper suitable for recycling and made from fully managed and sustained forest sources. Logging, pulping and manufacturing processes are expected to conform to the environmental regulations of the country of origin.

A catalogue record for this book is available from the British Library.

Library of Congress Cataloging-in-Publication Data
Names: De Silva Joyce, Helen. | Feez, Susan.
Title: Exploring Literacies / Helen de Silva Joyce, University of New
    England, Australia; Susan Feez, University of New England, Australia.
Description: Houndmills, Basingstoke, Hampshire; New York: Palgrave
    Macmillan, 2015. | Series: Research and practice in applied linguistics
Identifiers: LCCN 2015021828
Subjects: LCSH: Applied linguistics—Research. | BISAC: EDUCATION /
    Teaching Methods & Materials / Reading & Phonics. | LANGUAGE ARTS &
    DISCIPLINES / Literacy. | LANGUAGE ARTS & DISCIPLINES / Study & Teaching.
Classification: LCC P129 .D46 2015 | DDC 418—dc23 LC record available at
    http://lccn.loc.gov/2015021828

Typeset by MPS Limited, Chennai, India.

For Georgia and Ella
and the joy of your developing language and literacy skills

Contents

List of Figures and Tables

Figures

Tables

xiv

Preface and Acknowledgements

> Bringing up the question of learning to read and write reminds us of the comment by the primary-school teacher who remarked, 'It's lucky we're not responsible for teaching them to talk. If we were they'd never learn that either'. Nevertheless, a surprising number of people do become literate, mostly through being taught.
>
> (Halliday 2009/1978: 178)

The literacy educator or researcher preparing to undertake research into their own practice, or into literacy education more broadly, will find a vast terrain of research literature to traverse. So it was with some apprehension that we embarked on the task of adding this title on the topic of literacy to the *Research and Practice in Applied Linguistics* series. Our brief from the series editors was to present 'a concise historical and conceptual overview' of the literacy field and to identify the 'many lines of enquiry and findings, but also gaps and disagreements' in the field. We were to provide readers with 'an overall framework for further examination of how research and practice inform each other, and how practitioners can develop their own problem-based research'. Importantly, for us, we were also 'to ensure many, often, competing voices are heard' (Candlin & Hall 2011: xii.). The extent to which we have met our brief will be for you the reader to judge. Capturing every important and illuminating research and practice-based orientation to literacy and literacy education is clearly beyond the scope of one volume. Writing about literacy, to adapt Firth's famous words, is after all just turning literacy back on itself using constructs that are 'neither immanent nor transcendent' (Firth 1951, cited in Butt, 2001: 1815).

All literacy artefacts are located in a particular time and place (Barton, Hamilton & Ivanič 2000) and, likewise, this book is unavoidably a product of the time and place in which it has been written. We have necessarily drawn on our own experience as literacy educators and researchers. While our outlook is international, the reader will become aware that this snapshot of the field has been taken from our location in Australia, and from an orientation to language and literacy development and education that owes much to the 'appliable' linguistics of Professor Michael Halliday and his colleagues. From this perspective language is central to all aspects of social development across the human life span.

> In the development of the child as a social being, language has the central role. Language is the main channel through which the patterns of living are transmitted to him, through which he learns to act as a member of a 'society' – in and through the various social groups, the family, the neighbourhood, and so on – and to adopt its 'culture', its modes of thought and action, its beliefs and its values.
>
> (Halliday 1978: 9)

One valuable legacy of Halliday's language-based theory of learning in Australia has been that literacy researchers and practitioners from diverse contexts and educational sectors share ways of thinking and talking about language and literacy development. By traversing the boundaries between developmental stages, from the origins of language in infancy and early childhood, across primary and secondary school and into adult life, researchers and practitioners have been able to collaborate on studies of language and literacy development between and across contexts and sectors that are often kept apart. Numeracy, numerate practices and numeracy teaching are also important features of the social and educational contexts in which language is used. The quality of research and practice within each context and sector is the richer for insights shared across these boundaries.

Another boundary that is becoming less distinct in educational contexts is the one that differentiates speakers of standard English from speakers of other languages and dialects. An educational linguistics makes it possible to describe in principled ways the differences between standard English and other dialects, and between English and other languages. These descriptions can be used to map well-targeted language and literacy learning pathways that start with learners' current levels of language and literacy before leading them towards their language learning goals. All language learners are striving to expand their use of language to achieve personal, community, study and/or vocational goals that are important to them. Whether students are identified as learners of English as a second or foreign language (ESL/EFL), or learners of English as additional language or dialect (EAL/D), or as English language learners (ELLs), they are all on the language-learning continuum, but at different points along the way.

As we have been exploring the field of literacy research and practice, we have compared the task to searching for tracks through a rocky terrain. While our geographical and theoretical location remains the reference point to which we return regularly, as the reader will find, the book contains many excursions into complementary, contradictory and competing regions of this complex and uneven landscape. While we do not seek to persuade readers to one particular understanding or approach, we do acknowledge that in our journey through the terrain of literacy research we have regularly looped back to a contextualised and rhetorical view of literacy as social practice informed by a language-based theory of learning.

During the writing of this book we have become particularly aware of just how bewildering and intractable the literacy research landscape must be for those who are new to it, and even more so for practitioners immersed in 'the tasks of ordinary devoted teaching' (Macken-Horarik 2012: 180). Yet, knowledge about literacy and literacy development, gained through research, can only benefit students, if literacy practitioners are able to transform this knowledge into pedagogy. The application of research to practice in turn refreshes literacy research agendas and keeps them grounded. Bridges are needed to connect research and practice and these are built by practitioner-based enquiry and collaboration between teachers and researchers.

Readers are invited to follow our journey across the literacy research landscape where we hope you will find tools for thinking about literacy as social practice, the pedagogy of literacy, and literacy in its role at the core of human learning. We hope that readers will be prompted to investigate a selection of the different aspects of literacy, whether these relate to how people practise literacy in social contexts or to the practical issues that confront the literacy educator.

The book is divided into three parts to trace one of many possible tracks through this vast terrain. Part I – *Literacies Education: The Landscapes of Literacy Studies* – briefly introduces in Chapter 1 four orientations to the teaching of literacy, together with the views of literacy and learning that underpin these orientations. In Chapter 2, the role of literacy in human societies over time is explored, alongside ways in which the development of written language has been implicated in the development and teaching of specialised fields of knowledge. Part II – *Lifespan Literacies* – examines the teaching and learning of literacies across the human lifespan. This begins in Chapter 3 where literacy learning in the home is examined as the foundation for children's transition to the early years of school. The focus of Chapter 4 is the variety of methods through which literacy is taught in primary and secondary school. The final chapter in this part, Chapter 5, spans the social contexts of adult life, bringing into focus the ways people use literacy in community, further education and work contexts and the various forms of literacy education in adult contexts.

The final part of the book – *Literacy Research: A Continuing Project* – reviews a range of research methods, with examples of projects that have utilised these methods to research literacy in social contexts and in education (Chapter 6). The book concludes with Chapter 7, in which the voices of literacy researchers give us first-hand descriptions of their literacy research experiences. We are very grateful indeed to this group of researchers whose considered responses to the questions we posed are so encouraging and welcoming for newcomers to the community of literacy researchers and the practitioners with whom they collaborate.

We need to end this preface by thanking those who directly assisted us as we wrote the book. This includes Professor Christopher Candlin who extended the original invitation to contribute to the RAPAL Series and Dr Jonathan Crichton whose incisive feedback on various drafts provided valuable guidance as we finalised the book. And of course we must acknowledge Elizabeth Forrest of Palgrave Macmillan for her assistance and her patience, especially in the final weeks before the manuscript was submitted.

We again thank those researchers who enabled us to end the book with their insights and descriptions of their own journeys across the literacy terrain – James Gee, Maria Estela Brisk, Mary Schleppegrell, Annemarie Palincsar, Geoff Williams, Ruth French, Len Unsworth, Jenny Hammond, Anna-Vera Meidell Sigsgaard, Barbara Comber, Peter Freebody, Helen Nixon, Victoria Carrington, Anne-Marie Morgan, Debra Myhill, James Martin, Frances Christie, Beverly Derewianka, Claire Acevedo, Caroline Coffin, Carlos Gouveia, Ann-Christin Lövstedt, Rachel Whittaker, Brian Byrne, Anne Burns, Dave Tout, Stephen Black, Jo Balatti, Brian Paltridge, Sue Starfield, Louise Ravelli, Susan Hood, Jennifer Blunden, Helen Whitty and Nancy Jackson.

General Editors' Preface

Research and Practice in Applied Linguistics provides the essential cross-over between research in applied linguistics and its practical applications in the professions. Written by leading scholars and practitioners, the series provides rapid and authoritative access to current scholarship and research on key topics in language education and professional communication more broadly. Books in the series are designed for students and researchers in Applied Linguistics, TESOL, Language Education, Communication Studies and related fields and for professionals concerned with language and communication.

Every book in this innovative series is designed to be user-friendly, with clear illustrations and accessible style. The quotations and definitions of key concepts that punctuate the main text are intended to ensure that many, often competing, voices are heard. Each book presents a concise historical and conceptual overview of its chosen field, identifying many lines of enquiry and findings, but also gaps and disagreements. Throughout the books, readers are encouraged to take up issues of enquiry and research that relate to their own contexts of practice, guided by reflective and exploratory questions and examples that invite practical connections to their work.

The focus throughout is on exploring the relationship between research and practice. How far can research provide answers to the questions and issues that arise in practice? How should we warrant the relevance of research to practice? Can research questions that arise and are examined in very specific circumstances be informed by, and inform, the global body of research and practice? What different kinds of information can be obtained from different research methodologies? How should we make a selection between the options available, and how far are different methods compatible with each other? How can the results of research be turned into practical action?

The books in this series identify key researchable areas in the field and provide workable examples of research projects, backed up by details of appropriate research tools and resources. Case studies and exemplars of research and practice are drawn on throughout the books. References to key institutions, individual research lists, journals and professional organizations provide starting points for gathering information and embarking on research. The books also include annotated lists of key works in the field for further study.

The overall objective of the series is to illustrate the message that in Applied Linguistics there can be no good professional practice that isn't based on good research, and there can be no good research that isn't informed by practice.

Christopher N. Candlin and David R. Hall
Macquarie University, Australia

and

Jonathan Crichton
University of South Australia

Part I
Literacies Education: The Landscapes of Literacy Studies

Introduction

In this opening part of the book the field of literacy studies is surveyed from several standpoints. First, it is explored from an historical perspective to consider changing views about what it means to be literate over time, in different contexts and for different groups of people. The field as a whole is then examined to take into account influences from other discipline areas, and key sociocultural concepts that have emerged from research, for example, *literacy domains*, *practices* and *events*, and common misunderstandings are identified and re-interpreted. Key terms such as *illiteracy*, *literacy*, *literacies*, *multiliteracies* and *numeracy* are introduced and explained, as well as overlaps between these concepts and ways they are integrated within the field. Readers are encouraged to reassess their current ideas and concepts in relation to various aspects of literacy and literacy teaching, and to extend their interpretations of current debates and research evidence.

In Chapter 1 a range of views not only about literacy, but also numeracy, are explored using an historical lens, as well as in terms of the influence of research across disciplines and social and economic agendas, which, in turn, have influenced educational approaches to teaching literacy and numeracy. Changing views about how literacy and numeracy should be taught are also examined. This is important because contrasting pedagogical approaches developed for different times and contexts continue to have their advocates, which leads to recurring 'literacy wars' (Snyder 2008). Regularly, often on the basis of contested evidence, politicians, the media and public administrators claim there is a literacy crisis, and promote superficial solutions to an inadequately articulated problem. As the exploration in Chapter 1 confirms, Graff's (2001: 3) statement still resonates: '[a]s a student of literacy for over two decades, I cannot recall a time when literacy was not in a crisis'.

That literacy wars and crises can be so easily and regularly reignited in the public mind, no matter how disingenuously, is a reflection of how dependent post-industrial societies have become on literacy and numeracy to mediate all aspects of life, and how easily the community can be alarmed if access to this resource appears to be under threat. While literacy has been aligned with knowledge and power for millennia, access to literacy and the chance of a reasonable quality of life are becoming increasingly enmeshed for all levels of society. Fifty years ago, even in industrialised societies, people with low levels of literacy or with no literacy at all, could carve out dignified lives, but this possibility is receding at an accelerating rate for people in all parts of the world. An open question remains about what kinds of literacy, or configurations of different types of literacies, will be most highly valued as the 21st century unfolds. A re-examination of literacy and numeracy pedagogy, across the last century and into the early years of the 21st century, can provide a way of addressing the inevitable question of whether it is possible to deal with the 'enduring problems in literacy education, themselves a legacy of its history and of a time-honoured tendency to create false dichotomies or dualisms where none really exist' (Christie 2010a: 9). While the funding and resources available for addressing these enduring problems appear to be shrinking, there is no doubt of the expanding role played by literacy and numeracy in 'learning, in promoting personal development, in fostering self-expression and self-esteem' as well as 'conferring skills that build employability' (Christie & Simpson 2010: 4).

Chapter 2 offers a selective review of some of the many debates that have been generated by the study of literacy and literacy development over time and in different societies. Reviewing historical and cross-cultural perspectives and recurring themes is central to challenging fixed ideas about literacy and about becoming literate, as it enables us to see that studies of literacy are themselves products of specific times and places. As societies, cultures and technologies change, literacy and numeracy and what it means to be literate and numerate need to be re-evaluated. This chapter also examines systems of organised knowledge across academic disciplines, and how these are built through particular genres and language features, as revealed by literacy research. Understanding differences across academic discourses is crucial if literacy educators are to successfully apprentice students into the discourses of the academic disciplines that are key to achievement in educational contexts and subsequently in the world of work and social engagement.

1
Literacy: A Field of Evolving Terms, Definitions and Educational Approaches

Everyone has an opinion about literacy. When differing opinions about literacy are represented as conflicts in the media, through print and online newspaper articles and editorials, talk-back radio and online spaces, the spectre of a literacy crisis is raised, 'usually … in relation to socio-economic change of some kind' (Snyder 2008: 7). While commentary is sought from politicians, employer groups, teachers, teacher unions, experts and parents, rarely, if ever, are students consulted. Everyone who believes there is a literacy crisis can give an example of the crisis in action: young people glued to their various electronic devices using text language instead of *correct* language; the young woman at the local store who can't add up the prices on a few groceries, young employees who can't follow written instructions and schools that fail to teach grammar or that teach a grammar parents don't recognise.

Reasoned debate seems impossible when the loudest voices are aligned with the political stance of powerful media outlets and vested interests who want to redefine 'professional educators and students as consumers' (Luke 2004, 2011). Those who wish to voice alternative views, even when based on considered and extensive research, are often accused of undermining educational traditions designed to build literacy and numeracy skills that will enable students to obtain employment and contribute to the national economy.

Quotes

Although no one has died in these wars … there have been casualties. The persistent denigration of literacy teachers by the conservative critics in the media has damaged the morale of those charged with

---

the responsibility of educating the next generation of citizens. Hard-working and underpaid, without the social regard they deserve, literacy teachers have been bewildered, but also angered ... Moreover the collateral damage for the students in the classrooms of these battle-weary teachers and their confused parents cannot be underestimated

(Snyder 2008: 9)

Clearly, debates around literacy education have concerned much more than matters of classroom method or remediation strategies. These debates have dealt with the nature and consequences of an individual's or a collective's becoming literate, and, moreover, with the consequences of becoming literate in particular ways. That is, we can insert into debates a concept of literacy that entails a set of individual and social resources that enable certain kinds of practices, events and organisational arrangements, rather than a single trait that is either possessed or not, or that is possessed in some quantity.

(Freebody 2007: 15)

What it means to be literate, how literacy is defined and how best to teach literacy is difficult to determine because the answers to these questions have altered through history, are shifting in the present and will continue to change into the future. The term *literacy* is used as a label for a valuable 'set of behaviours' (Wignell n.d: 5) that enable people to learn and to participate in a range of social contexts, but as a concept it is complex to grasp and, as with all complex concepts, is reinvented in response to the context in which it is used, changing global and social structures, advancing technologies and individual aspirations. However, if the term *literacy* remains so value-laden for so many and at the same time is subjected to limited and limiting characterisations, then educators and community members are less likely to reconcile disparate views about literacy and its consequences. It is hoped that this book will assist readers to participate in considered and productive debates about literacy that account for its complexity and the multiple ways it can be developed.

Defining literacy

The terms *literacy* and *illiteracy* have shifted in meaning over the years. Traditionally literacy was, and still is in most dictionaries, defined as 'the ability to read and write', and *illiteracy* was defined as 'the lack of ability to read and write'.[1] However, now the term *literacy* has a number of definitions and has come to be associated with 'effective participation of any kind in social processes' (Halliday 2007/1996: 98), so that we refer to financial literacy, health literacy, media literacy and even emotional literacy (Steiner and Perry 1997). But as Halliday goes on to say '[t]he problem is that if we call all these things literacy, then we shall have to find another term for what we called literacy before'.

In this book we begin by adopting the following definition of literacy, proposed by UNESCO (2004), as the:

ability to identify, understand, interpret, create, communicate and compute, using printed and written materials associated with varying contexts. Literacy involves a continuum of learning in enabling individuals to achieve their goals, to develop their knowledge and potential, and to participate fully in their community and wider society.

This definition of literacy is then expanded to account for the shift over recent decades from paper-based to digital technologies as captured in the concept of *multiliteracies,* which means understanding 'how different modalities separately and interactively construct different dimensions of meaning' in texts (Unsworth 2001: 10). We also consider what it means to be numerate in the contemporary world, that is, having 'the ability to effectively use the mathematics required to meet the general demands of life at home and at work, and for participation in community and civic life' (NSW Department of Education and Communities 2013: 1).

Socially oriented research has revealed that different social contexts make different literacy and numeracy demands on people. Consequently people who are literate in some contexts may not be literate in others, and even people who are otherwise highly literate may have problems with some literacy tasks (see for example, research by Fawns outlined in Chapter 6). This has complicated what is meant by *illiteracy,* with many policy statements now concerned with levels of functional literacy and illiteracy in society. So while illiteracy is the total inability to participate in the literacy practices of the society, being functionally illiterate means being unable to use literacy skills to manage everyday social and work tasks.

In describing functional literacy, some assessment and educational programmes have focused on the literacy tasks people encounter in daily life, identifying three types of literacy (as defined by the National Assessment of Adult Literacy 2003 below):[2]

1. Prose literacy – the ability to search, comprehend and use continuous texts such as news stories, brochures and instructional materials.

2. Document literacy – the ability to search, comprehend and use non-continuous texts in various formats such as application forms, payroll forms, train timetables, maps, tables and labels.
3. Quantitative literacy – the ability to perform quantitative tasks such as computational tasks or recognising and using mathematical information embedded in printed texts.

It was assumed that dividing the literacy tasks in adult contexts into these three categories would result in a more fine-tuned assessment of adult literacy skills. Results of these assessments are compared across countries. For example, the Adult Literacy and Life Skills Survey, an international study, found that in New Zealand between 1996 and 2006 there were significant improvements in prose and document literacy over those years. In a national report, measures of document literacy, prose literacy and numeracy were compared with those of Australia, the United States and Canada (Education Counts).[3] International assessment studies, surveys and comparisons feed into continuing literacy debates in various OECD countries. Comparisons with other countries, such as the one above, are often used as an incentive to improve literacy levels within a country with the implication that particular country should be at the top of the scale.

Quote

The meaning of the term 'literacy' appears to live something of a dichotomous existence. While superficially it is a word widely understood and used by the public, 'literacy' lives a double life as the subject of intense academic debate that aims to attach a concrete definition to what is a complex, dynamic and often mercurial concept ... Scholars have used the term 'literate' to describe, not only the autonomous skills characterised as forming an integral part of literacy, such as writing and numeracy, but the application of such skills and how their acquisition affects learning processes.

The United Nations Educational, Scientific and Cultural Organization (UNESCO) regards 'literacy', in an attempt to recognise the diversity of definitions attributed to the term, as being beyond simply 'the set of technical skills of reading, writing and calculating ... to a plural notion encompassing the manifold of meanings and dimensions of these undeniably vital competencies. Such a view, responding to recent economic, political and social transformations,

---

including globalisation, and the advancement of information and communication technologies, recognises that there are many practices of literacy embedded in different cultural processes, personal circumstances and collective structures'.

'Literacy', throughout history and across societies, has encapsulated a varying range of skills and erudition, but its antonym, 'illiteracy', has always been synonymous with disadvantage. It is this definition that, perhaps, elucidates the concept best.

(United Nations Regional Information Centre for Western Europe (UNRIC) 2015)[4]

Failing to become literate

In various parts of the world literacy and education programmes form a significant part of the work of international organisations such as the United Nations and the World Bank. At the end of the United Nations Literacy Decade (2003–2012), according to UNESCO (2015), there are 775 million illiterate people in the world and about 61% of these are women. In addition, the 80 million children who are not in school 'are likely to encounter great difficulties in the future, as deficient or non-existent basic education is the root cause of illiteracy'.[5] It is probably not surprising, when viewing UNESCO statistics on literacy in the world that developing countries with low school participation rates have low average literacy rates and that countries with compulsory schooling have higher rates.

The current United Nations literacy strategy is the *Literacy Initiative for Empowerment* (LIFE) 2006–2015, which focuses on literacy as 'an indispensable means for effective social and economic participation, contributing to human development and poverty reduction' (UNESCO 2007: 11). The strategy focuses on 35 countries with the highest levels of illiteracy through 'advocacy, capacity, policy, country-led programs and knowledge sharing' (UNESCO 2007: 12). The aims of the LIFE strategy are to meet the learning needs of young people and adults, to improve adult literacy rates by 50% and to achieve gender equity in education.

Debates about literacy rates in Western countries may seem to be of a different order, when viewed from a global perspective, but nevertheless they have been part of continuing community discussion for over a century. In the Victorian era in the United Kingdom literacy was linked to social order and industriousness, as in the Sunday schools established by people such as Hannah and Martha More. In these schools students were to

> learn of week-days such coarse works as may fit them for servants. I allow of no writing for the poor. My object is not to teach dogmas and opinions, but to form the lower classes to habits of industry and virtue.
>
> (More 1859: 6)

There were also discussions about what materials to use to teach literacy and how to counter the influence of popular publications and radical literature.

Quote

... as an appetite for reading ... had been increasing among the inferior ranks in this country, it was judged expedient, at this critical period, to supply such wholesome aliment as might give a new direction to their taste, and abate their relish for those corrupt and inflammatory publications which the consequences of the French Revolution have been so fatally pouring in on us.

(More 1801 in Kelly 1970: 78)

The link between low levels of literacy and delinquency or crime is continually made. The Basic Skills Agency in the UK reported that 'one in two prisoners have problems with reading while two thirds have problems with numbers' (*The Independent* 17.2.2002). In Canada it is reported that 'almost 7 out of 10 prisoners in Canadian gaols before 1996 had low literacy skills' with low literacy affecting 'both procedure and outcome in the courtroom' (Canadian Association of Chiefs of Police 2008: 20). Similarly, Black, Wickert and Rouse (1990) found that prisoners in New South Wales had serious literacy problems requiring intervention through educational programs but that these same problems were a reflection of literacy patterns in the general population.

Many adults who have succeeded in becoming literate remember the way they were taught to read and write at school, childhood memories often embellished over the years with nostalgia and mythology. They assume that it was the half-remembered style of teaching at their school that led them to be successful readers and writers, and that this style of teaching should, therefore, be used to teach all children to read. Other influences that may have contributed to their success were so much part of their lives that they remain invisible, for example, family background, early access to written texts and extensive family conversations about books, newspaper articles and other printed material. At the same time, when adults who see themselves as successful readers find it difficult to read or write unfamiliar types of texts, they rarely perceive this in terms of their own lack of literacy. Instead, they perceive the literacy challenge posed by such texts to lie in the nature of the texts themselves. Recollections of their own school experience, and confidence in their own literacy practices, may blind them to the plight of others who may not have successfully achieved the same levels of literacy because of social and economic disadvantage or cultural and class differences. They may also be blind to the ways in which rapid social change has increased the complexity of what it is to be literate in a diverse and interconnected world.

While literacy and numeracy are placed front and centre in education policy statements, internationally, nationally and locally, the causes of 'enduring problems in literacy education' (Christie 2010a: 9) are often ignored in the quest for a simple one-size-fits-all pedagogic and/or assessment approach. For some it is a matter of returning literacy pedagogy 'to a simpler form' as a 'nostalgic retreat to a simpler apparently more literate society of the past' (Freebody, Morgan, Comber & Nixon 2014: 4), where, for example, literacy could be achieved through drilling a basic set of skills. Others perceive the reasons some students fail to develop literacy and numeracy skills as multidimensional, only offset by fine-tuned compensatory education and appropriate social support.

Current calls for education through which all students are *made* literate coincide with a shift in social attitudes, in which 'poverty and unemployment' are no longer seen as 'social problems but more to do with individual moral failings', a matter of individuals being lazy, spendthrift or lacking aspiration (Jones 2012: xii). According to the UK 2011 National Centre for Social Research Social Attitudes Survey,[6] 51% of people think child poverty will increase in the next ten years and over 60% now blame parents rather than social causes. While 79% of the people surveyed thought the central government should be responsible for reducing child poverty, a large minority said that the parents should be responsible. This shift in social attitudes has political and educational consequences because if people 'think poverty and unemployment are personal failings, rather than social problems' (Jones 2012: xiii), they will question why the government should provide compensatory education for what are seen as intractable individually induced problems.

> **Quote**
>
> Demonisation [of the working class and other groups in the society] serves a useful purpose in a divided society ... because it promotes the idea that inequality is rational; it is simply an expression of differing talent and ability. Those at the bottom are supposedly there because they are stupid, lazy or otherwise morally questionable. Demonisation is the ideological backbone of an unequal society.
>
> (Jones 2012: xiii)

The now well-known *Pygmalion in the classroom* research by Rosenthal and Jacobson (1968) claimed that teachers' expectations of students' capabilities affect teaching and student outcomes. There were many criticisms of the Rosenthal and Jacobson research method and the conclusions they reached (for example, Gumpert & Gumpert 1968, Jensen 1969, Thorndike 1968). However, despite the limitations of the original research, 'there is widespread acceptance of the existence of teachers' expectations and of their importance for students' learning'. Later researchers began to focus on teacher behaviours towards 'high and low expectation students' (Rubie-Davies 2009: 696). The overall conclusion is that 'although the factors that influence student performance are multiple and complex, teacher expectations do play a role in how well and how much students learn' (Cooper & Tom 1984: 76). Smith (1980), for example, found that teacher expectations had a much stronger effect on reading achievement than achievement in mathematics. This, Cooper and Tom (1984: 79) speculate, may be 'because reading curricula are less structured, allowing teachers to vary more in how they present material'.

Many current literacy research projects report improved achievement for disadvantaged children arising from classrooms where particular interventions are based on high expectations of students combined with high levels of support (see descriptions of research projects by Hammond, Myhill, Comber et al., Martin, Acevedo et al. in Chapter 7).

Across the world, schooling is seen as central to developing literacy. In the past, in industrialised countries, state sponsored compulsory education underpinned the 'positive, long-term civic consequences that arise from the distribution of literacy capabilities via strong educational programs' (Freebody 2010: 41). In literacy policy statements across countries with higher literacy rates 'we find literacy characterised variously as a set of interrelated capabilities, as a human capital resource that signals educability, (re)trainability and as an object inserted into debates about the performance of teachers, schools and governments' (Freebody 2007: 18).

Quotes

The two student characteristics that researchers generally agree have the greatest impact on teachers' expectations are student social class and diagnostic labels. Dusek and Joseph (1985) suggested that particularly for lower class students, teachers formed their expectations based on the students' social standing rather than on their academic performance. In a classic study by Rist (1970) he reported that in a first grade class he observed the teacher purported to group her students by ability whereas the students had actually been grouped by social class. The teacher then proceeded to seat the low 'ability' group furthest from her and interacted more frequently and warmly with the children in her high 'ability' group. It appears that time has not altered the findings from earlier studies. Reports that expectations for middle class students are much higher than they are for lower social class students (around a half a standard deviation higher) continue to be conveyed (Jussim, Smith, Madon & Palumbo 1998).

(Rubie-Davies 2009: 698)

The most important message is that any effects of teacher expectations tend to be oriented round attributes of teachers rather than with characteristics of students. Teachers differ in their beliefs and the degree to which they assimilate societal stereotypes. They differ in the degree to which they allow student characteristics to influence their expectations and the degree to which they allow their expectations to influence the ways in which teaching is implemented in their classrooms. It is the teacher who structures both the instructional and the socioemotional climates of the classroom. For these reasons it is important teachers set high expectations for all students, use dependable assessment feedback on a regular basis to correct any inappropriate expectations, and use this information to set meaningful and challenging targets for all students. Arguments about teacher expectations are debates about equality for students. Every student has the right to a quality education and should be given, therefore, the opportunity to make maximal learning gains while in the care of every teacher.

(Rubie-Davies 2009: 705)

Large-scale intervention programmes have been designed in response to perceptions of falling literacy standards in many industrialised societies, based on, for example, the three-yearly OECD *Programme for International Student Assessment* (PISA) results. Improvement in PISA ratings is the goal of many recent literacy interventions. Some early 21st century examples of these large-scale programs are the *No Child Left Behind Program* in the United States and the *Literate Futures Program* in Queensland, Australia (see Freebody 2007). Others include the *National Accelerated Literacy Program* (NALP) that aimed to address 'low levels of literacy in remote communities around Australia,[7] the *National Literacy Program* in Wales (2012)[8] and the *Family Literacy in Europe Program* (2009).[9] These programmes have generally been motivated more by economic human capital perspectives than equity considerations, as governments predict that falling literacy standards will make their countries less competitive in a transnational world.

Interventions to improve literacy levels occur at local, state and national levels across countries. This trend is illustrated by the 32 intervention schemes for mainstream students aged from five to 14 years and the 26 intervention schemes for students with special needs implemented within the United Kingdom in recent years (Brooks 2013). Other countries have adopted national literacy assessment strategies to monitor standards and to benchmark outcomes, as an incentive to raise literacy levels. One such programme is the Australian *National Assessment Program – Literacy and Numeracy* (NAPLAN), which annually assesses students in Years 3, 5, 7 and 9 through standardised tests in reading, writing, language conventions (spelling, grammar and punctuation) and numeracy.[10] There has been much criticism of NAPLAN from various quarters, for example, that it is a high-stakes assessment scheme with negative impacts as schools are compared, curriculum is narrowed, and teachers teach to the test. An interesting research project using participatory methods (Howell 2012) examined the impact on children who undertake the test by asking a representative sample to draw a picture of their NAPLAN experience and then write about their picture. This was followed by focus group discussions with small groups of children and classroom observations, where time spent on NAPLAN and the number of times teachers referred to NAPLAN were recorded. Howell (2009: 9) found that '[t]he contributions were overwhelmingly negative, with over 50% of students reporting an entirely negative response to their NAPLAN experience, compared with just over 10% who reported an entirely positive response'.

All interventions, whether by national or state governments or local authorities, to improve literacy outcomes in schools reflect varying degrees of concern for equity and for national economic advancement. Some interventions are aligned with particular pedagogic approaches and assessment instruments, while others are not. Unfortunately, many do not build into the programme design sufficient levels of professional development for teachers to implement the interventions effectively, and some try to *teacher-proof* the interventions by mandating a one-size-fits-all approach. Recent studies, however, for example, Rubie-Davis (2009) have found that quality literacy education relies on teachers developing the knowledge and skills required to respond to the needs of different students. This involves building an 'instructional and socioemotional' (Rubie-Davies 2009: 703) classroom environment that can provide students with appropriate support through explicit teaching while, at the same time expecting students to achieve high level results.

Quote

As an objective measure of our success, our national ambition is, that by 2015, Wales will be among the top 20 nations in the Programme for International Student Assessment (PISA). Setting ourselves an ambitious target for PISA 2015 is the right approach because PISA tests the skills that young people need in order to succeed ...

Unfortunately, literacy in Wales is not as well developed as we would wish it to be. The 2009 PISA results were a wake up call for all of us involved in education in Wales. The 2009 results for Wales were poor in terms of comparison to prior performance, to other UK nations, as well as internationally. In reading, our mean score was significantly lower than our UK counterparts and the OECD (Organisation for Economic Co-operation and Development) average, and our international 'ranking' was lower than in 2006.

(The National Literacy Programme – http://learning.wales.gov.uk – accessed 31.3.2015)

Educating for literacy

Only an encyclopaedic sized publication could cover the breadth of theoretical and research perspectives that have influenced the teaching and assessment of literacy during the 20th century and into the first decades of the 21st century. So in writing this book we have chosen to select those perspectives that have had the most direct, and in some cases, lasting influence on literacy education. These are listed in Table 1.1 as

Table 1.1 Changing approaches to literacy and literacy education

View of literacy	Approach to literacy development	Features	Text focus	View of teacher	Informing theories/authors
Literacy as learned practice	Learning through traditional rules (grammar and spelling) Text translation with focus on sentence level	Application of language rules to writing **Additional language** Belief in equivalence between L1 and L2	Literary texts	Teacher as learned authority	Classical studies tradition
Literacy as coding and skills practice	Basic skills – sound-letter correspondence (synthetic phonics) Study of discrete linguistic features (sounds, letters, words, sentences) From bottom-up (phoneme to whole sentence)	Repetition drills Programmed explicit teaching sequences	Word level reading Phonics-based readers	Teacher as behaviour modifier	Bloomfield & Fries – descriptive linguistics Skinner – behavioural psychology Cognitive psychologists (reading disorders) – Coltheart – Wheldall
	Cognitive approach based on knowledge of spelling and grammar rules Reading and writing represented as a hierarchy of skills	Drills, practice and rules memorisation Classification exercises Readers to support mechanical sentence level memorisation of text Whole-word look-say **Additional language** Situational language teaching	Flash cards Basal readers Reading programs	Teacher as skills developer	Chomsky – transformational grammar Cognitive psychology (nativist)

Literacy as individual practice	Learn to read and write by reading and writing (e.g. analytic phonics) Focus on strategic aspects of reading and writing Writing as personal creative expression Readers as individual seekers of meaning who bring individual schemata to the tasks of reading and writing Literacy as individually liberating	Progressive pedagogies – often implicit Free writing Problem-solving tasks and discovery learning **Additional language** Reduced emphasis on reading and writing – specialist literacy classes for higher spoken language proficiency level students	Authentic texts meaningful to students Student chosen texts Language experience stories Personal narratives	Teacher as facilitator	Rousseau – Dewey – Piaget Cognitive psychology (developmental) Sauvignon & Canale – communicative language teaching Frank Smith & Ken Goodman – psycholinguistic view of reading Donald Graves – whole language Cambourne – whole language Paulo Friere – literacy as individual liberation
Literacy as sociocultural practice	Text-based e.g. genre approach Explicit teaching of text structure and linguistic features Focus on link between texts and sociocultural purpose Developmental methodology – teacher provides scaffold for literacy development Attention to product and process within curriculum and methodology	Integration of written and spoken language Systematic and explicit instruction Conscious shifts between teacher and student centredness orchestrated by the teacher on the basis of the student's level of knowledge Emphasis on meaning and purposeful communication	Whole texts	Teacher as expert	Halliday – sociocultural view of language that relates language use to social contexts and culture; differences between spoken and written language; language-based theory of learning Vygotsky – non-separation of individual psychology from acculturation process Bernstein – individuals do not have equal access to powerful forms of language in society Freebody and Luke – four reader roles (integration of approaches within a principled framework)

Source: Adapted from earlier table by Helen de Silva Joyce and Anne Burns.

four views of literacy that have influenced literacy pedagogy through the decades. These we refer to as:

1. Literacy as learned practice
2. Literacy as a coding and skills practice
3. Literacy as individual practice
4. Literacy as sociocultural practice

Literacy as learned practice

Before compulsory schooling was introduced in most Western countries in the late 19th century, literacy was not only a province of the elite classes but was becoming more widespread as children were taught to read by relatives and also in day schools, dame schools and Sunday schools (Barton 2007: 129). According to Vincent (1989) a variety of approaches were used. When compulsory schooling was introduced, its primary aim was to teach children to read and write. This was seen as a way of developing social stability, reducing crime and teaching morality, although some believed that teaching the masses to read and write would lead them to become discontented and rebellious.[11] The main continuing influences from this period of literacy teaching include the issue of what grammar to teach in order to stabilise and maintain language standards and the role of literary texts in the literacy classroom.

Quote

Fluent native speakers of English quite often say that they 'don't know' any grammar, or that foreigners speak English better than they do ... which at first seem nonsensical ... It is certainly true that many foreigners can talk about English grammar more confidently than native speakers can, because foreign learners have usually acquired their knowledge in a conscious way. It is also true that many native speakers have little or no ability to describe their own grammatical knowledge. Either because they have never been taught to do so, or because the potential fascination of this task has been stifled by poor teaching methods. The pedagogical quest has long been to find ways of developing a person's 'knowledge about' grammar which are both enlivening and rewarding, and it continues to be an important goal of contemporary educational linguistics.

(Crystal 1995: 191)

In England from the 17th to the 19th century there were several attempts to systematise the grammar of English. The two most influential texts on English grammar at the time were Lowth's *Short Introduction to English Grammar* (1762) and Murray's *English Grammar* (1794). These texts are 'the origins of most of the grammatical controversies which continue to attract attention today' (Crystal 1995: 79). One such controversy that continues to excite debate in the English-speaking world is whether it is permissible to split the two parts of an infinitive. As early as the 18th century there were debates about whether grammars should reflect the way people actually used the language or be written as a set of rules to prescribe *correct* usage (de Silva Joyce & Burns 1999: 6). From the 17th century there were criticisms that English was being forced

> into the mould of Latin ... giving many useless rules about the cases, genders and declensions of nouns, the tenses, the moods and conjugations of verbs, the government of nouns and verbs, and other things of that kind, which have no bearing on our language, and which confuse and obscure matters instead of elucidating them.
>
> (John Wallis 1653 in Crystal 1995: 78

Many of the decisions made about grammar standards in that period were arbitrary, based on Latin grammar and on written, rather than spoken English. Grammarians would defend their decisions through 'philosophical, logical, aesthetic, historical and occasionally linguistic arguments' (Crystal 1995: 191).

Traditional grammars essentially adopt a rule-based view of language systems, related to such things as how we put words together (syntax) and how we change the form of words and their parts (morphology). Descriptions of the grammar of a language reveal 'a structure and regularity which lies at the basis of language and enables us to talk of the language system' (Batstone 1994: 4). Rather than describing this system and regularity as absolute rules, it is possible to describe typical arrangements of features that may vary across dialects, texts and contexts. In the end 'grammar is something of a *more or less* phenomenon, with some rules applying more consistently than others' (Batstone 1994: 7) and, over time, arrangements that may have been hard and fast *rules* begin to shift.

Quotes

The 'problem' of the split infinitive is the fruit of a misconception about English infinitives, the assumption they consist of two parts (*to* + the verb itself: *to read*), and that these two parts can never be split. In fact English infinitives do not necessarily come with the preceding *to* ... split infinitives were used for centuries before they became the bête noire of nineteenth century grammarians.

Reaction to the split infinitive still begs the question as to what is wrong with it ... Having an adverbial phrase between the *to* and the verb can make awkward reading, as in *I wanted to above all be near her* ... Yet there's no alternative place for the adverbial phrase in *He wanted to more than match that offer.*

(Peters 1995: 711)

When we need pronouns in the third person plural, **they** (and **them** and **their**) are there to serve our purpose. Yet being gender-free, they're increasingly used instead of he/she in singular applications as well: *Each member of the group must be prepared to bring in samples of their work to discuss.* **Their** avoids the need for the sexist *his* or the clumsy *his/her*.

(Peters 1995: 751)

In English-speaking countries, traditional ways of studying grammar, with a focus on the form of words in isolated sentences, was taught in the 20th century up to about the 1970s, when the formal study of grammar was largely abandoned in both schools and adult language and literacy education. Over the last three decades, however, grammar has re-appeared in curriculum documents at the same time as more contemporary functional grammars have begun to influence literacy education. Because the traditional approach to teaching about grammar in formal and prescriptive ways is more familiar to many older people, they will often vigorously defend the value of this approach.

Quotes

The classroom image of grammatical structure is something like the following. Language is made up of sentences (some of which have clauses in them) consisting of words (some of which are grouped into phrases). There is no need to reject this picture; we can build on it and enrich it.

(Halliday 1994: 23)

... there is a long tradition of taking content from linguistics in the form of 'school grammar', the version of classical and medieval linguistic scholarship that went into the making of humanist descriptive grammars. It is not a bad grammar, but it is not very useful in school. It is formal, rigid, based on the notion of rules, syntactic in focus and oriented towards the sentence. A more useful grammar would be one which is functional, flexible, oriented towards the text. Hence the recurrent cycle of love and hate for it; 'we thought it would help children to write; it doesn't so we abandon it; they still can't write, so we take it up again' and so on.

(Halliday 2007/1981: 336–337)

In the latter half of the 20th century a functional description of English grammar began to influence literacy teaching in schools and in adult contexts. The functional model for describing language and its use, derived from Systemic Functional Linguistics (SFL) (see Chapter 2), is now widely used in literacy education, particularly in Australia, but increasingly in other places, including the United States and the United Kingdom. This model is not based on rules but is used to explain how language varies in response to changing social contexts, and to describe whole texts in terms of function and meaning, including how the language of a text is used to talk about the world and our experiences in the world, how it is used to develop interpersonal relationships and how it is used to bind the various features of language into whole cohesive texts that make sense in the social contexts.

Quote

In educational contexts, the debate around the choice of grammar is often framed in terms of 'traditional' vs 'functional'. We will argue here that such a framing is misleading and simplistic. We could range most descriptions of language that are typically found in English-teaching contexts along a cline between 'form' and 'function' ... At the 'form' end of the continuum, we might find those traditional school grammars which focus primarily on the 'parts of speech' and syntax. At the 'function' end of the continuum, we could place the

> notional-functional syllabus – which, even though no longer in common use, has had a lasting impact on the field. And around the middle, we might find a number of contemporary reference grammars – including Halliday's systemic-functional grammar (SFG) – which endeavour to describe the relationship between grammatical forms and their functions.
>
> (Derewianka & Jones (2010: 6)

Using systemic-functional grammar to describe how meanings are made in texts encourages a non-judgemental stance towards different language varieties and acknowledges the complexity and effectiveness of the languages that students may bring to the classroom. Rather than comparing students' home languages unfavourably against a prescribed standard, literacy educators using a functional approach acknowledge each student's language background, and build from this starting point. Educational linguists using a functional approach have studied the types of texts students must read and write effectively to succeed at school, studies that have been extended to the types of text that are required in broader work and social contexts. This grammar model has influenced approaches that adopt a social practices view of literacy and literacy education that are discussed below.

Literacy as coding and skills practice

In the early decades of the 20th century, structural linguists were concerned with developing a scientific study of language. For these linguists, particularly Bloomfield (1914, 1933), 'linguistic study involved isolating and categorising the finite number of phonemes in a given language (its smallest significant units of sound) and describing how these units join together to form larger units of language' (Chapman & Routledge 2005: 37), ignoring meaning and contextual factors. Structural linguists were influenced by the expanding field of behaviourist psychology (Watson 1930) and by its most famous exponent B. F. Skinner (1938) who believed that human behaviour is related to a series of habits that have been learned through response to repeated stimuli.

Bloomfield criticised the way reading was taught in American schools and developed a four-step plan, the first two steps of which involved children in recognising letters and developing left to right scanning, followed by 'practice with reading material containing letters with only one phoneme value, for example, *b* in *bat, bun,* and *bin*' (Chapman

& Routledge 2005: 39). This led to the development of the phonics approach to teaching reading with students 'practising consonant and vowel combinations which they were expected to combine into whole words' (Hood, Solomon & Burns 1996: 17) using materials such as phonics-based readers in which the same sound combinations were repeated over and over again. In 1955, Flesch wrote a book entitled *Why Johnny can't read: And what you can do about it* in which he supported phonics-based approaches to the teaching of reading. In an article entitled *A surprise for Johnny* (30th June 1955) the *New York Times* 'declared the battle lines over teaching reading had been drawn' (Schantz & Zimmer 2005: 1). This battle still rages as advocates of phonics regularly raise the spectre of falling literacy standards if this approach is not used, and publishers continue to produce phonics-based reading schemes which they seek to promote to politicians and education systems (Morris 2015, Paris & Luo 2011). Of the many people who remember phonics lessons in school with books entitled *Run Spot Run* made up of reading impoverished sentences such as *'Look, Spot. Oh Look, Look and see. Oh, see'* (1956: 9), some remain convinced it was this process and only this process that taught them to read.

The assumption underlying the phonics approach was that once students could distinguish the sounds of the language, and match them to corresponding letter patterns, they would then progress with ease to reading larger stretches of language. Critics of this approach included those who argued that students learn to read by learning to recognise whole words. An alternative to the phonics-only approach was *language experience* advocated by educators such as Sylvia Ashton Warner (1963). This approach centred on developing literacy from the student's firsthand experiences through a four-step procedure: sharing an experience, talking about the experience, making a record of the experience in words and pictures and finally using the record of the experience to extend reading and writing in the classroom. Students were encouraged to create their own books as well as class books that became additional reading texts. This approach can still be seen in classrooms across school and adult contexts when, for example, students draw pictures or take photographs on an excursion and these images become the stimulus for writing once they return to the classroom. Language experience has also been adapted to digital environments where students use computers to upload digital photos, write captions for the photos and develop digital books (for example, Turbill 2001). This approach aligns with the view of literacy as individual practice, an approach explored in the next section.

Quotes

Correctly sounding out the words is not reading, it's barking at print, retrieving no meaning at all from the text. So it's disappointing to discover that many parents, politicians and even a few principals think that decoding phonics correctly is indeed reading ... Only 50% of the words in English are phonically decodable This is a nuisance, especially for the mad keen phonicators among us. It's my sincere hope that we're able to go beyond a 50% literacy level in Australia and New Zealand. We have, actually. We're always in the top four in the world after Finland, and sometimes Canada. The Finns have an unfair advantage over us: their language, like Indonesian and Italian, is phonically simple.

And if phonics is so important, so fundamental, so essential – as so many claim – and so crucial to our ability to make meaning from text, how come we can read the following with ease?

Aoccdrnig to rscheearch at an Elingsh uinervtisy, it deosn't mttaer in waht oredr the ltteers in a wrod are, the olny iprmoetnt tihng is that the frist and lsat ltteers are in the rghit pclae: the rset can be a toatl mses but you can still raed it wouthit a porbelm. This is bcuseae we don't raed ervey lteter but the word as a wlohe.

So, hey, waht does this say abuot the improtnace of phnoics in raeidng? Prorbalby that phonics ins't very imoptrnat at all. How apcoltapyic is that, in the cuerrnt licetary wars!

(Mem Fox 2008)

Literacy as individual practice

From about the mid-1970s, research by psycholinguists such as Kenneth Goodman and Frank Smith began to impact on literacy education. Goodman wrote a paper entitled *Reading: A psycholinguistic guessing game* in which he sought to refute the notion that reading 'involves exact, detailed, sequential perception and identification of letters, words, spelling patterns and large language units' (Goodman 1967: 1). For Goodman and Smith reading 'involves not greater precision, but more accurate first guesses based on better sampling techniques, greater control over language structure, broadened experiences and increased conceptual development' and as 'reading skill and speed' develop a reader 'uses increasingly fewer graphic cues' (Goodman 1967: 7). The impact of this research and its influence on literacy teaching was that in many classrooms learning to read and write became a matter of immersing children in reading and writing activities. Because young readers were individual seekers of meaning, they would bring their individual schema to the reading of a text, enabling them to make guesses that they would confirm as they read the text.

At the same time writing was also being promoted as a personal creative activity undertaken through process writing (Graves 1978). Process writing, associated with whole language approaches to literacy education, is based on the idea that 'language is more learned than taught' (Walshe 1981: 9) and the conviction that children would learn to write through writing. After teachers had taught a few *teachables* – the alphabet, handwriting, punctuation and spelling, a few grammar points and some formalities of usage – their responsibility shifted to providing a classroom where children could write, not through model texts but from their own creativity, where the novice writer could 'discover his or her own *process*' (Walshe 1981: 11).

It was also at this time that the work of Paulo Freire, the Brazilian educator and philosopher (1968 and 1985) had been translated into English and began to influence adult literacy education around the world. For Freire, literacy education should be directed at individual liberation from oppression through *conscientisation*, which is the process of developing a critical awareness of one's social reality in reflection and action. He was concerned that the oppressed and disadvantaged should come to understand the sources of their oppression and that teachers should understand education as a possible instrument of oppression. 'Attempting to liberate the oppressed without their reflective participation in the act of liberation is to treat them as objects that must be saved from a burning building' (Freire 1968/2000: 65). Teachers sought to assist students to reflect on their circumstances because '[w]ashing one's hands of the conflict between the powerful and the powerless means to side with the powerful, not to be neutral' (Freire 1985: 122). This humanist philosophy was particularly appealing to literacy educators working in adult basic education settings in which students had low levels of literacy and a history of school failure and disengagement from formal educational institutions.

An advocate of the whole language approach, Brian Cambourne (1984), identified eight conditions that he states are necessary for literacy development in children (Cambourne 1995):

1. *Immersion* by surrounding the child with texts of all types
2. *Demonstration* with parents and teachers showing children that they are also readers and writers

3. *Engagement* by establishing an environment where children feel free to experiment with texts
4. *Expectation* by setting realistic goals for children who know that their parents and teachers expect them to become readers and writers
5. *Responsibility* through allowing children to make choices about what they want to read and making a variety of written material accessible to them
6. *Approximation* by accepting children's mistakes and acknowledging their achievements
7. *Employment* to create possibilities for children to use their language skills
8. *Response* through listening to children and extending their oral and written language

Educators using the individual practice approaches described above attend primarily to the individual literacy learner and the ways in which teachers (and parents) could assist each learner to develop literacy skills. While the work of both Freire and Cambourne includes the recognition that literacy is learned in social environments, it was the next wave of literacy research and pedagogic development, from the 1980s onwards, that brought with it the idea of literacy as social practice along with tools for analysing the literacy demands of school, employment and other social contexts, so students could be taught explicitly how to meet those demands.

Literacy as sociocultural practice

Literacy education theory and practice took a new turn when it became the focus of multidisciplinary studies drawing on sociolinguistics, sociology, developmental psychology, and classroom-based action research and case studies. Literacy came to be understood as social practice, the role of the literacy teacher was redefined, and more explicit models of pedagogic intervention were devised (Candlin & Mercer 2001). Emerging from this broad research base is the genre-based approach to literacy education that aims to teach students about whole texts as the main unit of purposeful language use and about varieties of language to use in different contexts. This involves teaching students to predict what type of text, or *genre*, will be used to achieve a particular social purpose and what variety of language, or *register*, to adopt in a particular social context. Another important aspect of linguistic research that brought new insights to literacy education, at this time, was detailed and explicit explanations of the differences between spoken and written language, which made it clear what was involved in students moving from one mode to the other.

A genre is a general category of texts used to achieve similar social purposes, and is defined as 'a staged, goal oriented activity in which speakers [or writers] engage as members of our culture' (Martin 1984: 25). Texts belonging to the same genre can be recognised by recurring language patterns. The genres that have evolved over time to fulfil a range of social purposes in different disciplines within school curricula and different fields of work are listed in Table 1.2. Learning to recognise and to work with these genres enables students to understand how discourse is structured to meet educational and work purposes, to critique the texts presented to them, and to mould texts to their own communicative purposes. The concept of genre has been applied systematically to the analysis and teaching of written texts and more recently to the analysis and teaching of spoken language and multimodal texts. Wide ranging studies have identified the overall structure of spoken and written texts used in school, tertiary education, workplaces and the general community.

Beyond the primary classroom, genres are usually found as components of larger, more complex texts in educational, work and community contexts. These combined genres are referred to as *macrogenres*. Christie (2002) used the concept of the curriculum macrogenre to analyse the phases of classroom discourse, as illustrated in Table 1.3.

Similarly, Martin (2012/1994) analysed school textbooks as macrogenres structured to apprentice students into the language of particular disciplines by integrating different genres in mixed texts that tell stories, inform, instruct, evaluate and persuade. Macrogenres are also a feature of workplace texts, for which school education is expected to prepare students.

Genres can be seen 'as offering choice – a *menu* with several courses of social purpose to choose' from (Martin & Rose 2008: 258). The aim of genre-based pedagogy is to assist students to understand how knowledge of genres can be applied to the construction of texts in order to

Table 1.2 Genres and social purpose

To tell stories	recounts, anecdotes, exemplums, observations on events, narratives, news stories, biographical recounts, historical recounts
To inform	explanations, descriptive reports, reports, procedural recounts
To instruct	procedures, protocols
To evaluate	personal responses, reviews, interpretations, critical responses
To persuade	expositions, discussion, challenges

Table 1.3   Curriculum genre

Curriculum initiation	^	Curriculum collaboration/negotiation	^	Curriculum closure
Establishes overall goals for teaching and learning through teacher direction		Where essential work is done with teacher and student sharing the workload		Provides clear sense of closure with students working independently to complete task(s)
Each phase contains different genres and usually extends over more than one lesson.				

Source: Adapted from Christie 2002: 100.

achieve a variety of social purposes. Students can also use knowledge about genres to critique the use of genres by others and to adapt genre patterns for specific and complex purposes.

Quote

By following genres we can see both the complex regularities of communicative life and the individuality of each situated utterance. Awareness of robust types and purposeful individual variation responsive to local circumstances provides an antidote to oversimplifying models of writing instruction ...

The longer you work with genre, the more it reveals and the more it connects with – perhaps because genre is at a central nexus of human sense-making, where typification meets utterance in pursuit of human action. To communicate effectively we need to know what kind of situation we are in, what kinds of things are being said, and what kinds of things we want to accomplish. The evolving variety of human circumstances, the creative potentials of language, and the cleverness of human action challenge us to know where we are and where we are going in interactions, especially since we must be intelligible to other people equally struggling to make sense of communicative situations from their separate perspectives. Shared social attributions of genre help us, and those we communicate with, to be on the same page, or close enough for our practical purposes.

(Bazerman in Bawarshi & Reiff 2010: xi)

Research undertaken within the theoretical framework of Systemic Functional Linguistics (SFL) has provided a detailed description of the differences between spoken and written language. A useful tool for thinking about spoken and written language is the mode continuum,

Table 1.4 Texts located along the spoken-written mode continuum

Mode Continuum			
Text 1	**Text 2**	**Text 3**	**Text 4**
A: Put this here and move this to about here and then you can sit here. B: Here? A: Yeah that's about right.	A: Good morning tech services. B: Hi I'm having trouble with using the keyboard – it's too high. A: Do you have a desk with a keyboard extender? B: No. Can I get one? A: Get your supervisor to …	1 Relax arms at your side with elbows a few centimetres from your body. 2 Position your chair and keyboard to minimise reach.	… The work surface may need to be raised or lowered to keep the operator's arms in a comfortable position. This can be achieved by installing an adjustable keyboard extender or tray, by providing an adjustable working surface … (Adapted from www.medicinenet.com– 3.1.12)

◄──────── Spatial and interpersonal distance ────────►

Visual and aural contact with immediate feedback	Aural contact with immediate feedback	No visual or aural contact between reader and writer but reader can respond to instructions	No visual and aural contact between reader and writer

◄──────── Experiential distance ────────►

Language accompanying action	**Language as reflection**

as illustrated in Table 1.4, in which four texts about setting up an ergonomic workstation are placed along the continuum. Text 1, the most 'spoken' text, is an exchange between two workmates and Text 4, the most 'written' text, appears on a website giving health advice. Text 1 can only be fully understood by participants sharing the context in which it is being used and taking part in the accompanying actions. At the other end of the continuum, Text 4 is written to communicate its message to readers in different contexts across time and space. The speakers of Text 1 and the writer of Text 4 drew on the same language to construct these texts but used the grammatical resources of the language in different ways. Located between Texts 1 and 4 on the mode continuum, Text 2 is concerned with problem-solving via spoken language over the telephone and so the speakers must be more explicit by naming computer components and office furniture, while Text 3 is an instructional written text that is seeking to *advise* the reader in a direct way.

Halliday (1985a: 61) describes written language as being *lexically dense* because meanings tend to be expressed in expanding nominal (noun) groups. Nominal groups make it possible to package and condense information into texts, adding to the lexical density of written language, for example, *an adjustable keyboard extender.* Halliday (1985a: 76) describes spoken language as *grammatically intricate* because generally it is created jointly by a number of speakers and develops through intricate networks of interdependent clauses, as well as incomplete utterances, false starts, repetitions, hesitations, repairs and overlapping (See also Halliday 2002/1987). Because spoken language is usually used in dialogue with others it is characterised by constant feedback, everyday non-specialised vocabulary, and fewer content words than grammatical words. To illustrate, in the following examples boundaries between clauses are marked by vertical lines and content words are highlighted in bold.

Spoken example
Put this here | and **move** this to about here | and then **you** can **sit** here.

Written example
The **work surface** may need to be **raised** or **lowered** | to **keep** the **operator's arms** in a **comfortable position**

Quotes

Writing and speaking are not just alternative ways of doing the same things; rather, they are ways of doing different things ... the kinds of meanings that are transmitted in writing tend to be somewhat different from the kinds of meanings transmitted through speech.

(Halliday 1985b: iii and 45)

Written language – especially in its published form – is both more permanent and more prestigious than the spoken word. It is the written form most users will take as defining what counts as 'the language'.

(Cameron 1995: 56)

The genre-based approach to language and literacy education is based on the view that learning language is a process of 'learning how to mean' and expanding a language user's 'meaning potential' (Halliday 2007/1991: 274). It is not a process that is completed in primary school but begins with the development of a first language during infancy and early childhood, proceeds throughout the school years, and continues into adult social and work contexts. It has been derived not only from

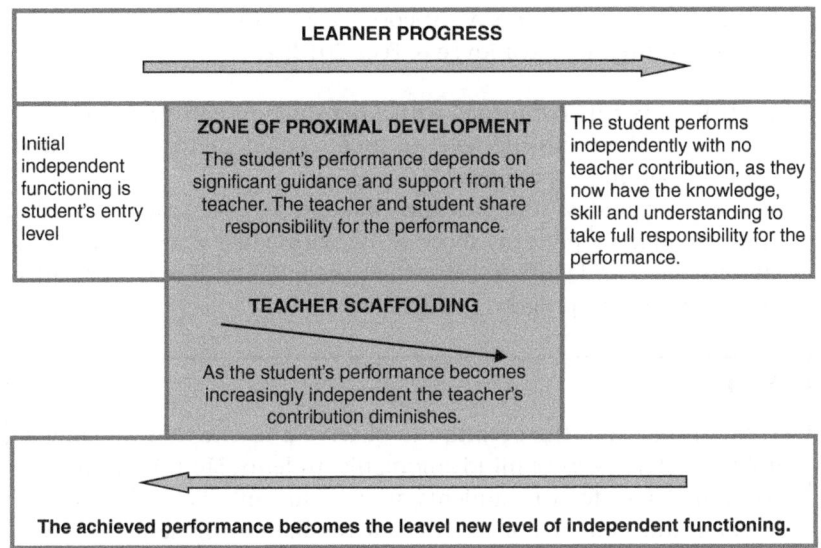

Figure 1.1 Zone of proximal development
Source: de Silva Joyce & Feez (2012: 49).

linguistic research but also from the work of the Russian psychologist Lev Vygotsky (1978/1934) who identified learning as a social activity involving interaction and collaboration between teacher and student. In any given domain of learning, where students are trying to develop skills, knowledge or understanding, the learner has two levels of performance:

1. A level of independent performance where the learner can think through problems and undertake tasks and activities without assistance
2. A level of potential performance where the learner, if supported to achieve higher levels of competence, could think through problems and undertake tasks and activities

The region between these two performance levels, Vygotsky labelled *the zone of proximal development* (see Figure 1.1). In this zone, educational instruction, social interaction and collaboration 'with more capable others' (Vygotsky 1978: 86) can lead the learner to new understandings and higher levels of capability. For Vygotsky (1987: 48) '[t]he only good instruction … is the one that precedes and guides development'. A view of learning based on Vygotsky's theory leads to two conclusions about language learning (de Silva Joyce & Feez 2012: 47):

1. If a teacher is only concerned with what students can already do with language – their existing level of independent performance – then students will never progress.
2. If a teacher guides, supports and collaborates with students so that they are able to perform successfully within the zone of proximal development and work towards their potential level of performance, real learning and progress is possible.

Quote

[My visit] provides the occasion to observe a teacher encouraging a problem-solving cast of mind among his students. His role is particularly important, for the students are in a juvenile justice diversion program and benefit especially from his mentoring style. But the interaction demonstrates, as well, the critical role of knowledgeable others in the development of systematic thinking. Furthermore, the teacher and the plumbing trade provide the opportunity for these young people to display intelligence so often missed, or misunderstood, in the typical classroom.

(Rose 2004: xxix–xxx)

In genre-based approaches to literacy education, the teacher is central to the process of literacy development, adopting an authoritative role similar to that of an expert guiding an apprentice and supporting the students to the degree needed for them to succeed. This process of collaborative support between teacher and student has been called *scaffolding* (Bruner 1986: 74). 'Effective scaffolding is support that is provided at the point of need' (Hammond & Gibbons 2001: 5) and is gradually reduced as the students become more and more independent. Scaffolding takes two forms in the classroom, with the first being *designed-in scaffolding* where the teacher builds it into the planning of units of work. The second form is *contingent scaffolding*, which occurs when the teacher identifies an immediate need and a 'teachable moment' in which intervention targeted at the need can 'maximise the learning potential of that moment' (Sharpe 2001: 33). As students move to new levels of independent functioning through collaboration with the teacher, these new levels become the starting points from which the students are supported to make further gains as illustrated in Figure 1.1.

Quote

[Scaffolding is] the steps taken to reduce the degree of freedom in carrying out some task so that the [student] can concentrate on the difficult skills she is in the process of acquiring.

(Bruner 1978: 19)

Genre-based pedagogy can also be seen as an application of the theory of pedagogy proposed by the British sociologist of education, Basil Bernstein (2000). Bernstein (1996) distinguishes between two types of knowledge (everyday knowledge and educational knowledge) and two types of pedagogy (invisible and invisible). The genre-based approach to language education is a visible pedagogy that can be oriented to learning everyday knowledge, for example, the knowledge needed by newly arrived migrants to participate in the everyday routines and practices of their new country, or to specialised educational knowledge, depending on the curriculum context and student learning needs. Genre pedagogy is used to build language and literacy competence systematically and incrementally through a shared pedagogic metalanguage that helps teachers and students to collaborate more effectively in the process of literacy learning. Ideally, this metalanguage is accessible, 'systematic and consistent' and 'can be used in teacher education, and by teachers in lesson preparation' as well as by teachers and students in the classroom (Rose & Martin 2008: 207).

Reconciling approaches to literacy education

Each of the four orientations to literacy education introduced above is a product of a different era. Each one has been supported by a variety of studies based on different methodologies, conceptual frameworks or theories. Each orientation has filtered into educational policy and classroom practice to varying degrees and in varying forms. Each has been introduced into the educational domain through publications whose authors have researched language, literacy and/or pedagogic practice from a variety of disciplinary perspectives. Over the years, different selections from these publications have been studied in teacher education programmes, and/or have been recast for public consumption by journalists, politicians and/or populist commentators, each with their own experience of literacy and literacy education. As those trained in one or other of these various orientations become classroom teachers themselves, and later teacher educators, or move into administrative positions, debates about the nature of literacy and how to teach it become inevitable. The processes through which successive research findings filter into bureaucracies, teacher education and classrooms are one reason why debates about what literacy is and how to teach it will continue to be so strident. Populist commentators, for example, will always be able to find an educator, for example, from an earlier generation or with experience teaching literacy to a particular social group, who will provide evidence in support of one particular approach and who will criticise other approaches.

It is difficult to come to a more balanced view that recognises that all these orientations to literacy have added to our overall understandings of what literacy is and how people use it. If the enduring challenges of literacy and its role in society are to be dealt with effectively, then setting up dualisms and dichotomies (Christie 2010a: 9) wastes an enormous amount of energy, resources and money. All the above orientations to literacy can be and perhaps should be part of literacy planning, programming and teaching. After all literacy is a learned practice that is developed largely through schooling, and decoding is part of the reading process but is not the only reading skill.

Over recent decades models have been developed that integrate disparate views of literacy in terms of complementary knowledge and skills. One such model is the framework outlined by Freebody and Luke (1990) in which reading was explained in terms of either four resources – code-breaking, participating in, using and analysing texts – or four reader roles – code breaker, text participant, text user and text analyst (see below). With the advent of this model of reading, educators were encouraged to take a more complex and sociocultural view of reading, beyond, but not excluding, decoding. Over recent years the model has been expanded or adapted to account for how viewers 'read' multimodal texts. Serafini (2012), for example, has applied the four reader roles to multimodal texts by re-naming them as text navigator, text interpreter, text designer and text interrogator.

Effective readers and writers also apply strategies such as skimming and scanning across pages of text to match what is on the page with an overall purpose, and they develop skills for using different writing technologies, each one demanding specific fine motor skills. The earliest writing technologies were slow to change, over millennia, from inscribing on stone, clay, wood or wax to scribing on animal skin or paper. Writing technologies developed more rapidly over centuries with the invention of the printing press and the typewriter, until the ways we use screens as writing instruments today, activated by keyboard, touch or voice, can change almost overnight. Learning how to read and write means learning how to integrate these strategies and skills while engaging with the various levels of language in texts, including structure, meaning, grammar, vocabulary and sounds and letters.

Quotes

Learning your role as code breaker

To be a successful reader, an individual needs to successfully engage the technology of the written script. There are two aspects to this technology: the nature of the relationship between spoken sounds and written symbols, and the contents of that relationship ...

Learning your role as text participant

By this term we mean developing the resources to engage the meaning-systems of the discourse itself ... the processes of comprehension call upon the reader to draw inferences connecting textual elements and background knowledge required to fill out the unexplicated aspects of the text ...

Learning your role as text user

Since reading and writing are nothing if not social, then being a successful reader is being able to participate in those social activities in which written text plays a central part ...

Learning your role as text analyst

... an awareness of the fact that all texts are crafted objects, written by persons with particular dispositions or orientations to the information, regardless of how factual or neutral the products may attempt to be ...

(Freebody & Luke 1990: 8–13)

As well as understanding literacy as a multidimensional phenomenon embracing literacy-specific knowledge, skill and practice across social contexts, what people bring to reading and writing processes from the wider context is also seen as important. That reading was more than a straightforward process of decoding was revealed in studies of the psycholinguistic processes that underpin reading (for example, Goodman 1996, Smith 1973 and 1990). These studies showed, through various experiments, that readers bring their (often unconscious) knowledge of grammar, as well as their life experiences (sociocultural knowledge) to the reading process. They then use the overall context of the texts they are reading to confirm their interpretation of the words in the text. Goodman's (1969, 1973) development and application of a reading diagnostic tool, miscue analysis, provided insights into what readers do as they read a text, enabling assessment of capabilities as well as identifying areas for pedagogic intervention.

The sociolinguistic study of spoken and written language has been extended to account for visual and multimodal texts. Most literacy curricula now include outcomes related to interpreting and/or creating multimodal texts. The four reader roles framework outlined by Freebody and Luke (1990) shifted the focus of reading pedagogy towards a concern for enabling students not only to decode written language but also to understand and participate in the sociocultural practices of reading. This framework has been recast to account for how 'an informed, literate citizenry ... must be able to navigate, interpret, design and interrogate the written, visual and design elements of multimodal texts' (Serafini 2012: 152). To prepare students for contemporary community, work and education contexts where multimodal texts abound, literacy programmes need to assist students to become text navigators who can decode written text and understand the elements of design, visual images and other multimodal elements in multimodal texts; text interpreters who can understand what has been written and depicted in multimodal texts; text designers who can decide how a particular multimodal text is to be read, in a particular time and place, according to the particular sociocultural context and the design, textual and visual elements within the text and finally text interrogators who can interrogate the meanings in a multimodal text beyond a literal reading/viewing.

Quote

Navigating multi-modal texts requires readers to attend to the grammars of visual design, in addition to the grammar, structures and typography associated with written language. The decoding processes outlined by Luke and Freebody (1999), for instance, delineate a reader's ability to break the code of written texts by recognising and using fundamental features and architecture, including alphabet, sounds in words and spelling, and structural conventions and patterns may be subsumed within the larger concept of navigating. In addition, non-linear structures, hypertext, visual images and multi-modal compositional structures need to be navigated by readers if readers are to be successful in today's educational, [community and work] settings. Navigating, including the decoding of written text, is an important skill and an equally important consideration for literacy educators, but it is an insufficient skill in and of itself to make readers proficient in new times ... The process of interpreting multi-modal texts requires readers to draw from their experiential reservoirs to generate viable interpretations to add to the interpretations made by others in a community of readers ... The interpretation of multi-modal texts requires readers to develop interpretive repertoires that address the visual images and design elements, in addition to the text itself, and the meaning potential across the various modes presented ... The images contained in multi-modal texts encountered in complex social contexts are created with particular semiotic resources, basic design elements and visual structures ... The act of interpreting may focus on the construction of knowledge by individual readers, but must also account for the sociocultural contexts of production, as well as reception, of multi-modal texts ...

The concept of reader as designer can be extended from the producer of texts to the process of navigating and interpreting multi-modal texts as well. Making a shift from designer as producer of multi-modal texts to navigator, interpreter of texts requires an expansion of the concept of design to include the active construction of meaning potentials during reader's transactions with multi-modal texts ...

Cultural theories of meaning assume a reading of a text to have idiosyncratic (personal) as well as culturally mediated (public) meanings. From this perspective, reading is re-conceptualised as a social practice that involves the construction of meaning in a socially mediated context, the power relationships inherent in any given setting and the readers' identity and available means of social participation. Although the term interrogator was chosen rather than the term analyst to connote a more aggressive stance to interpreting and designing texts, the two concepts are closely aligned. The concept of interrogator, like that of text analyst, includes the critical and sociocultural aspects of analysis espoused by Luke and Freebody in their original four resources model.

(Serafini 2012: 155–159)

Numeracy education

We will now move to a brief review of numeracy teaching and how it is currently viewed within the framework of literacy and numeracy education. Numeracy is another area that is assessed through PISA and there are also regular comparative social discussions and debates about numeracy levels across countries. The ability to utilise numeracy skills and understand mathematical ideas and information is essential to effective participation in contemporary community, employment and educational settings. There are two main perspectives that help to differentiate the way numeracy is approached, particularly in adult learning contexts. The first perspective is a focus on the mathematical information that is integrated into written texts such as graphs and tables, newspaper reports, etc. The other perspective is a focus on the development of mathematical knowledge and skills, which is, or should be, the province of specialist numeracy or mathematics teachers.

Numeracy is now also seen as a social practice as people 'employ mathematical content and techniques that vary according to the situation' and 'generate mathematical problems, skills or procedures depending on the purpose and context in which the numeracy takes place'.[12] Numeracy education focuses on how numeracy and mathematical language are part of meaning making in social contexts, developing relationships, and forming a numerate identity. Ginsburg and Gal (1996: 2–16) propose strategies for teaching numeracy to adults that include linking numeracy with literacy by providing opportunities for students to communicate about mathematical issues and developing skills in interpreting numerical or graphical information within texts.

Quote

Activities within an adult math class should serve to develop mathematical understanding as well as computational skills, and should target generalised problem-solving, reasoning, and communication skills. All too often, students work on one skill at a time and are told what algorithms to apply to contrived or context-free problems ...

However, in real life contexts, quantitative or quantifiable elements may be interspersed with other information, and it is seldom specified what to do or what knowledge is relevant. People have to *comprehend* a situation, *decide* what to do, and *choose* the right tool(s) from their 'mathematical tool chest' that will enable them to reach a *reasonable* solution ... For math education to be effective and meaningful for adults, we must broaden the contexts in which instruction is couched, widening the range of interactions among students and between students and mathematics content. This implies an expansion of the definition of essential math-related skills to include verbal and written communication about numbers, the interpretation of numerical information encountered in the media, and the knowledge to make decisions regarding the level of precision or the most effective mode of response needed for various tasks.

(Ginsburg & Gal 1996: 16–17)

Conclusion

The orientations to literacy described above – basic skills, the four roles model, literacy skills and strategies, psycholinguistic processing – all have a place in research, policy and institutional settings. While some educators understand each orientation as a product of its time contributing to our accumulating knowledge about literacy and its development, others will endorse one orientation as the definitive response to the often ill-defined literacy problems faced by society. Meanwhile, in the unsupportive context of the seemingly endless 'literacy wars' (Snyder 2008), classroom teachers typically select from a repertoire of instructional practices and resources to design programmes they believe best match the needs of their students, but which do not always align neatly with one particular approach (Freebody 2007). In the review of the series of orientations to literacy above, and their influence on literacy education, we have attempted to understand what they have contributed cumulatively to our understandings of literacy and to consider what they might bring to the contemporary literacy classroom.

When home language practices coincide with those of the school, children gain a foundation for successful educational learning but, for a variety of reasons, for some children there is only a partial overlap or no overlap between home and school language. Initial disadvantage often compounds over the school years and into community life and the workplace but text-based approaches to literacy development support teaching programmes that intervene in the language and literacy development of students of all backgrounds and ages, providing them with the tools they need to achieve their goals in educational, community and vocational settings. What is essential is enabling students to deal with the increasing abstraction that they will encounter as their learning moves into specialised disciplines and this requires the understandings that have come from SFL about spoken and written language and how technicality and abstraction are developed in the discourses of specific disciplines (see Chapter 2). To ensure that all people learning to be literate share these understandings requires explicit visible interventionist pedagogy that can apprentice them into these discourses.

Quote

In considering language and literacy in relation to school and work, secondary education distributes access to discursive resources, in differing proportions to different groups in society ... The economic roles that different groups of students go on to occupy depends on how successfully they engage with the reading and writing demands of secondary education.

(Korner, McInnes & Rose 2007: 10)

Literacy researchers continue to build our understanding of the many complex features of what it means to be literate and, more recently, what it means to be numerate in a variety of social contexts. Areas of enquiry include the intersection between literacy and numeracy, the intersection between power and disadvantage, and ways to tailor literacy teaching to meet the needs of particular social groups. Each orientation to literacy and literacy teaching reviewed above has afforded the literacy teacher one or more classroom roles: learned authority, behaviour modifier, skills developer, facilitator or expert. Each has privileged different types of texts in the classroom: literary texts, phonics-based readers, basal readers, authentic texts, student chosen texts, language experience stories, personal narratives and other whole texts representative of school and social genres

We hope revisiting the different approaches to literacy education will assist teachers to engage 'in a dialogue between past ways of understanding literacy [and numeracy] and present formulations' (Snyder 2008: 213). Realising how research over the decades has allowed us to accumulate understandings is perhaps a way of avoiding the pointless and wasteful literacy wars and allowing us to get on with the job of enabling all students to develop literacy and numeracy skills for participation in an increasingly complex world. This does require the type of explicit intervention as reflected, for example, in genre-based or text-based approaches because time is limited when children are in school and assisting those who are disadvantaged in school and adult educational contexts is an imperative if we want to 'make things better' (Gee Chapter 7).

2
Studies of Literacy over Time and across Disciplines

An exhaustive study of literacy in human society over time and space would require many volumes. A thorough examination of the many debates that have been generated by the study of literacy and literacy development in different historical periods and in different societies is not possible in a publication of this size. However, a broad review of the terrain makes it possible to reflect on recurring themes across different historical and cultural contexts and to challenge fixed ideas about what it is to be literate and how people become literate. Different historical and cross-cultural perspectives demonstrate that approaches used to study literacy are themselves products of specific times and places and continually need to be reviewed and re-evaluated as cultures, societies and their literacy technologies change over time.

Literacy can be defined as 'the ability to read and write in at least one language' (McArthur 2003), where reading and writing involve the use of texts that are meaningful and purposeful in social contexts. Since the time when writing first appeared in human societies, the contexts in which people have read and written texts have been astonishingly diverse. Recognition of this diversity and the changes that have occurred in the uses of literacy and the practices of literacy has the potential to reinvigorate discussion about literacy and literacy education. Reinvigorating this discussion is important in the context of ever-changing developments in communication technologies, which has meant that the uses and practices of literacy are changing at a more rapid pace than ever before. Literacy educators thus work under clashing external pressures, including the pressure to attend to new literacies while at the same time providing access to high value and high status traditional literacy practices.

Reviewing the terrain involves an exploration of the development of the different scripts, systems of graphic symbols and technologies used by humans for writing in different eras and in different parts of the world. It also involves exploring how these scripts, symbols and technologies have encoded the language spoken by their users, what meanings they made possible and in what sociocultural contexts. Providing a picture of diverse literacy possibilities also raises questions about what the people who used these scripts and technologies understood literacy to be and what they did with it. It is also useful to recognise the historical origins of views about literacy that retain their currency today.

Questions about literacy practices in different eras and in different parts of the world also have to do with who was 'entitled to read and write' in these societies and how reading and writing was transmitted from one generation to the next because 'ensuring that a script endures must involve the strategies of pedagogy and apprenticeship' (Houston 2004: 6). Ancient societies tend to be identified by archaeologists as civilisations if the people of those societies lived in towns and used a writing system, for example, societies in Ancient Mesopotamia and Egypt, or Imperial China (Greene & Moore 2010: 314). We can see this identification echoed in beliefs widely held to this day about the nexus between literacy and civil society (Gee 2012a).

Several recent reviews in the field of literacy and literacy education have turned their attention to the history of the field. From the vantage point of 'literacy-saturated and literacy-dependent' post-industrial societies (Freebody 2007: 4), the perspective on literacy education that history provides is 'a way of framing and assessing current debates, policies and practices' (Freebody, Barton & Chan 2014: 419–420). Looking back to see how 'what it means to be literate' has varied across time and cultures is one means of coming to grips with the complexity of study in this field. Barton (2007: 8) reviews both the archaeological and social history of literacy to gain insights into 'the learning of literacy, levels of literacy in society, literacy and technological change and literacy and power relations'.

Quotes

To be literate varies with history and culture; it is to be literate in a given time and place, to be literate here and now.

(Freebody 2007: 9)

... what passes for effective literacy education can differ depending on the culture, history and technologies of social groups, and that our centuries-long focus on teaching and researching English in print, however rich and challenging that project has been, represents only one possible scholarly tradition.

(Freebody 2007: 3)

Reading and writing are goal-oriented activities, so it is impossible to understand what counts as literacy in any context, without first asking the question: What do people read and what do people write? In contemporary post-industrial societies, the literacy required to interpret and respond to a text message is different from the literacy required to write a scientific journal article. In other times and places scientific and literary texts have not been written down but have existed in oral form only (Gaur 2000: 176), or they have been encoded in a visual form, in painting, song or dance. These different forms of 'literate texts' nevertheless 'require[d] specialised cultural knowledge to be *read*, that is, decoded, understood, responded to and interpreted' (Freebody 2007: 3).

The visual *italk library*,[1] developed in Alice Springs in Central Australia, is an example of how widening the view of what counts as literacy can lead to innovation. This library combines 21st century technology with a visual literate tradition stretching back through the millennia to create multimodal and multilingual resources. Stories and information texts are represented in visual form and spoken language, in up to 14 Australian languages, as well as in English. The stories and information, when written in English, open a path to literacy in the English language (Brocklebank 2002).

This chapter reviews a selection of studies of literacy from prehistory to the present and across the fields, or disciplines, of educational knowledge. Because the transmission of literacy from one generation to the next 'must involve the strategies of pedagogy' (Houston 2004: 6), literacy education is also woven into the discussion.

Literacy across time and space

Writing is possible because humans have the capacity to see and hear. What we hear is more transient than what we see, with the result that representing spoken language visually as writing 'allows for the preservation of feelings, facts and ideas through time and space. This power to conserve ... has changed the face of the world' (Robertson 2004: 20). The 'scripts that first represented sound and meaning in a systematic fashion' in ancient times (Houston 2004: 3) are studied using methods and insights from a range of disciplines including, among others, archaeology, anthropology, linguistics, history and sociology and often through very specialised fields within these disciplines. The study of the origins of literacy and its development generates another of the multidisciplinary research landscapes that are a feature of literacy studies. Identifying some key features of this landscape adds to our understanding of what literacy means, the extent of literacy variation in the contexts in which it is used, the purposes it has been used for and the ways it has been learned and taught. In addition, it has expanded the repertoire of approaches researchers use in the fields of literacy studies and literacy education.

Humans began making 'intentional semipermanent marks' more than 30 000 years ago, although the genesis of 'a true writing system dates back less than six thousand years from the present' (Barton 2007: 112–113). With the advent of writing, humans began to represent meaning in 'a sequence of conventional marks' (Barton 2007: 114). These scripts were in contrast to earlier representations of meaning in visual images, symbols and memory aids. The idea, however, that writing systems can only be based on a linear script is challenged by the complex organisation of abstract symbols into sequences and spatial arrangements by the Indigenous peoples of Australia and North America, representations that, like all writing systems, need to be *read* in their cultural context to be understood.

Quote

To understand the history of writing we must set aside our literate prejudices, our tendency to assume as natural and obvious that language is an object available for inspection; that we have a natural consciousness of language. This tendency comes to literate people primarily from their identifying language with the written form and in some cases as identifying language as a distinctive 'tongue'. For non-literate persons language is available to thought only in the most general sense, as answers to 'What did he say?' or for translating into a foreign tongue. Consequently, writing was never a matter of simply inventing a device for recording speech but rather a matter of discovering the properties of speech suitable for visual representation and communication. It was the latter task that required generations of borrowing and invention ... the study of writing is at the same time the study of reading and their histories are, if not the same history, at least rather intertwined ...

... what began as a useful mnemonic, a device for keeping records some four or five millennium ago, turned into a means of communication, writing, that was readily adapted to serve diverse social practices in different ways in different contexts and cultures. Writing did so by capturing not only the basic structures of speech but also by the capacity, more developed in some cultural contexts than others, the full range of functions that speech serves. By specialising some of these functions to serve special purposes such as science and government, writing put its imprint on much of the modern world.

(Olson 2009: 9–15)

Much early writing has been lost, especially everyday writing using impermanent materials, but specialist archaeologists study what remains. One specialisation within archaeology, epigraphy, is the study of inscriptions that have been scratched, carved, engraved or baked onto durable materials such as bone, stone, pottery or metal. A complementary specialisation, palaeography, is the study of old handwritten manuscripts. These have been composed using implements such as a stylus, brush or quill and materials such as ochre, chalk, ink or paint on less durable writing surfaces such as bark, bamboo, wax, papyrus, parchment, silk or paper. Identifying the materials used and the temporal and geographical contexts that constitute the provenance of these ancient inscriptions and old manuscripts involves the use of archaeological research methods.

Archaeology is a discipline within which researchers build knowledge of past human societies, from human origins to the recent past, by compiling and interpreting material evidence such as artefacts, built structures, the effects of interaction between humans and the environment and biological data. Archaeology is an interdisciplinary field that combines quantitative and qualitative research techniques from the sciences (for example, physics, chemistry, biology, geology and climate science), the social sciences (for example, anthropology, psychology, linguistics and geography) and the humanities (for example, history, languages, literature and the visual arts). Research methods begin with a review of existing archives and literature and this is followed by field surveys to identify, to report and to interpret (see for example, Greene & Moore 2010).

If an ancient society used oral language only, then past events and insights into these earlier societies and cultures are lost to us. However, writing, whether inscriptions or manuscripts, provides records of past events and gives archaeologists and historians the opportunity to gain a perspective on these cultures from those who lived at the time. Consequently, the advent of writing is often used to represent the boundary between prehistory and history (Schmandt-Besserat 2004). Investigating the provenance of a script and deciphering its graphemes, using research methods from linguistics and history, aids interpretation of the meanings made by the text and the cultural significance of each inscribed or handwritten text for the ancient writers and their audiences.

Writing as a means of recording and archiving information emerged with the first city-states about 5 000 years ago. Most famously the cuneiform of Mesopotamia was used in various forms for 3 000 years but this writing most likely derived from earlier forms of graphic representation (Gaur 2000). From the advent of agriculture, 5 000 years earlier, tokens had been used to record harvests and, for tens of thousands of years before that, hunter-gatherers had used tallies for counting, suggesting that numeracy predated literacy. This developmental trajectory has been interpreted in terms of increasing levels of abstraction. 'Whereas tallies translated quantities of unspecified items, tokens referred to particular sets and, finally, writing encoded abstract numbers' (Schmandt-Besserat 2004, *Writing and society*: paragraph 7).

Writing appears to have emerged in Mesopotamia for the purposes of trade and keeping accounts, and in China and India it developed for purposes of administration. Wherever writing emerged, and for whatever reasons, it soon became an instrument of political power that could dominate from a distance by controlling and manipulating the production, storage and distribution of goods and codifying the hereditary privilege of monarchs and the edicts of the gods. Power wielded through literacy became entrenched when the ability to decipher writing remained in the hands of an elite few. At the same time, the records of royal genealogies and deeds evolved into history, laws became codified to make possible equality before the law, the retelling of the exploits of the gods evolved into scripture and literature, and from records of the movement of the stars and planets arose science and mathematics. Meanings captured in writing could be disseminated, reflected upon, discussed, reviewed, extended and elaborated (Bowman & Woolf 1994, Gaur 2000). Yet, despite these advantages, the historical record shows that writing was not the only means by which humans conserved and transmitted complex cultures through millennia. The development of writing is not necessarily tied to the advance of civilisations with, for example, Mayan writing developing as the civilisation declined (Houston 2004). Over thousands of years, since humans first invented them, many systems of writing have developed, stagnated, regained vibrancy and disappeared.

Over a period of about 2 000 years, the cuneiform of Mesopotamia and the hieroglyphs of Egypt were overtaken by scripts composed of signs representing the sounds of speech. From about 1 500 BCE, the Phoenicians were trading their purple-red dye and other much sought after goods around the Mediterranean Sea. By this time they had streamlined earlier writing into a business-like script made up of symbols, or letters, each matched to a single syllable or consonant sound of the language, and named with a word beginning with that sound. This script was taken up and modified by the Mediterranean trading partners of the Phoenicians, giving rise to Hebrew, Arabic and Greek writing. The Greek alphabet added letters for vowel sounds and this gave rise in turn to the Latin and Cyrillic alphabets. The word we have inherited from Greek to name the alphabet fittingly immortalises the Phoenician contribution to literacy by reminding us of the names of the first two Phoenician letters – *aleph* (ox) and *beth* (house) (see for example, Fischer 2001).

The phonetic Phoenician alphabet and its descendants have proven to be effective for the societies that inherited this writing system. In contrast, the writing system, which originated in China at about the same time around 1 200 BCE, and which spread to Japan and Korea, is based on logographs or characters, each one representing a morpheme. Like the alphabet, this writing system coevolved with the rise of complex cultures and societies and is used by a third of the world's population. Questions have been raised about whether alphabets of less than 30 letters representing the discrete sounds of a language make literacy more accessible and the evolution of abstract thought and logic more possible than a writing system based on the thousands of characters needed to represent the morphemes of a language. This view is described by Harris (1986: 29) as the 'tyranny of the alphabet over our modern ways of thinking about the relation between the spoken and written word'. A contrasting view is that a logographic script has the advantage because it can be used to share meanings across languages that are mutually unintelligible when spoken. In response to these questions, Taylor and Taylor (2014: 418) provide evidence that while users of different languages might think in different ways as a result of differences in cultural and educational traditions, this is not 'necessarily because of differences in scripts'. They conclude that 'a writing system is not inherently efficient or inefficient, but is so when considered in relation to the characteristics of the particular language it represents' (Taylor & Taylor 2014: 421).

Many contemporary authors maintain, as Taylor and Taylor (2014: 418) do, that no matter what type of script is used the 'benefits to civilisation of writing are incalculable' because writing 'enables humans to record natural phenomena and commercial transactions and to transmit culture and knowledge across space and time'. Nevertheless, this view was not necessarily held by those experiencing the advance of literacy in ancient times. In many ancient societies the most-highly valued knowledge and literature were captured in specialised varieties of oral language (Trigger 2004), a tradition that continues in some cultures to this day. In Plato's *Phaedrus* (370 BCE) Socrates even argues that writing is inferior to spoken language and impairs memory, 'since if written words are asked a question, they always give the same answer … once words are written down, they tumble about anywhere among those who may or may not understand them'. Thus, writing, according to Plato's written record of Socrates's argument, gives 'the appearance of wisdom, not true wisdom'[2] and because writing gives the appearance of being final and unable to respond to questioning, even more danger-ously, it can close down dialogue (Gee 2012a).

The Greeks had begun developing their alphabet centuries before Plato's time, when 'the first literate Greeks were not aristocrats but rather a small nucleus of craftsmen' who inscribed epic poetry onto objects (Robb 1994: 252). Much of Greek law and culture remained in oral form for centuries and the education of the elite continued to consist of memorising, reciting and singing epics and other highly revered texts. The oral tradition appears to have been kept alive in Plato's Academy in Athens, even though the reason we know some of what Socrates and Plato taught is because Plato wrote it down. By the mid-4th century BCE, when Plato's student, Aristotle, was teaching at the Lyceum, most public institutions in Athens were based on written texts (Robb 1994).

From this time on, to be educated in Ancient Greece was equated with being literate. Literacy was acquired by being educated and being educated became a pathway to certain types of social opportunity. Restricting access to education, whether for women, non-citizens or the poor, became a means of controlling the distribution of that opportunity. This pattern endured, as classical Greece gave way to the Hellenistic period and the Roman Empire began spreading across Europe and beyond. Literacy levels in societies shaped by this expansion waxed and waned, but literacy did not necessarily become widely accessible until comparatively recently.

In Ancient Roman society many people, including women and slaves, achieved at the very least what we now might call *functional literacy* and could read everyday inscriptions and notices (di Renzo 2000). Following the fall of the Roman Empire, however, formal education and literacy became more restricted in Medieval Europe, with 'writing, education and book production' largely controlled by the church (Gaur 2000: 138). Being literate, at that time in Europe, was equated with reading and writing Latin, the *lingua franca* of the educated across Europe in the Middle Ages, so to become educated meant learning Latin grammar.

Quote

Levels of literacy were low in classical antiquity by comparison with those prevailing in the most educated countries of the last 200 years. That is entirely to be expected, for each society achieves the level of literacy which its structure and ethos require and its technology permits.

(Harris 1989: 331)

There is growing evidence that literacy, including multilingual literacy, was more widespread than previously thought in Europe during the Middle Ages (Barton 2007). Nevertheless, for those who could not read written texts, in certain contexts of the medieval world, for example in churches, there was an abundance of images in the form of stained glass windows, sculpture, icons and friezes. 'The notion of reading images has a long history: the metaphor was utilised throughout the Middle Ages, especially in the Latin West, where pictorial cycles in churches were defended on the grounds that they were the books of the illiterate' (Sears 2002: 1). It is difficult from a 21st century understanding of multimodality to appreciate how for the medieval *reader* of images 'materiality acquired meaning and how the real presence of an object had aesthetic ramifications, how medieval viewers encountered objects, became culturally attuned to particular types of objects, and learned to perceive differences within classes of objects' (Thomas 2002: 13).

The study of grammar, alongside the study of logic and rhetoric in the classical tradition, made up the Trivium of medieval universities. While the Trivium covered knowledge about language and its use, knowledge about the physical world was studied in the Quadrivium of astronomy, music, geometry and arithmetic. This way of organising knowledge continues to resonate today, not only in the structure of universities established in the Western tradition (Bernstein 2000), but also in the structure and types of knowledge studied in these universities. The discourse patterns for representing this knowledge are valued in societies where the education system is based on this tradition. For example, if a Western audience considers a spoken or written argument to be convincing, this is likely to be because the argument includes the three elements identified by Aristotle as essential components of rhetoric – logic (valid and reliable reasoning), pathos (an appeal to the emotions), and ethos (a demonstration of trustworthiness).

A parallel story can be told of the role of literacy in Imperial China, where for centuries written examinations were used to select candidates for the civil service. The influence of the knowledge of the classic texts that was needed to succeed at these examinations, coupled with the Confucian values that these texts embodied, shaped Chinese society for centuries. This influence continues to be felt in China, and in other countries where Confucian values were adopted in the past, including Vietnam and Korea, despite the more recent impact of Western models of education.

The appearance in Europe of cheaper paper, invented in China, combined with moveable type printing technology, perhaps based on printing techniques invented in China and Korea some centuries earlier, led to the rapid expansion of literacy in Europe during the Renaissance (Saenger 1987). This in turn promoted the spread of education and the increasing standardisation of written languages. The advent of printing meant that less effort was needed 'to recover and preserve traditional knowledge' and more time could be devoted to building new knowledge, although, as print became dominant, ideas that failed to be printed, by intention or neglect, were easily lost (Barton 2007: 125–126).

In the English-speaking world, the affordability and accessibility of books and other printed material jumped again during the Industrial Revolution. Children were taught to read and write in private homes, individually or in small groups, and a variety of methods were used. During the 19th century, as compulsory primary schooling was introduced with the aim of teaching all children to read and write (Barton 2007), practices that were developed to teach large groups of children to read and write became increasingly standardised.

In English-speaking countries, in particular, rising literacy levels and increases in mass schooling coincided with the Industrial Revolution of the 19th century, but the social historian, Harvey Graff 1987 and 2011 Graff (1987, 2010, 2011), warns against naively accepting the 'literacy myth', which originated during this time. This is the myth, expressed in an 'evolutionary framework' (Barton 2007: 120), that increases in levels of literacy automatically and directly result in increased economic, cultural and social well-being for individuals, as well as for democracy and society as a whole. Vague and inconsistent definitions of literacy make it impossible, Graff (2010) argues, to investigate empirically the relationship between literacy and social impacts. Furthermore, the impact of literacy is mediated in complex ways by social factors such as gender, ethnicity, class, and the geographical, historical and cultural context. For example, the effects of literacy may have been greater for skilled, rather than unskilled workers, and rising literacy levels may have been 'an effect rather than a cause of industrialisation' with, at the time, an immediate 'negative impact on schooling chances for the young' even if the long-term impact has been positive (Graff 2010: 641). Literacy and education may also be used 'to foster political oppression and maintain inequitable social conditions' (Graff 2010: 640). The corollary of the literacy myth is the fear generated by each advance in communication technology that the new technology threatens the quality of literacy and of education, a fear that echoes back through the centuries to the fears about writing technology expressed in Plato's dialogues, fears that are re-emerging in the present with the advent of digital technology.

The 'literacy myth' according to Graff (2010) remains remarkably resilient, for example, in the assumptions of politicians and administrators who prescribe uniform literacy standards and pedagogies. These assumptions conflict with the richness and diversity of the historical record in relation to literacy, a record that reveals 'multiple paths to literacy learning ... and the diversity of motivations for learning to read and write' (Graff 2010: 645).

Quote

The most striking continuity in the history of literacy is the way in which literacy has been used, in age after age, to solidify the social hierarchy, empower elites and ensure that people lower on the hierarchy accept the values, norms and beliefs of the elites, even when not in their self-interest, or group interest to do so.

(Gee 2012a: 57)

In summary, to 'avoid conferring on literacy the status of myth' and to assess both the benefits and limits of literacy on the basis of evidence, it is necessary to ground literacy research 'in specific, contextualised and historical particulars' (Graff 2010: 639). The task for researchers in the 21st century, in the context of the multiple literacies generated by digital technology, is not to disprove the literacy myth 'but to understand it, and re-interpret it to serve more equitable, progressive humane goals' (Graff 2010: 652). The historical dimension, Graff (1987: 4) argues, is important, and he supports ethnographic studies as a means of making us aware of the 'difficulty, complexity and limits of literacy'. Ethnographic studies can be used to investigate in detail the different types and uses of literacy in specific social and cultural contexts.

Ethnography is a research approach originally developed by cultural anthropologists in order to study, systematically and in detail, specific societies and cultures, or sub-groups within a society or culture. Pioneering ethnographic studies include the studies of Indigenous cultures and languages undertaken by Franz Boas (1911) in Canada and the study of the Trobriand Islanders of New Guinea by Bronislaw Malinowski (1922). Ethnographic approaches are also used by social historians, sociologists and linguists (see Chapter 6).

The most influential ethnographic studies of literacy, for example by Scribner and Cole (1981), Heath (1983), and Street (2001a), led to the field of study that has become known as *Literacy Studies* which, with the development of digital communication technologies, has been reconceived as *New Literacy Studies* (Pahl & Rowsell 2006). In their study of the multilingual literacies of the Vai people in Liberia, cognitive psychologists Scribner and Cole (1981) focused on the use of the script in which the Vai language is written down. This is the script taught and used in everyday contexts, in contrast to Arabic literacy, taught for religious purposes, and English literacy learned in the context of formal schooling. To investigate literacy in this complex sociocultural setting, Scribner and Cole conceived of literacy as a social practice, with three components: technology, knowledge and skills.

Quote

All practices involve interrelated tasks that share common tools, knowledge base and skills ... tasks constitute a social practice when they are directed to socially-recognised goals and make use of a shared technology and knowledge system.

(Scribner & Cole 1981: 236)

The study by Scribner and Cole (1981) also distinguished between the features of the language itself and the teaching and learning processes through which people were taught to be literate in the language. Learning to read and write not only involves learning how to decode the script but also involves learning how a particular written language is used to achieve social purposes, within the context of the culture (see Freebody 2007, Olson 1994). Finally, Scribner and Cole's findings challenged the idea, which was commonly held at the time, that being literate automatically confers the ability to reason abstractly. In their study, this ability was linked not with literacy learned in everyday and religious contexts, but was linked specifically with literacy learned in formal school settings. Moreover, this type of abstract reasoning was only useful, and sustained, if it was useful in contexts beyond the school (Gee 2012a).

Scribner and Cole (1981) designed their study using a 'culture-cognition model', which combined techniques from two disciplines in order to explore the relation between cultural context and individual cognition. They borrowed an ethnographic approach from anthropology to investigate the 'social organisation and characteristics of the culture' and 'the standard ... techniques of experimentation and clinical interview' from cognitive psychology to investigate 'individual psychological processes' (Scribner & Cole 1981: 16–17).

Cognitive psychology is a study of the processes of the mind that transform information from the external environment into knowledge and understanding (cognition). The mental processes studied by cognitive psychologists include perception, attention, memory, thinking and language, in other words, processes which mediate between the outside world and thinking about and responding to that world. Cognitive psychologists also study development and learning, as well as metacognition, the monitoring of one's own thoughts and self-regulation. Cognitive psychology is often contrasted with behaviourist psychology, which is the study of direct responses to external stimuli, through conditioning, reinforcement and punishment (for example, Skinner 1938, Watson 1930). Cognitive psychologists use a variety of research methods that include

- experimental design in which participants are randomly allocated to groups, one of which is a control group for comparison, and the variables are carefully controlled (see Debra Myhill's description of a literacy research project in Chapter 7 which combined experimental design with a design-based methodology and discourse analysis)
- quasi-experimental design in which the research compares naturally occurring groups
- correlational design, in which the researcher investigates the possibility of a relation between two independent variables
- case study, an intensive study of an individual or individual group to generate a detailed and principled description (see Chapter 6)
- naturalistic observation of people in real-life settings, such as at home or in the classroom (see Chapter 6)
- computer imaging of the brain during specified activities to model different types of mental processes in terms of brain function

The relation between a language and its use in particular sociocultural contexts is explored in the well-known ethnographic study by Heath (1983) into the uses of reading and writing in two small Piedmont Carolinas working-class communities during a period of significant social change in that part of the United States. For a decade Heath immersed herself in the culture of these two communities – one white and one African-American. She described the different ways people in the two communities used language, and how these uses of language differed again from the way the middle-class white and African-American townspeople used language. Heath linked the different ways language was used in these communities to the varying degrees of success that children from the three communities achieved at school. The more that language use at home, including the use of literacy, aligned with the way language was used in school, the more likely the children were to succeed. An ethnographic perspective, according to Street (2011: 580), challenges the idea of a 'single uniform thing called *literacy*', that can be separated from the 'local meanings and cultural variations' of the social context in which it is used.

Even this brief review of the history of writing, through studies in anthropology, archaeology and history, reveals an extraordinary diversity in literacy practices over time and place. This diversity is revealed in the technologies used to write languages down, the knowledge systems underpinning and represented by those technologies and in the skills needed to be literate. Reflecting on this same diversity, Barton (2007: 32) argues for researchers who want to apply research approaches from the field of linguistics to the study of language education to adopt an 'ecological approach' to literacy as a way of 'bringing together its different strands'.

Quotes

Rather than isolating literacy activities from everything else in order to understand them, an ecological approach aims to understand how literacy is embedded in other human activity, its embeddedness in social life and in thought, and its position in history, in language and in learning ... Instead of studying the separate skills which underlie reading and writing, it involves a shift to studying literacy, a set of social practices associated with particular symbol systems and their related technologies.

(Barton, 2007: 32)

To be literate is to be confident in the literacy practices one participates in.

(Barton 2007: 185)

An ecological view of literacy challenges two perspectives on literacy that have retained their currency in the field of literacy education. The first view is that literacy can be considered and learned in isolation from the social contexts in which it is used. This view continues to strongly influence policy and practice, even though it is not supported by linguistic studies demonstrating that language and literacy can be viewed more clearly when 'society, culture and values' are foregrounded (Gee 2012a: 1). The second is the evolutionary view of literacy as a 'natural linear progression towards the best' applied either to the development of writing over time or to the development of literacy in the individual (Barton 2007: 122). However, this does not align with either the social history of writing development nor the way educational linguistics has shown how individuals learn to read and write.

Linguistics is the study of language, including the study of the components of language and their organisation, the meanings made by language, and the uses made of language in sociocultural contexts. Sociolinguistics is the branch of linguistics concerned with studying the relationship between language use and sociocultural contexts. It is concerned with 'language variation and change' and the 'social uses of language' (Chambers, Trudgill & Schilling-Estes 2002: 1–3). Sociolinguists study how language use varies in relation to contextual variables such as gender, age, status, educational attainment, social class, ethnicity, geography and time, and how it varies across social groups or speech communities in particular locations, for example, adolescents at a secondary school or employees in a workplace. They also compare those varieties of language that are valued in specific social contexts, for example, in tertiary education or in the professional workplace, as well as varieties of language identified as standard or non-standard.

The linguist William Labov is credited with establishing the field of sociolinguistics and is best known for a study that challenges the idea that children who grow up speaking non-standard varieties of English are verbally deprived. Instead, he argued that these children are prevented from succeeding in school because educators do not pay attention to the children's home language and educational practices do not enable these children to display and build on the language ability they have developed prior to coming to school (Labov 1972).

Quotes

Teachers are now being told to ignore the language of black children as unworthy of attention and useless for learning. They are being taught to hear every natural utterance of the child as evidence of his mental inferiority. As linguists we are unanimous in condemning this view as bad observation, bad theory and bad practice ... That educational psychology should be strongly influenced by a theory so false to the facts of language is unfortunate; but that children should be the victims of this ignorance is intolerable.

(Labov 1972: 187)

Linguists are in an excellent position to demonstrate the fallacies of the verbal-deprivation theory. All linguists agree that nonstandard dialects are highly structured systems; they do not see these dialects as accumulations of errors caused by the failure of their speakers to master standard English ... Nor do they believe that the speech of working-class people is merely a form of emotional expression, incapable of relating logical thought ... There is no reason to believe that any nonstandard vernacular is in itself an obstacle to learning. The chief problem is ignorance of language on the part of all concerned.

(Labov 1972: 239)

Like anthropologists, sociolinguists use ethnographic techniques to investigate different contexts of language use. Sociolinguists also collect samples of the language variety they are studying through interviews and recordings of people using language, often building a corpus, a collection of naturally occurring samples. These samples are analysed using techniques such as discourse analysis or conversation analysis, as well as statistical analysis. For example, they may analyse the language samples for one or all of the following – the frequency of particular language features, the co-occurrence of features or correlations between language features and contextual variables.

When linguistics is applied in order to solve problems related to the use of language in social life, it is known as *applied linguistics*. Applied linguistics is relevant to research in many fields, including education, psychology, medicine, media studies and policy development.

The rationale for applied linguistics is exactly the reconnection of language not only... to the contexts of situation in which it occurs, but also, more generally, to the many social practices involving an understanding of language. This process, as many have observed, should not be a one-way imposition, but a dynamic interaction in which theories of language will also be illuminated by insights from practical activities.

(Cook & Seidlhofer 1995: 7)

How literacy is embedded in social and cultural contexts – its ecology – is undergoing rapid change, most obviously driven by the constant renewal of communication technologies. So, once again, what counts as literacy is under challenge, with new literacies and numeracies blurring the boundaries between what is understood as traditional reading, writing and mathematics, and the interpretation and composition of literacies and numeracies that combine multiple modes.[3]

Quote

In numeracy the issue of modality is central since numerical principles and procedures are always represented in a variety of modes – from oral and written (using symbols) to visual (in mathematics education terms 'iconic'), including layout and ordering as in a number square or number line, to action (or 'enactive'), as in the use of concrete apparatus for number or as in movement across diagrams.

(Street & Baker 2006: 219)

Even a brief and incomplete overview of literacy across time and in different parts of the world reveals that human societies have flourished in different parts of the world and in different eras with and without literacy. These societies include those in which valued social practices and cultural knowledge are conserved and transmitted in multiple modes, including oral language, as well as through visual arts and music.

An oral culture can be transformed into a literate one, gradually or more rapidly, in a variety of ways, not all of which are benevolent, and what counts as literacy also varies considerably across and within societies over time. In Ancient Greece, oral and literate traditions operated in tandem, before the written mode became dominant, while in developed societies, in the 21st century, valued knowledge is stored as written text. Increasingly, digital technologies are generating new types of texts globally, often in multilingual settings. These texts combine spoken and written language, still and moving images, and are interconnected through networked links. Digital text genres are emerging and adapting to contexts of use, which themselves are emerging and changing and thus generating the potential for representing existing knowledge in new ways and opening up possibilities for making new kinds of meaning and new kinds of knowledge. '[L]anguage as a resource for meaning-making has to date dominated the semiotic space' but this is a time when people are exploring the *semiotic margins* or the ways in which humans make meaning through non-linguistic resources (Dreyfus, Hood & Stenglin 2011: 1) and how these intersect with language. Looking back across the landscape of multiple literacies of the past may enable us to step into the dazzling and sometimes confusing world of the multiple literacies of the future with more confidence.

Literacy across academic disciplines

Traditionally, and most succinctly, the term *literacy* refers to the ability to read and write, but research across several disciplines, including archaeology, anthropology, history and sociolinguistics, has expanded this view. Scholars working within each of these disciplines, or systems of organised knowledge, have asked and continue to ask different questions about literacy and to attend to literacy in different ways by using different approaches. As a result, there is now a spectrum of literacy definitions to choose from, depending on the purpose for which a definition is needed. At one end of the spectrum is the view that literacy is a set of generic and portable skills for deciphering written language, skills most often learned in the early years of school, a view sometimes associated with studies from the field of psychology (Barton 2007). At the opposite end of the spectrum are more expansive multidisciplinary definitions based on the view that literacy is 'the flexible and sustainable mastery of a repertoire of practices with the texts of traditional and new communications technologies via spoken language, print and multimedia' (Luke, Freebody & Land 2000: 9), or more concisely 'how people use and produce symbolic materials fluently and effectively' (Freebody 2007: 9).

The idea of mastery is particularly relevant when considering the relation between literacy and academic disciplines. Gee (2012a: 173), for example, has defined literacy as the mastery of a 'secondary discourse', a discourse *learned* through teaching and apprenticeship in a public setting such as a school or, later in life, a workplace. This is in contrast to the primary discourse *acquired* at home during the first years of life (Gee 2012a).

Quotes

By 'discourse' I mean stretches of language which 'hang together' so as to make sense to some community of people ... what makes sense to one community may not make sense to another.

(Gee 2012a: 112)

When we write, read, speak or listen, on a particular occasion, we coordinate and get coordinated by other people, specific ways of using language, various objects, tools, technologies, sites and institutions. What is important is not words (oral or written) themselves, but the larger and specific coordinations of which they are a part and in which they gain their significance ... so 'discourse' is part of 'Discourse' – Discourse with a capital 'D' is always more than just language ...

Writing and reading are actions by which humans make meaning, and meaning is a complex phenomenon that continually criss-crosses the boundary between mind and society. If you were to come across strange marks etched in a rock, they would have no meaning for you. Why? Because you wouldn't know anything about how these marks were used in the sense making activities of the community whose symbols they are.

(Gee 2003: 5–6)

Apprenticeship into an academic discipline means learning how 'to participate successfully in the discourses of that discipline' (Hasan 1996a: 398), and becoming part of the community who make sense of that configuration of discourses. The discourses, and more specifically, the literacy practices, of each discipline are a function of the way knowledge is structured and produced in the discipline. Discipline-specific literacy practices have been productively investigated using Systemic Functional Linguistics (SFL) as a conceptual framework (see for example, Halliday 1985b and 1994, Halliday & Matthiessen 1999a, Halliday & Hasan 1989).

The conceptual framework provided by SFL is used to study *texts* in the contexts in which they are used, the *system* of language as a whole, and the relationships between texts and the language system. Text is the unit of analysis for systemic functional linguists, who understand a text to be 'a purposeful, harmonious collection of meanings relevant in the context, unified by *texture*, or the way the meanings fit together in the text, and *structure*, or the organisation of the elements of the text' (Butt, Fahey, Feez & Spinks 2012: 22).

When SFL is used to study a text, the first step is to analyse the sociocultural context in which a text is used in order to consider how the context shapes and is shaped by the meanings made by the text. The variables in the immediate social context – the context of situation – that directly impact language use are analysed in a systematic way in terms of three parameters of the context:

1. **field** – what is being talked or written about (for example, science)
2. **tenor** – the relationship between the producer of the text (speaker, writer) and the audience (listener, reader) (for example, a teacher and student)
3. **mode** – the kind of text, whether spoken, written or multimodal (for example, face-to-face spoken language accompanying a classroom activity or a textbook)

Using these three parameters to analyse systematically the context of situation opens up the possibility for a further analytical step, that is, an investigation of how the configuration of contextual variables constrain the meanings that can be made in the text, and, thus, the language features chosen to express those meanings. In other words, the framework can be used to show how contextual variables govern the language variety or register of a text, and how the words and grammatical structures of a text give these variables substance in the text.

Quote

These three variables [field, tenor and mode], taken together, determine the range within which meanings are selected and the forms which are used for their expression. In other words, they determine the 'register'.

(Halliday 1978: 31)

The three parameters of the context are reflected in the three main functions, or metafunctions, for which language is used in texts. Experiential meanings are meanings about our experiences of the world and logical meanings are how these experiences are related to each other logically. Together experiential and logical meanings make up the ideational meanings of a text, which are a reflection of field. Interpersonal meanings enable us to interact with others and to express a point of view, a reflection of tenor, and textual meanings tie ideational and interpersonal meanings together into a cohesive, comprehensible, and coherent whole, a reflection of mode. These three types of meanings are made real, or given substance in a text, through the choice and arrangement of language features. The relationship between meanings and the register variables is represented in Figure 2.1.

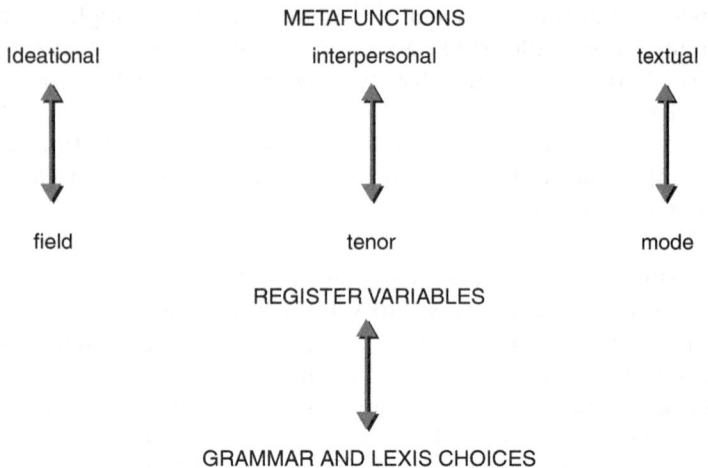

METAFUNCTIONS

Ideational   interpersonal   textual

field   tenor   mode

REGISTER VARIABLES

GRAMMAR AND LEXIS CHOICES

Figure 2.1   Relations between register variables and metafunctions

In this model there are two main layers of language – the layer of content and the layer of expression that gives the content a material form. The layer of content is further divided into two levels – meaning, or semantics, and words organised into grammatical structures, or lexicogrammar. In summary, the *content* layer has two sub-layers – systems of meaning made real by systems for organising words into grammatical structures, which, in turn, are made real by the expression layer that is made up of systems of sounds (phonology) and systems of graphemes (graphology) for representing the sounds[4] (Butt et al. 2012).

The SFL model (see Figure 2.2) can be used as a map to navigate, in a principled way, the different functions and elements of language. If a researcher wishes to focus attention on one small aspect of language use for detailed study, the SFL map makes it possible to keep in mind the relationship between the particular element, the varieties of language it is associated with and the language system as a whole.

When using this map, the researcher is not forced to choose between either a view of literacy as a narrow set of skills for managing print or an all-encompassing view of literacy as the mastery of multiple practices involving written, spoken and multimodal texts. For example, the researcher may want to focus on a specific print literacy skill associated with the system of graphology, at the expression level. The use of this skill can be studied in relation to its use in particular varieties

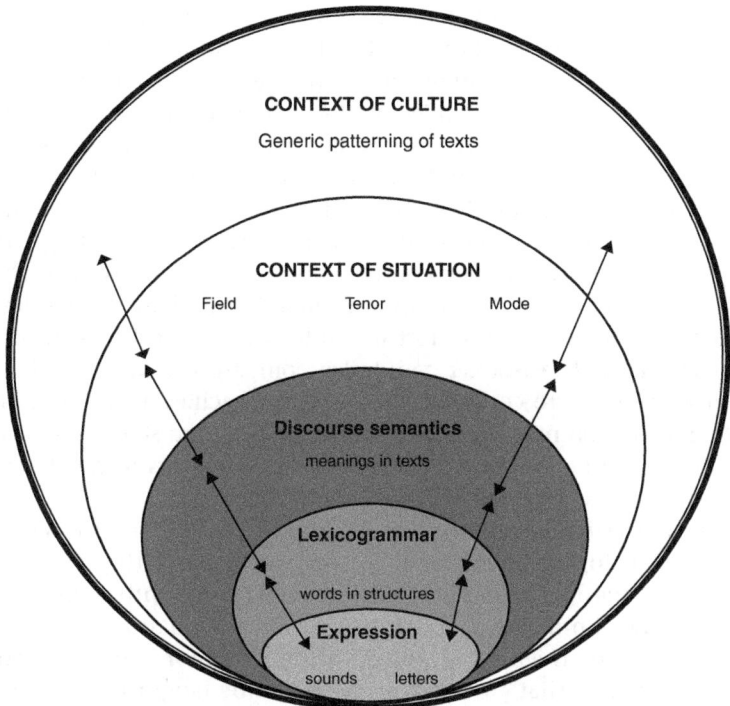

Figure 2.2 SFL language model

of written language, at the content level, in particular contexts. For example, a researcher may wish to study how varieties of written language associated with a particular print literacy skill are different from and interact with texts composed using other modes, including spoken texts, visual images and other written texts in a particular *language event* (Barton 2007: 35 – 36). A teacher, perhaps in collaboration with an academic partner, might design a small action research (practitioner-based enquiry) project to answer the question about which texts composed by students should be accepted as handwritten texts and which should be typed using a computer keyboard. The findings could be used to assist with programming the teaching and practice of handwriting and keyboard skills in the context of writing texts most relevant to these skills.

Over a school term, or other specified time period, the teacher could collect samples of texts written either by all students, or by a representative sample of students. The texts could first be sorted according to whether the writers used handwriting or a computer keyboard to prepare the texts for publication. The texts could be next categorised according to the activity type that generated the text (for example, in-class practice activity, guided writing, homework activity, end of term assignment, summative assessment task). Finally, the texts could be analysed for purpose, and therefore genre, for example, whether the purpose of each text is to tell a story, give instructions, organise information, explain or persuade. On the basis of the findings from this simple study, the teacher could identify, in the context of teaching about particular types of text, and/or preparing students for particular types of activity, when it is most useful to teach about handwriting or keyboard skills. The teacher could also compare the samples of high and low achievers to consider what aspects of achievement are linked to the publication medium (handwriting or keyboard skills), and if this knowledge can be taught explicitly to lower achievers to set them up for more success.

Such a research project might be useful in light of the current debate occurring in educational sectors, particularly the school sector, about whether or not to teach handwriting, with some countries having eliminated handwriting from core national curricula. For example, in the United States, '[t]he Common Core education standards dictate that cursive will no longer be taught in elementary schools' but individual states are 'fighting to keep cursive in the curriculum'.[5] Handwriting will no longer be compulsorily taught in Finnish schools from 2016 (*The Age* February 2, 2015) and Australian education systems are debating the issue. Some people think that it is irrelevant in the digital age to teach cursive writing, while others think that handwriting teaches fine motor skills and that students still need to be able to read handwritten texts. James (2012: 32) used brain imaging to show that in preliterate five-year-old children '[a] previously documented *reading circuit* was recruited during letter perception only after handwriting – not after typing or tracing' and she conjectures that handwriting 'may facilitate reading acquisition'. Hensher (2012: 15) makes a plea for the maintenance of handwriting as '[t]he shaping of thought and written language by a pen, moved by a hand to register marks of ink on paper has for centuries, millennia, been regarded as key to our existence as human beings'. Perhaps this is the next literacy battleground where another unnecessary dualism between teaching handwriting and keyboard skills will lead to endless arguments, when there is probably a need to teach both, for different social and aesthetic reasons.

Quotes

It sounds sold-fashioned when you put forth the arguments that you lose connection with the past ... But then there's also that scientific aspect of it. We don't know what's going to happen later on if you don't teach children how to write on paper or how to write cursive.

(Wright 2011 – http://indianapublicmedia.org – accessed 17.4.2015)

At some point, the ordinary pleasures and dignity of handwriting are going to be replaced permanently. What is going to replace them is a man in a well-connected electric room, waving frantically at a screen and saying, to nobody in particular, 'Why won't this effing thing work?' Before that happens, perhaps we should take a look at what we're so rapidly doing away with.

(Hensher 2012: 15)

Researching academic literacies

The term *literacy* is increasingly used to refer to 'effective participation in any kind of social processes' (Halliday 2007/1996: 98), but for research purposes it is still necessary to distinguish reading and writing practices from other practices such as speaking and listening and viewing and composing. Some may argue that the term *literacy* might more usefully be used to refer to reading and writing practices specifically.

Quote

The nature of the material environment, and the way our bodies were able to create patterns in it, opened up the possibility of writing, and also circumscribed the forms that writing took.

(Halliday 2007/1996: 99)

Michael Halliday (2007/2002), the linguist who designed the *architecture* of systemic functional linguistics (SFL), describes this type of linguistics as problem-oriented and applicable to questions relating to any context where language plays a role. Language plays a central role in the domain of academic disciplines and using SFL as a conceptual framework to study and describe varieties of language that represent knowledge within specific academic disciplines has proven to be a particularly fruitful application of the model (see, for example, Hyland

2009, Korner, McInnes & Rose 2007, Coffin 2006, Christie & Martin 1997, Ghadessy 1988, Halliday 2004/1988). As a first step, the varieties of language used in academic disciplines can be differentiated in terms of the three parameters of the context of situation, as explained below.

Technicality

The *field* of academic discourse varies with the discipline, whether, for example, History, Science or Geography, in terms of technicality. The dimension of technicality can be represented as a scale, or continuum, from everyday commonsense language to highly technical, specialised language. Similarly, the dimensions of *tenor* and *mode* can each be represented as a continuum, as seen in Figure 2.3. The register of any particular text can be plotted along these scales (see Eggins 2004).

Using the field, tenor and mode scales, researchers have been able to investigate and record the differences between the varieties of language people use in their everyday lives and the varieties of language, the secondary discourses, used to represent knowledge in academic disciplines. In summary, the language of everyday life is used to represent the objects and processes of daily life (field) and to build personal relationships (tenor) in the form of concrete spoken language accompanying habitual activities. This is language that makes sense through the material context in which it is produced (mode). In contrast, knowledge organised as an academic discipline is represented using specialised language varieties that build technicality (field) for specialist audiences (tenor) in the form of abstract written language that distances meanings from the material context in which they are produced (mode) (see for example, Halliday & Martin 1993). The contrast between everyday spoken language at one extreme and the discourse of an academic discipline, in this case science, at the other is illustrated by the two language samples in Figure 2.4.

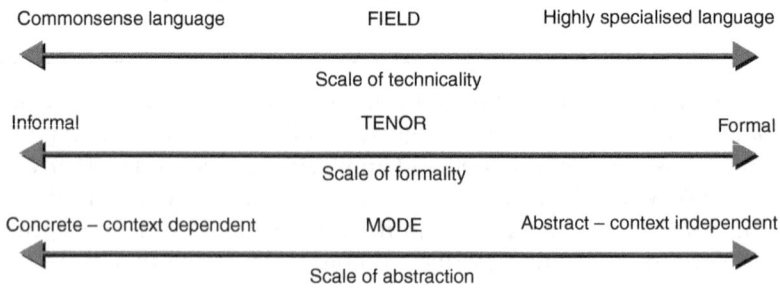

Figure 2.3   Field, tenor and mode dimensions of text

Everyday spoken language	Written language of science

←————————————————————————————→

Example 1

How shocking is this? How are people supposed to even breath? Look at them belching out all that muck! Why can't those lazy sods take a bus? My Nan'll be up all night wheezing for sure. I really worry about her when it's this bad.

Example 2

Air-borne vehicle emission pollution is a significant cause of geriatric respiratory morbidity.

Figure 2.4 Everyday spoken language and the written language of science

Most people will understand the gist of Example 1, and perhaps will even imagine gestures and intonation used by the speaker to intensify and punctuate the meaning, especially if this type of context is familiar to them. For anyone not sharing this specific immediate context, however, some meanings are not retrievable; for example, exactly who or what the pronouns *this, them, I* and *it* refer to. The people and things (participants), events (processes) and their circumstances, are not identified explicitly. In contrast, it is not necessary to be with the writer in person to understand the meanings made by Example 2, but understanding is enhanced if the reader shares the writer's knowledge of the discipline and the specialised participants and processes used to build that knowledge.

Between these two extremes – along a continuum from more spoken to more written – fall language varieties like the four examples in Figure 2.5.

Based on scales of language variation such as this, linguists using the SFL analytical framework have been able to develop increasingly fine-tuned descriptions of the differences between academic discourse in the sciences, in the social sciences and in the humanities. They have also been able to describe the distinctive literacies of specific disciplines and sub-disciplines, for example, biology, ancient history and modern history (for example, Matruglio 2015).

From the perspective of field, academic discourse is characterised by configurations of language features, alongside specialist images, that build technicality. In the science disciplines, technicality is a function of systems of technical terms organised in taxonomies of type

More spoken

Example 3

Cars make the air dirty so some people can't breathe properly and they can get sick and even die, especially when they are very old.

Example 4

Because cars pollute the air, some people have breathing difficulties. This can lead to sickness and even death, for example, if people are old and frail.

Example 5

Air pollution caused by cars can result in life-threatening respiratory disease in the frail aged population.

Example 6

More written   Air pollution caused by cars is a significant factor in the development of life - threatening respiratory disease in the frail aged population.

Figure 2.5   From more spoken to more written language

(classification) and/or parts of wholes (composition). The technicality in Example 2 above is drawn from three taxonomies – two classification taxonomies and a composition taxonomy, as shown here:

- Classification taxonomy – types of pollution: *air pollution, noise pollution, water pollution*
- Classification taxonomy – types of disease: *respiratory disease, cardiac disease*
- Composition taxonomy – the parts or stages of the human lifespan: *infancy, childhood, adolescence, early adulthood, middle age, older age*

Quote

It is not only [scientists'] tools which are technical; their words are technical too ... And it is not just the words. The grammar is special too. The text is not written in sentences, but in long nominal groups ... The point of both the technical terms and the grammar is to compress as much information as possible into a short space.

(Martin 1993a: 168)

Each technical term used in the discourse of science becomes part of its particular taxonomy on the basis of an explanation of the underlying processes (derived from evidence) and becomes technical through

Example 7

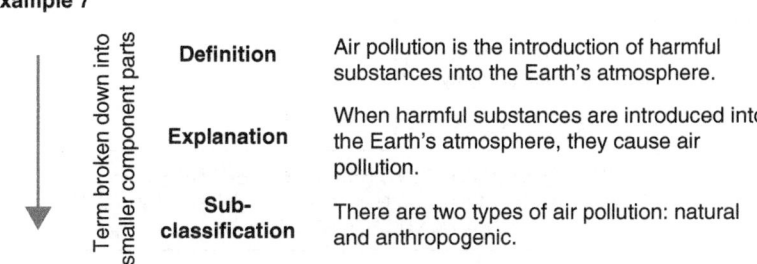

Figure 2.6 Defining, explaining and classifying a technical term

definition, if not in a particular text, then in reference texts from the same or related fields. Each term in a taxonomy can be further classified, or broken down into smaller component parts, through explanation and definition, generating the next level down in a taxonomic hierarchy (see Example 7 above (Figure 2.6)). The composition taxonomy might be accompanied by a visual image, a diagram, for example, showing the location and relative length of each component on the trajectory of a lifespan, as well as sub-components (for example, early adolescence or late adolescence). In this way the knowledge structure of science allows for increasing technicality and specialisation, and for adjustments on the basis of new evidence (see Martin 2007).

Abstraction

From the perspective of *mode*, academic discourse is characterised by abstraction, largely achieved through grammatical metaphor, a linguistic process 'whereby the meaning is cooked twice as it were, introducing a degree of tension between wording and meaning' (Martin & White 2005: 1). This process enables 'the drift from spoken to written discourse' (Martin 2007: 51) and can be recognised and explained when SFL is used as an analytical tool (see, for example, Halliday 1994, Halliday & Martin 1993; Halliday & Matthiessen 1999b, Taverniers 2004). The SFL model of language describes the content level of language in terms of two layers, a layer of meaning (semantics) made real, or realised, by a layer of wording (lexicogrammar), with each unit of meaning paired with a unit of grammar through which it is realised in the most straightforward or congruent way. The relation between the meaning and the grammar expressing the meaning can be shifted so the meaning is realised in a non-congruent way, as seen in Figure 2.7.

```
┌─────────────────────────────────────────┐
│ CONGRUENT                                │
│ Events and happenings –processes – are   │
│ congruently realised grammatically by    │
│ verbs.                                    │
│   ┌───────────────────────────────┐      │
│   │ Cars pollute the atmosphere.  │      │
└───┴───────────────────────────────┴──────┘

   ┌──────────────────────────────────────────────────┐
   │ CONGRUENT ALIGNMENT IS SHIFTED THROUGH THE        │
   │ GRAMMATICAL PROCESS OF NOMINALISATION RESULTING IN│
   │ GRAMMATICAL METAPHOR                              │
   └──────────────────────────────────────────────────┘

        ┌────────────────────────────────────────────────┐
        │ GRAMMATICAL METAPHOR                            │
        │ The dynamic process of polluting is held still by│
        │ representing it as an entity:pollution.         │
        │   ┌────────────────────────────────────────────┐│
        │   │ Most atmospheric pollution is caused by cars.││
        └───┴────────────────────────────────────────────┘┘
```

Figure 2.7   Sample shift with grammatical metaphor

In the most spoken text, Example 1, above – *Look at them belching out all that muck* – instead of choosing a literal expression, the speaker chose a figurative expression, *belching*, a physiological process that bystanders find unpleasant. The speaker uses this figurative expression to represent a mechanical process – the release of vehicle exhaust fumes. The word *belching* is an example of *lexical* metaphor, used to highlight the unpleasantness of the phenomenon. Lexical metaphors are common in everyday spoken language. In contrast, in Example 5, a more written text, grammatical metaphor is used,– *Air pollution caused by cars **can result in** life-threatening respiratory disease in the frail aged population* – where the congruent expression of cause, a logical meaning, usually expressed through conjunctions, is transformed into a verb – *results in.*

Grammatical metaphor is a process of abstraction critical to the construction of the technicality in academic discourse. Once a process such as *pollute* has been nominalised in the form of an abstract noun – *pollution* – it can be used as a technical term in a scientific taxonomy. It can then be expanded into a nominal group to add meanings that, for example, further classify (*air pollution*), measure (*air pollution index*) and evaluate (*carcinogenic air pollution*). In this way, meanings, which in more spoken language would be expressed in sequences of clauses, become condensed into nominal groups. The effect of grammatical metaphor in academic discourse is that meanings are packaged much more densely than in the language used in everyday life, making possible 'the accumulation, compacting, foregrounding and backgrounding of information and evidence so that the argument can move forward' (Christie & Derewianka 2008: 25).

Grammatical metaphor also underpins the technicality of disciplines in the humanities. The discourse of History, for example, is characterised by language features used to package not only processes, but also periods of time, as *things* that can be chronicled and explained (Martin 2007). Coffin (2006: 98–99) explains that 'calendar time makes it possible to develop timelines and chronologies, which in turn makes it possible to flesh out records of past events in the form of historical narratives … these constructs provide the means of locating, referring to, recording and explaining past events'. Nominalisation is used to package these chronological events into single nouns

> '[f]or example, the nominal group *the Industrial Revolution* does not denote a single instant of revolution, but instead summarises many events and activities. Grammatically, we know that this is a nominal group, but semantically, this nominal group refers to many events and actions'.
>
> (de Oliveira 2010: 192)

These nominalised processes can then be related through causal processes, as seen in this sentence – *The westward expansion led to the discovery of gold in the rivers of the western plains* – where the bundled events of *the western expansion* are causally linked to *the discovery of gold* through the verb group *led to.*

Quotes

… whereas … nominalising was functional in the language of science, since it contributed both to technical terminology and to reasoned argument, in other discourses it is largely a ritual feature, engendering only prestige and bureaucratic power. It becomes a language of hierarchy, privileging the expert and limiting access to specialised domains of cultural experience.

(Halliday & Martin 1993: 15)

Without grammatical metaphor then, technicality and abstraction would not be possible. And this underlines the significance of writing in the development of discipline-specific discourses – grammatical metaphor is primarily a resource for writing, not speaking. A different kind of consciousness is involved (Halliday 1985a). Without the technology of writing, science and history as we practise them would not exist.

(Martin in Halliday & Martin 1993: 228)

Thus, studies of written language by linguists, including studies of the language varieties in which the knowledge of academic disciplines is represented, reveal that the distinction between spoken language and written language is less to do with forms of expression, such as sounds or graphemes, but instead is a function of the expression of textual meanings in the words and grammar associated with these two modes. It is through distinctive word choices, and the way they are organised in grammatical structures, that spoken language and written language represent our experience of the world, and what we know about it, in different ways. Thus, when conversations online are typed using a keyboard, they unfold like spoken conversations, and when written language is read aloud using spoken language, it remains written language.

Quote

Texting has long been bemoaned as the downfall of the written word, 'penmanship for illiterates', as one critic called it. To which the proper response is LOL. Texting properly isn't writing at all – it's actually more akin to spoken language. And it's a 'spoken' language that is getting richer and more complex by the year.

(McWhorter 2013: *Time* April 25 2013)

Evaluation

Alongside technicality (field) and abstraction (mode), evaluation is the critical feature of academic discourse related to *tenor*. In Example 1 above, the speaker uses language to express personal emotions – *shocking, really worry about* – and judgements of the behaviour of others – *lazy sods*. The speaker's use of the lexical metaphor – *belching* – further intensifies the expression of the speaker's point of view. In contrast, instead of expressing and intensifying emotion or judgement, the writer of Example 2 evaluates an abstraction – *a significant cause* – which, in the context of evidence and reasoning generated by accepted scientific methodologies, enables the writer to present an *objective* evaluation of the object of study.

One aspect of the appraisal system, a linguistic framework used to analyse the expression of evaluation in language (Martin & White 2005), is appreciation and within this is a set of resources for conveying social valuation. Coffin (2006: 141–142) explains that these are 'particularly relevant to historical discourse' and can be 'thought of as the institutionalisation of feeling but with reference to norms for valuing processes and products rather than behaviour'. For example, in the discipline of history time is frequently evaluated 'in terms of significance, and cause and effect in terms of the degree of causal impact' (Coffin 2006: 142). To distinguish between interpersonal meanings that express emotions, judgements of others and evaluations of phenomena, linguists use appraisal theory as an analytical tool (see Martin & White 2005).

Quotes

... written language tends to be more removed from – or less **directly** related to – the categories of our experience. This in turn, if we are literate, affects our perceptions of what the world is like ... Written language is *synoptic*. It defines the universe as product rather than as process. ... The written language encodes [it] as a **thing** that **exists**. In principle we can freeze it, attend to it, and take it as a whole. The cost of this perspective may be some simplifying of the relationship among its parts, and a lesser interest in how it got to be the way it is, or in where it is going next. Spoken language presents a *dynamic* view. It defines the universe primarily as a process ... In spoken language phenomena do not exist; they **happen**. They are seen as coming into being, changing, moving in and out of focus, and as interacting in a continuous onward flow. The cost of this perspective is that we may have less awareness of how things actually are, at a real or imaginary point in time; and a lessened sense of how they stay that way ... these different properties are inherent in spoken and written *language*, in whatever form the text is actually presented to us ... Similarly, spoken language is spoken language even if it is presented to us in the form of a transcription, as a text in writing. Although the special features of each variety clearly derive in the first place from the medium and the functions it serves, once it has evolved the variety becomes independent of the medium and can be transposed into the other form. We can all learn to talk in written language, and even (though this is harder) to compose conversation.

(Halliday 1985a: 96–97 – emphasis in the original)

In a non-literate society, spoken language performs all the functions that language is called upon to serve ... In a literate society, the functions of language are shared out between speaking and writing; there is some overlap, but by and large they fill different roles. They are both forms of a language; it is the same linguistic system underlying both. But they exploit different features of the system, and gain their power in different ways.

(Halliday 1985a: 99–100)

Genre

Texts that fulfil the same social purpose share the same general structure, a structure that is given substance through similar configurations of words and grammatical structures. These patterns are called *genres* or *text-types*. A genre is a category of texts with similar language patterns used to achieve similar social purposes. For Martin (2007) these conventional generic patterns are a function of the cultural context in general – the *context of culture* (see Figure 2.8).

It is the immediate social context in which a text is produced that determines the language variety of the text – the texture of the text, the word choices and the patterning of the words into grammatical structures. This is demonstrated in Figure 2.9 (de Silva Joyce & Feez 2012: 20), which provides a general picture of procedures in terms of

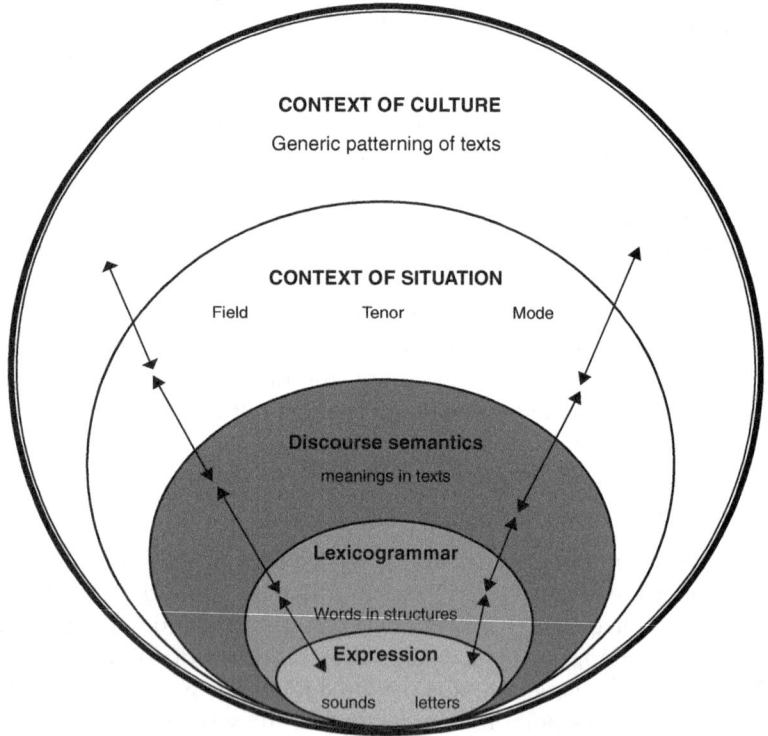

Figure 2.8   Texts in context

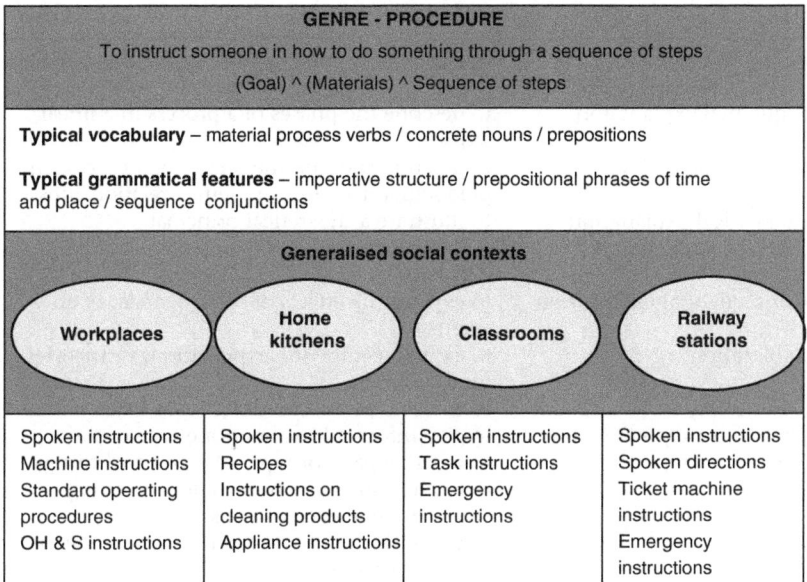

GENRE - PROCEDURE

To instruct someone in how to do something through a sequence of steps

(Goal) ^ (Materials) ^ Sequence of steps

Typical vocabulary – material process verbs / concrete nouns / prepositions

Typical grammatical features – imperative structure / prepositional phrases of time and place / sequence conjunctions

Generalised social contexts

Workplaces | Home kitchens | Classrooms | Railway stations

Spoken instructions	Spoken instructions	Spoken instructions	Spoken instructions
Machine instructions	Recipes	Task instructions	Spoken directions
Standard operating procedures	Instructions on cleaning products	Emergency instructions	Ticket machine instructions
OH & S instructions	Appliance instructions		Emergency instructions

Figure 2.9   Procedural genre across social contexts

generic structure and typical vocabulary and grammatical features. In Figure 2.9 this picture is projected onto four general social contexts, with lists of different types of procedures typically found in these contexts.

Procedural texts, of course, occur in a range of other contexts and in each of the contexts presented in the table other procedural texts occur. The table illustrates that using the concept of genre in literacy programmes can take students beyond preparing for the language and literacy needs of specific contexts towards preparing them to 'use language beyond specific instances' (de Silva Joyce & Hood 2009: 244). Using genre theory, which 'is concerned with how a culture maps ideational, interpersonal and textual meaning onto one another in phases as a text unfolds' (Martin 2007: 55), each academic discipline can be mapped as a system of conventional text patterns, or genres. Ways of combining the patterns produce the texts through which the knowledge of the discipline is structured, as seen in Table 2.1 (adapted from Korner et al. 2007: 47), which lists the genres relevant to secondary school science.

Table 2.1   Secondary school science genres

Genre	Purpose
Sequential explanation	to describe the phases of a process in a linear sequence
Causal explanation	to describe and link the phases of a process in predominantly cause-and-effect relationships
Theoretical explanation	to illustrate a theoretical principal
Factorial explanation	to explain the effects of consequences of an event
Consequential explanation	to explain the effects of consequences of an event
Exploration	to explore competing explanations or theories for a situation
Description	to describe what something looks like
Descriptive report	to give information about one type of thing
Taxonomic report	to describe parts or types of a group of things
Procedure	to instruct someone how to do something through a sequence of steps
Protocol	to establish the conditions to enable someone to do something
Procedural recount	to retell the aim, method and outcome of an activity
Experimental record	to enable scientific activity to occur and to retell the results and conclusion

Multimodal literacy

Quote

Multimodal literacy explores the design of discourse by investigating the contributions of different semiotic resources (for example, language, gesture, images) co-deployed across various modalities (for example, visual, aural, somatic) as well as their interaction and integration in constructing a coherent text.

(O'Halloran & Lim 2011: 14)

The mastering of academic literacies includes being able to make meaning from 'a great deal of visual information that is clearly not writing, and yet has to be processed along with a written text: maps, charts, line graphs, system networks, diagrams and figures of all kinds ... although these are not made of language, they are semiotic resources whose texts can be translated into language, and that offer alternative resources for organising and presenting information' (Halliday 2007/1996: 114–115).

In the academic disciplines, non-linguistic representations of knowledge are not a new feature of literacy practices, as illustrated, for example, in the diagrams, graphs and mathematical symbols that are central to meaning-making in the sciences. Digital technologies have, nevertheless, greatly enhanced the capacity of writers to compose texts that integrate visual information with language, without relying on visual artists or specialist graphic designers, and with an expanding range of meaning-making resources, including sound and animation.

Quote

We have progressed from realistic pictures on cave walls and now know that abstractions can represent numbers, processes or animals. But abstract or not, **pictures** are what designers still produce when they set about the work of explaining something. Charts and diagrams **are** pictures – pictures of information. Keeping the picture from overwhelming the information it represents is the problem that diagram designers face with every job. With each new project, the gulf between information and design has to be bridged.

(Holmes 1993: 7 – emphasis in original)

Analytical tools from the field of linguistics have been used to analyse images and the relation between images and verbal texts for several decades, initially in studies of advertisements, news media, film and music (van Leeuwen 1999, 2006). Kress and van Leeuwen (2006/1996) adapted the metafunctional architecture of SFL to design an analytical framework for exploring meanings in visual images that represent patterns of experience (ideational or representational meanings), enact social interaction (interpersonal or interactive meanings) and organise these meanings into a whole unified text (textual or compositional meanings). This framework makes it possible to analyse how these meanings reflect variables in the immediate context (field, tenor and mode), how they are realised in a visual *grammar*, and how they interact with accompanying verbal text.

Quotes

When a semiotic mode plays a dominant role in public communication, its use will inevitably be constrained by rules, rules
enforced through education, for instance, and through all kinds
of written and unwritten social sanctions. Only a small elite of
experimenters is allowed to break the rules – after all, breaking
rules remains necessary to keep open the possibility of change.
We believe that visual communication is coming to be less and
less the domain of specialists, and more and more crucial in the
domains of public communication. Inevitably this will lead to
new, and more rules, and to more formal, normative teaching.
Not being 'visually literate' will begin to attract social sanctions.
'Visual literacy' will begin to be a matter of survival, especially in
the workplace.

(Kress & van Leeuwen 1996: 1–2)

Gradually it has become evident that it was no longer viable to focus
only on the verbal aspects of such texts, not only because they use
images as an integral part of the text but also because visual composition (layout), colour and typography play an increasingly important role in structuring them, through the use of space, typography
(including special typographic signs such as bullet points) and colour
coding. As a result, linguistic or linguistically inspired methods for
integrating the analysis of the linguistic and nonlinguistic aspects of
written text have begun to emerge.

(van Leeuwen 2006: 624)

Multimodal literacy explores the design of discourse by investigating
the contributions of different semiotic resources (for example,
language, gesture, images) co-deployed across various modalities
(for example, visual, aural, somatic) as well as their interaction and
integration in constructing a coherent text.

(O'Halloran & Lim 2011)

This is not the place to outline the full range of elements within visual
images but readers can follow up the summary below, as illustrated in
Figure 2.10, and through the references given in this section and
in Chapter 7. How meanings interact in a visual text to achieve a
social goal determines whether the text has a narrative or conceptual
structure. Visual texts with a *narrative structure* show the unfolding of

Narrative image	Conceptual image
	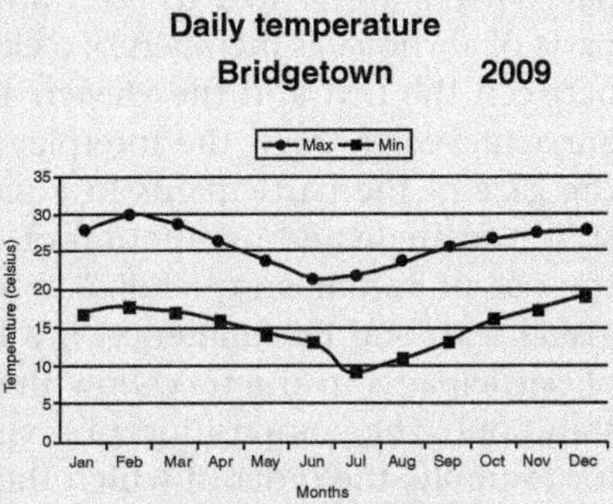 **Daily temperature** **Bridgetown 2009** (Courtesy of NSW AMES)
In this narrative image, the participants, the father and the child, are the salient aspects of this image, as emphasised by the vertical line they form through the centre of the frame. The trees, the driftwood and the sand set the narrative on a beach. The surrounding trees and driftwood replicate the curves of the father's arms around the child. The viewer is placed at a social distance from the two participants who are not engaged with the viewer as their gaze is directed away, presumably towards the sea. So the viewer is distanced from the participants as an observer of the scene.	This conceptual, or analytical, image is a record of temperatures in Bridgetown in 2009. Time is shown moving from left to right. The maximum and minimum temperatures have been plotted along the axes and remain static.

Figure 2.10 Narrative and conceptual images

events over time, specific participants involved in these events and the settings in which the events are happening, while visual texts with a *conceptual* structure represent generalised participants in terms of their classification, their composition, their temporal or spatial relations, or what they stand for or symbolise. Participants in visual texts structured as narratives engage in dynamic events, while in conceptual texts the participants are related to each other in static ways, for example, as parts of a whole, as members of a class or as a symbol. The relationship between the text and the viewer, along with expressions of attitude, are achieved through the interplay of choices from resources such as the gaze of the participants in a narrative image, the distance of the shot, the angle and orientation of the line of vision and variation in the use of colour and detail. The organisation, or composition of a visual text, and its coherence, is a function of the relative placement of participants in the text, how they are framed and how much they stand out. The composition of a visual text influences how it is *read*, for example, the order in which the viewer attends to the elements of the image.

Kress and van Leeuwen's framework for analysing visual texts is one among a suite of approaches from several disciplines used to analyse multimodal meaning-making or multimodality. These include conceptual frameworks and methods for collecting and analysing meaning-making in multiple modes, not only in spoken and written language and visual image, but also in the resources of sound, space and gesture. They enable analysts to think about the affordance of each mode, that is the meanings that can be expressed using the mode, and how modes combine and interact in different communication contexts, especially in digital environments.[6]

The nature of specialisation

The distinction between the discourses of everyday life and those of the academic disciplines can be further explored using approaches from the field of sociology, which has been described as 'a social science that aims to empirically appreciate the complexity of daily life ... and ... of everyday experience' (Marvasti 2004: 2). Sociologists study social processes and institutions, the relation between culture, social structures and individual agency, and social systems, including language and education. The sociology of education is the study of education systems, knowledge structures, socialisation and social reproduction, and relations between these.

Research methods in sociology overlap with those used in the other social sciences, for example, anthropology and linguistics. These methods include quantitative analysis of responses to surveys by people sampled from specific populations, historical and/or content analysis of documents, interviews, longitudinal studies of social groups, conversation analysis and ethnographic techniques, for example, direct observation and participant observation. Data may be analysed on the basis of conceptual frameworks from existing traditions, or conceptual frameworks may emerge from the analysis of data, an approach known as *grounded theory* (see for example, Darity 2008, Marvasti 2004).

The technical and abstract specialised meanings of educational knowledge extend beyond the immediate material context in time and space, and intervene between the material world and the consciousness of those who learn the specialised knowledge. How this is done, however, differs across the academic disciplines. The knowledge structures that lie behind the differences between everyday language and specialised academic discourses have been described by the sociologist, Basil Bernstein. Everyday, or commonsense, knowledge is 'knowledge that appertains to the visible, material world, that is functional for the routine living of daily life, that is non-specialised, shared by all members of the culture/community and realised through everyday forms of talk' (Painter 1999b: 68). *Everyday knowledge* is contrasted with the specialised academic knowledge, or *official educational knowledge* (Bernstein 2000). Everyone potentially has access to everyday knowledge, which is learned in local settings through spoken language. Its meanings are habitual and dependent on the context in which they are made, and they are oriented to building personal relationships. Bernstein (2000: 157) describes everyday knowledge as being organised horizontally, in segments. In contrast, specialised educational knowledge is technical and abstract, independent of the immediate context and organised vertically. Access to this type of knowledge is not available to everyone.

In general, academic disciplines are classified as either belonging to the sciences or the humanities. Bernstein described the discourses of the humanities as *horizontal knowledge structures*, a series of specialised languages, each one based on different principles and assumptions, in contrast to the *hierarchical knowledge structures* of the sciences in which knowledge is organised hierarchically on the basis of explicit and systematic principles (Bernstein 2000: 157–163).

Bernstein's conceptual framework for describing how knowledge is structured and produced in the disciplines can be used to investigate the literacy practices of each discipline, as well as how and to what extent these practices are distributed to different social groups through education (see for example, Christie & Martin 2007). This framework has been further developed by Maton (2014) to enable principled investigations not only of the knowledge structures of specific disciplines, and how they differ, but also of the distinctive beliefs, attitudes and dispositions, or *knower structures*, that give specialists in each discipline legitimacy in their field. This analytical move makes it possible to investigate what it means to be socialised into the literacy practices of a particular discipline. To illustrate this point, Gee (2012a: 168) uses the example of autodidacts, who while extremely knowledgeable, rarely gain legitimacy as discipline specialists because they are trained 'outside of a process of group practice and socialisation'. This indicates that learning the content knowledge of a discipline, the 'body of facts and theories' that distinguish that discipline, is not enough for a person to be recognised as a specialist in that discipline.

By using the analytical tools of SFL for describing language variation across social contexts alongside the conceptual frameworks that have emerged from the sociological tradition of Bernstein (see Hasan 2005c), researchers have been able to generate rich descriptions of the language varieties and literacy practices of specific academic disciplines and how these relate to specialised knowledge and knower structures. These descriptions make it possible to investigate how specialised academic literacies are produced and distributed in educational contexts, by and to whom, and how distribution of this knowledge might be achieved more effectively and more equitably.

How knowledge is distributed in educational contexts can also be studied using analytical tools developed by Bernstein for examining the social systems through which knowledge, and its expression in academic discourse, is recontextualised from the fields of its production, for example in research settings, to its reproduction in educational settings. Using this framework, which Bernstein (2000) named the *pedagogic device*, research settings and educational settings can be studied to establish how clear a distinction is made between everyday knowledge and specialised knowledge, and between the different disciplines and content areas within disciplines.

The framework can also be used to investigate how discipline content is selected and re-organised, or recontextualised, in *pedagogic discourse*, the discourse through which the relationship between teachers and learners is constructed. Within pedagogic discourse are embedded two discourses – *instructional discourse*, relating to the content and *regulative discourse*, which is used to manage social order. Who has control of these discourses in any educational setting is analysed using the concept of framing. In classroom practice, maintaining the distinction between different areas of content (strong classification) and making explicit the different social roles of the teacher and student (strong framing) constitutes, in Bernstein's terms, a *visible pedagogy*. In contrast, an *invisible pedagogy* is one in which neither the classification of knowledge nor the framing of social relations is obvious. Invisible pedagogy can pose problems for students, when, as Hasan (2005a: 29) points out, 'the rules of the game are not transparent except to those who have experience of this particular form of communicative strategy'. If everyday interactions at home and in the community do not prepare children to recognise the communicative strategies needed to access invisible pedagogy, then those children are at a disadvantage at school.

Quote

In the case of invisible pedagogic practice it is as if the pupil is the author of the practice and even the authority, whereas in the case of visible practices it is clearly the teacher who is the author and authority.

(Bernstein 2000: 110)

Critical literacies

Written language, whether carved into stone, handwritten on paper, or typed onto a screen, pins meanings down, stabilises and preserves them, and, in the process, meanings written down gain an authority, which may or may not be warranted or benevolent. This is at the heart of Socrates's warning, which echoes down to us through the centuries (because Plato wrote it down). The Brazilian philosopher, Paulo Freire, in designing a reading pedagogy for disadvantaged adults, understood reading to be critically important, but Freire's focus was not the type of reading that accepted, in a 'fatalistic way', texts which gave authority to injustice (Freire & Macedo 1987: 36). Instead, his critical pedagogy teaches reading as a process of questioning and interpreting written text, and of transforming the meanings in written texts in ways that empower the reader in their world (Barton 2007, Gee 2012a).

> **Quote**
>
> Reading the world always precedes reading the word, and reading the word implies continually reading the world. ... this movement from the word to the world is always present; even the spoken word flows from our reading of the world. In a way, however, we can go further and say that reading the word is not preceded merely by reading the world, but by a certain form of writing it or rewriting it, that is, of transforming it by means of conscious, practical work ... this dynamic movement is central to the literacy process ... ... reading always involves critical perception, interpretation and a *rewriting* of what is read.
>
> (Freire & Macedo 1987: 35–36)

The legacy of Freire can be seen in sociolinguistic approaches to literacy research, especially the understanding that literacy is not an accumulation of skills but a social practice embedded, or situated, in social structures. From this perspective, literacy practices are never neutral or random. They are always used in social contexts and are aligned to the routines and expectations of the culture, and thus involve 'values, attitudes, feelings and social relationships' (Barton, Hamilton & Ivanič 2000: 11).

The study of socially 'situated literacies' begins by locating literacy practices in literacy events, events in which 'literacy has a role' often as written text accompanied by texts in other modes (Barton et al. 2000: 8). This approach is used to study literacy practices in different 'domains of life', for example, home, school or work, how these are 'historically situated' and re-interpreted across 'discourse communities', and the degree to which particular sets of literacy practices are 'more dominant, visible and influential than others' (Barton et al. 2000: 12–13).

Studies that investigate literacy as social practice belong to the New Literacy Studies (NLS) tradition. Researchers in this tradition also explore ideologies that shape different understandings of what counts as literacy, and the impact particular literacy ideologies might have on communities and individuals. Learning new literacy practices results in changes in identity and consciousness, changes which may clash with, diminish and delegitimatise pre-existing ways of being in the world. For example, the literacy practices of the school may conflict with the way the world is experienced at home and in the local community, or influential literacy practices used productively in one domain may be transferred to another domain in ways that result in those practices being used to constrain access and entrench inequality (see for example, Blommaert 2005, Fairclough 1992a, Gee 1992).

The body of NLS research supports the proposition that academic language is not neutral, but involves a series of social practices embedded in uneven power dynamics. 'NLS, then, takes nothing for granted with respect to literacy and the social practices with which it becomes associated, problematising what counts as literacy at any time and place and asking *whose literacies* are dominant and whose are marginalised or resistant' (Street 2003: 77).

Quote

There is a very real need for schools to support emergent bilinguals in their acquisition of academic language and literacy, but a criticism is how the very definition of academic language and literacy privileges some while marginalising others.

(Menken 2013: 445)

Studies of literacy as situated social practice have reconfigured traditional views of literacy education. This begins with the shift away from viewing literacy teaching as the teaching of a set of generalisable autonomous skills and towards the design of different pedagogies. These pedagogies are designed to enable literacy learners to build knowledge and skills for controlling texts across diverse contexts, in language varieties both standard and non-standard and realised in forms comprising multiple modes, especially in the context of digital media.

As sociolinguists continue to investigate literacy use, they expand their descriptions, and our knowledge, of socially situated literacy practices. Once these descriptions are written down, and are thus rendered authoritative, a critical orientation demands that this knowledge too is viewed through a critical lens, in particular, in terms of the way it is applied in educational and other institutional contexts. Without this step, new literacies and multiliteracies, will become merely the latest vehicle for entrenching inequality and injustice.

Conclusion

This chapter has reviewed a selection of literacy studies, which have investigated what it meant and means to be literate from prehistory to the present and across the fields, or disciplines, of educational knowledge. Because the transmission of literacy from one generation to the next 'must involve the strategies of pedagogy' (Houston 2004: 6), the next part of the book takes another path through the literacy terrain and reviews studies of literacy education from the early years of emergent literacy, through primary, middle and secondary school to adult contexts of literacy use and education.

Part II
Lifespan Literacies

Introduction

The focus of this part of the book is the learning and teaching of literacy throughout life. A *lifespan* approach provides a holistic perspective on literacy development. It enables researchers, including practitioner-researchers, to think about the literacy needs of the student profile of concern to them, in relation to language and literacy development over a lifetime. The research examined in this part does not focus solely on educational settings but will include studies undertaken in community and work contexts, studies which have informed definitions of what it is to be literate and our understanding of how people put literacy to use.

This part begins with Chapter 3, which reviews the broad and intricate landscape of early years literacy development and how literacy development and participation in school contexts are influenced by the discourse and the practices of the home. This awareness of early literacy development, that is, how literacy skills develop in young children, stretches back to ancient times with, for example, 1st century Roman children playing with ivory figures of letters. Different research perspectives, through to the present century, have been adopted to investigate the development of language in children and the ways in which children are equipped to participate in the literacy practices of schooling and the broader culture. These have inevitably influenced the various approaches to literacy development and the debates and oppositional positions adopted by educators and policy makers. The chapter proposes that social semiotic frameworks can be used to account for the meaning-making of young children as they first learn to control spoken and written language and when later they engage with the discourse of schooling. It also puts forward the idea that a theory of language can help to reconcile semantic and phonological perspectives on literacy development, seeing them as complementary rather than incompatible, with literacy pedagogy diminished if one perspective is favoured at the expense of the other.

Chapter 4 continues the journey through the continuum of school education and tracks literacy demands through the phases of schooling, which takes students from the language of everyday experience to the technical and abstract language of educational knowledge. Beginning in the early years of school, with initial instruction in reading and writing, students navigate two critical literacy-dependent transitions. The first is in the middle years of the primary school as teaching and learning increasingly revolve around learning in the subject areas. This is followed by the transition into the secondary school where the focus is on the educational disciplines.

The final chapter in this part scans the terrain of adult literacy contexts in the community, further education and workplaces. Beginning with ways adult literacy levels are assessed across countries, the chapter focuses on how people practise literacy and numeracy differently in different social domains to achieve different purposes. There will always be some adults who fail to develop their literacy skills at school to a level that can enable them to participate in the literacy domains of adult life. There are also people who need to develop their literacy skills further, as they move into new domains of practice, the chapter reviews the types of literacy provision that seek to assist adults to become part of communities of literacy practice in the various domains.

3
Literacy from Home to School

Children learn to talk at home before they are taught to read and write at school. The spoken language (or languages) children develop during interaction with close family members at home becomes the foundation on which their learning continues to develop beyond the home, in the wider community, in early childhood settings and eventually when they begin to learn to read and write formally at school. Similarly, the ways children learn to use other meaning-making resources at home, for example, images, numerical symbols and gesture, lay the foundation for the more specialised and more formal uses of these meaning systems in educational contexts.

Outside the home, and through media such as television and the Internet, children also encounter variations of the home language, or languages, including different dialects and registers. Many, perhaps most, children will also encounter additional languages. Children experience different dialects of their first language when interacting with people in their community who are, for example, from a different generation, region or social group. From an early age children gradually become aware, at some level, of how the dialect spoken in their home is valued in the wider community. This is particularly the case, if the home dialect is perceived as a non-standard language variety by the wider community.

Children encounter different registers of their first language as their sphere of experience, their interests, and the circle of people they interact with, broaden through a variety of communication channels. At home and in the wider community children will experience the ways language varies when used in different situations for different purposes – to accompany the routines of family life, to interact with others in conversations, to tell stories about what happened, to explain how things work, to give instructions, to talk on the telephone, to argue and console, to make transactions in shops and offices and to take part in celebrations. If there is no physiological, cognitive or emotional barrier to language learning, by the time children arrive at school, they have developed a rich repertoire of culturally mediated ways to act on and learn about the world, to represent their experience and to interact with others using language and image.

For many children, language use at home includes taking part in inter-actions involving not only spoken language, but also written language and visual images. Written language and visual images surround many children, in relation to at least one language but perhaps more than one. Long before they attend school and take part in formal lessons to learn to read and write, these children already know what written language can be about, who communicates with writing, and some of the ways this is done. They will have observed, or taken part in, the purposeful use of written language and images, and seen how these can be used to achieve practical, informative and entertaining goals. Their daily activities will include looking at picture books with family members, hearing information and stories read out loud, checking pro-cedures for completing everyday tasks presented in images and words, and observing other family members reading, writing and viewing a variety of media. These children will have learned how to behave when reading a list or a note, or when reading and viewing a book or a screen. They will have used drawing and writing implements such as paint-brushes, pencils, a keyboard or a touch screen, and many will have used these implements to mimic, or even approximate, writing. Among this group are children who are able to write and read to some degree before they arrive at school, perhaps in more than one language.

Other children grow up in families where, culturally and socially, the use of one or more spoken languages, accompanied by gesture and images, meets all the everyday communication needs of the family. These children are likely to develop a rich and vibrant repertoire of spoken language and they bring these diverse language repertoires to school. Some children come from homes where written language plays little or no role in daily life, or may even be viewed as a means by which disadvantage becomes entrenched. Their pathway to mastering the language of the school is necessarily not as straightforward as it is for children whose family life echoes the language of school and where written language is part of the everyday experiences and accomplishments of family life.

Thus, there are a variety of developmental trajectories followed by children as they make the transition from spoken language at home to written lan-guage at school. Approaches for investigating these trajectories, and the experiences of children who follow them, is the topic of this chapter. There is a vast literature devoted to the field of language and literacy development in early childhood, an international literature that stretches back decades, and arguably centuries. It is beyond the scope of a single chapter to cover all possible and legitimate approaches to researching children's language development from home to school. Instead this chapter will draw attention to some key features of the trajectories of children's language development from home to school, as well as selected approaches for investigating these features separately and in relation to each other in principled ways.

Parallels can be drawn between studies of the pre-history and history of writing systems and studies investigating the task of the young child, or non-literate adult, in learning to master the valued literacy practices of their society (see Chapter 2). This includes mastering the use of writing implements, decoding graphemes, recasting spoken grammar and vocabulary as writing, interpreting and composing written texts and recognising the purposes for which written language is used in the culture.

Lessons from the past

An area of research that deserves to be pursued is the ways reading and writing have been taught in the past, not least of all to put into perspective some of the entrenched positions that characterise contemporary debates about how to teach young children to read and write. Over the centuries and across the world young children have been successfully taught to read and write in many different ways (Fischer 2001, Murphy 2012, Rosen 2013) and some age-old concerns continue to reverberate in the literacy debates of the 21st century.

In 1st-century Rome, for example, a retired 'teacher of eloquence', Marcus Fabius Quintilianus, or Quintilian (1856/2006: 25–29) as we know him today, drew on 20 years of teaching experience to document, in 12 volumes, the 'education of an orator' from infancy to old age, anticipating by two millennia a great many of the themes of interest to 21st century literacy educators. Particularly compelling are the images provoked by Quintilian's description of very young children in Ancient Rome being given 'ivory figures of letters to play with'. Children were also given boards with letter shapes cut out so they could learn to write the letters without assistance, the 'stylus ... guided ... along grooves ... as on wax'. This was followed by the learning of syllables they could form into words, which then could be joined into phrases.

Quintilian writes about topics such as the nexus between nature and nurture in children's education, memory training and children learning the alphabet, handwriting, spelling, vocabulary, grammar and rhetoric (or genre as we might call it today), together with study of the literary canon, music, geometry and astronomy (disciplinary knowledge). He promotes quality early childhood education delivered by well-educated mothers and 'eminent' and not 'inferior', teachers (Quintilian 1856/2006: III.1.1–3). He promotes public, rather than private education, and bilingual literacy, with children learning to write Greek before Latin, the language of Ancient Rome. He argues that children should learn the shape of letters (graphemes) before letter names and that the teaching of grammar and rhetoric 'should be in some degree united' (II.1.4). For him, children should learn to read and write narratives (fables, comedies and histories) before 'facts' (information texts) and 'pleadings' (persuasive texts) (II.4.2–4). He proposes that 'the pupil should have but moderate assistance, not too much or too little' (II.6.1) and that 'variety of talent and disposition in pupils requires variety of treatment' (II.8.1–5). He does not give rules from which there is no departure, as seen in the following direct quote.

> ## Quote
>
> ...for rhetoric would be a very easy and small matter if it could be included in one short body of rules, but rules must generally be altered to suit the nature of each individual case, the time, the occasion, and necessity itself ... and the different bearings of [the] subject.
>
> (Quintilian 1856/2006 II.13.1)

In 1658, a Czech theologian and educator, John Amos Komensky, better known by his Latin name Comenius, published a bimodal (words and pictures) and bilingual (German and Latin) textbook 'to delight' young children learning to read both their first language and the European language of scholarship, Latin. The book, *Orbis sensualium pictus (The world of things obvious to the senses, drawn in pictures)*,[1] uses pictures with bilingual captions to illustrate the sound made by each letter of the alphabet (see Figure 3.1). These are followed by an encyclopaedic progression of diagrammatic images, each one a scene in which things and processes are captioned using categories and relations that match the way knowledge was structured at the time. Over subsequent decades this picture book was republished in multilingual versions, which always included Latin accompanied by up to three languages, including French, Italian, Dutch, English or Hungarian. This 400-year-old work put words and pictures within the reach of beginning readers from the perspective of

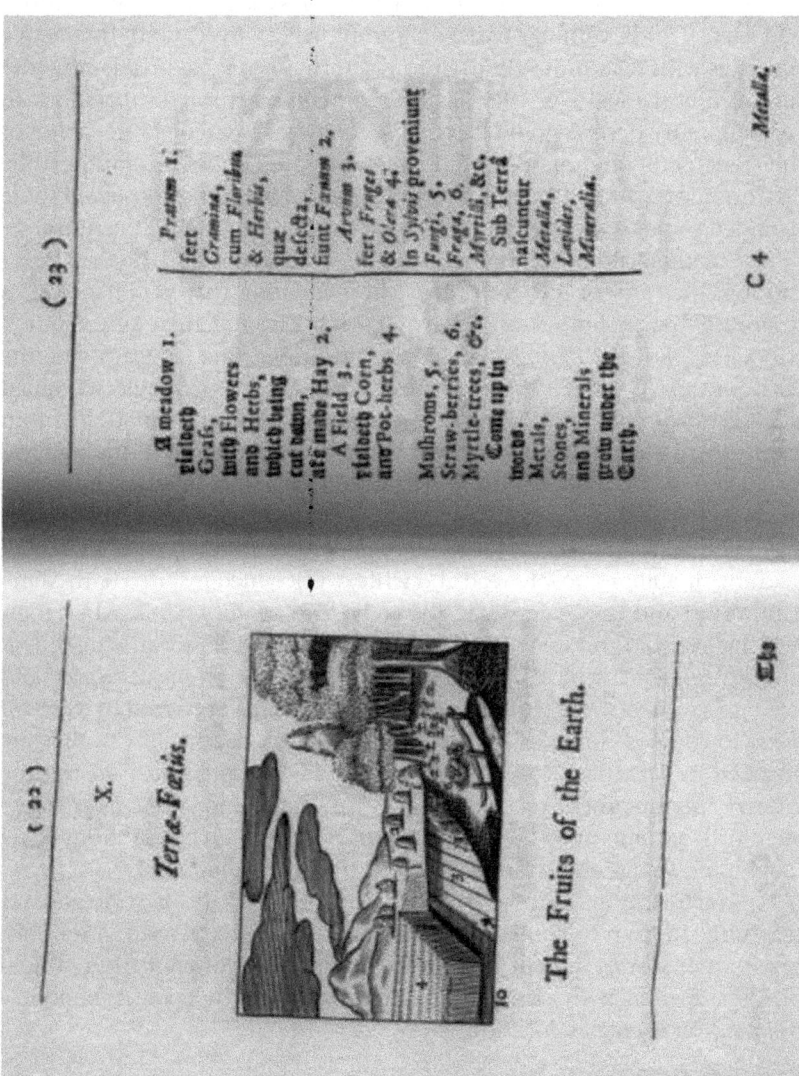

Figure 3.1   Page from *Orbis sensualium pictus* by Comenius
Source: From Facsimile of third London Edition 1672 – Sydney: Sydney University Press 1967.

both multilingual literacy and educational knowledge. Are there 21st century literacy educators who can claim such an achievement?

In the mid-18th century, in Paris, Jacob Rodrigues Pereire, in the steps of Quintilian, used a 'manual alphabet', 'a syllabic manual of forty-odd signs' and grammar-based 'pantomime' in lively and interactive activities with deaf-mute children to teach them to speak, read and write successfully (Lane 1976: 196). Such an outcome appeared miraculous to contemporary observers and Pereire's school was visited by philosophes of the French Enlightenment, including Jean-Jacques Rousseau and the Abbé de Condillac, whose different interpretations of what they observed there heralded some of the contentious literacy debates of the 21st century.

The manual alphabet was scorned by Rousseau (1974/1762: 81) for turning 'the nursery into a printer's shop', arguing that 'a better way' is to arouse 'the desire to learn … in your scholar' and then 'any method will serve'. Rousseau's ideas would inspire progressive educators of the 20th century (Cremin 1961). In contrast, the Abbé de Condillac designed sequences of teaching strategies to lead young children systematically from interactive sensory activity to the reading and writing of abstract educational knowledge (Knight 1968: 211). Condillac's curriculum was developed through the 19th century by two French doctors, Jean Itard (1972/1801) and Edouard Séguin (1971/1866), to teach young children with a range of learning disabilities how to read and write, work which inspired both Maria Montessori and Lev Vygotsky in the early 20th century. Thus, when four- and five-year old children in 21st century Montessori classrooms are shown how to sequence moveable letters of the alphabet to make words, and six- and seven-year-old children combine word cards organised in *grammar boxes* to compose text (Feez 2010, 2011, Kalantzis & Cope 2012), they are engaged in activities with a provenance that can be traced back via the French Enlightenment to Quintilian in Ancient Rome. These approaches align with arguments by literacy educators that children benefit from being taught knowledge about language explicitly and systematically.

The historical account above briefly tells the story of strategies for teaching children to read and write that continue to be used in schools. Many such stories remain to be told by historians of education, a field of research rich with possibilities for throwing light on contemporary practices in literacy education.

Conceptual frameworks for research

To investigate any aspect of the trajectory of children's language use from the spoken language of the home to the written language of the school requires a conceptual framework, or theory, as a lens through which to view the phenomena under investigation. This also provides a means of thinking systematically about, and analysing in principled ways, language and language development. A conceptual framework is based on a *theory* the researcher can use to explain phenomena and a theory is often represented as a *model*, a tool for thinking about, analysing and relating elements. The choice of conceptual framework will both shape and depend on the nature of the investigation and the questions being posed by the researcher.

Quotes

Theories are explanations that are grounded in belief systems usually supported by extensive research and databases, and often held by large groups of people. Competing theories are often studied, tested and held over long periods of time ... People may be conscious or unconscious of the theories they use in daily living. When individuals are conscious of their theories, or belief systems, they are able to label them, think about them, talk about them with others, and compare their own theories with alternative ones ... When the term 'theory' is used in the field of education, it refers to a well-documented explanation for a phenomenon related to teaching and/or learning. This explanation (i.e., theory) then becomes part of the body of content knowledge that constitutes the field.

(Tracey & Morrow 2006: 2–4)

Teachers with a firm grasp of educational and psychological theories have a clear basis for making instructional decisions. Their understanding of educational theory provides them with a foundation for understanding why they are choosing the instructional practices they use ... The reason that theories are central to educational research is that they are the concepts by which scholars explain their research ... Theories also provide the frameworks through which various research studies can be linked both within and between fields of study ... In addition to providing a basis for hypotheses, explaining research findings, and linking research studies to each other, theories allow variables to be generated and evaluated.

(Tracey & Morrow 2006: 6–7)

The general overview of the development of meaning-making from home to school provided at the beginning of this chapter could not have been written without a theory of language and language development. In this case the conceptual framework is a social one, based on the premise that language is the way it is because of the purposes it achieves in social contexts. From this perspective, language varies with the contexts in which it is used and language, as a resource for making meaning, is learned through interaction with others and through putting language to use as a tool for thinking and learning about the world, in concert with other semiotic resources, for example, visual images (see for example, Gibbons 2006, Halliday & Hasan 1985, Painter 1999a, 1999b, Painter, Derewianka & Torr 2007).

The conceptual framework through which language and literacy development is viewed by researchers determines the aspects of literacy and literacy development they perceive as relevant and significant, and so worth investigating. It shapes the questions they ask, the data they collect, the analytical tools they use and the teaching approaches they promote. The breadth and complexity of the terrain researchers find themselves traversing in order to assemble a framework for thinking about language and literacy, however, is daunting. The intractability of the field from the perspective of researchers is illustrated by the increase in new editions of research handbooks, some extending to multiple volumes, in which different approaches are showcased. Such handbooks provide overviews of theories, methodologies and studies organised in relation to one aspect of the field, for example, one life stage, as in the *Handbook of early literacy research – Volume 3* (Neumann & Dickinson 2011), or one set of related analytical approaches, as in the *Routledge handbook of discourse analysis* (Gee & Handford 2012).

Systematic reviews of the literature and meta-analysis are also used to find principled pathways through the literature. These techniques have been borrowed from the health sciences, which in recent decades have privileged evidence-based approaches, approaches based on scientific experimental methods such as randomised controlled trials, as a means of improving clinical decision-making and practice. The push for evidence-based decision-making and practice has now spread to the field of education in general, and language and literacy education in particular (Hempenstall 2006, Wyatt-Smith & Gunn 2007). Systematic reviews contribute to the evidence base by reviewing and synthesising a selection of related studies (for example, Chall 1967, Freebody 2007, Snow, Burns & Griffin 1998), while a meta-analysis is an application of statistical methods to synthesise the results of related studies, often to compare the effect sizes of different treatments or interventions (for example,

Hattie 2009, Myhill & Watson 2014). Even though advocacy for evidence-based approaches to language and literacy education has become commonplace in the literature, a consensus about what this might mean remains elusive, especially in relation to the features outlined in the following quote from Freeboody.

Quote

...what counts as 'rigour in evidence', that is ... research methodology ... what the concept of literacy entails, what aspects of human knowledge, skill and disposition it brings into play, or how learners should be taught how to use these, and what they mean for learning and social participation in school.

(Freebody 2007: 21)

Despite handbooks, systematic reviews and meta-analyses providing inventories of possibilities, the researcher is still faced with the task of navigating the complexity of the language and literacy field in order to select and assemble elements in a way that is apposite to the issues under investigation. The researcher's task is to make principled choices from the array of possibilities along several dimensions, including theoretical frameworks, data collection procedures and analytical tools. This is necessary so that the design of any particular study is unified conceptually and unified conceptually and remains dynamic enough to account for the many variables of any situation in which language is being used and learned. It is also necessary so that a study produces results that provide insights for practice and which have the potential to be generalised to other teaching and learning contexts. In other words, researchers in the field of language and literacy need a conceptual framework through which to view possible theoretical and analytical orientations. A first step towards building such a framework is to consider the spectrum of theoretical perspectives on offer from an historical perspective.

A century of theoretical perspectives

Taking into account the historical dimension of available approaches to language and literacy research makes visible the provenance of each approach, including its disciplinary origins, the era in which the approach originated, the issues of significance in the era that generated the approach, and how the approach may have been overtaken or overlaid with new knowledge and new or expanded analytical tools over time and in response to new challenges. Intermittently, over the last century, scholars have reviewed developing understandings about literacy education and related literacy teaching practices (for example, Chall 1967, Freebody 2007, Huey 1908, Smith 2002, Snow et al. 1998). Many contemporary texts providing introductions to the field also provide historical overviews of both theory and practice (for example, Kalantzis & Cope 2012, Lightbown & Spada 2013).

At the most general level, distinctions can be made between behavioural, cognitive, social and biological views about language and literacy development, views that emerged and retreated as the 20th century unfolded. A variety of these adaptations and combinations remain influential in education today, each one intersecting with ideas about whether language development is a function of innate (nature) or environmental (nurture) factors, or a combination of both. The extent to which two or more of the views described below have been applied productively together, or whether in the research literature they have remained in separate silos, is partly determined from three angles. These include the extent to which they can be aligned in terms of their initial premises or axioms (axiology), the phenomena that they recognise and how these are categorised and related (ontology) and how knowledge and learning knowledge are understood (epistemology).

The overview below necessarily omits many of the ways in which these perspectives have overlapped or diverged over the century. It does, however, provide a starting point for weighing up the relevance of each view to the investigation of specific language and literacy issues (see also Rassool 2002).

The behaviourist view

In the first half of the 20th century the view of language development promoted by behaviourist psychologists prevailed. The behaviourist perspective is based on the premise that children learn by responding to external stimuli in the environment, and by imitating the behaviours of others, in this case, language behaviours. When children's behaviour is reinforced, for example, by the positive response of caregivers, it is repeated and practised, and further developed through more imitation. Conversely, behaviour that is ignored or punished falls away. The object of study from a behaviourist perspective is external behaviour that can be observed and measured empirically using experimental methods (Skinner 1974, see also Lightbown & Spada 2013).

Cognitive views

To explain aspects of language development not accounted for by the behaviourist view, cognitive psychologists have described language development in terms of developmental stages, such as those proposed by Rousseau (1974/1762) and Piaget (1970), and in terms of internal mental or cognitive processes. In his attempt to 'answer questions about the nature and origin of knowledge' (Elkind 1974: 130), Piaget theorised that a child's construction of knowledge, and its expression in language, only happens after the maturation of the relevant innate internal mental structures, which emerge in a series of lock-step developmental stages, independent of the child's material and social setting. With each developmental stage, children become ready to learn particular types of knowledge, by either *assimilating* new experiences into the frameworks that organise their existing understanding of the world in their minds (*schema*) or by adjusting this mental organisation to *accommodate* new experiences.

The view of developmental stages often linked to Rousseau, and his story of the education of the fictional child, Émile, suggests that children's development unfolds naturally through maturational stages, if the context is materially rich and interesting. This view is associated with child-centred progressive pedagogies which emerged in the early 20th century and which are often aligned with the educational philosophy of John Dewey. These pedagogies, in their purest form, leave children 'free to pursue their path at their own pace along the universal road of cognitive development' (Painter 1999a: 18). A more contemporary view is that developmental achievement is constructed through children's own activity under the guidance of and in collaboration with adults. This constructivist view draws on aspects of Vygotsky's (1978) social theory of cognitive development, where the development of the internal processes of a child's thought are a consequence of activity in the external social environment.

A cognitive view of learning accounts for the internal mental or cognitive processes children use to mediate information from the environment and transform it into knowledge. These cognitive processes include attention, perception and memory. Language is also understood as an internal cognitive process, through which concepts are mapped onto language forms (see for example, Bloom 1993). Cognitive processes are studied using observational and interview techniques, experimental studies and case studies.

The nativist view

By the mid-20th century, the linguist Noam Chomsky claimed that language development was different from other aspects of children's development. To explain the capacity of human children to generate the complex syntactic forms of their first language so accurately and so early in their lives, despite the very different environments in which children learn language, and the inconsistent and unpredictable language input they experience, Chomsky (2006) proposes that children have an in-born capacity to *acquire* language. Using a set of innate universal grammatical categories and principles, children instinctively know how to combine words to generate the correct forms and structures of their language (see also Pinker 1996). This has become known as the *nativist* view.

Studying language and language acquisition from a nativist perspective involves hypothesising and investigating idealised grammatical categories and forms. This includes studying how, and in what order, all children acquire the forms of their language, the generalised processes through which they work out for themselves the rules for combining these correctly, and the optimum amount and nature of language exposure or input necessary for children to acquire language. The focus is on the universal characteristics of language acquisition in children.

Interactionist views

By the second half of the 20th century, the view that children's language is not acquired because of an innate facility, but instead originates and develops through interacting with others in the external social environment, has increasingly gained ground. According to this view, children's language develops as they strive to communicate with family members and others in their community, who in turn support them to achieve their communicative goals. Like constructivism, the interactionist view of language development and learning has its origins in the theory of development proposed by the Russian psychologist, Lev Vygostky, who argued that intellectual development is a function of interaction with others in the external social environment. The American psychologist, Jerome Bruner, (Wood, Bruner & Ross 1976) coined the term *scaffolding* to describe the type of interactive support provided by adults to help children use language to achieve social and intellectual goals they could not achieve on their own (see also Hammond 2001).

For Vygotsky (1929/1994: 58) language is the 'principal weapon of logical reasoning and the formation of concepts' and children's development is a function of their interaction with people and things in the environment. In early infancy, when children's involuntary actions merge with meanings made in interactions with others, they are able to bring their actions increasingly under voluntary control. With this step, speech is 'beginning ... to precede action and throw light on the conceived of but as yet unrealised action' (Vygotsky & Luria 1994/1930: 120). Similarly, the involuntary functions of children's minds, for example, perception, attention and memory, are also mediated socially when children interactively share the mental *know-how* of others in order to be able to achieve socially what they could not achieve in isolation. In this way, involuntary functions are reorganised into analytical and logical functions increasingly under the voluntary control of the mind. What begins as an external, interpersonal or social, phenomenon evolves into the internal phenomenon, thought, which retains the social, dialogic nature of the speech from which it has evolved. In other words, the young child's developing language becomes a mental tool through which the child's developing consciousness is structured. This idea has been developed by Rogoff (2003: 52), who describes human development as 'a process of people's changing participation in sociocultural activities of their communities' in which people both contribute and 'inherit practices invented by others'.

Detailed accounts of the social origins and drivers of infant language development have been produced by linguists using social semiotic and sociocultural analytical tools (for example, Halliday 1975, Painter 1984, Torr 1997). By recording and analysing the meaning-making of infants and young children, this group of linguists has been able to describe the development of language from its origins in 'the gradually elaborated cooperative exchange of attention between infant and caregiver during the first six months of life' (Painter 1999a: 38). From about the age of nine months, this exchange of attention evolves into a 'protolanguage', a system of 'invented vocalisations or gestures' used by the child to address others and to draw their attention to 'objects and happenings around them' (Painter 1999a: 38). Because the child uses this personal system consistently, caregivers can interpret the meanings the child makes and respond in ways that satisfy the child, but the protolanguage can only be used to express limited meanings about specific people and things in the child's immediate environment. As the child strives to communicate more fully, family members respond in kind by recasting the child's emerging meanings in the words and grammar of the home language. In this way, words and grammar appear in the child's language, and the child makes the transition into using the full language system used by the family and shared with the wider community. Once children master the system, around the age of two years, they will spend the rest of their lives 'learning the language itself' (Halliday 1975: 32). From this starting point, social semioticians have mapped the way language and learning develops interdependently through early childhood and the school years, from spoken language to written language and multimodal representation (for example, Christie & Derewianka 2008, Christie & Unsworth 2005, Djonov 2008, Djonov, Knox & Zhao 2015, Halliday 2007/1993, Painter 1999a, 1999b, Painter, Derewianka & Torr 2007, Zhao 2008).

Biological views

> ### Quote
>
> Literacy and numeracy change the human brain, but also enable human beings to perform feats that would not be possible without these cultural tools, including the achievements of science.
>
> (The Royal Society 2011: 9)

Over the last two decades researchers have begun investigating the influence of biological factors such as genetic endowment and brain development on young children's ability to learn to read and write. These studies suggest that 'learning outcomes are not solely determined by the environment' and that '[b]iological factors play an important role in accounting for differences in learning ability between individuals' (The Royal Society 2011: v). Such studies have the potential to help us understand specific learning difficulties and the way the brain is changed by learning. They may also provide sound means for evaluating so-called 'brain-based' teaching methods, often marketed to worried parents and teachers of young children struggling to read on schedule (see Geake 2009, Howard-Jones 2014).

To address the question about why children differ in their development of reading and related skills, researchers have undertaken a series of longitudinal behaviour-genetic studies of twins in Australia, the United Kingdom, the United States and Scandinavia, comparing similarities and differences between identical and non-identical twins (Olson,

Keenan, Byrne & Samuelsson 2014). Statistical analytical methods, including factor analysis and biometric modelling, were used to compare the relative influence of genetics and environment on pre-reading and reading development. These studies have revealed that genes have a role 'in influencing the course of reading development', particularly by the end of the first year at school, and further suggest 'that some of the high genetic influence on reading ability is due to a gene-environment correlation for reading practice' (Olson et al. 2014: 51), although exact causal relations have not been identified (see Chapter 6).

Within the field of developmental cognitive neuroscience, researchers also investigate interrelations between the developing brain, cognitive processes and the environment. For example, Diamond (2014) reports on research that strives to understand how executive functions and language development mutually support one another, research that employs complementary methods from the sciences and social sciences.

Quote

To study [the] neural bases [of executive functions] and [their] modulation by genes and neurochemistry, we use functional neuroimaging (MRI) & molecular genetic techniques. To study their modulation by the environment, we look at detrimental factors such as poverty or stress, and we look at facilitative factors such as school programs, and hope to start looking at the possible benefits of dance, music and storytelling.

(Lab of Adele Diamond – at http://www.devcogneuro.com – accessed 12.4.2015)

Executive functions are 'a family of top-down processes needed when you have to concentrate and pay attention, when ... relying on instinct or intuition would be ill-advised, insufficient or impossible' (Diamond 2014: 7). Executive functions depend on 'a neural circuit in which the prefrontal cortex plays a prominent role' (Diamond 2012: 335). This family of processes include three core executive functions, inhibitory control, working memory and cognitive flexibility, and three higher order functions, reasoning, problem solving and planning. Studies evaluating interventions for improving executive function use methods that include 'random assignment', 'an active control group and pre- and post-intervention measures' (Diamond 2012: 336). Working memory is the process of 'holding information in mind and manipulating it' and is an executive function of particular relevance to language and literacy development. This is because it is 'necessary for making sense of spoken and written language whether it is a sentence, a paragraph or longer' and is also 'critical for understanding what you are reading because even at the level of a sentence it is rare to see all the words at once' (Diamond 2014: 7–8).

Activities that contribute to children's development of executive function, their ability to concentrate and think, appear to be those that require discipline and practice. They are also activities that children love, so they commit time and effort to them, including activities that build physical fitness (Diamond 2012). Two early childhood programmes have also been shown empirically to contribute to the development of executive functions. These are Montessori programmes (Lillard & Else-Quest 2006) and the Tools of the Mind Program, an approach inspired by Vygotsky (Bodrova & Leong 2007). Both these programmes are designed to build children's independence and intellectual development through socially mediated structured activity (Feez 2011).

Quote

[Both Montessori and Tools of the Mind] (a) help children exercise their [executive functions] and constantly challenge them to do so at higher levels; (b) reduce stress in the classroom; (c) rarely embarrass a child; (d) cultivate children's joy, pride, and self-confidence; (e) take an active and hands-on approach to learning; (f) easily accommodate children progressing at different rates; (g) emphasise character development as well as academic development; (h) emphasise oral language; (i) engage children in teaching one another; and (j) foster social skills and bonding.

(Diamond 2012: 338)

Understanding working memory and neural functioning is central to assisting underachieving students master basic literacy and numeracy, according to Pegg (2013). Through deliberate practice, sustained effort and valuing of errors as a means of building expertise, Pegg argues, underachieving students can work towards automaticity in basic skills, freeing up their working memory to make way for higher order skills. Neuroimaging evidence shows that 'successful reading requires the integration of multiple neural processes' (Geake 2009: 134). As more is understood about neural processes, and how they interact with and respond to environmental conditions, inevitably this knowledge will impact the field of literacy research in ways that are as yet difficult to predict.

Conceptualising initial literacy instruction

Each of the theoretical perspectives reviewed above, albeit all too briefly, generates a different perspective on initial literacy development and how it might be researched. Each perspective leads to research findings that point to different ways of approaching early literacy learning and teaching. With this in mind, Wyatt-Smith, Elkins and Gunn (2011: 3) argue that 'a sound basis for action is converging evidence from multiple sources and different perspectives'. This is because '[e]vidence-based convergence lends strength to findings as no single study, methodology, finding or view is considered, in and of itself, a sufficient basis for action'.

From a behaviourist perspective, learning, whether at home or at school, involves explicit demonstration and teaching of behaviours, which children imitate and practise, behaviour that is reinforced when it is correct or effective. This approach is often aligned with a skills-based orientation and explicit instruction of those skills in a fixed sequence. In the context of initial literacy teaching and learning, skills-based approaches focus on 'teaching literacy as a generic set of portable skills' (Wyatt-Smith & Gunn 2007: 3). Imitation, practice and reinforcement of portable literacy skills all feature in a discussion of cognitive perspectives as well.

Intensive phonics instruction

Since the mid-20th century, cognitive perspectives have generated divergent views about what counts as the foundation of successful literacy development, particularly in relation to the teaching of reading, resulting in 'one of the most contentious debates in literacy pedagogy ... the *skills* versus *whole-language* debate' (Wyatt-Smith & Gunn 2007: 3) (see also Chall 1967, Snyder 2008). The skills approach is aligned with intensive instruction in phonics based on a 'narrow view' of literacy as 'the ability to read and write; nothing more and nothing less. By *reading* we mean the ability to decode text accurately and fluently with understanding of what has been read' (Wheldall & Beaman 2011: 256). When reading is understood as 'the ability to decode, recognise and draw meaning from the printed word' (Buckingham, Wheldall & Beaman 2011: 22), initial instruction in reading typically involves explicitly and systematically teaching the component sounds of the language and their correspondence with letters of the alphabet.

Quote

... in order to be able to progress with reading instruction, children need to acquire the basic building blocks for reading, including letter knowledge (the names and sounds of the alphabet), phonological awareness (explicit appreciation of the sounds of language and how words are composed of these sounds) and a grasp of the alphabetic principle (the principle that the individual sounds of language can be represented by individual marks on the page – letters).

(Coltheart & Prior 2007: 4)

Skills-based reading instruction has two main dimensions: instruction in phonemic awareness, 'the ability to focus on and manipulate phonemes in spoken words' (Ehri, Nunes, Willows, Schuster, Yahgoub-Zadeh & Shanahan 2001: 253), and systematic instruction in phonics, the correspondence between the phonemes in spoken words and the letters used to write the words down. Quantitative meta-analyses of experimental studies undertaken between 1970 and 2000 show that, in comparison with other types of reading instruction, explicit, systematic instruction in phonemic awareness and phonics has a more positive effect on the word-level reading and spelling of younger children than other methods when measured by standardised texts, while also protecting against later reading difficulties (Ehri et al. 2001, Xue & Meisels 2004).

Several types of phonics instruction have been identified, including synthetic (blending) and analytic (segmenting) approaches, decoding by analogy with known words or by using onset-rime syllable patterns, phonics learned through spelling activities, and phonics instruction embedded in authentic language use. One of these, synthetic phonics, is promoted as having the highest effect size (Buckingham et al. 2013, Coltheart & Prior 2007, Rose 2006). Synthetic phonics is defined as 'a highly structured, sequential and explicit method that teaches beginning and remedial readers how to construct words from the smallest language *building blocks* of letters and letter combinations and their corresponding sounds' (Buckingham et al. 2013: 23), a definition that brings to mind children in 1st century Rome constructing words with letters carved from ivory.

While meta-analyses show that systematic phonics instruction helps younger children with word-level reading and prevents later reading difficulties, it is less effective for older readers facing difficulties with reading. While systematic phonics instruction is necessary, for maximum effect the teaching must be 'engaging and enjoyable' and combined with other strategies related to building fluency and comprehension (Ehri et al. 2001: 433). The evidence for the sustainability of the impact of intensive phonics instruction is limited, however, because it is 'based on achievement measures that typically test letter-sound knowledge and word knowledge in isolation ... not on reading whole texts and developing reading strategies and skills in the context of reading' (Xue & Meisels 2004: 194–195). This limitation is underscored by studies that suggest the ability of preschool age children to attend to speech units larger than phonemes, that is, syllables, onset and rime, is a more reliable indicator of future reading success across all languages (Goswami 2006).

Quote

Systemic phonics instruction by itself does not help students acquire all the processes they need to become successful readers. Phonics needs to be combined with other essential instructional components to create a complete and balanced reading program ... fluency, vocabulary and reading comprehension strategies.

(Ehri et al. 2001: 433)

In English-speaking countries, experimental evidence supporting intensive, systematic phonics instruction has strongly influenced early literacy policy development (for example, the National Early Literacy Panel [NELP] 2008, Rose 2006, Rowe 2005) and the design of high-stakes testing regimes in early childhood contexts (Meisels 2007). Generalisations about optimum teaching practice made on the basis of this evidence, however, have been challenged Freebody (2007: 21). For example, questions have been raised about the rigour of the evidence when ethnographic and observational studies of literacy teaching and learning are not taken into account. Determining the degree of equivalence between specific instances of 'explicit phonics teaching' in diverse real-life classroom settings is also challenging (Freebody 2007: 29–30).

> ### Quote
>
> Understanding the limitations and possibilities of statistical reasoning provides a way of refining debates between practitioners committed to contrasting paradigms and forms of inquiry, and is thus a way of containing the potentially debilitating effects of those debates on a field of study ... research needs to include careful descriptive documentations of current practice in any comprehensive research base, in order to be able to inform the teaching and learning of literacy in schools. Otherwise, the research is aiming to reform phenomena in evolving contexts about which it has not bothered to systematically inform itself ... The implication here is that, because we cannot avoid these 'many factors' that 'leave one wondering about', we should set about isolating them from confounding factors, and measuring them as separate, non-interactive entities, without losing the 'real-world validity' of the project. This balancing act is beyond the capacity of experimental research alone.
>
> (Freebody 2007: 28–59)

The evidence base that has driven the emphasis on phonics over other types of literacy instruction, according to Paris and Luo (2010: 321), is compromised by faulty analysis in which 'differences in the developmental trajectories of different reading skills' are not taken into account. These authors distinguish between *constrained skills*, such as decoding, which are learned relatively quickly during initial reading instruction, and *unconstrained skills*, such as reading comprehension, which develop much more slowly over the years of schooling and beyond (see also Luke & Woods 2008, Paris 2005).

> ### Quote
>
> Conclusions that decoding skills deserve greater or earlier instruction for beginning readers than do unconstrained skills are not warranted, and there are liabilities for early reading pedagogy that overemphasises decoding skills at the expense of vocabulary, comprehension, oral language, writing, and critical analyses of literacy.
>
> (Paris & Luo 2010: 321)

The consensus 'that many young readers in the early years of schooling need explicit instruction in alphabetic knowledge and ... phonemic awareness' was largely established by 1990, as Freebody (2007: 44) points out, although not always in 'naturally occurring classroom settings'. Since then, according to Freebody (2007: 45), rather than building on existing knowledge, many studies merely reconfirm 'basic propositions about how children do and can learn aspects of the English written code' and grapheme-phoneme correspondence, and what still deserves further investigation are 'the longitudinal consequences of various kinds of early literacy education settings and experiences'. Longitudinal studies in real classrooms would help establish more nuanced understandings of the following questions:

• What types of phonics instruction in the early years are more likely to support sustained literacy achievement for different cohorts as they progress through school?
• In the developmental continuum, when are specific types of phonics instruction most effective, for which groups of students and in what settings?
• How are difficulties in early literacy achievement best addressed in different settings?
• What types of testing of early literacy gains might predict sustained achievement over time?
• What wider definitions of literacy and of evidence-based literacy research are required to identify predictors of sustained achievement from different starting points?

(See for example, Campbell, Torr & Cologon 2014, Mills 2005, Soler, Wearmouth & Reid 2002, Wyatt-Smith, Elkins & Gunn 2011.)

For practical reasons, and in response to pressure to include phonics in their programmes, some early years teachers report they are resorting to pre-packaged commercial phonics programmes, without having access to the professional training or research evidence needed to evaluate the effectiveness of such programmes in different contexts (Campbell et al. 2014). The relations between competing sources of research evidence, mandated content, high-stakes testing, commercial gain and the reality of early years' classroom practice continue to demand attention from researchers.

Identifying phonics, and specific strategies for teaching phonics, as the most important components of initial literacy teaching is often accompanied by accountability measures based on standardised assessment, and a discourse of deficit and difficulty. This was the approach implemented in the United States in 2001 with the No Child Left Behind Program,[2] which was seen as a means of improving the quality of early literacy acquisition for children from all social groups. Despite increased time spent on phonics instruction, as well as on vocabulary, fluency and comprehension, subsequent research suggests standards of reading comprehension have remained the same in the United States (see Luke & Woods 2008 for a review). This suggests that wider definitions of literacy instruction and of evidence-based, scientific, research might be required.

> ## Quote
>
> The scientific approach assumes that any phenomenon can be observed from a detached, objective point of view with researchers exploring the relationships between component parts through a series of studies utilising a deductive process.
>
> (Wyatt-Smith & Gunn 2007: 3)

Whole language

A wider definition of literacy is used by those who promote literacy teaching practices that align with the whole-language approach, drawing variously on cognitive and nativist views of learning. The whole-language approach, with its origins in the 1960s, is based on the idea 'that written language [is] learned naturally in the cultural context, just as oral language is' (Ken Goodman in Harste & Short 1996: 508). After analysing the miscues made by beginning readers while reading authentic texts, Goodman (1997: 596) described reading as a 'psycholinguistic guessing game' in which 'a tentative reader processes information from three cueing systems: graphophonic, syntactic and semantic'. The emphasis in the whole-language approach is on beginning readers being given opportunities to draw on the cueing systems to construct meaning from text when reading and writing.

> ## Quote
>
> In this guessing game, the reader uses strategies to sample and select from the information in the text, makes predictions and draws inferences, confirms or disconfirms and regresses when necessary to make necessary corrections. Starting with visual input the reader forms perceptions, assigns wording and syntax and brings meaning to the text, all the time keeping focus on making sense, constructing meaning.
>
> (Goodman 1997: 596)

The value of cueing systems for beginning readers who have not yet 'cracked the spelling-to-sound code', however, has been strongly challenged in a systematic review of the literature undertaken by Stanovich (1986). This review argues that while cues may help with comprehension, they do not help with initial word recognition. Children who fall at this initial hurdle are in danger of falling increasingly behind their more successful peers. Beginning readers who successfully crack the code read more, and build vocabulary and comprehension skills, which further improves reading through a reciprocal relationship.

The idea that written language is learned best in conditions similar to those in which spoken language is learned reappears in the 'seven conditions of natural language learning' proposed by Cambourne (for example, 1995). These conditions include immersing learners in rich and meaningful language use, demonstrating and modelling how texts are used, expecting that learners will be successful, leaving decisions about learning to the learner, celebrating learners' approximations, providing frequent opportunities for learners to use print with more knowledgeable others providing learners with feedback (see discussion in Chapter 1)

Towards balanced and responsive approaches to initial literacy instruction

> **Quote**
>
> The challenge for the expert literacy teacher is not simply about choice of one approach over the other in all pedagogical contexts. Instead, it is to design literacy learning opportunities that deliberately draw on elements of each approach, separately and in combination, taking account of needs of individual students.
>
> (Wyatt-Smith & Gunn 2007: 7)

Proponents of explicit and systematic phonics instruction in the early years continue to claim that teachers who use whole-language approaches do not teach phonics explicitly or systematically (for example, Buckingham et al. 2013). However, this claim, along with 'the dichotomy between code/skill emphases and meaning/integrated emphasis' in general, is not supported in the 'scholarly literature on whole language', which includes phonics as 'an expected feature of instruction' (Dahl, Sharer, Lawson & Grogan 1999: 317). Nor is it supported in longitudinal studies that document actual classroom practice from various disciplinary perspectives (Bowyer-Crane, Snowling, Duff, Fieldsend, Carroll, Miles, Giotz & Hulme 2007, Dahl et al. 1999; Meiers & Khoo 2006, Morris, Bloodgood, Lomax & Perney 2003, Xue & Meisels 2004). The studies listed above variously show that:

1. Classroom teachers select from a repertoire of both skills-based and meaning-based teaching strategies in response to the developing needs of their students and the demands of their teaching context.
2. Different approaches make different contributions to students' literacy development.
3. Development of decoding skills and the ability to make meaning in the context of both reading and writing are mutually supportive.
4. Students' achievements are highest when teachers explicitly incorporate the two techniques – phonics instruction and whole language – together in balanced and responsive ways (Freebody 2007: 47).

Moreover, following Morris et al. (2003: 48), a focus on word meaning 'provides a generative bridge between decoding ... and ... making meaning'. The study of 'young children in real reading situations' by Morris et al. (2003: 322) 'suggests an interactive relationship between beginning readers' concept of word in text and phoneme awareness'.

> ### Quote
>
> In order to learn to read effectively, children need a balanced instructional approach that includes learning to break the code and engaging in meaningful reading and writing activities.
>
> (Xue & Meisels 2004: 222)

To help with navigating research and debates in the field of literacy development in the early years, Snow (2004) has recast contrasting views of literacy and literacy development as a framework of complementary perspectives. Questions emerging from this framework will only be resolved on the basis of research evidence demonstrating the 'relative effectiveness of code-focused versus language-focused early literacy instruction' for specific groups, such as children learning

English as an additional language and those 'growing up in poverty' (Snow 2004: 290).

The argument for developing effective 'balanced and responsive ways' of teaching initial literacy is compelling, in an era when demands for accountability are closely aligned with standardised, often scripted and mandated, skills-based early literacy programmes and narrowly focused high-stakes testing (Comber & Nichols 2004, Pressley 2002). Balance implies the integration, for instructional purposes, of disparate elements and processes related to code-breaking and meaning-making, while responsiveness implies instruction differentiated to accommodate the individual needs of students. The design and implementation of programmes that aim for balance and responsiveness, however, pose practical challenges for teachers, just as investigating how this might be achieved in real classrooms poses theoretical, methodological and analytical challenges for researchers.

The study by Dahl et al. (1999) cited above exemplifies the complex methodology and analysis required to study specific teaching approaches, when these are enacted in real early years classrooms. The teaching approach under investigation must be defined to establish criteria for selecting classrooms as research sites on the basis of their fidelity to the approach within a specified range. Types of achievement must be distinguished (for example, decoding, in isolation and in context, and encoding, in isolation and in context) and instruments selected to measure each type of achievement. Extensive observational and transcript data are required and these must be coded accurately to distinguish between what is being taught (content), how it is being taught (instruction) and associated skills and strategies.

Terms that are often confused, or used interchangeably, such as *strategy* and *skill*, also need to be disentangled and realigned for effective analysis of classroom data. As a first step, strategies can be defined as 'general methods used to address an issue or solve a problem' (de Silva Joyce & Feez 2012: 135), either by the teacher (teaching strategy) or by the learner (learning strategy), whereas a skill is a learned action that becomes automatic with practice. This distinction has been elaborated by Afflerbach, Pearson and Paris (2008) in their discussion of reading strategies and skills. They define reading strategies as 'deliberate, goal-oriented attempts to control and modify ... efforts to decode text, understand words, and construct meanings of text' and reading skills as 'automatic actions that result in decoding and comprehension with speed, efficiency, and fluency and usually occur without awareness of the components or control involved' (Afflerbach et al. 2008: 368).

Strategy use requires conscious effort, involves metacognition, and with practice over time can evolve into an automatic skill. This clarification 'situates our understanding of skill and strategy in an historical context – one marked by the dynamic of new knowledge generated by research, and one that is subject to ongoing discussion and revision' (Afflerbach et al. 2008: 372).

Quote

When we are teaching strategically, we help students to analyse tasks, to consider various approaches to performing the task, and to choose among alternative actions to reach the goal. Teaching skills involves practice and feedback to improve speed and efficiency, which taken together amount to what we call fluency. One challenge for teachers of reading is fully investigating the strategy-skill connection and determining how an effortful strategy can become an automatic skill. A related challenge is designing instruction that makes clear the steps of strategies while providing practice so that strategies may transform themselves into skills.

(Afflerbach et al. 2008: 372)

In summary, navigating the extensive and divergent literature on initial literacy teaching and learning generated from a cognitive point of view over recent decades can leave the researcher, and the practitioner, with unstable inventories of items that are extremely challenging to relate and unify, especially when some elements have been identified as antithetical to others in some contexts. Such inventories include lists of language content (phonemes, graphemes, syllables, words, sentences, texts, topics), cognitive processes (perception, attention, memory, phonemic awareness, vocabulary building, comprehension, fluency, strategies and skills, cueing systems, learning continua, knowledge building) and teaching approaches (explicit, implicit, synthetic, analytic, intensive, balanced, embedded). Increasingly, however, there is evidence that isolating these elements one from another in teaching contexts is not optimal. Palincsar and Schutz (2011: 91), for example, argue that strategy instruction isolated from knowledge building achieves little and that strategies only become helpful when used as 'tools for thinking' in response to 'the demands of the text ... [and] in the service of ... knowledge building'.

To prevent reading failure for the approximately 25% (or more in disadvantaged populations) of children who find learning to read difficult, Morris (2015: 502–506) proposes a framework in which 'complementary principles' are used to combine 'disparate instructional approaches (for example, word-control basals, whole language, intensive phonics)' into 'a balanced approach to teach beginning reading'. The framework Morris develops for this purpose has three components: the selection of reading material, systematic instruction in phonics and teacher training. Reading material is selected by controlling for difficulty not only at word level with texts that repeat high frequency words and decodable word patterns (the intensive phonics approach), but also at sentence level with interesting texts that repeat sentence patterns to lead 'the beginner to anticipate upcoming words', alongside 'pictures that complement a meaningful storyline' (the whole-language approach) (Morris 2015: 504). Systematic phonics instruction in a balanced approach combines both synthetic phonics (blending individual sounds into words) as the starting point, and analytical phonics (segmenting words into sounds and syllables) to 'foster automatic recognition' of syllable patterns for fluent reading, alongside 'copious amounts of contextual reading at the appropriate difficulty level' (Morris 2015: 505–506). Beginning readers also 'require extensive exposure to more challenging text – that is, text that they cannot read themselves ... [and] time spent actively listening to challenging stories' (Morris 2015: 509) within a literacy programme that includes writing.

Quote

...a balanced classroom literacy program must also include writing, an important language art in and of itself. Writing plays a role in learning to read. Children's earliest writing efforts (e.g., picture captions, single sentences, short notes) help them to understand that sentences are composed of words and that words are composed of sounds that match to letters. Later on, writing allows children to tell a story or make an argument; it affords them opportunities to read and reread text (both their own and that produced by classmates); and it provides them a purposeful arena for experimenting with, practising, and eventually internalising the letter sounds, spelling patterns, and sight words that are of crucial importance in learning to read.

(Morris 2015: 507)

To integrate disparate elements into a balanced literacy programme, teachers require knowledge of both the content and a 'developmental continuum of ... instruction' related to that content and they must 'decide where a child (or a small group of children) needs to be taught along this continuum' [and] 'have a method for teaching the content' (Morris 2015: 504–505). Developing this knowledge and skill requires 'quality pedagogical training' (Morris 2015: 506) in what might be described as 'pedagogical content knowledge', following Schulman (1986). The next section reviews how the disparate elements surveyed from a cognitive perspective might be unified in frameworks developed from interactionist perspectives.

Quote

The ability to read fluently requires the integration of many complex skills and concepts, including phonemic awareness, the alphabetic principle, a rich vocabulary, background knowledge of the world, and knowledge of the grammatical features of different genres including narrative and explanation.

(Campbell et al. 2014: 40)

Socially informed initial literacy education: integrating skills, knowledge and pedagogy

Since the 1980s, balanced and responsive approaches to initial literacy education have been pursued by researchers who are 'oriented towards a view of language as social or interactional in character' (Painter 1999a: 19). Researchers working from this point of view do not isolate the development of specific cognitive and linguistic skills, such as phonemic awareness, sound-letter correspondence, vocabulary building, comprehension and composition, from meaningful interactive language use in social contexts.

Ethnographic views

When researchers view the development of cognitive skills and the development of linguistic skills as interdependent, and a function of interaction with others, their interest turns to the ways different interactive experiences in childhood might shape this development. Detailed eth-nographic descriptions of social life in different cultural settings reveal how the culturally specific interactional experiences of children growing up in these settings shape how they perceive and think about the world, how they use language, and experience literacy, and how they learn (for example, Heath 1983, Scollon & Scollon 1981, Scribner & Cole 1981, Street 2001a).

For a retrospective look at studies undertaken over several decades into formal and informal language socialisation, includ-ing socialisation into literacy practices, across diverse social and cultural contexts, see Duff & Hornberger (2008). This volume exemplifies the richness of the intellectual heritage in the field of language socialisation studies, and the strength of the foundation on which researchers can build, as they investigate ways language and literacy development is mediated socioculturally. Importantly for literacy research, ethnographic and sociolinguistic studies into early language and literacy development over several decades have demonstrated that ways of perceiving, thinking, meaning, valuing and learning considered to be the *norm* in dominant cultural groups, for example, middle-class English-speaking cultures, may be experienced as foreign, even alienating, by those from different cultures and subcultures. This becomes significant when children from non-dominant cultural backgrounds enter classrooms where they are faced with literacy instruction shaped by a dominating culture.

A sociocognitive lens

Quotes

Viewing literacy as situated within social contexts stands in opposi-tion to the view that literacy is a set of skills, isolated from contexts of use.

(Purcell-Gates 2013: 69)

Within a sociocognitive lens, all instances of reading reflect both (a) mental processing and skill application and (b) the contexts within which they occur.

(Purcell-Gates 2011: 470)

When viewed through a sociocognitive lens, the cognitive processes involved in reading and learning to read are *nested* inside the socio-cultural contexts in which reading occurs (Purcell-Gates, Jacobsen & Degener 2004). For Purcell-Gates (2011: 469–470) this approach 'accounts for both informal and formal (school) instruction ... and reflects a dialogic relationship among student, teacher and pedagogy' and she extends this idea by arguing that reading research is also socially and culturally situated and 'contexts within which research takes place need to be acknowledged' and accounted for as variables within both the research design and the interpretation of results. Furthermore, descriptions of the context in which research has been undertaken, for example, ethnographic descriptions, provide teachers with greater access to research findings because teachers always read and use research on the basis of their own classroom experiences (Purcell-Gates 2011: 471).

Purcell-Gates (2013) reports on a study that explains why an English language Migrant Head Start Program in the United States, designed to support academic achievement in preschool age children from a marginalised subculture of Spanish-speaking migrant farm workers, failed to achieve its goals. This failure was the result of 'a school-based focus on only surface features of early literacy, delivered in an unfamiliar language and reflecting culturally specific beliefs and values about literacy practice that did not match those of most of the children' (Purcell-Gates 2013: 68). For the purposes of her study, she adopted a sociocognitive perspective and used an ethnographic case study design, in which she was a participant-observer. She focused her attention on the children's literacy development because 'literacy achievement is so basic to academic achievement and to social upward mobility' and is 'something that is highly desired by the migrant farmworker families for their children' (Purcell-Gates 2013: 70). One of the aims of the study was to model for educators 'who care about the perpetual underachievement of children from marginalised communities' how to 'begin to see and know the men, women and children who populate their classrooms' and 'the nature of their community-based knowledge' (Purcell-Gates 2013: 69). By assuming that 'all students bring with them to formal literacy instruction socioculturally con-structed bodies of knowledge that can be productively built upon', educators avoid 'the devaluing of children's culture, language and knowledge' that leads to this 'devastating' underachievement (Purcell-Gates 2013: 70).

Quotes

...emergent literacy theory asserts that young children acquire their foundational understandings of literacy within their own communities of practice before they begin formal literacy instruction in school ... literacy achievement in school is built on [the] foundation of early literacy concepts that children acquire in their literacy practice communities. Thus, educators wishing to provide beginning literacy instruction that is meaningful and productive of future literacy development and achievement must adopt a learner stance ... toward their students' home literacy environments.

...our understanding of children's literacy development, including the instruction we provide them, must derive from a systematic and real attempt to uncover the multiple and diverse language and literacy practices familiar to individual children.

(Purcell-Gates 2013: 69–73)

The analysis was based on 'grounded theory, where explanations of phenomena are grounded in data provided by participants', and the researcher used 'meta-matrices' to 'compare literacy practices in the homes and communities' with those of the education programme (Purcell-Gates 2013: 80). Purcell-Gates found a 'lack of congruence between the programme and the children in terms of language and literacy instruction', exemplified by the contrast between the children's disengagement during story reading, a literacy practice completely unknown to the children and from which they regularly tried to escape, and their total absorption later the same day when making greeting cards, a literacy practice familiar to them from home (Purcell-Gates 2013: 88–91). The children's disengagement from story reading served to confirm the teachers' preconceptions that literacy was not valued in the children's homes and community, preconceptions the ethnographic study demonstrated were incorrect. To build on the 'many hidden literacies' that her ethnographic study revealed to be embedded in the lives of the children, Purcell-Gates (2013: 91), citing Gutiérrez (2008), proposes the creation of a 'third space' in classrooms for children who are marginalised 'socially, culturally and linguistically, where the languages, cultures and funds of knowledge' of the children are 'as equally represented and respected as those of the teacher'.

The social semiotic tradition

Literacy researchers working within the social semiotic tradition use a linguistically informed sociocultural approach to model the relations between early literacy development and the contexts in which children become literate. When analytical tools derived from social semiotics are used to study initial literacy development, polarised views claiming **either** meaning (whole language) **or** phonology (phonics) as the best entry into literacy become unsustainable (Schleppegrell 2004). Instead, social semiotic frameworks can be used to account for all types of meaning-making in social contexts. This includes the meaning-making of young children as they first learn to control spoken and written language, as well as meanings made through other modalities such as images or symbols, and the ways these modalities combine with language in multimodal texts.

As introduced in Part I, the starting point for a social semiotic analysis of literacy development is Systemic Functional Linguistics (SFL), developed by M. A. K. Halliday (see Halliday & Matthiessen 2014). This theory organises otherwise disparate language features into a three-layered model representing language as a unified resource for making meaning, with text as the unit of meaning. At the top layer of the model is meaning (the layer of semantics), which lies at the interface between language and context. The context is integrated into the meanings chosen by language users and the ways these meanings are woven into texts. The meanings in texts are expressed in words organised into grammatical structures (the layer of lexicogrammar). Words find their expression in the sounds of the language, and in the letters and letter combinations used to write down the sounds (the layer of phonology/graphology). This multi-layered model of language makes it possible to study language in use, including developing language, from three different perspectives:

1. from top-down to examine the way meanings are woven together into whole texts
2. at the intermediary level to examine how words are structured into clauses
3. from bottom up to examine how words are expressed as sounds and written down using letters corresponding to the sounds.

This model reveals that semantic and phonological perspectives are complementary, rather than incompatible views of language, and this suggests that possibilities for literacy pedagogy are diminished, if one perspective is favoured at the expense of another. Representing words in grammatical structures (lexicogrammar) as the intermediary between meaning and its expression in sounds (or letters) is a feature of this model that has proven to be particularly valuable for literacy researchers and practitioners (see Part III).

In any context of language use, including pedagogic contexts, three sets of immediate situational variables shape the language choices that distinguish the varieties of language used in texts in that context. These variables are *field,* the social activity taking place, *tenor,* the relationship of the people taking part in the interaction and *mode,* the role language is playing in the context, including the channel being used to communicate (see Chapter 2). Here is an example of how these variables might be applied to analyse the register of a particular educational context: learning about volcanoes (field) through reading an] information text (mode i.e. written text accompanied by labelled diagrams and pictures) written for children (tenor i.e. the relationship between the author and the child readers).

In the SFL model, language features, including structural and cohesive devices, words and grammar, are labelled for their function, and the type of meanings they make. Unlike, for example, traditional and formal grammars, in the SFL model, language features are not listed in inventories, but instead are organised into networks, or systems, of meaningful choices, at increasingly delicate levels. These systems cluster under general metafunctional headings, and each metafunction is understood as an expression of a related situational variable. In this way, it is possible to analyse how the three situational variables of any context – field, tenor and mode – are expressed in the choices of language features in texts used in that context. Language features that represent ideas about our experience of the world (experiential meanings) and relate these ideas logically (logical meanings) are an expression of field. Language features used to interact with others and to express attitudes and feelings (interpersonal meanings) are an expression of tenor. Language features used to compose spoken and written texts so they are well organised and cohesive (textual meanings) are an expression of mode (see Chapter 2). A multifunctional approach to describing the meanings made in images has also been developed (Kress & van Leeuwen 2006), making possible complementary analyses of language and image in multimodal texts (see Chapter 2).

> **Quote**
>
> These meaning strands, or metafunctions, produce 'a poly-phonic composition in which different semantic melodies are interwoven, to be realised as integrated lexicogrammatical structures'.
>
> (Halliday 1978: 112)

The SFL model of language embraces a rich description of language elements at each level of language, generating a proliferation of technical terms. Thus, for example, the substantial set of technical terms, or metalanguage, used by proponents of intensive phonics instruction to talk about phonological and graphological items and processes can be mapped onto the SFL model. At the same time, SFL descriptions of language elements at the level of lexicogrammar and semantics can be used to expand, in principled ways, the comparatively sparse and far less specialised set of terms used by proponents of both intensive phonics instruction and whole-language approaches. This enables researchers and teachers to pay closer attention to the language elements in play when the focus of literacy research and instruction is on vocabulary building, reading fluency, reading comprehension and written composition in educational contexts. The capacity to generate comprehensive descriptions of language use, in theoretically principled ways, is the key to reconciling unwarranted and distracting oppositions in early literacy research. It also provides ways of building tools fit for the purpose of investigating, in genuinely balanced ways, literacy demands and literacy development at the sentence (lexicogrammar), text (meaning) and context layers, the layers implicated in the building of vocabulary, fluency, text comprehension and composition.

Depending on their research goals, literacy researchers can choose whether to use the full descriptive and analytical power of the rich and complex technicality developed by systemic functional linguists (for example, Halliday & Hasan 1976, Halliday & Matthiessen 1999b, 2014), or they can draw on SFL apprenticing texts or pedagogical grammars, which may be more effective for guiding classroom-based research in collaboration with teachers (for example, Butt, Fahey, Feez & Spinks 2012, Derewianka 2011, Eggins 2004, Humphrey, Droga & Feez 2012, Jones & Lock 2011, Thompson 2014).

Social semiotic research frameworks: discourse analysis and ontogenetic trajectories

Social semiotic research frameworks have been used as both discourse analysis tools and to trace trajectories of children's language development from infancy and through the years of schooling. Studies undertaken using social semiotic analytical tools, however, are not designed using experimental methodologies. Researchers using social semiotic frameworks collect naturalistic data, by recording and transcribing spoken language, taking notes while observing, and collecting written and visual texts. They then select from the repertoire of analytical tools generated by the functional model of language, or, if demanded by the data or research questions, extend or add to that repertoire within the parameters of the model.

Quotes

Systemic functional linguistics (SFL) offers a means of exploring meaning in language and of relating language use to social contexts so as to contribute to our understanding of language in social life.

(Schleppegrell 2013: 21)

Experimental approaches to data collection have an appeal within theoretical approaches which seek 'clean', 'objective' data to test specific hypotheses in a context where it is believed all variables other than those under attention can be identified and carefully controlled. However, researchers conceiving of language as a social practice have ... argued against the very premises upon which experimental data collection takes place ... Certainly, simply to recognise that an experiment to elicit linguistic data is itself a semiotic context that will have a strong bearing on the language produced is to appreciate the extreme difficulty of obtaining data which will provide insights into how language is used outside that experimental situation.

(Painter 1999a: 70)

Hasan (1990, 1996b, 1996c) and Hasan and Cloran (1990), for example, developed networks that enabled her to focus on the level of semantics as a starting point for analysing talk between mothers and preschool age children during everyday routines at home. These networks were further extended by Williams (1998, 2001, 2005b) to analyse turn-taking between parents and children during joint book-reading at home. Cloran (1999) added to the analytical power of semantic networks by proposing a new unit of semantic analysis, the rhetorical unit, based on patterns of cohesion. By applying these analytical tools to naturalistic data, this group of researchers has generated linguistic evidence of how children, growing up in families positioned differently in society, learn to make different kinds of meanings, through interactions with their caregivers. These and related studies of semantic variation provide both evidence and explanation for the proposition by the sociologist Bernstein (2000) that access to specific types of meanings are differentially distributed to different groups within a society, depending on their social position, and that, because of this differential access, children entering school from some social groups will find it easier to engage with the literate meanings of the classroom than others. If everyday interactions at home and in the community do not give children experience with the communicative strategies needed to access educational meanings, these children are at a disadvantage (see Chapter 1).

Painter (1999a), as participant-observer, recorded samples, and observed and took notes, of her son's everyday conversational interactions between the ages of two and a half and five years. These data were the basis for a longitudinal case study of 'one child's grammar in use, with the aim of describing the way language was mobilised and developed as a resource for learning during the preschool years' (Painter 1999a: 69). Painter used the SFL model of language to analyse, at the level of lexi-cogrammar, the child's developing language use within a middle-class English-speaking family. This study draws attention to developments in the grammatical patterns of the preschool child's everyday interactions with others, developments which act as a 'semiotic preparation' for learning educational knowledge at school (Painter 1999a: 332–333) and which prepare the child for later facility with written language. These developments include discussing what is typical about different classes or categories of things, talking about letters and words in written texts, classifying and defining concrete and abstract ideas, and reasoning and inferring logically. The case study was 'used to support an argument that at least for some children, their linguistic experience involves developing an orientation to those ways of learning that are best tuned to the demands of educational knowledge ... and that learning is a linguistic process' (Painter 1999a: 333–334).

In summary, studies of naturalistic data show how children's everyday interactions are as much contexts for learning that support literacy development as interactions at school. Children from backgrounds where language use at home is echoed in the literate practices of the school typically achieve better educational outcomes than those for whom language use at home is less in harmony with these practices (Compare Snow 2004: 275–276).

The studies of young children's everyday social interactions provide evidence for a language-based theory of learning, as proposed by Halliday (2007/1993: 342), for whom 'language is the essential condition of knowing, the process by which experience becomes knowledge'. Understanding learning as a linguistic process complements Vygotsky's view of human development as socially and so semiotically mediated (for example, Vygotsky 1978), as well as Bernstein's (2000) sociology of pedagogy that proposes a system of principles through which knowledge is given reality in learning contexts. These three complementary approaches have been integrated very productively by researchers striving to understand the mechanisms that underpin children's successful and unsuccessful engagement with the literacy demands of educational knowledge, as will be explored further in subsequent chapters.

Vygotsky (1978) identified the origins in infancy of two genetic pathways of particular relevance to language and literacy development. The first begins when an infant intentionally points at something, and the second originates when an infant intentionally imitates the actions of others. When infants point, or indicate, they are both regulating their own attention, and sharing attention collaboratively with others. Indication is the origin of a developmental trajectory that leads to later use of language for labelling, generalising and categorising. When infants imitate, they are collaborating and interacting in shared social activities under guidance. In Vygotskian terms, imitation demonstrates infants are in the *zone of proximal development*, because imitation enables them to achieve beyond what they could do on their own (see Chapter 1).

These Vygotskian genetic pathways are retraced by Halliday (2004/1993) in semiotic terms (Wells 1994). Halliday lists 21 features he considers to be critical to a language-based theory of learning. The identification of these features is 'based on natural data rather than experimental data: that is, on language that is unconscious, not self-monitored; in context, not in a vacuum; observed, not elicited'

(Halliday 2004/1993: 328). By attending to these features, it is possible to trace pathways through which

> children successively generalise contexts and meanings in ways that ultimately transform the semiotic into one that allows all the disparate specificity of lived experience to be construed into more general categories and relations of meaning; a semiotic with an unlimited potential for learning about the world in interaction with others.
>
> (Painter, Derewianka & Torr 2007: 569)

Quotes

When children learn language, they are not simply engaging in one kind of learning among many; rather, they are learning the foundation of learning itself. The distinctive characteristic of human learning is that it is a process of making meaning – a semiotic process; and the prototypical form of human semiotic is language. Hence the ontogenesis of language is at the same time the ontogenesis of learning ... during the past hundred generations or so ... [a] new form of expression has evolved, that we call writing, and following on from this a new, institutionalised form of learning that we call education. Children now learn language not only in home and neighbourhood but also in school; and with new modes of language development come new forms of knowledge, educational knowledge as distinct from what we call commonsense. At the same time, the process of language development is still a continuous learning process, one that goes on from birth, through infancy and childhood, and on through adolescence into adult life.

(Halliday 2004/1993: 327)

When children begin to read they cannot tell others how they do it because they don't know. But the sense that, somehow, there is a kind of dialogue going on with a voice on the page. Learning to write seems to be easier to understand; it comes later and is visible. As they watch others doing it, children see words appearing. Yet the puzzles remain: how to make the pen move, and how to know which words to write. Watch the efforts of a three-year-old. See the concentration on the tip of a crayon and wonder, again, how it all happens.

(Meek 1991: 70)

Relations between the concepts young children learn through everyday interactions and abstract literacy and numeracy concepts have also been investigated by Fleer and Raban (2007a) from a cultural-historical perspective. They collected photographic, video and interview data to document the 'everyday practices of families ... in order to gain insights into the everyday knowledge children gained at home and in the community' and to explore the 'conscious interlacing of everyday and academic thinking in literacy and numeracy' by families and early childhood practitioners' (Fleer & Raban 2007a: 107–109).

Fleer and Raban (2007b) provide examples from their research to illustrate how everyday experience can be transformed into abstract knowledge, for example, when children's activity is scaffolded by adults. Literacy concepts are learned everyday through activities such as playing with the sound patterns of language (songs, rhymes, word games), using books (sharing books, turning pages, pretend reading from a picture book), engaging with and thinking critically about environmental print (advertising, signs, logos), sequencing events (enacting, telling, retelling stories) and drawing, taking messages and using lists. These activities teach children that 'writing can carry meanings across time and space' (Fleer & Raban 2007b: 9). Similarly, numeracy concepts are learned through everyday interactions in which children build vocabulary to talk about measurement (*big/little, high/ low, heavy/light, full/empty*), spatial and shape awareness (*straight, curved, bent, upside down, triangle, square, circle, top, edge*), number (counting, *share* [division], *half/quarter* [fractions], *how much/long/many*) and classifying (*same/different*, sorting by colour/size) (Fleer & Raban 2007b: 7). Links identified by Fleer and Raban (2007a: 116) between 'everyday home learning and later learning' provide evidence that these concepts are not learned in isolation and, to illustrate this point, they cite Vygotsky's metaphor of sewing where 'the stitch (concept) can only exist when it is connected to the fabric (system)'.

Everyday concepts, learned in the language of the home, are a resource young children bring with them to school. If a different language or dialect is used at school, or if the child has learned these or equivalent concepts from within a sociocultural orientation different from that of the school, the challenge for educators is to provide school-based literacy and numeracy instruction to link with and build on the child's achievements outside the school. There remains considerable scope for researchers working within a variety of conceptual frameworks to explore how this might be best achieved in the interest of equitable educational outcomes for all children.

Conclusion

This chapter has reviewed the broad research landscape of early years literacy development and how this has influenced views of beginning literacy education. The importance of the link between the discourse and the practices of the home and the discourse and the practices of school has been clearly demonstrated through sociocultural and sociosemiotic research. Those educators and researchers who remain concerned about why some children succeed and others fail when they enter school recognise the need to 'provide beginning literacy instruction that is meaningful and productive of future literacy development and achievement' and that they 'must adopt a learner stance ... toward their students' home literacy environments' (Purcell-Gates 2013: 69). The next chapter will examine how research approaches have examined literacy at school and how this research has informed school literacy teaching and learning practices.

4
Literacy at School

Quote

In contemporary schooling, students' learning is comprehensively and unrelievedly dependent on the development of their literacy capabilities. So mapping the relationship between literacy and curriculum would mean navigating through almost an entire corpus of educational research and theory.

(Freebody, Chan & Barton 2013: 304)

We now continue our journey through the continuum of school education and track literacy demands through the phases of schooling, as students move from the language of everyday experience to the technical and abstract language of educational knowledge. This phase of the journey begins in the early years of school with initial instruction in reading and writing. It then follows students as they navigate two critical literacy-dependent transitions: the first during the middle years of the primary school as teaching and learning increasingly revolves around learning in the subject areas, followed by the transition into the secondary school where the curriculum and the school day is organised in terms of educational disciplines (Shanahan & Shanahan 2014b). There is no clear pathway visible through the tangle of perspectives, theories, methodologies, evidence, claims and practices that is the terrain of research into literacy at school. Sometimes the most strategic tactic is to pause and look around carefully before deciding which direction to choose when taking the next tentative step. Such a tactic has guided the path taken through the field of school literacy in the chapter to follow. The path taken in this chapter, of course, is just one of the many possible ways through this crowded and at times disorienting terrain.

Foundation literacy skills in the context of initial reading instruction and reading difficulties have been the focus of attention in the field of literacy teaching and research in English-speaking countries since 2000 with the publication, in the United States, of the National Reading Panel Report (2000). In this report the five essential components of reading are listed as phonemic awareness, phonics, fluency, vocabulary and comprehension (see also Snow, Burns & Griffin 1998). Later, these were more succinctly represented in the United Kingdom as two components – word recognition and comprehension (Rose 2006). Public attention has been fixed, in particular, on the explicit and systematic teaching of phonemic awareness (knowledge about how to segment spoken words into phonemes) and phonics (the correspondence between phonemes and the letters of the alphabet). Teachers have been provided with a rich technical metalanguage for talking about phonemic awareness and phonics, and have been encouraged to build a repertoire of related systematic instructional approaches. There is also an increase in commercially available teaching resources and assessment instruments that focus on these skills.

There is much less of a public call for teachers to build specific and detailed knowledge about what counts as fluency, vocabulary building and comprehension, and about how these components might be taught systematically and assessed in a valid and reliable way. Nevertheless, those who advocate balanced literacy instruction include instruction in decoding as an essential component of their approach, in the same way as those who foreground systematic instruction in decoding also recognise that reading fluency and the ability to comprehend and compose texts are essential goals of literacy instruction (Wheldall & Beaman 2011). This recognition has been built into recent curriculum initiatives, such as the *Australian Curriculum* and the *Common Core State Standards* in the United States.

Quote

... reading comprehension, being able to understand written language, is dependent upon both accurate decoding of the written word and understanding of spoken language; neither will lead to reading comprehension in the absence of the other. There is little point being able to read, even fluently, if there is no understanding of what has been read. Instruction in phonemic awareness and phonics leads to effective decoding of text, reading fluency instruction promotes automaticity that aids comprehension, along with appropriate specific instruction in vocabulary and listening comprehension skills.

(Wheldall & Beaman 2011: 260)

The spotlight on phonemic awareness and phonics in recent years has at times overshadowed instruction in fluency, vocabulary and comprehension. The emphasis on phonemic awareness and phonics as generic threshold skills and in high-stakes testing can leave the impression that, if these skills are addressed successfully in the early years of school, all that is required for students to achieve fluency, build vocabulary and to comprehend what they are reading is to provide them with further practice as they move through the middle years and beyond. It would be easy for literacy practitioners, researchers and policy developers to assume that direct literacy instruction is no longer necessary past the early years, except for those students deemed in need of remediation.

In some jurisdictions, it has been argued that an emphasis on the teaching of initial reading skills has also meant that the field has neglected the teaching of writing (Mo, Kopke, Hawkins, Troia & Olinghouse 2014, Myhill 2012, National Commission on Writing 2003). In this chapter, ways for integrating all components of literacy instruction into all areas of the curriculum throughout the school years and beyond will be explored. To do this effectively requires knowledge of the texts students must read, write and view, and the literacy practices they must engage in, to meet the demands of each curriculum area.

The technicality of the terms *phonemic awareness* and *phonics* also makes these components of literacy instruction stand out when compared with the terms *fluency*, *vocabulary* and *comprehension*, terms which are much more amenable to everyday explanations. Fluency, for example, is readily understood as reading at a steady rate and with expression, perhaps usefully augmented by a more specialist recognition of the role of accuracy and automaticity in this process. Fluency instruction is one of the most iconic of classroom practices, familiar to the many generations of school children who have been asked to read out loud in class and then received feedback from teachers and peers. In contemporary classrooms, teachers are more likely to organise this activity in ways that are less humiliating and more supportive for struggling readers, for example, by using differentiated guided reading techniques. Instruction that is equally familiar to school students, past and present, includes vocabulary building either directly taught, or *caught* through reading, as well as comprehension lessons, during which students recast what they have read, perhaps as an illustration or diagram, in a spoken retelling or as a written paraphrase or summary.

Despite being in the background in the public domain, research into fluency, vocabulary building and comprehension has continued to build on these enduring foundations. This research has continued to refine what we understand to be the essential elements of each skill, while also expanding repertoires of related instructional models, practices and strategies for each skill (see for example, Samuels & Farstrup 2011). What remains a challenge for literacy researchers and practitioners is how best to integrate reading fluency, vocabulary and comprehension instruction, alongside writing instruction, into sequences of systematic and explicit teaching and learning across all areas of the curriculum.

Rather than consider literacy and literacy development throughout the school years, and beyond, in terms of the five essential components separately and one by one, in this chapter we take a different approach. We turn our attention to research that explores literacy development and literacy instruction in more integrated ways that are oriented towards 'bringing together a connective web of theory and approaches' (Gunn & Wyatt-Smith 2011: 40). Bringing together all the elements that demand attention, when literacy becomes a topic of research, requires principled organisational tools. In the next section, we will review frameworks that organise literacy elements, the *what* of literacy education, in complementary ways and consider how these might be used to plot the literacy demands of school and post-school contexts. In subsequent sections, we consider ways in which literacy has been framed in terms of trajectories of development across the years of schooling, as well as frameworks for designing comprehensive and integrated sequences of literacy instruction, learning and assessment, the *how* of literacy education.

Quote

... the field of literacy research, including the term 'literacy' itself, reveals a complex and rich phenomenon that can be viewed from multiple theoretical and disciplinary perspectives ... several literacy scholars have provided frameworks that attempt to capture the multiple perspectives and dimensions of literacy to make available to students the full repertoire of skills and competencies required in contemporary society.

(Gunn & Wyatt-Smith 2011: 27)

Frameworks for integrating literacy elements: the *what* of literacies education

Over recent decades, a series of frameworks has been developed that can be used to organise, in complementary ways, the array of literacy knowledge, skills, resources, practices and demands that are characteristic of school and post-school contexts. Frameworks of this type can also be useful for navigating the vast field of literacy research findings, based as they are on understandings of literacy as being situated in, or an expression of social contexts (Barton, Hamilton & Ivanič 2000). Many are derived from educational linguistics, the study of language in teaching and learning. While part of a 'broader linguistic theory', educational linguistics is specifically concerned with developing 'a theory of language in education' as a means of investigating the role of language in learning and of identifying the kinds of knowledge about language to teach students to support their learning (Christie & Unsworth 2005: 217). The linguistic theory that has generated a particularly rich collection of conceptual tools for thinking about the role of language in learning is Halliday's Systemic Functional Linguistics (SFL), the foundation of the broader field of social semiotics. This theory has been productively applied to literacy research in tandem with Vygotsky's social theory of 'the genesis of consciousness' (Hasan 2005b: 131; see also Hasan 2005/1995) and Bernstein's sociology of pedagogy (Hasan 2005a).

From inventories to binaries

A first step in developing a framework for organising the disparate elements of literacy education is to list them as an inventory, or menu. For example (Snow et al. 1998: 2–3) argue that 'effective teachers make choices' from 'a common menu of materials, strategies and environments'. To this menu can be added skills, practices, modalities, language features and technologies. Such inventories become intractable, however, not only because of the almost limitless number of items that can be added to the list, but also because the view of literacy that underpins an inventory is not always visible. In other words, an inventory does not make visible the principles for selecting, distinguishing, categorising and relating items, or for determining whether the list is comprehensive, relevant to specific contexts or focused on one area of literacy development alone. Moreover, inventories do not provide researchers with a principled means for critical comparison or for identifying gaps or weaknesses in the knowledge base that might be worthy of further investigation.

The previous chapter introduced some ways for thinking about elements of literacy education as complementary pairs. These include relating literacy *strategies* and literacy *skills*, by thinking about literacy strategies as a means of consciously practising actions that, once they become automatic, will evolve into literacy skills (Afflerbach, Pearson & Paris 2008). Literacy skills can also be related in terms of whether they are *constrained* skills, learnt comparatively quickly during initial literacy instruction, or *unconstrained* skills that develop more slowly throughout the school and post-school years (Paris & Luo 2010).

A further binary distinction has been made by Freebody et al. (2013: 304) between *generic* 'foundational, stable literacy resources that are recognisable across the curriculum areas' and *contextualised* 'resources that are specific to each curriculum domain'. The five essential components of reading are typically presented as generic skills. As students move through the school years, these generic literacy skills are taught in terms of strategies, or in the form of intensive interventions, and assessed through standardised testing. While research investigating early years initial instruction of generic literacy skills is extensive, Pressley (2002) argues that much more research is needed to understand the literacy skills demanded of students in the middle and senior years, particularly in the area of fluency, comprehension and writing.

On the basis of a meta-analysis of the literature on writing interventions for adolescents, Graham and Perin (2007) have developed an inventory of 11 generic interventions to support the writing development of adolescents. This list includes instructional approaches (process writing, writing in the content areas), the explicit teaching of strategies and skills (writing strategies, sentence combining, summarising), scaffolding activities (pre-writing, inquiry and collaborative writing) and alternative modes of composing (word processing). The meta-analysis by Graham and Perin (2007: 462) demonstrates that instruction in sentence combining as a discrete generic skill enabling students 'to construct more complex and sophisticated sentences' makes a positive impact on students' writing. Teaching other aspects of grammar and text structure in this way showed no beneficial effect.

In contrast to the findings of the meta-analysis by Graham and Perin (2007), studies of grammar instruction 'within a purposeful context for writing' (Myhill, Jones, Lines & Watson 2012: 161) have found explicit teaching of grammar to have a beneficial impact on student writing in the middle years (Jones, Myhill & Bailey 2013). A meta-analysis of studies in contextualised grammar instruction by Myhill and Watson (2014: 49) suggests that this beneficial impact occurs when grammar instruction supports learners in 'making authorial decisions in the composition of a particular text' and when grammar is theorised on the basis of an educational linguistics. Thus, a comparison of the meta-analyses undertaken by Graham and Perin (2007) and by Myhill and Watson (2014) suggests research findings will vary, depending on whether researchers choose to investigate instruction based on an inventory of generic literacy skills or whether they choose to investigate contextualised literacy instruction organised on the basis of a theory of language.

From binaries to integrated relational frameworks: an educational linguistics

The French word *bricolage* is used in the visual arts to describe a unified work created from a variety of available elements. This term has also been used by Kincheloe (2003) to describe educational research that draws on multiple theoretical orientations, perspectives and frameworks to enhance the rigour and impact of the research. People who create *bricolages* are described as *bricoleurs* (Lévi-Strauss 1962). Honan (2004: 37) uses the term *bricoleur* to describe literacy teachers who routinely draw on 'a variety of resources around them to create a meaningful assemblage of practices' creating 'a *bricolage* of practice that makes specific and particular sense for each group of students with whom they work'.

Quote

The teacher as *bricoleur* is someone who carefully and thoughtfully makes a series of professional judgements about **what** and **how** to teach.

(Honan 2004: 39 – emphasis in the original)

To make professional judgements in response to the needs of their students, and the challenges of their classrooms, the teacher *bricoleur* must make selections from and connections between theories of language and literacy, literate contexts, language features, literacy practices, teaching strategies and classroom activities. They must then reflect critically on the impact of the resulting *bricolage*. Honan (2004: 45) describes how teacher researchers have used the 'four resources model' as a framework for mapping, connecting and reflecting on existing approaches, and for filling 'the gaps in the map of practices they have created', in order to create a balanced literacy programme.

The four resources model

The four resources model is a 'generic framework for reading and writing' designed to address 'the confusion of necessity and sufficiency' that has generated so many unproductive literacy debates (Freebody 2004: 3–6; see also Chapter 1). The model organises literacy resources and practices into four categories, according to whether they are used to break the code, participate in texts, use texts or analyse texts. Sometimes these four categories are represented in terms of reader roles (for example, Freebody 2007: 34). The four categories for organising literacy resources are summarised here:

- Resources for breaking the code are those that readers and writers use to relate the sounds of spoken language with the graphic symbols (letters) that represent those sounds in written language. These resources include punctuation, as well as formatting and layout conventions.
- Resources for participating in texts are those that readers and writers learn about and use to comprehend and compose the meaning patterns of written and multimodal texts. These include the conventional structures of texts used to achieve particular purposes (genres), as well as patterns of cohesion, grammar and vocabulary.
- Resources for using texts are those that readers and writers learn about so they can use written and multimodal texts in context, to achieve and respond to 'social and cultural functions of various kinds' (Freebody 2004: 7) in ways that reflect sociocultural expectations.
- Resources for analysing texts are those that readers and writers use to investigate, critique, challenge and transform 'the cultural and ideological bases on which texts are written and put to use' (Freebody 2004: 7).

The framework was first proposed by Freebody and Luke in 1990, when they 'speculated on what categories of resources would come close to a "statement of sufficiency" for a literacy programme' (Freebody 2004: 6). The framework continues to be used by literacy teachers and researchers, perhaps because it not only provides a 'non-technical vocabulary for naming the collection' of existing and potential literacy resources and practices (Freebody 2004: 4), but also because it can be used to organise, in a principled way, what would otherwise be a burgeoning inventory of disconnected elements.

Quotes

... to read is to know that text materialises sound, sound materialises language, language materialises textual activity in the world, and textual activities materialise cultural meanings and practices. The problems that learning to read calls upon are material (breaking the codes), semantic (applying and participating in the meaning structures of the text), sociocultural (using a text in its sociocultural context) and ideological (analysing the interaction of the text with the ideological position of the reader and the consequences for both). Working with these problems is what is acted out, for and with learners, in literacy learning settings.

(Freebody 2007: 37)

... we attempted an accessible outline of the kinds of resources that any theory of literacy education and any pedagogy or assessment regime aimed at that education should address, precisely because it is those categories of literacy resources that contemporary societies require of their members.

(Freebody 2004: 6)

The basic proposition of the 'four roles' model is that effective literacy in complex print and multimediated societies requires a broad and flexible repertoire of practices. This repertoire we have characterised as a set of 'roles', later 'practices', that participants in literacy events are able to use or 'resource'.

(Freebody & Luke 2003: 56)

The 'four reading roles' framework also provides a means of evaluating literacy approaches and programs to determine whether they offer 'a *balanced* set of programs for learners of literacy' that will prepare them for 'the complex everyday demands of text-based societies and economies' (Freebody & Luke 2003: 57). For example, the four resources model can be used to link 'theories of literacy education to daily planning and classroom activity' and has been used to reveal whether, in classroom practice, different types of resources are 'intermixed in unpredictable and arbitrary ways' or whether students' attention is focused systematically on each set of resources to support sustained literacy development (Freebody & Luke 2003: 58).

The four resources model is a *generic* framework researchers can use to navigate in a principled way the expanding literature and recurring debates that continually push out the boundaries of the literacy terrain. The whole of this vast and rocky terrain is beyond the reach of any one individual, study or publication, and so literacy teachers, literacy researchers, and authors of books such as this one, can only ever be *bricoleurs*, creating their work from the elements that are within their reach. One means of unifying these elements in principled ways, often used in tandem with the four resources model, is to focus attention on the contexts in which *specific* types of literacy use are situated. This approach will be explored below.

Types of literate practice

The 'multiple perspectives and dimensions of literacy' have been captured in frameworks, such as the four resources model, to make available to teachers and students 'the full repertoire of skills and competencies required in contemporary society' (Gunn & Wyatt-Smith 2011: 27). Unsworth (2001) has integrated several of these frameworks into a typology of literate practices as the basis for developing literacy pedagogy that accounts for the complementary work of language and visual images in texts across and within curriculum areas. This typology aligns with the four resources model and with three dimensions of literacy education identified by Hasan (1996a).

The first dimension of literacy identified by Hasan is *recognition* literacy, which attends to resources used for breaking the code. If recognition literacy is the sole focus of literacy education, Hasan (1996a: 387) argues, then 'the issue of meaning can and often does get ignored' leading to a 'fragmentation of linguistic facts'. Action literacy, in contrast, equated by Unsworth with resources for participating in and using texts, 'has the aim of enabling the pupils to do something with their language' (Hasan 1996a: 399). Action literacy covers a spectrum from 'the more traditional practices of getting the pupils to produce some form of connected writing to the more linguistically-informed text-based approaches' that are designed to enhance students' chances of success by teaching them explicitly how to produce the types of texts that are valued in schools (Hasan 1996a: 399). Importantly, in action literacy, students' 'learning and their doing' are not 'isolated from each other', and all learning is 'harnessed to some act of meaning' (Hasan 1996a: 401). Unsworth aligns resources for analysing texts with Hasan's proposal that students should also be taught 'reflection literacy', that is, literacy for producing knowledge, which students learn in order to question and examine the norms and standards of current knowledge.

Unsworth (2001: 14–15) integrates the four resources model and Hasan's three facets of literacy education into three 'dimensions of literate practice' – recognition, reproduction and reflection. Reflection literacy in Unsworth's framework includes the idea of critical literacy that is used to interrogate 'the visual and verbal codes to make explicit how choices of visual and verbal resources privilege certain viewpoints and how other choices of visual and verbal resources could construct alternative views' (Unsworth 2001: 15). He argues that metalanguage is important for teaching all three dimensions of literacy. The metalanguage he proposes is one that links the 'visual and verbal elements of texts' with 'how they make meanings and their relationship to the parameters of the social contexts in which they function', yet one that does 'not make unrealistic demands on teachers and students' (Unsworth 2001: 16).

Quote

Recognition literacy involves learning to recognise and produce the verbal, visual and electronic codes that are used to construct and communicate meanings. ... Reproduction literacy involves understanding and producing the conventional visual and verbal text forms that construct and communicate the established systematic knowledge of cultural institutions. Reflection literacy necessitates an understanding that all social practices, hence all literacies, are socially constructed ... [and so] selective ... including certain values and understandings, and excluding others. Reflection literacy means learning how to read this inclusion and exclusion.

(Unsworth 2001: 15)

Unsworth (2001) cites the following call for a multimodal metalanguage by the New London Group (2000: 24) and then addresses this challenge in relation to the teaching of multiliteracies across the curriculum:

... an educationally accessible functional grammar; that is, a metalanguage that describes meaning in various realms. These include the textual and the visual, as well as the multimodal relations between different meaning-making processes that are now so critical in media texts and the texts of electronic multimedia.

He presents a conceptual framework incorporating 'sociocultural, semiotic and pedagogic perspectives on key issues in literacy learning and teaching and emerging dimensions of change' and draws on research to document the 'technical knowledge' that teachers need (Unsworth 2001: 221–222). This technical knowledge relates to the way meanings are made in verbal and visual texts, in the distinctive multimodal literate practices of different subject areas, and in children's multimodal literature. Significantly, he takes the all too rare step of showing how these understandings might be transformed into practice, beginning by overlaying the three dimensions of literate practice onto the three dimensions of learning contexts to create a Curriculum Area Multiliteracies and Learning (CAMAL) framework. The three dimensions of learning contexts in the CAMAL framework are based on a description by Macken-Horarik (1996) of three domains in which learning occurs – the everyday, specialised and reflexive domains (see Table 4.1). Each domain is characterised by a different type of learning and each makes different

Table 4.1 Domains of learning

Domain	Type of learning
Everyday	Knowledge learnt in the everyday domain is the commonsense and functional knowledge of everyday life learnt through observation and participation. It is built on the shared understandings and expectations of the home and community. What counts as everyday knowledge for different groups of students varies and depends on their cultural and social background. Most classrooms include students with diverse understandings of the everyday.
Specialised	The knowledge of specialised domains builds on the diverse prior learning of everyday life but is learnt in formal educational contexts. Specialised knowledge is learnt through conscious design and intervention (Macken-Horarik 1996: 238), mediated by a teacher or instructor. Students are required to reproduce and display this knowledge as they learn it. Applied specialised knowledge is technical but practical knowledge used to carry out specific tasks. Theoretical specialised knowledge is the discipline knowledge of experts and academic education.
Reflexive	Knowledge in the reflexive domain problematises, synthesises and critiques specialised knowledge. It encompasses divergent, contradictory and competing views.
	In the reflexive domain, we are dealing with the intersection of the everyday and the specialised in a society which is culturally diverse and in which power is distributed unevenly. And it is here that we can see how value-laden both discipline and commonsense knowledge are. (Macken-Horarik 1996: 239)

demands on students. As students progress from one domain to the next, new language and literacy demands are placed on them in the form of new genres and varieties of language. In any educational context the genres and language varieties, or registers, students are required to comprehend and compose can be distributed across these domains.

By describing shifts in the dimensions of learning contexts in terms of the three learning domains, Unsworth (2001) presents a principled and comprehensive approach to the teaching of multiliteracies (see Table 4.2 – following Unsworth 2001). When the sequence of teaching attends to the reflexive domain, students consider 'how other choices of visual and verbal resources could construct another view' and might be used to produce new knowledge (Unsworth 2001: 227).[1]

Table 4.2 A curriculum area multiliteracies and learning framework (CAMAL)

Domains *Dimensions of context*	Everyday	Specialised	Reflexive
Knowledge of content (field)	Everyday knowledge	Systematically organised specialised knowledge	Transformative knowledge
Pedagogy (tenor)	Interactive teaching to build on students' existing knowledge	Direct teaching of systematic specialised knowledge	Collaborative reflection, critique and 'creative application' of the knowledge (Unsworth 2001: 226)
Multiliteracies (mode)	Spoken language images making concrete and familiar meanings narrative forms	Technical and abstract language and images 'conventional visual and verbal text forms that construct and communicate the established knowledge of the discipline area' (Unsworth 2001: 227)	Visual and verbal texts 'that deal with controversial and competing points of view' (Unsworth 2001: 227)

The content, pedagogic and multiliteracies dimensions of learning contexts are integrated by Unsworth (2001) in an arrangement of strategies and implementation steps he calls the Literacy Development Cycle (see below). He then provides examples of these teaching strategies in the form of lesson sequences, lesson plans, model texts analysed for critical language features and visual elements, teaching resources and classroom management techniques.

In the decade and more since Unsworth published his book, the research literature in all dimensions of multiliteracies education has expanded enormously in rich and linguistically-informed ways, opening up huge potential for innovative, socially-responsible and contextually-responsive literacy teaching practices and pedagogies. This literature has been very influential in the design of new curriculum documents, most notably in Australia. Many studies contributing to this literature are grounded in educational practice, often in collaboration with teachers.

Unlike Unsworth, few authors have taken the step of including programming frameworks and classroom resources of practical use to teachers. The process of translating research findings into widely available professional learning for teachers and research-informed classroom practice remains an area that deserves much greater attention in the field of literacy research. Representing these findings in the form of accessible multimodal workshop and classroom resources is one particularly promising avenue for this work, and one that would benefit from research-driven initiatives. If research is not guiding the production of teacher education and classroom resources, teacher *bricoleurs* may only have at hand sketchy and fragmented resources designed on the basis of naïve or commercial, rather than evidence-based considerations. In this case, they are at risk of creating a pedagogical *pastiche*, rather than a developmentally coherent *bricolage*. The demands of the contemporary educational workplace are too great for teachers in isolation to be able to integrate the many strands of contextualised literacy teaching into quality programming and resource development without the support of research-driven professional learning and resource production.

Teaching about texts in context

Where literacy research has proved to be of particular value to teachers of literacy in recent decades is in helping them to make judgements about *what* to teach. This includes judgements about which types of texts and which varieties of language students must comprehend and compose effectively to meet the literacy demands of specific areas of the curriculum.

Over the last three decades educational linguists, using systemic functional linguistic theory, have researched and mapped in detail the literacy demands of school education in English-speaking contexts in terms of *register* and *genre*, a project that is ongoing.[2] Samples of written texts used in schools are collected and analysed to identify the genres that are most highly valued and the contexts in which the genres are used. These analyses have also established which genres students need to control to be successful at each stage of schooling and in each curriculum area (see Chapter 2 for analysis frameworks of genre and register).

Quotes

When talking about texts, the French word 'genre' is often used. It comes from the Latin 'genus' meaning a class or category. The term genre contains within it the idea of 'convention': it has been used in Australian education to refer to the structural and grammatical written conventions of the literary or factual text type under scrutiny. The conventions construe the different social purposes of the text type and indicate different ways of reading and composing literary and factual texts.

(McDonald 2013: 8)

Field, tenor and mode are woven together at the level of genre: for example, in an explanation genre the field may be a natural process such as a life cycle, or a social activity such as a global financial crisis; its mode may be spoken or written; and its tenor may be personal and entertaining or cool and objective.

(Rose & Martin 2012: 22–23)

... genre theory is concerned with how a culture maps ideational, interpersonal and textual meaning onto one another in phases as a text unfolds.

(Martin 2007: 55)

Each genre is named for its social, or communicative, purpose and described in terms of the stages that texts belonging to the genre typically go through to achieve their purpose. The one-size-fits-all generic stage labels of introduction, body and conclusion are familiar to many generations of school students. Genre descriptions elaborate these generic stages, by labelling each one according to the specific

Table 4.3   Genre example: exposition

Genre stage	Traditional stage	Purpose
Thesis	Introduction	Position statement and a preview of the arguments
Arguments	Body	Series of arguments each made up of a statement of topic with supporting elaboration and evidence
Restatement of the thesis	Conclusion	A review of the arguments and restatement of position

function it fulfils in the overall social purpose of the text. Table 4.3 shows the conventional stages of the exposition genre, which is used to persuade readers to adopt a point view (Rose & Martin 2012: 68), and how these align with the traditional one-size-fits-all staging of an *essay*.

Collectively, genres identified as critical to success at school have been organised and related in systems that map the culture of schooling in terms of literacy (see Rose & Martin 2012: 128). This genre *map* has the potential to support systematic and explicit literacy instruction that develops students' literacy capacity cumulatively from one year to the next. Genre descriptions identify patterns of language and image that recur in texts used to achieve similar purposes. When this knowledge is applied in a specific teaching and learning context, the categories of field, tenor and mode are used to analyse the language variety demanded by that context. In this way, teachers can identify the language features and visual elements that students will need to control in order to *represent* specialised knowledge at the required level of technicality (field), to *interact* effectively with the audience, whether examiners, teachers, peers or community members, and *express attitudes* (evaluation) at the appropriate level of formality (tenor) and *organise* meanings at the required level of abstraction, whether in a written text such as an essay, in a bimodal text combining written language and diagrams, or in a multimodal digital text (mode).

Genre theory has been easily, and comparatively inexpensively and uncontroversially, appropriated by the designers of curriculum and syllabus documents, commercially-produced teaching resources and high-stakes testing schemes, for example, in the writing assessment component of the Australian National Assessment Program: Literacy and Numeracy (NAPLAN). Nevertheless, in practice, teachers need training and support to be able 'to do close readings of language patterns realising genres' (Rose & Martin 2012: 57). Providing teachers with the knowledge about language, in particular the knowledge about grammar, they need to teach literacy effectively, has been much more challenging and controversial (Carter 1990). This has been exacerbated in English-speaking countries where knowledge about English grammar has not been explicitly and systematically taught in schools for many decades (Myhill 2010: 142).

While genre theory, often represented as text-types, has become a feature of literacy programmes in many English-speaking contexts, two criticisms of the use of genre to map the literacy demands of the school have emerged (Freedman & Medway 1994, Luke 1996, Reid 1987, see also Christie 2010a for a discussion). The first criticism is that teaching genre forces 'the potentially creative individual to conform to a restricting, constraining recipe' but the counter argument is that genre patterns have evolved over time because that particular 'way of achieving the goal has worked well in the culture' and these patterns are not arbitrary or prescriptive rules but 'functional and enabling' (Painter 2001: 170).

The second criticism is that teaching the genres of power denigrates other non-mainstream genres and runs 'the risk of subsuming non-mainstream students into mainstream ... cultural norms' (Painter 2001: 170). For example, Luke (1996: 334) argues that '[c]riticism, contestation and difference is not a genre' but a strategy for challenging power 'unless dominant cultures and pedagogical practice, however intentionally or unintentionally, silence it'. The response to this argument is one of social justice, in that it is 'important to make genres required for success in education and life beyond school as widely available as possible' (Rose & Martin 2012: 67). One response to these criticisms has been that those using genre approaches to literacy instruction are encouraged to strengthen their pedagogy by including opportunities for students to exploit creatively genre patterns they have mastered in their writing and to develop a critical orientation to the use of generic patterns in texts they are reading (see discussion below).

A further criticism raised by Freedman and Medway (1994) is that 'there is no adequate evidence that overt teaching of knowledge about genres makes a difference to students' progress as writers' (Christie & Unsworth 2005: 225). There is a great deal of anecdotal evidence from practitioners who can attest to improvements in students' literacy when they know about genre patterns, supported by findings from case studies and classroom-based action research projects. The design of studies to measure this impact, however, is more complex than the design of studies measuring the impact of teaching about one isolated language variable. Nevertheless, evidence of the impact over time of cumulative learning about the configuration of meanings that constitute genre patterns is emerging, in particular from longitudinal studies, such as those reported below and in Chapter 7 of this volume.

Quotes

Creativity can build on the fact that generic patterns are uncon-
sciously expected by native speakers and hearers, making it possible
to play with these patterns in various ways, to be ironic or outra-
geous and so on. Such effects are only possible against a background
of what is expected, and are only possible from a speaker/writer who
has good control of the predictable generic form.

(Painter 2001: 171)

... a critical perspective on genre depended on both mastery of
the genres being critiqued and mastery of the genres being used to
critique.

(Rose & Martin 2012: 67)

As for genre theory, this also has achieved greater prominence over
the years, and several schools of genre theory are now recognised
(Christie 2008, Hyon 1996, Johns 2002), though it does not follow
that they all agree. However, what is apparent is that the notion of
genres is established in the wider studies of texts and social practices,
and among the several approaches, SFL genre theory continues to
evolve. The SFL genre theory is still used and taught in many parts
of Australia, and though its influence waxes and wanes, I doubt it
will disappear any time soon.

(Christie 2010a: 67)

Teaching knowledge about grammar

If we are to teach about how the stages of a text unfold to achieve the purpose of a text, we have to explore with students how patterns of meaning
in words and grammar give substance to those stages. Meanings in texts
are organised as lexicogrammar, that is, words patterned into grammatical structures, which in turn are given material form in sounds and letters. So learning about texts in context includes not only learning how
texts are structured to achieve their purpose (rhetoric) or the correspondence between sounds and letters (graphophonics), it also means learning
about the grammatical patterns at the heart of textual meaning-making.

In the three-layer systemic functional model of language, lexicogrammar is the intermediate layer of language. Lexicogrammar organises
meanings so that they can be expressed in sounds and graphic symbols.
Educational linguists working with the SFL model of language consider

the lexicogrammar layer central to the organisation of meanings in texts. For this reason, they support the idea that the knowledge students need for literacy development at school includes knowledge about lexicogrammar, the way words are organised as clauses. Students also need knowledge about the way meanings extend across texts to build cohesion and coherence, for example, through lexical cohesion, conjunction, speech functions, evaluative meanings, reference and information flow (Halliday & Hasan 1976, Rose & Martin 2012).

The view that teaching students knowledge about grammar has value contrasts with research findings, such as those reviewed by Andrews, Torgerson, Beverton, Freeman, Locke, Low, Robinson and Zhu (2006) and Graham and Perin (2007). These findings are that explicit teaching about grammar, apart from sentence-combining activities, does not have a significant impact on the development of literacy. However, the conclusions drawn from these meta-analyses have been challenged by Myhill et al. (2012) and Jones et al. (2013) on the basis of 'conceptual and methodological flaws' in the research (Myhill et al. 2012: 140). They argue that the studies included in the analyses do not account for different types of grammar, are often based on the teaching of elements of grammar isolated from the use of that knowledge in meaningful contexts, and do not 'theorise an instructional relationship between grammar and writing, which might inform the design of an appropriate pedagogical approach' (Jones et al. 2013: 1243). A comprehensive review of the ways questions in relation to the teaching of grammar have been addressed in the research literature over past decades, particularly in Anglophone countries, can be found in Locke (2010).

Quote

The pivotal question, of course, is: What is meant by knowledge about language? Once a meaning is attributed to the term, then claims can be made for a relationship between either explicit or implicit knowledge and the enhancement of some aspect of literacy acquisition, for example, writing. If a positive relationship is claimed, more particular claims can be made in respect of whether explicit or simply implicit knowledge is needed for students to develop the sorts of literacies deemed to be desirable in terms of an intended curriculum or the requirements of a fulfilling life and citizenship, and the kinds of explicit knowledge deemed to be a desirable aspect of a teacher's content and pedagogical content knowledge (Shulman 1986).

(Locke 2010: 5)

Historical reviews collected in Locke (2010) trace the pendulum swings that have been a feature of the role bestowed on grammar instruction in literacy education in different eras. The starkest contrast in the orientations reviewed in this collection is between explicit and implicit approaches to knowledge about grammar in the classroom. The explicit approach emphasises instruction in traditional grammar, as a means of error correction, in order to maintain perceived language standards, most recently a feature of *back to basics* movements. Students learn inventories of grammar forms and rules, and using this knowledge to analyse and label the grammatical components of sentences, with a focus on correctness in activities isolated from meaningful use in whole texts. From this perspective, non-standard language varieties tend to be regarded as *incorrect*, rather than functional in their own contexts of use, and are sometimes also linked to declining standards of behaviour (Clarke 2010).

The implicit approach treats grammar as knowledge that students gain through engagement with reading and writing under motivating conditions, for example, the conditions identified as optimal by proponents of *whole-language* methodologies. The resulting incidental, unsystematic or non-existent grammar instruction leaves students, even those who have learned to write effectively and without error, lacking knowledge and a metalanguage to think and talk about the language choices that constitute the texts they are reading and writing. While these orientations appear to be in opposition, both reflect a view of language as a set of formal *rules*.

Quote

Perhaps the main weakness in the whole-language approach is the lack of accountability within the system and in the progressive diminution of knowledge it brings about over time. There is no way of blaming the teacher for not teaching grammar, when it has already been 'proven' that teaching grammar is harmful. The fault then lies within the students' failure to somehow soak it up from exposure or from the teacher's non-technical remarks. Or perhaps, because everyone grows at their own pace, that student is simply on a path that will lead them toward maturity somewhere down the road. Unfortunately, some of those students, unschooled in an understanding of grammar, become English teachers in their own right. Even if they have become writers not prone to error, they do not carry into teaching a deep grounding in knowledge of the language. Editing student writing becomes more a

matter of what 'feels right'. They don't have the knowledge base necessary to put the quirks of textual convention into perspective. They
don't see a connection between formal choices and rhetorical effect.

(Hancock & Kolln 2010: 34)

The key question to emerge from the volume edited by Locke (2010)
is not *whether* knowledge about grammar should be taught, but *which*
grammar to teach. The type of grammars considered of most value to
students are 'rhetorically friendly grammars', those 'that show a close,
dynamic connection between the forms of grammar and the meanings
they convey, including the meanings we most often associate with
discourse' (Hancock & Kolln 2010: 35). Rhetorically-oriented grammars provide students with tools to enhance their reading and writing
'through the skillful use of language conventions' and to build appreciation of language variation 'according to time, place, purpose, and
audience, in addition to factors such as home language or dialect, socioeconomic status and social opportunities, peer pressure and education'
(Weaver 2010: 203). From this perspective, knowledge about grammar
becomes part of a larger canvas of knowledge about language, within
which grammar is taught in the context of language use (Myhill 2010).
Christie (2010b: 60) describes this type of grammar as 'text or discourse
driven' and cites Systemic Functional Linguistics (SFL) as the source of
such a grammar. Janks (2010) reports on the application of systemic
functional grammar in a multilingual educational context in tandem
with the four resources model. Unsworth (2010) and Burn (2010) use
systemic functional grammar as a starting point for developing a metalanguage to accommodate the comprehension and composition of
multimodal texts in educational contexts.

Quote

The future of grammar probably depends on people who can draw
on advances in linguistics and can describe a basis for understanding language that can be both practical and accurate. Perhaps grammar can be embraced by progressive educators, if they can see that
it is not meaning neutral or discourse neutral, but deeply bound
up within the effectiveness of text. Perhaps it will also appeal to
traditionalists because increased understanding of language, a more
highly developed metalanguage, should make formal conventions
much easier to understand and master. Knowledge about language

> can empower us in many ways. It can help us resist standards as well as follow them. It helps make the power and effectiveness of non-traditional dialects incontrovertible fact, not just a political assertion. It can help guide us in thoughtfully nuanced expression, in recognising the inherent connection between formal choice and rhetorical effect. The questions should be about which grammar, not about if or when.
>
> (Hancock & Kolln 2010: 36)

To augment the limited quantity of research evidence relating to the effectiveness of contextualised grammar teaching, Myhill and her colleagues in the UK designed a mixed-method study based on an experimental intervention complemented by the collection and analysis of qualitative data (see research response in Chapter 7). They adopted this approach 'to investigate specifically complex causal relationships between pedagogical support for teaching grammar, teacher subject knowledge and improvement in writing' (Myhill 2010: 143–144). The complexity of their research design illustrates the challenge faced by literacy researchers wishing to provide robust evidence to support claims about the value of contextualised grammar teaching (see Jones et al. 2013, Myhill et al. 2012, 2013).

Quote

Teaching is a complex, multifaceted and situated endeavour which resists simplistic causal explanations between pedagogical activity and learning outcome; equally, writing is perhaps the most complex activity learners undertake, drawing on cognitive, social and linguistic resources. Accordingly, this study adopted a mixed method approach located within an inter-disciplinary conceptual framework, combining a cluster randomised controlled trial (RCT) with multiple regression analysis and a complementary qualitative study.

(Myhill 2012:144)

A recent review of the literature by Myhill and Watson (2014: 54) shows that a consensus is emerging in relation to 'theorising a role for grammar in the writing curriculum as a functionally-oriented endeavour, developing students' metalinguistic thinking and decision-making in writing'. Nevertheless, 'more well designed studies in this area are much needed to provide richer and broader understanding of how children develop metalinguistic understanding, how that learning transfers into their own language use, and the pedagogies that support the development of that understanding' (Myhill & Watson 2014: 54). The need for studies of this type has gained momentum with a re-emphasis on grammar content in current curriculum documents.

In Australia, functional approaches have had considerable influence on curriculum design for some decades (Christie 2010a, 2012). The *Australian Curriculum: English* (ACARA 2015, 2009) is informed by 'a Hallidayan functional model of language' (Derewianka 2012: 129) and incorporates knowledge about language in the Language Strand and in the identification of literacy, alongside numeracy, as a cross-curricular general capability. The implementation of the curriculum has focused attention on the task of relocating, or recontextualising (following Bernstein 2000), knowledge about text and grammar from the academic contexts in which it is produced, to the classroom. This recontextualising task has been described in terms of four challenges in that whichever type of grammar teachers use, whether 'traditional, structural or functional', their task is to bring 'coherence, continuity, portability and rhetorical power to classroom work on language' (Macken-Horarik, Love & Unsworth 2011: 20). When referring to knowledge about grammar, Macken-Horarik et al. use the term *grammatics*, as proposed by Halliday (2002/1996), to distinguish the language we use to think and talk about grammar (*grammatics*) from the phenomenon of grammar itself.

Quote

The first challenge relates to the development of coherent knowledge about language as a resource for meaning – a professional knowledge base about language that is systematic and makes sense to teachers. The second concerns the contribution of a rhetorical grammatics to improve student compositions – how to turn 'knowledge about' language into 'know-how'. The third is one facing any curriculum that aims to provide continuity of learning about language from kindergarten through to Year 12. Students will need to develop cumulative understandings about language and teachers will need a shared metalanguage that is relevant to early and later years of English. And the final challenge emerges from the palpable presence of multimodal texts in the English curriculum and the need for a toolkit for exploring the contribution to meaning of non-linguistic resources. New meanings call for new tools of analysis.

(Macken-Horarik et al. 2011: 11)

Recognising that many teachers need to build their expertise in grammar to implement the *Australian Curriculum: English* effectively, Jones and Chen (2012) used a small case study of primary and secondary teachers to investigate the current level of teachers' knowledge about grammar and to foreshadow the expertise teachers would need to develop to be able to *enact* the curriculum effectively in classrooms. The study included a survey, teacher interviews, workshops and classroom observations. The findings confirmed earlier studies suggesting that, in general, teachers' knowledge about grammar is 'piecemeal' and that teachers' ability to translate the knowledge they do have into 'effective pedagogic practice' is not consistent (Jones & Chen 2012: 150–154).[3] Classroom observations revealed that while the teachers used 'authentic quality texts', the analysis of such texts places considerable demands on teachers' knowledge about language. Texts must be analysed accurately for teachers to provide productive explanations, but many will require 'expert assistance with such analysis' (Jones & Chen 2012: 166). In summary, the 'Australian Curriculum implementation will require a sustained professional learning programme that includes extending teachers' grammatical knowledge at the same time as they are redesigning their teaching to incorporate the more complex grammar content of the curriculum' (Jones & Chen 2012: 166). Teachers also need expertise to evaluate the quality of classroom resources developed, often commercially, in response to the grammar content of the new curriculum. When these encourage grammar teaching that focuses on descriptions of grammatical elements in isolated sentences, or in short impoverished texts, they can 'establish strange ways of thinking about writing' and the description by Myhill (2010: 142) of grammar teaching that has emerged during the implementation of the National Curriculum in England acts as a warning:

> In England, the emphasis on grammatical constructions without the corresponding understanding of effect and meaning-making is leading many children to believe that some grammatical features have intrinsic merit. We are nurturing a generation of children who believe that complex sentences are good, that connectives are ace, and that adjectival pile-up before a noun is the path to good description!

Exploratory action research case studies in Australian schools have demonstrated that teaching contextualised functionally-oriented grammar in meaningful ways in the primary school can be accessible, useful and enjoyable (Cochrane, Reece, Ahearn & Jones 2013, French 2010, Williams 2004 and 2005a). In each of these case studies, in collaboration with the researchers, teachers implemented engaging, playful games-based pedagogies linked to the reading of literary texts (picture books) and the writing of whole texts. In each case, language patterns were made tangible for students during activities in which language features were coded using colour and shape, and labelled using a functional metalanguage. The resulting displays mediated children's learning of grammar by 'making the abstract more visible and manageable' (French 2010: 221) and keeping the 'cognitive demand ... in check' (Cochrane et al. 2013: 6). Grammar teaching that incorporates playful and game-based activities enables children to push against the limits of meaningful and functional language use and in the process to build new understandings about language. Such play, following Vygotsky (1978) and Williams (1999), is at once serious, collaborative, engaged, effortful and future-oriented. A forerunner of games-based pedagogies that encourage young children to engage playfully with the grammatical patterns of their language can be found in the grammar-based reading pedagogy designed in the 1920s by Maria Montessori, a pedagogy that remains a feature of Montessori classrooms today. In this pedagogy, abstract language patterns and choices are contextualised and made tangible and manipulable in games that involve dramatisation and coding by shape and colour (Feez 2008).

The games-based pedagogy implemented by Cochrane et al. (2013: 2) was contextualised in the sense that it was designed 'to enable us to work with the texts, activities and routines of our existing literacy programs', to be a first step in 'a cumulative approach to teaching grammar across the school' and to foster 'students' use of a shared metalanguage'. Familiar picture books, 'rich texts with ... dynamic images', were used to generate language that students could 'recast and manipulate' as they experimented with different ways to arrange clauses (Cochrane et al. 2013: 2). The games-based pedagogy encouraged students to use the metalanguage in purposeful ways at increasing levels of difficulty.

Quotes

Metalinguistic knowledge is to language as standing on a patch of ground is to seeing the world for the first time from the air. Or an even better analogy: to being able to visualise the world as a globe – an abstraction which we do not hesitate to put in any and every primary school classroom ...

(French 2010: 228)

> ... when students are confident and familiar with the metalanguage, and can analyse their own writing, they are able to assess their own work and make improvements more independently. Through their knowledge and understanding of functionally oriented grammar, students can bring their writing under more conscious control, and make specific, targeted improvements.
>
> (Cochrane et al. 2013: 11)

To meet the demands of the curriculum as the school years unfold, students must develop academic literacies that enable them to control texts that deploy meaning-making resources in increasingly complex and specialised ways. From this perspective, the re-inclusion of grammar in the curriculum presents teachers with both the challenge of building knowledge, expertise and confidence, and the opportunity to use knowledge about language to support students' literacy development across the different areas of the curriculum. As Christie and Unsworth (2005: 233) have noted, however, '[d]eveloping a technical language about language among communities of teachers who have lost the facility for handling such a phenomenon is at times quite hard'.

In the context of the school subject English, Macken-Horarik (2012: 185) argues that rather than providing teachers with 'more grammar', a more productive and sustainable approach is to provide them with a 'good-enough' grammatics in the form of 'an adaptive toolkit' that they can use to assess student's literacy achievement across the multiple levels of language. As a first step, she advocates showing teachers how to apply diagnostic and planning frameworks based on the *big picture* categories of genre and register, an approach which allows teachers to attend to students' strengths as well as their weaknesses. She then demonstrates how students' literacy development can be supported when teachers judiciously select *smaller picture* sentence-level aspects of grammatical knowledge. Building on the evidence that sentence combining supports literacy development, she illustrates this argument by recasting sentence combining in terms of functional categories derived from SFL. She likewise emphasises the value of providing students with opportunities to play and experiment with the language patterns of literate language.

A further contribution to the design of a multilevel pedagogical grammatics that can be adapted to school contexts has been made by Humphrey (2013). In the context of teaching subject English in the junior secondary school, Humphrey proposes a contextually-responsive toolkit represented in the form of a matrix, or 4 × 4 framework. The horizontal dimension of the matrix spans four levels of language: whole text, paragraph, sentence and word. The vertical dimension is organised in terms of four categories of meaning (metafunctions) linked to the context: language for expressing ideas (experiential meanings linked to field), language for connecting ideas (logical meanings linked to field), language for interacting with others (interpersonal meanings linked to tenor) and language for organising ideas (textual meanings linked to mode).

The 4 × 4 framework can be used to gather together, organise in a principled way and extend, if necessary, the knowledge and metalanguage teachers already have about the language resources students need to marshal in order to meet the demands of any particular curriculum-generated literacy task. It accommodates a metalanguage derived from a variety of sources, whether from functional approaches or from 'traditional grammar and classical rhetoric' (Humphrey 2013: 47). The matrix makes connections between literacy resources and specialised subject area knowledge in a way that can be shared with colleagues and students. It also serves teachers as a text analysis tool for diagnosing learning needs, planning teaching and assessing achievement.

The 4 × 4 framework has been used in classroom-based action research studies to analyse and identify the critical language features of target texts, and to build an accessible metalanguage for talking about these features, relevant to the specific literacy demands across several curriculum areas. This use of the framework also draws attention to portable language resources that can be used to meet literacy demands across more than one curriculum area (Humphrey & Robinson 2012, Humphrey, Droga & Feez 2012).

Quotes

A grammatics that is adequate to the rhetorical demands of writing in school English will need to attend to both form (e.g. subject-verb agreement) and function (managing the exchange with others via the mood structure). It should assist students to combine clauses to produce compound and complex sentences logically and to extend, enhance or elaborate on messages in rhetorically apposite ways.

A good enough grammatics should enhance teacher dialogues with students about grammatical patterns in texts and the ways in which they can play with and innovate on these patterns. It should also contain enough guidance on social expectations and standards of literacy education as this is regulated by the larger social world.

(Macken-Horarik 2012: 182–185)

Such a perspective supports teachers and ultimately students to avoid reductive accounts of the language resources needed to achieve their literacy goals in subject English while maintaining a clear and manageable framing for these resources.

Knowing which grammatical resources are relevant to the particular contexts of learning in the curriculum and knowing how resources combine to form multi-level meanings provides teachers with a robust, but also flexible platform to systematically describe the key language resources their students need to learn effectively across the contexts of their secondary English studies.

(Humphrey 2013: 54–55)

Teaching knowledge about spelling

Alongside grammar, spelling is an area of literacy education where research suggests teachers lack confidence, knowledge and expertise (Adoniou 2014, Herrington & Macken-Horarik2015). In schools, spelling tends to be taught in isolation from meaningful language use. Spelling programmes implemented in schools often involve students in memorising graded spelling lists or, even more commonly, rely on phonics knowledge only. When phonological knowledge is emphasised without taking into account other types of spelling knowledge, or the relation between spelling and meaning-making, the result can be 'inaccurate teaching' (Adoniou 2014: 145–146). Recent studies have revealed that teaching students about morphemes can have a positive impact on their spelling. Morphemes are the parts of words that are meaningful (for example, Nunes, Bryant, Hurry & Pretzlik 2006).

An intervention study designed on the basis of these findings was undertaken in ten primary school classrooms (Years 3, 4 and 5) in rural Australia (Herrington & Macken-Horarik 2015). Teachers participating in the intervention were provided with a *teaching toolkit* that included a metalanguage for talking about morphemes and phonemes, and information about how morphemes in words relate to the sounds (phonemes) in the words, as well as a list of common morphemes. The teachers were also given strategies for teaching children explicitly how to *look inside* words in order to identify morphemes and then how to map the morphemes onto sounds (phonemes) and letter patterns (orthography). In addition, children were shown how to group words that share a common morpheme, even though the morpheme is not necessarily pronounced in the same way in all the words used. The authors use the example of the words *native, nature, natural* and *nation* that share the morpheme *nat,* meaning *source, birth* or *tribe.* Pre-test and post-test data were compared and children's spelling approximations were analysed to record how children used knowledge about morphemes to reason about spelling.

The findings of the study reported in Herrington and Macken-Horarik (2015) show that providing young children with knowledge about the relations between morphemes and sounds results in improved spelling accuracy. Furthermore, following the intervention, struggling spellers attended more closely to both phonemes and morphemes. Knowledge of morphemes also gave students confidence to try to work out for themselves the meaning, pronunciation and spelling of unfamiliar words. This multilevel approach to spelling aligns with other functional approaches to literacy education. Such an approach becomes even more significant as students move towards the middle years of school, when increasingly they are required to decode, comprehend and spell special-ised vocabulary. Many specialist terms across the discipline areas of the curriculum are of Graeco-Latin origin, with orthographies unsuited to simple sounding out strategies. Knowledge about morphemes of Graeco-Latin origin not only helps students with the spelling of technical terms but also aids in their comprehension (Shanahan & Shanahan 2014a).

Quotes

Spelling is a linguistic skill that develops through, and for, inter-actions with others. It is an integral component of reading and writing, allowing us to make meaning from, and with, texts ... An effective speller draws upon the entire rich linguistic tapestry of a word to spell it correctly. The threads of this tapestry can be identi-fied as phonological knowledge (including phonemic awareness), orthographic knowledge, morphological knowledge (which includes semantic knowledge), etymological knowledge and visual knowl-edge ... As a morphophonemic language, English is quite systematic and unendingly fascinating. The system, and the storying, behind English spelling should be shared with children from the time they begin to engage with print. Orthography, morphology and etymol-ogy are not the sole precinct of the advanced learners. They are necessary skills, especially for the children who are finding spelling difficult. They may just be the roads into spelling that they have, thus far, been left to find themselves.

(Adoniou 2014: 144–152)

... technical words in science often are built from Greek and Latin roots and combining forms. This often means that scientific names not only reveal what a word means but also its relationship to other words (e.g., *annual, perennial*). Scientists use such words because it helps other scientists anywhere in the world figure out the words' meanings and relationships.

(Shanahan & Shanahan 2014a: 638)

If children can be taught to make use of form-function-meaning connections in spelling, grammar and even images, they have access to powerful portable knowledge that can be applied across contexts.

(Herrington & Macken-Horarik 2015)

Teaching knowledge about visual grammar

The metafunctional categories that are used by functional linguists to organise language resources have been adapted by Kress and van Leeuwen (2006) to identify and organise resources used to make meanings in visual images. This visual grammar provides literacy educators with a metalanguage for thinking and talking about the contextually-motivated meanings made by visual images. The same functional semiotic approach has been extended to the development of *grammars* for other modes, including gesture (Hood & Forey 2005), space (Stenglin 2004) and music (van Leeuwen 1999). Using these complementary descriptive tools, researchers have begun the task of investigating how different modes interact in multimodal texts in both paper-based and screen-based environments (for example, Macken-Horarik & Adoniou 2008). Multimodal texts include literary texts, such as picture books and graphic novels, and texts in which language and image are used to apprentice students into specialised knowledge (Callow 2013, Chan & Unsworth 2011, Painter, Martin & Unsworth 2013, Unsworth 2010). From the point of view of literacy educators the task is to understand 'how different modes interact and interface with one another in multimodal texts and how these interactions affect comprehension, composition, and learning' (Freebody, Barton & Chan 2014: 428).

Quote

Even before the advent of paper, books and computer screens, the world for most people was a visual text.

> Written text has always held and will continue to hold a key place in our cultures. However many commentators note the rise of the visual as part of cultural and technological change. In one sense, the written word has to share the limelight with the visual. But do they have a closer connection than we realise?
>
> In the same way that teachers have a set of skills or metaphorical 'tools' for understanding and teaching reading and writing, that toolkit needs to be flexible enough to take on new types of texts and concepts ... a toolkit that goes beyond written text to include images and multimodal texts.
>
> (Callow 2013: front matter and 6)

Unsworth and Macken-Horarik (2015: 56) describe a study in which primary and secondary school teachers took part in a professional learning programme to build 'explicit knowledge about verbal and visual grammar as a resource for text interpretation and text creation'. The professional learning was also designed to build teachers' expertise, or *know-how*, in applying this knowledge in the classroom. The teachers incorporated this knowledge into the planning and implementation of a literary study based on a picture book. Students explored 'the what, the how and the why of choices in classroom discussions of images and words in picture books' (Unsworth & Macken-Horarik 2015: 62), before composing written responses interpreting the meanings represented in the words and images. This study represents a first exploration of 'the need for explicit teaching of written interpretive responses to multimodal literary texts, drawing on an articulated visual and verbal grammatics appropriate to the teaching of English in primary and secondary schools' (Unsworth & Macken-Horarik 2015: 56).

Literacy and the school curriculum: increasing specialisation

Literacy development can be considered in terms of three language learning processes (Halliday 2007/1981). One is learning the language itself, whether a first or additional language. From this perspective language is what is being learnt, as learners expand the meanings they can make through interaction, instruction and use. Another process is learning about the target language, or language variety, and how it works. From this perspective, language is the object of study, and a specialist metalanguage is used to think and talk about it. Finally, language is the primary medium or instrument of learning; in other words, we learn through language across all areas of the curriculum.

Quotes

... it would be difficult to draw a distinction between the pupils' knowledge of an academic discipline and their discursive ability to listen/read, speak/write the discourses of that discipline. Academic disciplines are, after all, largely a constellation of certain types of discourse, and, in the end, what counts as knowing a discipline is the ability to participate successfully in the discourses of that discipline.

(Hasan 1996a: 398)

The success with which ... learners can engage in analysis, discussion and critique will depend on how well they have engaged with the field as a specialised domain in the first place.

(Macken-Horarik 1996: 249)

These three processes are reflected in the way literacy is located in the *Australian Curriculum* ACARA 2015. Literacy is the strand of the *Australian Curriculum: English* concerned with 'expanding the repertoire of English usage' available to students. The Literacy Strand is interwoven with a Language Strand, concerned with building students' knowledge about the English language, and a Literature Strand with a focus on students' appreciation and creation of literary texts (Hasan 1985, McDonald 2013, Simpson, White, Freebody & Comber 2013). Elements of the Language and Literacy Strands reappear throughout the curriculum as general literacy capabilities applicable to all learning areas across the school years. Alongside common literacy capabilities, which are portable from one learning area to the next, each learning area also places on students literacy demands which are discipline-specific.

As students move through the school years, they must engage with the discipline-based literacy demands of different curriculum areas, if they are to be successful. Students learn in each curriculum area *through* the specialist literacy of that discipline, yet for many students subject-specific literacy demands can become barriers to learning and success at school. On the basis of design-based studies in middle-years classrooms, Freebody and Morgan (2014: 53) established, for example, that in Mathematics 'what students found most difficult was the language of mathematical problems, rather than the mathematical and arithmetic concepts themselves' (see Chapter 5 where this is discussed in terms of adult EAL). Knowledge about the language used in each subject would help students manage this type of difficulty. Once students know how to attend to the specialist meaning-making of each discipline, they can learn to represent discipline content in ways that are recognised and valued by specialists in the field. A focus on discipline-specific literacies represents a significant shift away from what Freebody and Morgan (2014: 52) represent as:

> ... a view that literacy involves only the 'basic skills' of reading and writing, measurable in generic decoding and comprehension tests, and that the work in establishing school-ready literacy skills is complete by the end of the early years.

Shanahan and Shanahan (2008: 43) propose a three-level model of literacy progression through the school years represented as a pyramid, with the base of the pyramid accounting for 'the highly generalisable basic skills that are entailed in all or most reading tasks'. These skills, typically developed in the early years, include decoding, fluent reading of high frequency words and knowledge of basic conventions of text organisation. While a solid early foundation in these skills is essential, it does not automatically lead to the development of subject-specific literacy skills in later years. The intermediate layer of the pyramid accounts for generic literacy skills that students use across the curriculum, including increasingly fluent and automatic reading of less frequent and more specialised words, and comprehension of longer texts organised in more complex ways. These skills typically develop in the middle years, although not necessarily for all students. At the apex of the pyramid is disciplinary literacy, involving 'more sophisticated but less generalisable' literacy skills and routines (Shanahan & Shanahan 2008: 45). To master the specialised reading and writing of each discipline, whether Literature, Science, History or Mathematics, students 'need explicit teaching of sophisticated genres, specialised language conventions, disciplinary norms of precision and accuracy, and higher level interpretive processes' (Shanahan & Shanahan 2008: 43). Generic literacy skills applicable across the curriculum, including reading strategies such as summarising and paraphrasing 'that can be used no matter the field', can help low-achieving students with comprehension, but by teaching disciplinary literacy the academic achievement of all students can be enhanced (Hynd-Shanahan 2013: 93–97).

Quotes

[Disciplines] have been resources for gearing young people into an 'explicable' world beyond the touchstones of the tribe – common-sense and *dogma*.

(Freebody & Muspratt 2007: 46 – emphasis in the original)

Disciplinary literacy ... emphasises the differences among the disciplines. The differences lie in what is important to pay attention to, what counts as evidence for an argument, what level of confidence the field has in the knowledge it produces, how texts are organised, how sentences are constructed, and so on.

(Hynd-Shanahan 2013: 94)

Disciplinary literacy refers to the idea that we should teach the specialised ways of reading, understanding, and thinking used in each academic discipline, such as science, history, or literature. Each field has its own ways of using text to create and communicate meaning. Accordingly, as children advance through school, literacy instruction should shift from general literacy strategies to the more specific or specialised ones from each discipline.

(Shanahan & Shanahan 2014a: 636)

Mapping the evolution of knowledge-building through texts across the middle years and developing more connected, cumulative and curriculum-specific ways of teaching across that process is an urgent matter for literacy researchers.

(Freebody 2007: 64)

To describe differences between disciplines in terms of literacy, Shanahan and Shanahan (2008: 57) studied how disciplinary experts approached literacy in their field and how these 'approaches might be translated into instruction' for students in secondary school. The different ways knowledge is structured and represented in language and image from one discipline to the next has also been investigated from the perspective of applied linguistics and the sociology of knowledge. The focus of this line of research is 'the relation between curriculum knowledge and the language of that curriculum knowledge' because discipline knowledge and discipline literacy are 'touchstones by which students' work is evaluated and their subsequent pathways marked out' (Freebody, Maton & Martin 2008: 188–196).

Emphasis on discipline-specific literacies counters the idea that the teaching of literacy is the province of English teachers alone, a view that has been challenged since the 1990s by those working in the field of genre-based literacy education. Martin (1993a: 167), for example, argues that, in order to prepare students for the literacy demands of studying Science, 'we have to be very clear about the kind of knowledge science is trying to construct and also about the ways in which scientists package this knowledge into text'. At the time, however, traditional textbooks with the potential to mentor students into the language of science had been replaced with textbooks that provided only fragmented models of the texts valued by scientists, and often included stories and personal observations that were more appropriate to subject English. What teachers needed, according to Martin (1993a: 202) was 'an understanding of the structure of the genres and the grammar of technicality' used in Science. To build this understanding, 'the nature of disciplinary knowledge' needed to be studied 'from a linguistic perspective' and the foundation for this work were the descriptions of the key 'genres students should master by the end of primary school' (Rose & Martin 2012: 55–82), which included factual texts and arguments. This collection of genres provides a linguistic description of the generic literacy skills that Shanahan and Shanahan (2008) place at the intermediate level of their model of school literacy progression. Mastery of these genres in the context of different learning areas represents preparation for the specialised literacy demands of specific disciplines that necessarily should begin in the primary school (Shanahan & Shanahan 2014a, Freebody & Morgan 2014).

Analysis of disciplinary literacy in the curriculum areas of the secondary school, the apex of the Shanahan and Shanahan (2008) pyramid, has been an ongoing project in the field of genre studies for two decades. This work has been particularly exhaustive in the context of Science (for example, Halliday & Martin 1993, Martin & Veel 1998) and History (for example, Coffin 2006), exemplifying the contrast between the literacy demands of the sciences and the humanities. Other curriculum areas in which the literacy demands have been described linguistically, with a particular focus on writing, include English (for example, Christie & Macken-Horarik 2007, Macken-Horarik 2011), Mathematics (for example, O'Halloran 2005, Schleppegrell 2007), languages education (Byrnes 2009), Music (Weekes, forthcoming) and Business Studies (Weekes 2014). A feature of many of these descriptions is that they describe the literacy demands of the subject areas in terms of the way knowledge is represented in language and image, and in other modalities (Jewitt,

Kress, Ogborn & Tsatsarelis 2001). An extension of this work is being undertaken by Matruglio (2015), who is focusing attention on linguistic variation within disciplines, specifically differences between the literacies of ancient and modern history in the senior years of school. Shining the spotlight onto reading, Fang and Schleppegrell (2010) demonstrate how teachers might apply to reading instruction in the secondary school knowledge about 'how content experts use language to present meaning in discipline-specific ways'. (see also Fang & Schleppegrell 2008).

Quote

As educational knowledge becomes more specialized and removed from students' everyday experiences, the language that constructs such knowledge also becomes more technical, dense, abstract, and complex, patterning in ways that enable content experts to engage in specialized social and semiotic practices. This means that each secondary subject has specialized ways of using language that may pose comprehension challenges to adolescents. By making discipline-specific ways of using language explicit, teachers can help adolescents, especially those who have little access to these ways of making meaning outside of school, better engage with school knowledge and more effectively develop disciplinary literacies across academic content areas.

(Fang & Schleppegrell 2010: 596)

The genres identified as critical to success in the secondary school have been organised as a map in which they are classified according to whether their purpose is to engage (through telling stories), to inform (by chronicling, explaining, reporting or instructing) or to evaluate (by responding to texts or persuading) (Rose & Martin 2012: 128). Each genre is named for its purpose and described in terms of stages (Rose & Martin 2012: 130), and different configurations of genres are aligned with different subject areas. Further differentiation is achieved through linguistic descriptions of the ways experience is represented differently across the subject areas. This includes differences in the aspects of experience which become the focus of attention and how these are classified, as well as how sequences of time and cause are represented. The language of evaluation used to establish significance and worth is also specialised in different ways across disciplines. Central to these differences is the way grammatical metaphor is used to build the types of technicality and abstraction characteristic of the different disciplines. Linguistic perspectives on discipline-specific literacies complement and interact with insights from sociology relating to the ways knowledge is structured in different disciplines and the attitudes and dispositions that give specialists in each discipline their legitimacy in the field (Christie & Maton 2011, Maton 2014).

Knowledge about the literacy demands of specific subject areas has been generated through collaborative studies involving both researchers and practitioners. These studies have expanded our knowledge of the language varieties that are the keys to success at school. At the same time, these studies demonstrate that teachers need knowledge about language to transform what is known about discipline-specific literacies into pedagogy. Teachers also need to be able to talk confidently about the language and literacy demands of their subject area in ways that support their students' achievement.

The transformation of knowledge about subject-specific literacy demands into pedagogy, and the associated professional learning demanded of teachers, can be studied using a system of principles devised by Bernstein (2000). These principles are used to analyse how educational knowledge, typically produced in universities, is relocated, or *recontextualised*, in school classrooms as pedagogic discourse, which is at once regulatory and instructional. This system of principles distinguishes between everyday commonsense knowledge and abstract specialised educational knowledge, and between visible and invisible pedagogies.

Everyday commonsense knowledge is organised segmentally and is context-dependent, that is, it is closely aligned with a specific material base. In contrast, abstract, specialised educational knowledge is organised hierarchically and systematically. Teaching approaches that blur distinctions between commonsense and specialised knowledge, between disciplines, and content within disciplines, and between the roles of teacher and students, are said to be invisible pedagogies. On the other hand, pedagogies in which the teacher controls what is to be learnt and how it is learnt, and which also highlight the distinctions between subject-specific literacies, is a visible pedagogy. An important feature of visible pedagogies is that teachers select content and control the pace of learning in order to contribute to cumulative learning over the course of a lesson, from one lesson to the next, and over the years of schooling. In this way visible pedagogies have the potential to contribute to more equitable access to specialised knowledge for students from all social groups (Delpit 1988, Hasan 2004).

Bernstein's system of principles provides researchers with a conceptual framework they can use to investigate literacy development over the years of schooling. This is an area of literacy research where much remains to be done. Researchers, in collaboration with practitioners, continually need to review literacy pedagogies as the literacy demands of school education shift in response to curriculum and technological change and the expansion of knowledge, and even more significantly in light of the diverse needs of different groups of students. A further task is to design assessment instruments teachers can use to diagnose need, monitor progress and assess achievement in subject-specific literacy. As Uccelli and Snow (2008: 638) argue 'in the accountability driven world of education, developing assessments for these more sophisticated language skills is key, because if they are not assessed, they are unlikely to be attended to in the classroom'. Customising frameworks such as those developed by Humphrey (2013), Love, Sandiford, Macken-Horarik & Unsworth (2014), Rose and Martin (2012) and Unsworth (2001) to discipline-specific literacy demands provides a way forward with this work.

The crucial shift in the middle years

In the previous chapter we outlined the three-stage model of children's learning proposed by Halliday (2004/1993), a model based on the development of meaning-making. At the first stage, the infant transitioning from protolanguage to the language of the home is at the same time learning to generalise. From about three, preschool children begin to make abstract meanings, a step that prepares them for learning to use written language in the early years of school. From about the age of nine, children begin to make specialised meanings, a step that prepares them for the literacy demands of the secondary school. Some children, of course, grow up in contexts where steps they have made into abstract and specialised meaning-making do not align neatly with the literacy demands of school because the language or dialect used for everyday talk in their home is different from the language used at school (Hasan 1996b, 1996c).

Links between children's home circumstances and literacy achievement at school were investigated as part of a longitudinal study by Hill, Comber, Louden, Rivalland and Reid (2002). The study combined a case-study approach with quantitative analysis of literacy outcomes to explore 'children's literacy development over a five-year period in a range of Australian contexts' from the year before school to the fourth year of school (Hill et al. 2002: 2). The children came from diverse contexts, geographically and socioeconomically. Most children in the study made 'substantial growth in literacy' over the five years, but there was considerable variation in children's performances in all contexts. Those who did not achieve substantial growth came 'overwhelmingly from schools serving families living in poverty' (Hill et al. 2002: 5). Trajectories of literacy development varied a great deal and were not always predictable or linear. It was harder for late starters to catch up, if their life circumstances were difficult, and early progress did not guarantee later success. Children achieving at lower levels benefited, not from one-size-fits-all approaches, but from teachers with a broad repertoire of pedagogic and communicative strategies who were responsive to each child's particular needs. The study found that for some children a second safety net was needed by the age of nine years, before the curriculum becomes 'more strongly knowledge based' (Hill et al. 2002: 9).

The shift around the middle of primary school, from an emphasis on initial literacy skills to the use of those skills for learning curriculum content, places new literacy demands on children. Children's literacy achievement is increasingly assessed in terms of their ability to manage written language in order to engage with content across the learning areas. For some children, this transition can be difficult. Children who have already engaged with a wide variety of texts, including both stories and information texts, are more prepared for this shift in orientation. Research has confirmed that direct, systematic literacy teaching is equally necessary for children in the upper primary years as it is in the early years, if children are to be prepared for the literacy demands of secondary school (Sanacore & Palumbo 2009). Sample classroom resources to support such teaching have been developed by de Silva Joyce and Feez (2004) and de Silva Joyce (2005).

Quotes

What seems compatible with findings from many research studies then, is that different aspects of print and language knowledge mutually inform one another's development, particularly as learners progress beyond the acquisition phase of literacy learning, generally through the middle primary years.

(Freebody 2007: 49)

The 'new forms of literate practice' that children were asked to display in this fourth year of school required significantly different understandings, strategies and techniques to construct and understand texts. As the study progressed many children were assembling a range of literacy practices such as understanding the relationships between information, selecting appropriate details, and using differing forms of modality, tense and text structure. As children progressed through school these new forms of literate practices required overt instruction similar to the overt instruction that occurred in the early years of school.

(Hill et al. 2002: 6–7)

Literacy across the secondary school years

A corpus of 2,000 texts produced by primary and secondary school students was used by Christie and Derewianka (2008: 5) as the basis for 'a comprehensive and systematic study of [writing] development from childhood through to adolescence in a range of curriculum areas across a variety of genres employing all three metafunctions'. From this corpus, representative texts were chosen as benchmarks of 'what is possible at each phase of development' (Christie & Derewianka 2008: 6). These texts were written in the context of three contrasting curriculum areas, English, History and Science. To be successful in each of these subject areas, students were required to use written language in different ways to make different types of meanings. Each representative text was analysed in detail and described in terms of the language resources the writer deployed to compose the text.

Tracking the development of these resources in texts from the three subject areas across the school years revealed that learning to write at school followed a broad trajectory of four stages, which are subject, of course, to individual and social variation. Each phase is described in terms of the types of meanings most commonly made by students of that age in their writing, and the language resources they deploy to make those meanings. These meanings include the purposes the students achieved in writing (genres), as well as how experience and logical relationships were represented (ideational meanings realising field), how language was used to interact and evaluate (interpersonal meanings realising tenor) and how the text was organised to be cohesive and to guide the reader (textual meanings realising mode).

The phases identified by Christie and Derewianka (see Table 4.4) echo the three-stage linguistic model of learning proposed by Halliday, while also providing a detailed linguistic description of how those stages are manifested in student writing. Specifically, detailed descriptions of each phase provide insights into the grammatical development required of students, if they are to transform the everyday (commonsense) knowledge of home and community into the specialised (uncommonsense) knowledge of the school (Bernstein 2000).

In the senior secondary school, from 16 to 18 years, students are required to write about specialised knowledge and to make informed judgements demanding a grammar that expresses abstraction and technicality. This phase marks a consolidation and 'completion of schooling and the entry to adult life, though in principle the phase lasts throughout life' and how this phase extends beyond school depends on the literacy demands placed on students in the post-school years (Christie & Derewianka 2008: 243).

Table 4.4   Three-stage linguistic model of learning

Stage 1–6 to 8 years	Students write about everyday knowledge and express simple attitudes using a congruent grammar matched to concrete experience.
Stage 2–9 to 12 years Shift predicted by Halliday (2004/1993)	Students elaborate everyday experience with some technicality and expand the attitudes they express and grammatical metaphor emerges. Students move into secondary and are faced with a curriculum based on subject specialisation, at the same time as they are faced with the physiological changes of puberty.
	[This phase is] in many ways critical, for it marks an important transitional passage away from the forms of language like those of speech, towards forms closer to mature writing, and the grammatical organisation of children's texts must change if children are to succeed ... many students begin to fall behind. (Christie & Derewianka 2008: 240)
Stage 3–13 to 15 years	The representation of knowledge and expressions of attitude become increasingly specialised and abstract requiring commensurate grammatical resources deployed in subject-specific ways in longer and more complex texts.

The detailed linguistic description of the trajectory of writing development across the school years developed by Christie and Derewianka (2008) represents a valuable resource for literacy educators from several perspectives. Because it reveals the linguistic resources students need to control at each phase of schooling, differentiated according to subject area, it can be used to guide the development of subject-specific writing programmes. It can also be used diagnostically to determine the specific knowledge about written language needed by individual students facing barriers to writing development in different subject areas at different stages of schooling, thus enabling the development of targeted and differentiated programmes. Moreover, it provides researchers with benchmarks that can be applied and tested in diverse educational settings.

Importantly, a detailed trajectory of development such as the one that emerges from the study by Christie and Derewianka (2008) encourages teachers to match writing tasks and expectations to their students' phase of development. For all students, but particularly those who have slipped behind, this should be done in the context of appropriate pedagogies that support students as they approximate benchmarks commensurate with their stage of schooling. Lowering expectations too far below these benchmarks, even if for well-intentioned reasons, will only ensure struggling students fall behind at an ever-increasing rate. If adjustments need to be made, these are best achieved by designing pedagogies to bridge the gap between current levels of achievement and achievement aligned with benchmarks.

Literacy outside school

At the same time as students are navigating literacy trajectories in school, such as the one traced by Christie and Derewianka (2008), they are also engaging in parallel literacy practices outside the school. The intersection, or otherwise, between students' literacy development at school and their parallel literacy practices outside the school is a terrain that deserves the attention of researchers.

As we have seen, some students from the earliest age collaborate in shared print literacy practices for practical purposes and for enjoyment, in ways that foreshadow the literacy practices of the school, but for some students the rich fabric of everyday life at home will not prepare for or sustain literacy development at school. It is well established that such students respond to pedagogies that bridge the gap between home and school literacy practices in culturally and interpersonally responsive ways, although how this is executed in practice continues to deserve attention.

The gap between literacies outside the school and the literacies rewarded at school has become even more complex with the advent of digital technologies. The literacy experience of many students outside school is mediated not only through print, film and television, but also through sound, image and written language in interactive multimedia environments. Students might encounter and seek out related content, whether about fictional characters, scientific knowledge or an advertised product, represented in print and image, in books, graphic novels, comics, on television, in film and in interactive digital environments. Students may also communicate in text and image through email, messaging, blogs and other varieties of social media (Bus & Neuman 2009). The ways so many school-age students immerse themselves in digital media have led some to label them 'digital natives' (Prensky 2001, Zevenbergen 2007).

Quote

While students engage with this vast array of textual materials in a variety of settings, many classroom contexts continue to reflect a more static and traditional view of what 'counts' in literacy practices. Given the speed with which technologies advance, there seems to be an ever widening gap between the literacy experiences offered in school, and those available for students outside school walls.

(Flint, Kitson & Lowe 2013: 5)

The *digital native* tag has been questioned by Bennet, Maton and Kervin (2008). They caution against naïve attempts to close the gap between students' perceived immersion in digital media and classroom literate practices. Levels of digital immersion and skill among young people are not universal or uniform, so there is a danger that 'those less interested and less able will be neglected, and ... the potential impact of socio-economic and cultural factors will be overlooked' (Bennett et al. 2008: 779). Moreover, much interactivity in screen-based environments is shallow, random, passive, indiscriminate and uncritical, and may not apply to the learning of educational knowledge. While the interactivity of computer games can be engaging and motivating for many, but not for all students, the evidence that this type of interactivity supports the effective learning of educational knowledge remains inconclusive.

In an extension of these concerns, Gee (2012b) argues, that just like traditional literacy, there are different grades of digital literacy. Like premium traditional literacy, premium digital literacy is based on specialised forms of meaning-making and leads to 'more meaningful work and more financial success' (Gee 2012b: 418). And, just as with premium traditional literacies, some students develop premium digital literacies more effectively than others, depending on the nature of early socialisation and mentoring.

Quote

Premium digital literacy is the ability to use specialist/technical language connected to digital tools. Premium traditional literacy is being able to use academic language connected to institutional and public-sphere knowledge-building and argumentation. At the premium level, the digital brain and digital natives are not a new

'new thing', but an even higher octane version of an old thing, the literate brain. But now that brain has, for some young people, though not all, left the gardens of academe and the professions and is flourishing among young 'pro-ams' (amateurs with professional skills) producing all sorts of media, citizen science, and knowledge in competition with experts via collaborative problem-solving communities on the Internet.

(Gee 2012b: 419)

Students tend to become 'heavily embedded in a tech-rich world' as they approach adolescence, but Lenhart, Arafeh, Smith and Macgill (2008: ii) report that these students do not necessarily recognise digital communication as literacy. Yet, a significant number of students write journals and music lyrics, not only electronically but also by hand. The most prolific out-of-school digital writing undertaken by students, however, is blogging.

The distinctive characteristics of the blog, 'an online journal that contains entries, or posts, presented in reverse chronological order', as Adlington (2014: 2) argues, make this mode a particularly valuable means for students to connect and engage with others. Adlington (2014) cites the example of rural students using blogs to overcome geographical isolation. Developing students' use of the 'range of tools with which the blogger may present content and elicit interaction with readers' (Adlington 2014: 3) to the standard of a premium digital literacy is an example of how teachers can link a literacy practice outside the school in 'meaningful and motivated ways' with literacy at school (Lankshear & Knobel 2011: 252). Teachers can provide students with knowledge about specialised blogging skills such as designing non-linear spaces composed of both verbal and visual texts (Kress & van Leeuwen 2006), designing hypertextual relations for multilinear reading by embedding video and links (Djonov 2008), inviting reader coauthorship through comments, and tagging to enable simultaneous links to multiple blog posts organised in logical ways (Adlington 2014).

Quotes

... digital media and books share important properties ... and come in different grades with different implications for young people's success in school and mainstream society thereafter.

(Gee 2012b: 420)

> ... it is important in formal education, particularly at school level, not simply to transcend decontextualised, abstracted knowledge but, also, as much as possible, to ensure that the 'situatedness' of school-based learning – since it is situated – is 'onside' with the kinds of related situated practices students encounter beyond (spatially, temporally, and culturally) school.
>
> (Lankshear & Knobel 2011: 252)

The distinctive properties of interactive digital games represent a potential contribution to literacy development when adapted for educational contexts. For example, digital games involve students in problem solving and collaboration, and, as students modify games, they learn to think 'like a designer' (Gee 2012b: 420).

An under-explored aspect of literacy research identified by Freebody et al. (2014: 428) is online youth culture in which 'young people from diverse cultural and economic backgrounds now communicate globally and locally through new textual forms, developing local and transnational identities, and participating in hybrid social worlds'. The online communication and multimodal performance texts favoured by many young people are particularly well-suited to the domain of human experience that Humphrey (2010) describes as the civic domain. The civic domain is an additional domain added to the three domains of learning identified by Macken-Horarik (1996) – everyday, specialised and reflexive. The civic domain is a space for debate on issues of public concern, oriented to social action and change (Humphrey 2010) and making the world a better place.

To understand how young people use literacy in the civic domain, Humphrey (2010) analysed the stories and persuasive texts composed by a group of adolescent activists in support of refugees. The activists, all of whom were themselves once refugees and used English as an additional language, wrote texts that included speeches, blogs, essays and letters written to politicians. These texts were less stable structurally than the equivalent texts valued at school, and they foregrounded interpersonal meanings more than would be appropriate in educational contexts. Nevertheless, the young writers skilfully used rhetorical resources to build solidarity with their audience and to appeal to shared values and emotions. Humphrey argues that students can engage with the civic domain at any stage of their literacy development as issues emerge that galvanise their interest and desire to be agents of change. Humphrey (2010) points out that literacy in the civic domain needs to be clearly distinguished from the specialised literacy of educational knowledge, that students need to build a critical orientation to texts that use emotion to persuade, and that literacy activities at school must not intrude into young people's personal out-of-school communication. Nevertheless, her study does open up a space in which teachers can 'broaden the range of resources beyond those of the academic domain' and 'develop literacy pathways which enable young people to engage with, and perhaps subvert the discourses of power' (Humphrey 2010:18).

Quotes

Language is not a domain of human knowledge (except in the special context of linguistics, where it becomes an object of scientific study); language is the essential condition of knowing, the process by which experience becomes knowledge.

(Halliday 2004/1993: 328)

All learning-whether learning language, learning through language, or learning about language-involves learning to understand things in more than one way. In a written culture, in which education is part of life, children learn to construe their experience in two complementary modes: the dynamic mode of the everyday common-sense grammar and the synoptic mode of the elaborated written grammar. Any particular instance, of any kind of phenomenon, may be interpreted as some product of the two-once the adolescent has transcended the semiotic barrier between them.

(Halliday 2004/1993: 349–350)

Comprehensive literacy teaching frameworks: the *how* of literacy teaching

In previous sections of this chapter, knowledge about literacy content and knowledge about literacy development have been surveyed. Effective teachers of literacy have been identified as *bricoleurs* who select and connect elements of content on the basis of their students' current levels of development, and who then strive to fashion these into a balanced and unified teaching programme. To be able to do this, teachers need knowledge about pedagogy. Over recent decades practice-based research has expanded the knowledge about literacy pedagogy available to teachers. This knowledge has also generated frameworks teachers can use to organise the many elements of literacy teaching into an integrated programme.

Pedagogy is knowledge transformed into teaching practice. From the perspective of the sociology of education, different types of pedagogy can be described in terms of contrasting relations between everyday and educational knowledge, and invisible and visible pedagogy (Bernstein 2000). From a social semiotic perspective, pedagogical practice has been analysed in terms of three categories:

1. Relations between teachers and students (tenor)
2. Teaching activities and sequences (field)
3. Modalities of practice, for example, spoken and written language, images and objects (mode) (Rose & Martin 2012: 304).

On the basis of these three analytical categories, Rose and Martin (2012) argue that inequitable educational outcomes are a function of teachers relating to students as either successful or unsuccessful learners of educational knowledge. Inequitable outcomes are 'sustained' when teachers do not select teaching activities and sequences that make content and learning goals visible to students and when they fail to 'explicitly teach all students the skills they need to independently read and write the curriculum at each stage of school' (Rose & Martin 2012: 305). Unequal outcomes can be reduced, however, 'by adequately preparing all students for each learning task' and learning activities can become even more effective when different modalities are used in complementary ways (Rose & Martin 2012: 306–309).

The macro and micro levels

Effective literacy pedagogy, according to Hammond and Gibbons (2005: 9–10), interweaves two levels of practice: the pre-planned and the contingent. The pre-planned 'macro' level is the level at which the teacher plans, selects and sequences activities into a teaching programme that is launched from students' current levels of achievement, and the contingent 'micro' level is the level at which the teacher makes 'the most of the teachable moment' (Hammond & Gibbons 2005: 11).

Quote

It is this combination of the pre-planned and the contingent that enables teachers to provide new learning challenges for their students, while at the same time providing necessary support for meeting those challenges.

(Hammond & Gibbons 2005: 11)

The distinction between the pre-planned and contingent levels of pedagogy emerged from a three-year study undertaken by Hammond and Gibbons (2005). They documented, from a sociocultural viewpoint, the pedagogical practices used by teachers to support students who speak English as an additional language (EAL) in mainstream classrooms in Australian schools. The students were fluent in everyday spoken interactions in English, but continued 'to grapple with the language and literacy demands of academic study across the curriculum' (Hammond & Gibbons 2005: 6). To use terms coined by Cummins (2008), while these students had developed *basic interpersonal communication skills* (BICS) in English, they were still developing *cognitive academic language proficiency* (CALP).[4] Pedagogic practices used to support EAL students and students at-risk in mainstream classrooms are 'also good for the wider student body as a whole' because 'in one sense, *academic English* is nobody's mother tongue' (Miller 2015 emphasis in original). The success of all students faced with the challenge of mastering the academic literacy of school depends on the support they are given in the teaching program. Nevertheless, the challenge faced by students who have already achieved high levels of literacy in one or more languages is not the same as for those who have not yet learnt to read and write in any language (Hammond & Miller 2015).

Teaching English as an additional language is a field of education in which knowledge about language has a high profile (Nunan 2015, Ur 2012). Traditionally in this field, however, the different layers of language (text-level discourse, sentence-level grammar, vocabulary) and the different language skills (listening, speaking, reading, writing) are treated separately, and teachers are given little guidance about how to integrate these elements into pedagogy that is cumulative and responsive to the contexts in which students need to use the language, for example, in the school curriculum areas. For this reason integrated rhetorically-oriented and contextually-responsive approaches, as described by Hammond (2008 and 2012) and Rose and Martin (2012), are increasingly used to provide EAL learners with the support they need to succeed at school (for example, Schleppegrell 2004 and 2010).

The teachers who participated in the study by Hammond and Gibbons (2005) set learning goals, planned the organisation of whole class, group and individual work, and selected and sequenced teaching activities. They provided students with the type of support, Hammond and Gibbons called *scaffolding,* a term derived from interpretations of Vygotsky's (1978) theory of learning (see for example, Bruner 1986). Activities that scaffold learning present students with a challenge, for example, a task based on academic language commensurate with the students' stage at school, while also providing them with the support they need to be able to complete the task successfully and to undertake similar tasks independently in the future.

Many activities and resources documented by Hammond and Gibbons (2005: 16–17) were selected and designed to enhance *message abundancy*. Message abundancy occurs when the same or similar information is represented in a variety of ways generating a 'cross-calibration' of multiple modes with augmented potential for insight (Butt 2004: 233). This might include hands-on activities, spoken language, written notes and visual support such as images, diagrams or maps, or other 'modalities of practice' (Rose & Martin 2012: 304). Teaching resources also included 'texts or artefacts that were pivotal across sequences of lessons [and that] became an important point of reference' throughout the teaching programme (Hammond & Gibbons 2005: 17) Teachers planned for the systematic teaching of specific knowledge about language, including 'the rhetorical structures of particular genres, subject-based vocabulary and sentence-level grammatical patterns' (Hammond & Gibbons 2005: 18) and a metalanguage shared with students for talking about this knowledge.

Micro-level pedagogy unfolds in the interactions between teachers and students. During these interactions teachers provide scaffolding by recapping significant points, reformulating student contributions in the target language, and using feedback moves to elicit and prompt students so they have a greater chance of contributing to the interaction in a meaningful way (see also Gibbons 2009 and 2014). At both the macro and micro levels a characteristic of the teaching documented by Hammond and Gibbons (2005: 13–14) was that it looked in 'two directions', at 'students' current levels of knowledge' and abilities, and also at curriculum goals.

Genre-based pedagogy

Since the 1980s, educational linguists have worked with teachers to research and refine cyclical patterns of literacy teaching and learning designed to guide students towards successfully writing 'the genres of schooling' (Rose & Martin 2012: 308). These pedagogic patterns, also known as curriculum genres (Christie 2002), are a sequence of stages teachers can use to plan the selection and sequencing of literacy teaching activities at the macro-level. The stages are represented as a cycle 'which could be entered at different points'. Specific stages can be recycled 'depending on the needs of the students' (Rose & Martin 2012: 63).

The first of these linguistically-informed learning models was designed in Australia as an alternative to process writing, one of the best known teaching strategies in the *whole-language* repertoire. Process writing is an approach to early writing development that focuses on writing processes rather than writing conventions. Children choose their own topics, plan and draft their own writing, share it with classmates and the teacher during writing conferences, then use this feedback to edit and proofread their writing before it is published (see, for example, Graves 2003). Process writing, however, does not provide students, especially those whose home language does not match the language of the school, with the instruction and support they need to be effective writers in the learning areas. Genre pedagogy was designed to address this problem with the aim of making 'the distribution of knowledge in schools more equitable' (Rose & Martin 2012: 5).

The design of genre-based teaching and learning cycles is informed by studies in language development (for example, Halliday 1975, Painter 1999a) showing that successful language learning depends on 'guidance through interaction in the context of shared experience' (Rose & Martin 2012: 58). When applied to the teaching of writing, interactive guidance takes the form of teaching students about the purpose, stages and language features of a genre, then giving them opportunities to deconstruct prototypical model, or mentor, texts before students jointly construct another text of the same genre, with the teacher acting as guide and scribe. It is only *after* students have enough preparation to be successful that they embark on the writing process to draft a text of the target genre independently and are given opportunities to exploit the rhetorical pattern of the genre creatively and critically (Rothery 1996).

A feature of genre-based pedagogy is the shifting relations between teacher and students at each stage of the cycle (Martin 1999). At the beginning of the modelling stage students are given opportunities to display their current level of knowledge, to engage with a context in which the target genre is used and to build knowledge of the topic. Next, the teacher takes an authoritative role, providing direct instruction and practice in the knowledge and skills students need to write texts of the target type successfully. In the joint construction stage the students contribute ideas while the teacher as scribe interacts with the students to elaborate their ideas in ways that match the demands of the writing task. During students' independent construction of a text, the teacher provides support only as needed, for example, in writing conferences, but reclaims an authoritative role when assessing student achievement and providing feedback. Once students know how to write a text in a particular genre, they explore critical and creative adaptations of the genre pattern in different contexts.

Coevolving alongside the genre approach to writing has been an approach that integrates the teaching of reading and writing in detailed step-by-step sequences of teaching strategies and interactions. Initially named *Scaffolding Literacy*, this pedagogy was first developed by Gray (1987) and his colleagues as a means of breaking the cycle of low-achievement that leaves struggling readers falling further and further behind their peers. The main aim of this approach is 'to make explicit to struggling or confused learners the strategies effective readers and writers use' (Axford, Harders & Wise 2009: 9). The texts selected for students to read are interesting, challenging, age-appropriate and 'contain examples of complex and syntactically-rich language' (Axford et al. 2009: 28). A first sequence of activities prepares the students to read the text. This is followed by a teaching sequence to scaffold students' fluent reading of a passage from the text. The next sequence engages students in close analysis of the selected passage at the sentence and word levels. The final sequence links the text to a scaffolded writing task.

Scaffolding Literacy (Axford et al. 2009) has been renamed *Accelerated Literacy* (Cowey 2005), and has been adapted for EAL learners (Adoniou & Macken-Horarik 2007). It is also the forerunner of the *Reading to Learn* pedagogy (Acevedo 2011, Culican 2005, Rose & Martin 2012). This family of pedagogies is distinguished by the attention paid to the design of the teaching sequences, the activities that make up each sequence and the micro-level interactions through which the scaffolding is achieved. To implement these pedagogies effectively, teachers must participate in intensive training.

Teachers implementing genre-based pedagogies require knowledge about language and pedagogy. They also need to apply that knowledge to the design of rhetorically-oriented assessment (Love et al. 2014) for diagnosing need, monitoring development and assessing achievement. In the context of discipline literacies, this means writing assessment criteria specific to each literacy task in ways that attend to each layer of language and each strand of meaning (Rose & Martin 2012: 323).

Quote

... students' writing progress is dependent on the extent to which their teachers can identify students' achievements and challenges, attending both to correctness at word and sentence level and rhetorical effectiveness across the text. Furthermore, student progress is assumed to rely on a cumulative diagnostics across all levels of language, whereby teachers build in principled ways on language informed work of earlier years and anticipate the work of later years.

(Love et al.2014: 52)

Expanding literacy teaching repertoires

Since the advent of genre-based pedagogy, successive collaborations between educational linguists and practitioners implementing the pedagogy in different educational contexts, alongside critical re-evaluations of the approach, have led to development, refinement and adaptation of the framework.

Genre-based pedagogy has been adapted for teachers working in the context of the Australian Curriculum (ACARA 2015) to introduce them to 'the language that students encounter in the various curriculum areas as they move through the years of schooling' (Derewianka & Jones 2012: xiii). Reading has a role in the pedagogy and 'intensive guided reading' of a model text in the first stage of the pedagogy can be used to build 'shared knowledge' about the genre (Derewianka & Jones 2012: 44). Similarly, in response to curriculum reform in the United States, Brisk (2015) foregrounds genre pedagogy as an approach teachers can use to teach academic literacies from Kindergarten to Year 5.

Derewianka and Jones (2012), Brisk (2015) and Gibbons (2009) have drawn on years of classroom-based practice and research to provide teachers with model texts relevant to the curriculum, an accessible metalanguage for talking about the purpose, stages and language features of different types of texts, and a rich repertoire of teaching activities and resources for teaching about language at whole text, paragraph, sentence and word levels. Brisk (2015) is particularly concerned with using genre-pedagogy and knowledge about language to support EAL students learning to read and write in the curriculum areas. She demonstrates how the use of the students' first languages can be integrated productively into cycles of teaching and learning to build students' knowledge of academic literacies in English.

Quote

... an intellectually challenging and real-life-oriented curriculum presents many more opportunities for language learning (and for explicit teaching) precisely because such skills and knowledge are presented within meaningful contexts, are used in the service of broader educational goals and integrated into authentic tasks, and involve students in language based collaborative work.

(Gibbons 2009: 12)

Recently researchers studying the implementation of genre-based pedagogies in classrooms have been concerned with extending the language
knowledge and teaching repertoire of teachers so they move beyond
a 'focus on the formulaic structure of narratives, procedures and persuasive writing forms' (Freebody & Morgan 2014: 68), a focus that is
exacerbated when these forms become the basis of high-stakes testing
(Love et al. 2014: 48–49). The consequence of attending to formulaic
text structures only is that students do not build subject-specific knowledge about the role played by grammar in constructing the meanings in
texts in each discipline, which limits their capacity to comprehend and
compose written texts at school. Likewise, the formulaic study of grammar in the form of 'easily teachable language (for example, connectives
and a limited, atomistic range of persuasive devices)', again often in
response to one-size-fits-all testing regimes, is unlikely to contribute
'transparently and cumulatively' to 'linguistically informed scaffolding'
(Love et al. 2014: 51).

One way of addressing this issue is to pay attention at sentence level
to language used to express particular domains of meaning of significance to specific disciplines, but 'always contextualised within the study
of the relevant text' (Love et al. 2014: 46). Palinscar and Schleppegrell
(2014) report on a case study in which EAL students closely analysed,
at word and sentence level, and across whole texts, the ways scientists
express likelihood in their writing, for example, through modality.
Similarly, Unsworth and Macken-Horarik (2015) describe primary and
secondary students attending to the resources used to express interactive
meanings in the images of literary texts. These included resources for
representing social distance and point of view in images, and the use of
colour as a resource for creating ambience in an image. The researchers
found that students were able to apply the understanding they gained
through studying these resources to the writing of interpretative
responses to the images.

A further addition to the genre-based teaching repertoire is a teaching
sequence that has become known as the 'semantic wave' (Maton 2014).
In a study of knowledge-building practices in secondary classrooms,
Macnaught, Maton, Martin and Matruglio, (2013: 50–51) observed
a pattern commonly used by teachers in which they moved 'from
generalised, abstract and highly condensed meanings, often in technical
language, towards more context-dependent and simpler meanings,
often in everyday language', which they achieved by 'unpacking' the
technicality into 'more familiar commonsense language for students'.
Macnaught et al. (2013) argue that unpacking abstract meanings is

only half the teacher's task. The next step, during joint construction activities, is to guide students as they repackage the commonsense meanings into the dense specialised abstract language of the discipline. This type of teaching requires skill and is 'strongly dependent on shared metalanguage, supportive rapport between the teacher and students (and between students themselves), and careful mediation of students' suggestions' (Macnaught et al. 2013: 62).

A pedagogy of multiliteracies is 'more appropriate for today's world of change and diversity', according to Kalantzis and Cope (2012: 188). These authors describe literacies as 'multimodal designs for meaning' that 'bring together written, visual, spatial, tactile, gestural, audio and oral modes' in fluid and dynamic ways. The pedagogy they advocate is a *design pedagogy* that accounts for meaning-making as an 'active, transformative process' (Kalantzis & Cope 2012: 173–188).

> ## Quote
>
> ... in putting available designs to use, the meaning-maker never simply replicates or copies found designs, even if the raw materials they use seem to have been largely reproduced from well-established patterns of meaning-making. The meaning-maker always creates a new design, a design like no other ever made before. Their design is inevitably an expression of their voice, which draws upon the unique mix of meaning-making resources: the codes and conventions they happen to have had available in their contexts and cultures.
>
> Kalantzis and Cope (2012: 184)

Conclusion

In this chapter the journey has taken us into the years of schooling, where students are, ideally, apprenticed into the forms of discourse that will enable them to succeed across the school disciplines. All children deserve to succeed, and this means understanding that not all children begin their school life on the same footing, and that some may need compensatory pedagogic interventions to bridge the distance between the language(s) of the home and the language(s) of school. Sharing knowledge about language and how it is used to build discourse for different purposes is the fundamental task of education because 'language is the essential condition of knowing, the process by which experience becomes knowledge' (Halliday 2004/1993: 328). We share the vision of Palinscar and Schleppegrell (2014: 617) 'that children develop and hone the use of metalanguage as a tool in the context of lively discussion, argumentation, and collaborative talk about text', made possible through explicit, visible pedagogies that are informed by the wealth of research into literacy in the classroom, a fraction of which has been reviewed in this chapter. Ideally, language and literacy learning at school successfully equips students to participate in tertiary education and the world of work, as well as to contribute, as citizens, to the community and a civil society. We will explore the degree to which this occurs for different groups of students in the next chapter as we continue our journey into contexts beyond the school.

5
Literacy in Adult Life: Community, Further Education and Work

In the past it was assumed that people learned to read and write at school and that was the end of the matter. The belief was that school-based literacy skills would enable people to move on to and participate in further education and the workplace. However, in the 1980s and 1990s, researchers (for example, Barton, Hamilton & Ivanič 2000, Barton & Ivanič 1991, Baynham 1995, Clark and Ivanič 1997, Hamilton, Barton & Ivanič 1994, Heath 1983) began to turn their focus to the social purposes and practices of literacy in contexts beyond the school, including tertiary education contexts, home contexts, community contexts and work contexts. These socially oriented researchers began to investigate 'the different literacies associated with different domains of life' (Barton et al. 2000: 11) and this led to an interest in how adults managed in different contexts with varying levels of literacy skills and how these could be measured (for example, Black 1989, Wickert 1989).

Quote

Contemporary life can be analysed in a simple way into domains of activity, such as home, school, workplace. It is a useful starting-point to examine the distinct practices in these domains, and then to compare, for example, home and school, or school and workplace. We begin with the home domain and everyday life. The home is often identified as a primary domain in people's literacy lives, for example, by James Gee (1990), and central to people's developing sense of social identity. Work is another identifiable domain, where relationships and resources are often structured quite differently from in the home. We might expect the practices associated with cooking, for example,

---

to be quite different in the home and in the workplace – supported, learned and carried out in different ways. The division of labour is different in institutional kitchens, the scale of the operations, the clothing people wear when cooking, the health and safety precautions they are required to take, and so on. Such practices contribute to the idea that people participate in distinct discourse communities, in different domains of life. These communities are groups of people held together by their characteristic ways of talking, acting, valuing, interpreting and using written language.

(Barton et al. 2000: 11)

Many social, demographic and economic changes and issues over the past three decades have brought adult literacy and numeracy levels into sharper focus – workplace changes, globalisation, and the transnational movement of people as refugees, economic migrants, providers of professional and expert services and students. This chapter will proceed from the concept of literacy domains and briefly examine how research has informed our understandings of literacy in adult contexts beyond school and how these understandings have influenced approaches to adult literacy and numeracy teaching and assessment. The chapter will focus on the literacy demands of community contexts, tertiary education, and the workplace. This will mean considering different groups of adults or 'discourse communities' (Barton et al. 2000: 11) in these different domains of adult life and those adults who seek to develop their literacy skills in tertiary preparation courses, adult basic education provision and second-language programmes. It will also mean considering issues for adults who fall outside these domains such as the homeless and prisoners.

Measuring adult literacy levels

International surveys of adult literacy and numeracy were conducted throughout the latter half of the 20th century and there have been three more recent international surveys that governments, administrators and the media refer to when discussing the literacy skills of their country's adult population. The first survey is the *International Adult Literacy Survey* (IALS), which was conducted between 1994 and 1998 in 21 countries. This was followed by the *Adult Literacy and Lifeskills Survey* (ALL), which was conducted between 2003 and 2008. It defined literacy as 'the knowledge and skills needed to understand and use information from text and other written formats' and numeracy 'as the knowledge and skills required to manage mathematical demands of diverse situations'.[1] The first round of the ALL sought to measure the literacy and numeracy skills of a representative sample of 16 to 65 years olds in Bermuda, Canada, Italy, Norway, Switzerland and the United States, with four additional countries – Australia, New Zealand, Hungary, and the Netherlands – participating in the second round.

The latest international survey of adult literacy and numeracy – the *Program for International Assessment of Adult Competencies* (PIAAC) – was conducted in 2011 and 2012 in 24 countries. The PIAAC survey comprises three components – direct assessment, skills use and a background questionnaire. The direct assessment component assesses four areas of competency – literacy, reading components, numeracy and problem solving in technology rich environments. These 'are considered to constitute *key* information processing skills in the sense that they provide a foundation for the development of other, higher-order cognitive skills and are prerequisites for gaining access to and understanding of specific domains of knowledge. In addition, these skills are necessary in a broad range of contexts, from education through work to everyday'.[2] Table 5.1 is adapted from an OECD table that summarises the assessment domains in the PIAAC survey and gives a sense of how literacy and numeracy skills are defined and what is considered, by international organisations, important in terms of purposeful use of these skills by adults and in what contexts. The PIAAC extended the areas to be assessed and, unlike the earlier surveys, asked adults in employment about generic skills they use in the workplace. It also collected information in four broad categories of work skills – cognitive skills, interaction and social skills, physical skills and learning skills.

Quote

As part of its Program for the International Assessment of Adult Competencies (PIAAC), the OECD collects and analyses data that assist governments in assessing, monitoring and analysing the level and distribution of skills among their adult populations as well as the utilisation of skills in different contexts.

(http://www.oecd.org/site/piaac/ – accessed 30.4.2015)

Table 5.1 Assessment domains in the survey of adult skills (PIAAC) – OECD 2015[4]

	Literacy	Numeracy	Problem solving
Definition	Ability to understand, evaluate, use and engage with written texts to participate in society, to achieve one's goals, and to develop one's knowledge and potential.	Ability to access, use, interpret and communicate mathematical information and ideas in order to engage in and manage the mathematical demands of a range of situations in adult life.	Ability to use digital technology, communication tools and networks to acquire and evaluate information, communicate with others, and perform practical tasks.
Content	Texts are characterised by Medium – print-based and digital Texts are characterised by Format • Continuous or prose texts (narration, argumentation or descriptions) • Non-continuous or document texts (tables, lists, graphs) • Mixed texts (combination of prose and document elements) • Multiple texts (juxtaposition or linking of independently generated elements)	Mathematical content, information and ideas: • Quantity and number • Dimension and shape • Pattern, relationships, change • Data and chance Representations of mathematical content: • Objects and pictures • Numbers and symbols • Diagrams, maps, graphs, tables • Texts • Technology-based displays	Technology: • Hardware devices • Software applications • Commands and functions • Representations (text, graphics, video) Nature of problems: • Intrinsic complexity (number of steps, alternatives required for solution, complexity of computation and/ or transformation, number of constraints) • Explicitness of the problem statement (largely unspecified or described in detail)
Contexts	Personal Work-related Community Education	Everyday life Work-related Society & Community Education	Personal Work-related Community

It is often the case that national media report the findings of these surveys in alarmist terms and often blame is sheeted home to schools, for what are seen as poor results, ignoring the fact that a country might have lower results because of factors such as higher migration intakes. In one example, from Australia, following the release of the 2013 PIAAC results, the media reported that half of all Tasmanians were functionally illiterate and innumerate. This type of reporting ignores the facts that *functionally illiterate* and *functionally innumerate* are 'crude and sensationalist versions of the standard described' and that, in this particular survey, Australians 'performed significantly above the average' and were only outperformed by three countries (Mendelovits 2014). However, misreadings of the results from such international surveys are often used to fuel the literacy wars that have been discussed in other parts of this book.

Results of such international measures of adult literacy and numeracy often lead to national or state government policies or initiatives but the following four questions, adapted from Hamilton, Macrae and Tett (2001: 24) arise from such initiatives and policies:

1. What concept of literacy underpins national or state policies?
2. How are teachers and learners positioned by the policies?
3. What kinds of learning activities/processes are programmes or initiatives expected to engage in?
4. What outcomes are literacy programmes and learners expected to achieve?

Different countries put different funding and policy frameworks around adult basic education (ABE) and adult migrant language programmes, with some countries, like Australia, funding adult language, literacy and numeracy programmes nationally by distributing funds through regular cycles of tendering and with public and private providers bidding for the funds. In other countries, as in the United States, funds for ABE and migrant language programmes are allocated to states through a formula, and the states (See for example, Fieldhouse 1996) distribute funds to local organisations to provide courses for adults.[3]

Despite broader views of literacy development as a lifelong process, many politicians, journalists and business people still expect 'school literacy to equip students for varied roles and literate competence in post-school life' (Lo Bianco & Freebody 1997: xv) and do not focus on other broader issues. This attitude ignores the fact that some students do leave school and require assistance, through ABE, because the literacy teaching in schools has failed them as they may be socioeconomically disadvantaged or have physical or intellectual disabilities. There will always be some underperformance in literacy and numeracy among some groups and individuals in the adult population. This group may include migrants who speak a language other than the main language of the society, those who may have had disrupted schooling or Indigenous people who live in remote locations. The fact that 'these same groups and individuals are often seriously disadvantaged in their occupational and educational opportunities is sufficient cause to warrant a targeted policy on literacy' (Lo Bianco & Freebody 1997: xvi).

Quote

The goal of enhancing literacy capability is not merely one for education. Literacy capability for all is a compact of citizenship, securing for all ... the principal means for participation in democratic institutions and processes. Universal and broad literacy capability is also an investment in human development to strengthen ... social and economic progress. Finally and ultimately it is an achievement of ... civilisation and culture since literacy is the principal avenue for the enrichment, diversification and ongoing development of a lively, distinctive and cohesive nation.

(Lo Bianco & Freebody 1997: xvii)

There are a number of high-stakes schemes for assessing the language and literacy skills of people who seek to study in English-speaking countries. The two most best known schemes are the International English Language Testing System (IELTS) and the Test of English as a Foreign Language (TOEFL). According to the IELTS website,[5] the system is administered 'in more than 1 000 test centres and locations in over 140 countries' and 'is accepted as evidence of English-language proficiency by over 9 000 organisations worldwide'. In 2014,' more than 2.2 million tests were taken globally'. The TOEFL website[6] states that this testing system 'is the most widely respected English-language test in the world, recognised by more than 9 000 colleges, universities, and agencies in more than 130 countries, including Australia, Canada, the UK and the United States'.

Both systems assess the language macroskills of speaking, listening, reading and writing, with IELTS differentiating between general-training reading and writing and academic reading and writing. Tertiary education institutions set entry levels against these assessment systems, with many academics claiming that the levels are often set too low, particularly when tertiary institutions are keen to expand their business by enrolling students from overseas. Even more worrying is the corruption and misconduct reported in test results and in pass rates at some universities. This has been seen as the result of universities relying on the fees of overseas students for an increasing percentage of their income and the desperation of some overseas students to gain a qualification and, once enrolled, not to disappoint their families (NSW Independent Commission Against Corruption 2015).

Some research indicates that there is a level below which students are more likely to fail (Barthel 2007, Elder 2003, Graham 1987). However, English-language skills are seen as only one indicator of success in tertiary education and a number of researchers have investigated other factors that contribute to or limit student success in tertiary education (for example, Dooey & Oliver 2002, Miller 2006). These include study skills, understanding academic culture, the role of persuasive writing, the role of judgement in academic writing (see below) and the meaning and consequences of plagiarism.

Quote

[A critical stance involves] systematic analysis based on a questioning attitude to the material being analysed and the methods being used, and governed by the overall purpose of reaching a judgement.

(Clanchy & Ballard 1997: 47)

Some universities have developed their own assessment schemes in an attempt to identify students who may experience difficulties during their studies and to provide these students with targeted support. One such assessment programme is the University of Auckland's Diagnostic English Language Needs Assessment (DELNA) programme, 'a post-entry diagnostic programme administered to all first-year undergraduate students, regardless of their language background' (von Randow 2010: 172). The DELNA involves an 'initial 30-minute online screening assessment made up of an academic vocabulary task and a text-editing task', which all students take. Student are then notified if their language skills are appropriate for university study, they need to go to the Student Learning Centre to improve their language skills or they need to undertake the diagnostic assessment 'so that we can identify their language needs' and be guided 'to specific language enrichment programs' (von Randow 2010: 174). The diagnostic tool is a 'two-hour pen and paper diagnosis of listening, reading and writing' (von Randow 2010: 173). The results are reported against a six-band scale, with Bands 4 and 5 indicating a risk of failing. In one study of DELNA, Bright and von Randow (2004) explored why students do not access language support and the reasons included 'time, timetable restraints, family commitments, and the fact that they expected their lecturers and tutors to provide language support' (von Randow 2010: 172).

Quote

When asked to supply a metaphor to describe their first-year experience in an English-medium university, interviewees talked of drowning, being buried alive, being in a black hole, struggling uphill with a heavy pack, and in short, suffering and feeling unable to do anything to help themselves.

(von Randow 2010: 175)

Research within the frame of Systemic Functional Linguistics into academic discourse (see Chapter 2 and Chapter 4 and the section below) clearly indicates that language develops discourse within a specific discipline in particular ways. This indicates that the most effective and efficient language support programmes in tertiary contexts would be developed to provide support directed to the specific discipline that students are studying and that this support would best be provided with faculties working closely with language support staff.

Literacy domains, practices and events

In an ever-changing world that is driven by rapid changes in communication technology, the ability of adults in a society to be able to access information depends largely on their literacy skills. As people go about their daily lives, they 'are constantly encountering literacy' which is 'carried out in a wide variety of settings' (Barton 2007: 3–4). Literacy is not a separate activity undertaken apart from the everyday social and mental activities that people participate in. Literacy and numeracy are in fact embedded in these activities and are themselves 'a set of social practices associated with particular symbol systems and their related technologies' (Barton 2007: 32). This social orientation has led to three concepts that have influenced adult literacy research and education – literacy domains, literacy practices and literacy events (see Barton 2007).

Literacy domains

Adults use their literacy skills in a variety of social domains, each one requiring them to use these skills in different ways. Research into the social uses of literacy tracks the activities people engage in within the different domains of their lives and how and why they use literacy to participate in these activities. This type of data is usually gathered through ethnographic research with researchers spending time observing people in the various domains, making recordings, gathering texts and interviewing people. (see Chapter 6).

Adult students attending English-language and literacy programmes are often placed into classes that aim to prepare them for a particular social domain. These include Adult Basic Education (ABE) programmes that prepare adults for community participation, English for Academic Purposes (EAP) courses that prepare them for further study, as well as programmes that teach literacy skills and knowledge for employment and workplace participation. The domain-specific focus in such courses gives rise to 'a major tension' between 'a pressure to respond to a diverse range of specific and immediate needs for language use' and 'an imperative to build the potential of learners to use language beyond specific instances' (de Silva Joyce & Hood 2009: 244). This tension can be addressed through realising that various text-types or genres will recur across different domains and social contexts, albeit customised to different fields (see Table 2.1 for an example of procedural texts across different literacy domains) and for different specific purposes.

The concept of literacy domains was used as the basis of a research project undertaken in the Adult Migrant English Program in Australia (Burns & de Silva Joyce 2000a) to investigate how migrant students use reading in the private domain of their daily lives and how this use might relate to reading in the educational domain of their adult language classes. The researchers focused on three migrant groups in their home contexts – Arabic-speaking students from Lebanon, Chinese-speaking students from the People's Republic of China and Spanish-speaking students from El Salvador. One interesting finding from the project was that the students were keen to 'replicate their reading practices in [their first language] in the new language'. This learning goal requires teachers 'to think about a range of texts which they can make available to their students as well as introducing them to sources of texts in the community' (Burns & de Silva Joyce 2000a: xiii).

Literacy practices and events

For three or more decades researchers have been investigating the uses of literacy and literacy practices in local contexts, and how these relate to literacy practices across the society more generally. For example, 'vernacular literacies' or 'literacies associated with people's private, home and everyday lives, outside the domains of power and influence' (Barton 2007: 52) have been investigated through a variety of studies (for example, Barton & Hamilton 1998, Breen 1994, Gregory & Williams 2004). These studies have been undertaken to build a broader view of literacies across diverse societies and subgroups within societies, to make connections between private literacies and people's awareness and ability to use literacy in broader social contexts, and to link these literacies to learning. Other studies have investigated literacy in the workplace (for example, Belfiore, Defoe, Folinsbee, Hunter & Jackson 2004, Diehl & Mikulecky 1980, Joyce 1992, Street 2001b). In recent years employment-focused literacy research has been concerned with how changes in workplaces, resulting from new forms of production and distribution, have affected workers and literacy practices on the job (for example, Gee, Hull & Lankshear 1996). The workplace literacy practices of professionals, and the literacy demands of academic study, are a particular focus of the field of English for Specific Purposes (see below).

Studying literacy as a social practice involves 'studying literacy as it happens, looking both at specific literacy events and at how these events are embedded in social contexts. A literacy event is an 'occasion in everyday life where the written word has a role' (Barton 2007: 35). This idea of literacy events can be taken up in literacy programme planning where teachers can plan units of work around the occasions in everyday life in which their students will need to use literacy. Table 5.2 illustrates how this concept has been used to plan units of work. The units of work that feature in this table are centred on taking leave, as a component of a workplace language course, and on health in a community access programme for newly arrived migrants.

Drawing up a literacy event sequence, as part of course planning, clarifies the range of texts that students are likely to encounter in these literacy practices. When teaching migrant students, it also clarifies any knowledge about cultural practices involving literacy and the spoken language that accompanies written texts in these contexts, which may also need to be taught.

Table 5.2   The literacy event as a planning tool in adult language/literacy courses

Applying for leave						
Discuss leave plan with supervisor	Clarify leave owing with HR department	Download leave form from workplace intranet	Complete leave form	Submit leave form via workplace intranet	Phone HR to check leave has been approved	Talk to workmates about leave plans

Going to the doctor						
Make an appointment by phone	Greet the receptionist at doctor's surgery	Complete patient information form	Consult with the doctor	Sign medical insurance form	Take prescription to chemist	Read medicine instructions

The concept of a literacy event, where written texts are embedded in social activities, highlights how spoken and written texts are interrelated in these events. For example, when visiting the doctor we may need to engage in a telephone appointment-making exchange and in a service encounter with a receptionist, fill in a patient information form, participate in a doctor's consultation, engage in a chemist shop service encounter to dispense a prescription and then read the instructions on the medicine packaging. This interrelationship between prior texts and simultaneous texts is referred to as *intertextuality* (see Chapter 2). The question for teachers is whether they need to teach these other texts in order for their students to successfully participate in the literacy event sequence and broader literacy practices.

The classroom itself is a place of intertextuality and literacy events, where spoken and written language interweave as the teacher introduces activities that progressively move students towards control of the written text that is the focus of the literacy class. The teacher organises activities that shunt the students up and down the mode continuum (see Chapter 1) and systematically incorporate students' oral language into the learning process (Joyce 1992: 48). Figure 5.1 illustrates this intertextuality and movement along the mode continuum in a particular class where students were learning to complete workplace accident forms which incorporate a recount of the accident.

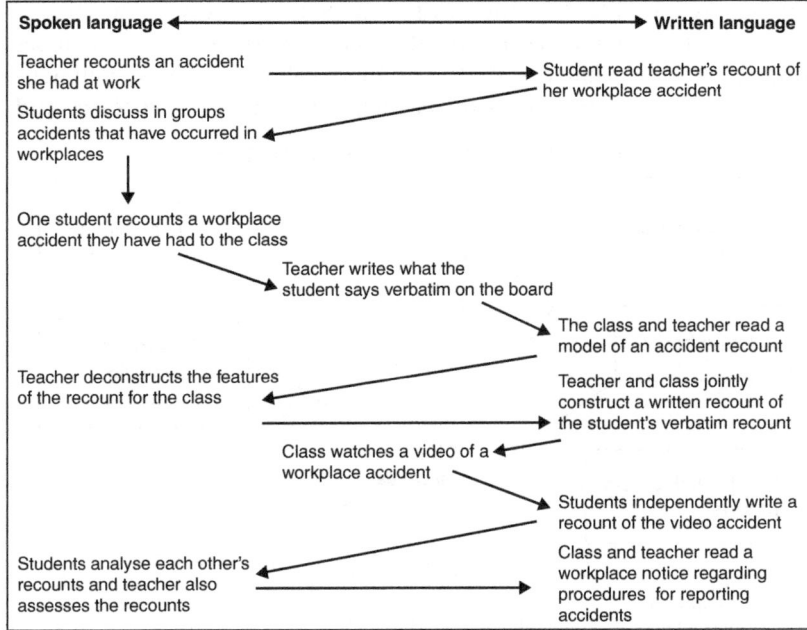

Figure 5.1 Intertextuality and the mode continuum in a literacy classroom
Source: Adapted from Joyce 1992: 48.

An adult literacy programme, no matter what the focus and endpoint, should aim to enable students to participate in the literacy practices of the society by focusing on the 'common patterns in using reading and writing' in particular situations (Barton 2007: 36). This means that instead of teaching programmes being based on single isolated texts, programmes should provide students with knowledge about how the texts they are studying are integrated into specific social contexts and how they align with culturally determined literacy practices. This knowledge is drawn from ethnographic research. Ethnographic research tools can also be used prior to teaching by classroom teachers to analyse the literacy learning needs of their students, for example, by investigating the written texts their students must engage with to participate successfully in particular contexts, as well as what people do with these texts and what cultural assumptions underpin successful use of these texts in the context.

An ethnographic research tool that can be applied to course planning is the communication network. A communication network can be used to identify the texts and people involved in literacy practices of particular contexts. It is particularly useful in courses conducted in workplaces that aim to develop employee language and literacy skills for successful participation in work processes and

CHILDCARE WORKER TEXT NETWORK

Staff handbook

Safety instructions

Daily sing-in sheet

Picture books

Emergency evaluation procedures

Childcare worker

Child development reports

Hygiene instructions

Equipment instructions

Workplace forms

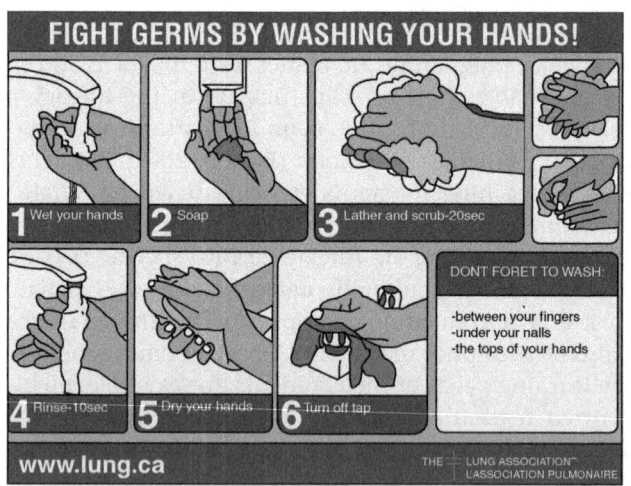

Figure 5.2   Communication network
Source: From de Silva Joyce 2014: 63.

procedures. For example, as part of the planning process for a linked skills course that incorporated language support while students were undertaking vocational training, a communication network was drawn up for childcare workers (Figure 5.2). This network was used by the literacy teacher, working in collaboration with a vocational trainer, to identify texts that the students would need to master as they undertook training to become childcare workers and where difficulties might arise as they began to use these texts in the classroom and in workplace placements (de Silva Joyce 2014). The literacy teacher's role was to teach the students about the texts identified by the network and their use, and how to participate in the literacy events in which these texts are used in the workplace. Texts in the childcare context identified on the network included the multimodal hand-washing instruction poster seen above.

Numeracy as social practice

The ethnographic concepts of literacy domains, literacy practices and literacy events have also been applied to numeracy. Knowledge about the use of numeracy, and the ways in which numbers and mathematical language are embedded in social contexts, is a particularly important aspect of Adult Basic Education (ABE). In adult education and training contexts, the planning of effective numeracy teaching accounts for the social use of mathematics from two perspectives: the mathematical language used to embed mathematical information in texts and the diverse needs of students studying numeracy.

Examples of how mathematical language is used to embed mathematical information in a text are highlighted in the following short extracts taken from the Transport NSW, Sydney Trains website, under the heading *Trip Tips*.[7]

Peak periods

> Our busiest services are those arriving in the Sydney CBD **between 6.00am and 9.00am** and departing the Sydney CBD **between 4.00pm and 7.00pm** on weekdays.

> Around **one million train trips** are made each weekday, and **around two-thirds of these** occur during **the peak periods**. We understand that **peak capacity** is a major concern for our customers. Sydney

Trains is working to **increase capacity** across the network, but there are **a few things** you can do to avoid the crowds:

The **middle carriages of a train** tend to be the most crowded – **the ratio of seats to passengers can vary by as much as 50% within a single train.** If your train is crowded, try boarding nearer **each end of the train** ...

For your personal safety

Arrive at your station **a few minutes earlier** than **your timetabled service** to allow **sufficient time** to board your train. Train doors may begin closing **up to 20 seconds before** the **scheduled departure time** to assist with **punctuality**...

Students undertake the study of numeracy in adult education for diverse reasons and with different needs. Some adults have failed to develop adequate mathematical understanding at school and so may not understand mathematical language and mathematical concepts as these apply to everyday activities. Such students may also be very anxious about learning mathematics. Adult students studying English as a second language, after perhaps migrating to an English-speaking country, may understand the mathematical concepts and use them with confidence, but do not know how these concepts are expressed in English. Given the diverse starting points and learning goals of adult students, numeracy teachers require training to work with all students in ways that make mathematics both relevant and accessible.

An issue addressed in adult numeracy research is the transferral of mathematical knowledge and understandings from one context to another (for example, Evans 2000, Harris & Evans 1991, Lave 1988, Nunes, Schliemann & Carraher 1993). Studies in the field of adult numeracy training have revealed that 'mathematical skills learned in one context, for example, school, cannot be assumed to transfer in a straightforward, unaided manner to new contexts' and that 'in workplace contexts mathematical skills may be deeply embedded in practices that are not manifested as clearly bounded tasks or problems' (Black, Yasukawa & Brown 2013: 10). Consequently, the need to apply mathematical knowledge learned in other contexts, such as school, may not be immediately visible to employees who lack relevant training or experience In other words, numeracy, like literacy, is part and parcel of the social activities in which people participate across the different social domains of their private, community, education and working lives.

Quote

1. Literacy is a social activity and can best be described in terms of people's literacy practices which they draw upon in literacy events.
2. People have different literacies which they make use of, associated with different domains of life. Examining different cultures or historical periods reveals more literacies.
3. People's literacy practices are situated in broader social relations. This makes it necessary to describe the social settings of literacy events, including the ways in which social institutions support particular literacies.
4. Literacy is based upon a system of symbols. It is a symbolic system used for communication, and as such exists in relation to other systems of information exchange. It is a way of representing the world to others.
5. Literacy is a symbolic system used for representing the world to ourselves.
6. We have awareness, attitudes and values with respect to literacy and these attitudes and values guide our actions.
7. Literacy has a history. Our individual life histories contain many literacy events from early childhood onwards which the present is built upon. We change, and as children and adults are constantly learning about literacy.
8. Literacy events and practices have a social history.

(Barton 2007: 34–49)

Literacies in the community

For many decades, researchers have undertaken long-term and detailed ethnographic studies of whole communities and their literacy practices. Examples of these include Shirley Brice Heath's (1983) study of Piedmont Carolinas communities, the study by Barton and Hamilton (1998) of a community in Lancaster (UK), Cheffy's (2007) study of a Cameroonian village, the 1981 Scollon and Scollon study of the Vai people, and Fishman's (1991) study of writing in an Amish community. Other researchers have worked closely with individuals. After tracking the development of literacy in a mother and son, for example, Victoria Purcell-Gates (1997) has produced a touching account of this journey, as the mother sought for her son the social capital she believes literacy holds, a task complicated by their move from a poor rural setting to an urban setting. The accumulation of ethnographic studies has shown that literacy is not a simple set of skills practised by all people in the same way. People use literacy skills in complex ways to fulfil different social purposes reflecting their sociocultural identities and circumstances, and they seek to develop these skills in different ways and through different means.

Quote

There are opportunities to develop further the important human capital rationale for adult literacy and numeracy provision, but also, as we have indicated, a social capital rationale which in turn complements skills development and enhances the socioeconomic well-being of individuals and communities. There are considerable opportunities for extending the influence and value of adult literacy and numeracy skills into other sectors with partnerships, but without national policy and subsequent sustainable funding, they will remain largely unfulfilled opportunities. And finally, those who work in the adult literacy and numeracy field, and for those who are new entrants, new opportunities and support mechanisms are urgently required for their professional learning and for re-building a sustainable and strong professional community.

(Black & Yasukawa 2010: 53–54)

In school contexts the connection between home literacy practices and literacy development in class has been made clear (see Chapter 3) but in adult education contexts this connection is often ignored. It is important to understand that, although adults in adult basic education programmes often assess themselves as illiterate or innumerate, this is rarely the case. Taking time to explore with students how they use written texts and numeracy at home or in the community can reveal skills that can be further developed in the classroom. It is often the case that people, who say they know no mathematics, in fact, play darts, sew dresses, knit jumpers, gamble by, for example, betting on horses, or complete many DIY projects at home. All these involve to some extent reading, writing and numeracy. Nevertheless, these learners have come to believe that mathematics is a subject people do at school and is not connected with their daily lives, and similarly, what they do with print around the home is not reading because they believe reading means reading novels and other *thick* books. Exploring how learners use written materials, mobile telephones, tablets and computers in their homes, can provide a starting point for teachers to engage students in the literacy work of the classroom.

In 2007, in collaboration with academic researchers, six teachers implemented a new approach to the teaching of reading in part-time adult basic education classes that were delivered in varied teaching spaces and with limited resources. The teaching contexts were further complicated by irregular student attendance and mixed-level class groupings made up of students from multiple language backgrounds. After a series of professional development sessions delivered by the researchers, the teachers introduced a detailed and intensive approach to reading pedagogy (Reading to Learn – www.readingtolearn.com.au). The study was designed to accommodate the complexity of the teaching context. This included collecting data from multiple sources. Sources included recordings and transcriptions of regular group discussions, classroom observations, teacher records of practice, student feedback, assessments of student reading and writing performances, and audio-and video-recordings of lessons (de Silva Joyce, Hood & Rose 2008).

A particularly relevant finding emerged when teacher expectations of the reading levels this cohort of basic education students could achieve were compared with actual assessments of that achievement. It was found that the reading abilities of students were frequently underestimated by teachers. This appears to be a consequence of the nature of initial reading assessment, which is often based on unchallenging texts. Subsequently, in many teaching contexts, there is 'no move towards the use of more challenging texts to extend students sufficiently', so the initial assessments do not 'provide adequate data for indicating progress' (de Silva Joyce et al. 2008: 8). In contrast, when students are taught systematically and cumulatively on the basis of a detailed, intensive pedagogy to use challenging texts, as in this study, they are able to attain levels of achievement beyond those indicated by the limited evidence gathered during initial testing. The study demonstrated the value of challenging the typical reluctance in adult basic education programmes to support students' use of challenging texts appropriate to the needs and interests of adults. Instead, most reading tasks in adult basic education are those used to *test* rather than to *teach* reading. This may be a consequence of teachers lacking both confidence and knowledge about research-based reading pedagogies. Action research as a collaboration between teachers and researchers is discussed in Chapter 6 (see also the Anne Burns entry in Chapter 7).

When policy makers emphasise the economic impact of low levels of literacy, rather than the social or individual impacts, the consequence can be that classes in community contexts are not afforded the funding or the status of programmes designed to prepare students for work. This is despite the fact that low levels of literacy and numeracy are flagged as concerns in broader policy areas such as health. Health policy rhetoric has shifted over recent decades from one of patients complying with medical regimens and treatment and medication instructions to one of patient empowerment, reflecting a 'more collaborative, rights-based model where people are provided with information and choices about their healthcare' (Australian Commission on Safety and Quality in Healthcare 2014: 8). The idea of health literacy has emerged from the field of social literacy studies and is seen as an important aspect of social participation. It is defined as the ability of 'people to understand information about health and healthcare, and how they apply that information to their lives, use it to make decisions and act on it' (Australian Commission on Safety and Quality in Healthcare reference in list 2014: 2). Non-adherence to prescription medication regimens and recommended treatment is considered a threat to individual health but is also seen as contributing to increased costs in the overall health system.

In terms of adults participating in literacy programmes in community settings and the impact of these programmes on their literacy practices in the community, there has been little systematic research. According to Reder (2011: 1) '[m]ost prior research has examined change in adult literacy in a single context over relatively short periods of time in which adults participate in basic skills classes and ... the follow-up intervals are too short to observe meaningful change'. The Longitudinal Study of Adult Literacy Development (LSAL) was conducted from 1998 to 2007 and followed 1 000 people who had dropped out of high school in the Portland (Oregon) metropolitan area and were aged from 28 to 44 years, when the project began (Reder 2011). The research project addressed four main questions (Reder 2011: 1):

1. To what extent do adults' literacy abilities continue to develop after they are out of school?

2. What are adult learners' patterns of participation over time in literacy training and education? In other learning contexts?
3. What life experiences are associated with adult literacy development? How do formally organised basic skills programmes contribute to these learning trajectories? Workplace training? Other contexts and activities?
4. What impacts does adult literacy development have on social and economic outcomes?

The study conducted 'a series of six periodic *waves* of in-depth interviews and skills assessments in respondents' homes. In every wave, literacy proficiency, engagement in everyday literacy practices and self-perceived wave-to-wave changes in literacy skills and practices were assessed. Other skills – such as oral vocabulary, reading fluency and holistic writing – were assessed only in particular waves. Interview questions during the first wave gathered background information (e.g., demographics, family-of-origin characteristics, K–12 school history). A series of interview questions repeated in each successive wave captured information about social, economic and educational status and activities (e.g., participation in basic skill programmes, post-secondary education and training, employment, job characteristics and earnings, household and family composition, life goals and aspirations). Administrative data about programme participation, education and employment/ earnings were also collected with permission from the individual' (Reder 2011: 2).

The study found that literacy skills and engagement in literacy and numeracy practices continue to develop but that this development varies, depending on factors such as demographics and background, experiences and age. Two interesting findings arise from this study. The first is that most of the participants had tried to improve their literacy and numeracy skills through self-study, which often preceded participation in courses. Participation in courses did not seem to improve proficiency very much but '[i]n sharp contrast, the data exhibit a strong positive relationship between programme participation and changes in literacy and numeracy practices measures. With many statistical controls in place, there are strong relationships between participation in adult education programmes and increased engagement with literacy (e.g. reading books) and numeracy (e.g. using math at home) practices' (Reder 2011: 3). It is clear from this study that narrow measures of literacy and numeracy gains do not show the true value of community programmes in terms of increasing participation in social literacy and numeracy practices and, and while these measures continue to be used to evaluate adult basic education literacy programmes, these programmes are likely to continue to be undervalued and underfunded.

A recurring theme in adult literacy education, particularly in community programmes, is that of power. Power determines 'what it means to be literate' which itself 'is socially constructed and cannot be seen outside the interest and powerful forces that seek to fix it in particular ways', and power determines the distribution of literacy (Crowther, Hamilton & Tett 2001: 1). Many adult literacy educators see adult basic education as a way of realigning the power relations and they talk of empowering their students through literacy. It was this approach that led many teachers in the community education sector to embrace the work of Paulo Freire, the Brazilian educator and philosopher (1968 and 1985). His orientation to literacy education as a means of individual liberation from oppression appealed to teachers who saw themselves as teaching the disadvantaged. It reflected an appealing humanist approach to literacy education for adult basic education teachers who were working with adults with low levels of literacy and who were disengaged from educational institutions.

The issue of power and literacy is a complex one, particularly in rapidly changing societies. If adult basic education is to be a means of challenging the power relations that work against students, then teachers need to be informed about research into literacy as social practice, which challenges simplistic deficit models of literacy development. Teachers need to look beyond narrow assessments of their students' literacy and numeracy levels towards what their students can do, and what they have the potential to do, rather than what they cannot yet do. They need to see the teaching space as negotiable in that it should recognise the validity of the student's own 'definitions, uses and aspirations for literacy' (Crowther et al. 2001: 2). To achieve this, teachers must strive to build meaningful and challenging uses of literacy at levels commensurate with students' aspirations into programmes, while also providing the support students need for success.

Adult literacy in the context of adult basic education is often aligned to concepts of social inclusion and exclusion, with governments, particularly in the first decade of this century, establishing social inclusion agencies or developing social inclusion strategies that sought to provide a range of support services to address health, mental illness etc. (for example, The European Social Inclusion Strategy 2000, Australian Social Inclusion Agenda 2007). Many researchers have extended definitions of social exclusion as they have shifted the focus onto 'the factors that contributed to the precariousness that often accompanies unemployment or disengagement from the labour market' (Saunders, Naidoo and Griffiths 2008).

At this time two orientations to literacy development and the benefits this brings to individuals and society were debated: literacy as social capital and literacy as human capital. The social capital orientation was more centred on the individual and emphasised connection to society through informal networks of friends and family, community networks in the broader community and institutional networks to schools and government agencies etc. Literacy development was seen as a way of strengthening these networks that were understood as important in countering the effects of social disadvantage. The other orientation, which has come to dominate debates about the benefits of literacy development, and one that government policies tend to emphasise, is the human capital orientation. This focuses on developing those skills that contribute to the productivity of the nation. It emphasises attributes, skills and abilities that increase an individual's value to the labour market and aligns formal education to a skills development agenda, with the gain to the individual from training and employment seen as a bonus. Black and Yasukawa (2010) propose that an effective literacy and numeracy policy approach should incorporate both orientations.

Literacy and disadvantage

This concept of power is brought into stark relief in affluent societies when considering the circumstances of those in extreme disadvantage, most canonically represented by the homeless and those in prison. Literacy, or lack of it, figures in any analysis of the situation of people in each of these situations, with many people moving between both (Vinson 2010).

Homelessness does not reflect a single category of people but includes 'people who are homeless, transient, staying in emergency shelters, or underhoused in substandard apartments and rooming houses' but in general they 'tend to be living in extreme poverty and excluded from opportunities for employment, education, recreation and social contact' (Trumpener 1997: 7 in Castleton 2001: 56). Castleton studied homelessness by interviewing clients and staff of a welfare centre in a major Australian city. She used the concepts of apparent need, perceived need and expressed need for literacy in order to analyse the literacy needs of people in this context. Apparent need for literacy is estimated from quantitative data sources such as census data; perceived need for literacy is based on interpretations of qualitative data by researchers and those who deliver services to people and expressed need for literacy is voiced by the clients themselves.

Overall, Castleton (2001: 62) found that 'rather than seeing lack of literacy skills as a precipitating factor in homelessness, informants generally identified limited literacy skills as an integral part of a range of characteristics of homelessness that included low socioeconomic status, poor employment opportunities, limited disposable income, poor accommodation, lack of self-esteem and motivation for learning'. Literacy was not seen as a panacea for the problems of the homeless but the informants did indicate areas that could 'provide some directions for the type of literacy provision that may be worthwhile for homeless people'. Castleton (2001: 63–64), for example, recognises the value of literacy in enabling people to take more responsibility for their health and wellbeing, but this would require literacy educators to work collaboratively with the social agencies who provide related social support services.

Collaboration with social support services has been identified by Vinson (2010) as a way of dealing with the range of problems children from disadvantaged backgrounds experience when they enter school. In a study mapping locations and characteristics of concentrated extreme disadvantage across Australia, Vinson (2007 63–64) identified the main 'connecting threads' in 'localised webs of disadvantage' as 'limited education and information skills' and 'low family income and employment-related skills', all of which align with low levels of literacy. These threads connect indicators of disadvantage such as disability and sickness, unemployment and prison admissions.

Prisoners are a group of people who sit outside the normal structures of society. In most countries, lack of literacy skills is given as a reason for levels of incarceration and many countries include an assessment of the literacy levels of prisoners in their national statistics. The United States administered a supplementary PIAAC survey in 2014 to a sample of 1 200 prisoners but the results have yet to be released. The UK National Literacy Trust states that '48% of offenders in custody have a reading age at or below the expected level of an 11-year-old' and that 'for prisoners with sentences under one year, 63% of offenders who had been expelled or permanently excluded from school were reconvicted within a year, compared with 44% of offenders who were not' (Morriscoe 2014: 7). The Australian Medical Association in 2012 stated that the prison population 'experience profound disadvantages in health compared to the wider community, with markedly elevated rates of mental illness, substance dependence, chronic disease and engagement in health risk behaviours' and proposed that the prison setting should address elements of disadvantage, which includes low levels of literacy.[8]

Many prison literacy programmes have tried innovative approaches to encourage prisoners to become engaged in literacy training in prisons. One programme, called the *Shannon Scheme*, is a peer mentoring approach to teaching reading that began in Wandsworth Prison in England in 2001, and in 2013 was operating in 150 gaols.[9] Another programme in the United States, *Read to Me*, operating since 1998, helps prisoners to learn to read for their children. The prisoners record themselves reading a story and the recording is sent to their children, which links the children to their parents and shows them a value in reading.[10]

In 1961 a mass literacy education campaign, inspired by Freire, was undertaken in Cuba. This model, *Yo sí Puedo* (Yes, I can), 'identifies low levels of literacy as a social, rather than an individual problem' and has been implemented 'to overcome low literacy in countries of the Global South', including Argentina, Bolivia, India, Venezuela, Grenada and Timor-Leste (Boughton, Ah Chee, Beetson, Durnan & Leblanch 2013: 8–9).

Quotes

Throughout the world, over 800 million adults are illiterate, of whom the majority are women, and international development agencies and scholarly opinion regularly identify this as a major obstacle to efforts to overcome poverty and marginalisation (Archer 2005). While literacy scholars associated with the New Literacy Studies (for example, Street 2001b and 2011) rightly question the simple equation of literacy with development, the extension of literacy continues to be a major goal of international agencies and national governments (Wagner 2011).

(Boughton et al. 2013: 8)

Where adult basic education programs focus on functional literacy and numeracy training preparing individuals for employment, mass literacy campaigns are designed to initiate social transformation in communities of marginalised people with little or no literacy. Each lesson of the mass literacy program developed

> in Cuba begins with a discussion of a 'positive message'. Students learn the letters of the alphabet by associating them with numbers in a method called 'alphanumeric', imitate literate behaviours modelled on video, and 'undertake exercises to build words, phrases and, eventually, sentences and texts of different genres'.
>
> (Boughton et al. 2013: 16)

While aspects of this model have attracted criticism, there is some case study evidence of its value in marginalised communities as a first step towards increased advantageous social participation, including in adult basic education. For example, in Australia, the *Yes I Can* model has been piloted in a remote Aboriginal community to address very low levels of English literacy in the adult population. The pilot was evaluated using a participatory action research model, which found a noteworthy rise in literacy levels of participants, with 'significant impacts on the lives of the individuals involved, their families and the whole community' and these outcomes were 'sufficiently compelling to warrant the continued development of the model for use in Aboriginal communities' (Boughton et al. 2013: 28) (see also Boughton & Durnan 2014).

Literacy and the experience of migrants and refugees

In many countries, migrants and refugees comprise a large group of students within community literacy provision. Some countries provide separate programmes to teach the language of the country but overall these students are integrated into programmes with other students. These students come to classes from a range of backgrounds and with a range of literacy skills. They may be literate in one or more languages or they may come from cultures with no written language. They may have extensive education or they may have experienced disrupted schooling or have had no schooling. All these characteristics present different pedagogic challenges for literacy teachers, particularly if the students are integrated into the same classes.

Australia has been accepting major intakes of settlers throughout its history and after World War II established the national Adult Migrant English Program (AMEP) to provide newly arrived migrants and refugees with English-language provision. For a number of years, the AMEP was supported by a National Centre for English Language Teaching and

Research (NCELTR), which undertook research into various aspects of language curriculum, pedagogy and assessment. It also focused, over the years, on the needs of particular students and the issues that teachers were facing in the classroom in relation to teaching language and literacy to particular groups.

Literacy was a major focus in a variety of AMEP projects and the findings have relevance to all literacy programmes for migrants and refugees or to literacy teachers who are teaching diverse language groups. One project, of particular relevance to literacy teaching, used a collaborative action research approach to explore issues in teaching disparate groups (Burns & Hood 1997), a perennial challenge in community provision. The teachers began by defining the characteristics of disparate groups that might impact on teaching and learning. These characteristics included:

- Proficiency levels in spoken and/or written English, or learning outcomes already achieved
- Levels of education and varied experiences in formal learning
- Literacy in a first or other languages
- Preferred learning pace
- Length of residence in Australia; knowledge of social systems, etc.
- Expectations about the course
- Goals and interests for language learning
- Contact with English outside the classroom
- Cultural values and attitudes
- Preferred learning styles
- Confidence, personality, motivation
- Health factors and personal circumstances
- Age
- Gender

The teachers then identified the problems they faced in teaching disparate groups, which fell into three categories:

1. **Time factors**: planning to accommodate different needs; developing and adapting activities so that the same core materials can be used across different levels; encouraging group rapport and mutual support; liaising with work colleagues or a support teacher
2. **Materials and support resources**: finding appropriate materials for the diverse needs; identifying content, topics or themes which appeal to all learners; needing more support in the classroom (team-teachers or aides)

3. **Classroom management issues:** deciding how best to group students; teaching in physical environments which limit flexibility in learning arrangements and methodologies; balancing the attention given to one group or another; ensuring that no student feels they are missing out; ensuring that higher level students are not frustrated; monitoring and record-keeping especially where multiple activities or group work are going on; avoiding cultural clashes or value clashes; resolving conflicts that arise

During the action research, the teachers explored various ways to work with disparate groups. Returning to the idea that teachers need to examine how students view the classroom and what they are learning, an interesting finding from the project was that students placed a very high value on developing and maintaining good relations with others and feeling that they were accepted in the group. They expressed bewilderment at the proposal that they could be seen as disparate and some viewed the wide variety of different personalities, skills and levels in the classroom as a positive aspect of the class (Burns & Hood 1997: 11).

Language focused programmes for migrants and refugees place different emphases on literacy, depending on the students and their needs for learning language and literacy. In English for Academic Purposes (EAP) courses, the development of reading and writing skills will be the prime focus of the programme (see below). Some courses will be targeted at students who have good spoken language skills and who have enrolled to focus on their literacy skills. Programming will rely on the teacher's knowledge of the kinds of texts and literacy practices that are important in the context in which the students want to operate but it should also be based on an identification of what students read and write in their first languages, as a starting point. This will give a sense of the students' first language literacy skills as a basis for developing literacy skills in the additional language. Teachers may also decide to incorporate texts that they know are important for participation in the general community.

Literacy for specific purposes

Adults use literacy to achieve social goals in the different domains of their lives, each domain requiring a different configuration of literacy knowledge and skills. English is increasingly used as a global *lingua franca* in specialist domains, for example, Science and Commerce, Medicine, Aviation and International Law. This has driven the demand for researchers to reveal more about the English literacy demands of these domains, and to consider how those who use English as an additional language might build the specific English literacy knowledge and skills required for high-level participation. This research focus tends to fall under the heading of English for Specific Purposes (ESP). Approaches used to investigate the language of specific specialist discourse communities include corpus studies of specialist discourses and ethnographic studies of their contexts, as well as studies of the construction of the disciplinary and cultural identities of those who use these discourses (Paltridge & Starfield 2013).

ESP research is concerned with describing language use in specialist domains for those who need to participate in those domains. For this reason, the conventional patterns that recur in texts used in those domains, or genres, are of particular interest in the ESP field. One of the most high profile branches of ESP is English for Academic Purposes (EAP). To help improve the academic English literacy of international students undertaking research in universities in the United Kingdom, Swales (1990) investigated the schematic structures of research articles, analysed in terms of rhetorical moves, so discourse-level knowledge could be taught, alongside knowledge about grammar and lexis, to international students. This study became the foundation for one branch of ESP genre studies (Paltridge 2013, Tardy 2011). Genre studies in the Systemic Functional Linguistics (SFL) tradition have also contributed to knowledge about the literacy demands of specialised domains.

There is a proliferation of specialist domains that have been studied from the perspective of ESP. These include academic study in the fields of humanities, social sciences and science, as well as professional employment in fields such a medicine, aviation, law and commerce. In the next sections, literacy for specific purposes will be considered from the perspective of two overarching domains: further education and employment.

Literacies in further education

> **Quote**
>
> Throughout the world there are many different approaches to knowledge. No one approach is better or worse than another but they do reflect differences in thinking. The values and beliefs of different cultures influence approaches to knowledge. In some cultures

> reproduction of knowledge is valued, while in others, extending knowledge – pushing the boundaries of what is known – is valued.
>
> (Thomson 2012: 3)

The literacy demands of further education are an extension of the subject-specific literacies that students have developed, if they have successfully completed 12–13 years of school. Successful completion of secondary school will be understood variously by students, depending on whether, through school completion, students have gained entry into an institution providing technical and further education or into a university.

Learning to write academic texts begins in secondary school as students learn how to structure essays using the language features of technicality, abstraction and evaluation, and the related use of nominalisation and grammatical metaphor (see Chapter 2). However, this knowledge is not evenly distributed among school leavers and in many post-school educational settings these students need assistance with literacy for further education and academic purposes. Students enrolled in technical colleges and universities, where English is the language of instruction and research, include those who use English in their everyday lives but who need assistance with developing academic language skills, as well as international students building literacy skills in English as an additional language. These students study English for Academic Purposes (EAP). The field of research into English for Academic Purposes (EAP) in general, and academic writing in particular, according to Hyland (2014: 392), has expanded due to 'three major developments: the increased diversity of students entering universities in many countries as a result of widening access policies; the increased attention given to effective teaching by funding bodies as a result of the shift to a "customer-service" view of higher education; and the incentives of offering EAP courses to fee-paying students from around the world'.

As discussed in Chapter 2, there has been much research undertaken into the rhetorical structure and language features of academic discourse across the disciplines, particularly within the frame of Systemic Functional Linguistics. For example, the texts and literacy practices of academic contexts have been analysed and documented by Coffin (2006), Hyland (2002) and Paltridge, Harbon, Hirsh, Phakiti, Shen, Stevenson and Woodrow (2009). This type of research involves the analysis of texts gathered from academic contexts in order to identify structural, grammatical and vocabulary choices. This has led to the identification of academic genres within specific disciplines. For example, Coffin (2006) identified the following sets of genres in the discipline of History: recording genres (autobiographical recounts, biographical recounts, historical recounts and historical accounts), explaining genres (factorial explanations and consequential explanations) and arguing genres (exposition, discussion and challenge). Korner, McInnes and Rose (2007) classified four groups of genres within Science as taxonomic genres (recounts and taxonomic reports), instructing genres (procedures), reporting genres (technical notes) and research articles that have a role in producing science. This has led to identification of overall language resources that students need to master in the various disciplines (Table 5.3).

Other researchers categorise academic genres in different ways. Hyland (2009), for example, groups genres according to the two main levels of higher education: undergraduate (essays, dissertations and oral presentations) and postgraduate (theses and dissertations, the viva voce or the oral defence of a dissertation and acknowledgements). Nesi and Gardener (2012) also analysed a corpus of academic texts from different academic levels and across disciplines. They identified 13 genre families, which vary according to their use across different disciplines for different purposes and with discipline specific language. These include: case study, critique, design specification, empathy writing, essay, exercise, explanation, literature survey, methodology recount, narrative recount, problem question, proposal, research report.

Table 5.3 Language features of the disciplines

Science, Technology and Maths	→	Linguistic resources of specialised discourse and technical discourse
Social Sciences and to a certain extent English	→	Linguistic resources of abstraction
History and Geography	→	Linguistic resources to read and write reports and accounts of social processes using abstraction
Social Sciences and English	→	Linguistic resources to write essays of argument and discussion requiring the manipulation of abstract discourses of social contestation
English and Creative Arts	→	Linguistic resources for expressing personality, particularly true of the complex demands of personal narrative in English

Source: Korner et al. (2007: 8).

Quote

... it is now apparent that acquisition of disciplinary knowledge involves students encountering a new and dominant literacy, which often differs considerably from their previous experience. While disciplines rely on different genres, and to some extent on different strengths in communication, academic ability is frequently evaluated in terms of competence in this 'essayist literacy' so that students often find their own literacy practices to be marginalised and regarded as failed attempts to approximate standard forms.

(Hyland 2009: 151)

It is clear that the changing demographics of universities means that courses in academic literacy will continue to be a feature of the broad field of literacy education. Different approaches to this have been adopted in various tertiary institutions. Hyland (2009: 151) states that 'supervisors and teachers seem to be uncertain of their responsibilities in terms of literacy support and their responses vary widely.' He notes that some teachers take an autonomous view of academic literacy, assign a grade, and send students with problems off to a writing support centre to learn generic academic literacy skills. Others sympathise with students' problems but do not know how to assist them, and yet others rewrite sections of students' assignments. Academics often complain about the low standard of their students' academic writing and that the universities do not support students with lower levels of English-language skills to the extent that is required, particularly fee-paying students, to develop their academic literacy skills to an appropriate level.

Quote

Prospective international students who do not reach the English-language proficiency requirements set by universities in NSW can apply for intensive English-language courses. It is estimated that around 28% of international students used this pathway. Provided that students succeed in the pathways program, they are guaranteed entry into the university course. This allows universities in NSW to accept an intake of students who they would otherwise reject due to English-language proficiency concerns ...

The effectiveness of such courses is unclear. Data indicates that, at least in the case of short preparation courses, they are not necessarily effective in improving the English-language proficiency of all students … A senior academic from one institution with whom the Commission spoke, commented that students attending IELTS preparation courses tend to lag behind academically compared to those who gain direct entry, as they begin with lower English-language scores. The pathways programs are very attractive from a revenue perspective but are likely to be widening the gap between the capability of the student cohort and the demands of the university.

(NSW Independent Commission Against Corruption 2015: 28–29)

Academic literacy support in tertiary contexts is usually provided through learning assistance centres where students can attend classes on academic writing or can seek individual assistance, but rarely do universities implement a whole of organisation approach to raising literacy standards. One exception is the University of South Australia, which in 2009 introduced a university wide approach to support academic English literacy development for all course work students (Harper 2013). The approach focused on diagnosing students' development needs early in their studies through an optional online language screening tool and integrating English-language teaching within course design, assessment and delivery. Academic language and learning staff work with discipline-based staff in this integration process but academic staff do not refer students to language and learning staff for support, unless they have performed below a threshold on the assessment screening tool. Harper (2013) reports on a mixed method study of the project to record its consequences and problems. While staff supported a model to address problems with students' literacy levels, there were issues that worked against developing a collegial model between language and learning staff and discipline-based staff. This research raises questions about how early assessment of students should occur, whether through an optional assessment tool, or whether undertaken by the staff though assessment of early assignment responses.

A recent research project focused on the academic literacy support provided in health science faculties in Australian universities. Language and literacy support in the health science field is seen as important 'with an increasing number of culturally and linguistically diverse students enrolling in degree programs' (Fenton-Smith & Frohman 2013: 61). This type of support is particularly significant because the students need to undertake clinical practicums. The project commenced with a fact-finding process to identify the issues faced by practitioners teaching academic language and learning to health science students. This was followed by a ten-point online questionnaire answered by 25 language and learning respondents working across various health science specialities. Despite the small number of respondents the project raises a number of issues that apply to all discipline areas, including the fact that international students received more assistance than domestic students, which begs the question of whether the needs of domestic students, who also require levels of assistance, are being recognised. Academic language and learning practitioners usually work outside faculties and this makes dealing with discipline-based staff difficult. They deal with students from across a range of disciplines and have no specialist knowledge of particular disciplines. This can be problematic when academic knowledge and literacy are so interwoven within academic genres.

Reading and writing academic texts is often described as challenging for those new to academic writing because of the dense packaging of meaning in abstract concepts and technicality, either in academic writing in general, or in writing used in the context of specific disciplines. While objectivity is also a feature valued in academic writing, a study by Hood (2010: 1) has drawn attention to 'the difficulties that novice academic writers face in adequately expressing a critical or evaluative stance in their written texts'. Using the Appraisal system (Martin & White 2005) from within the field of Systemic Functional Linguistics (SFL) (Hood (2010: 29) analyses patterns of evaluative meanings in research article introductions, as well as 'the variation across disciplines in the ways in which writers work to persuade readers of the legitimacy of their own study', variations which are a consequence of 'the knowledge structures the discipline represents'.

Literacies in the workplace

Researchers interested in the social and political dimensions of literacy have been tracking the implications of the 'new work order' (Gee et al. 1996) for literacy practices and education. This term refers to the changes that have been occurring in industrial economies over the past half a century. Lankshear (1997) outlines five features of the 'new capitalism', following Castells (1993) as:

1. Sources of production depending increasingly on the application of science and technology, information, and quality management
2. An increasing proportion of material production shifting to information processing
3. The shift from standardised production to specialisation and flexible production with flatter hierarchical structures and interchangeable tasks and jobs
4. Globalisation of capital and enterprises
5. The information technologies revolution spearheading and also responding to contextual changes

Workplaces and their employees, over the past three to four decades, have been undergoing enormous changes related to the five features outlined above. From a social practices view of literacy it is obvious that these changes have brought about new literacy demands in the workplace, new literacy events and new literacy practices.

Quote

To have a whole working environment, we need many threads, including literacy threads. But if we take individual literacy threads out of their place in the weave of everyday working life, extracting them from situations in which they are lived, we lose the meaning they derive from being part of a whole.

(Belfiore et al. 2004: 2)

If employees appear to fail in responding to change, then often their literacy skills are blamed and they are required to attend literacy courses at an external institution, or literacy courses are provided in the workplace. International adult literacy assessment surveys are often used to highlight perceived low levels of workplace literacy. At a national level the perception of a literacy crisis attributed to low employee literacy and numeracy levels becomes headline news as governments voice concern over the nation's ability to compete in the globalised marketplace. Some see the promotion of a literacy crisis as a way of blaming workers for broader social and economic issues (Graff

1979). What is rarely acknowledged is the increasing complexity of literacy tasks at work, perhaps because is easier to fall back on blaming the workers for the inability of a company to move forward financially and competitively.

An ethnographic approach was used by Black et al. (2013) to investigate more closely the idea of a crisis in workers' literacy skills by focusing on how the workers, in three workplaces undergoing change, managed the literacy and numeracy practices embedded in workplace practices. Overall, the findings revealed that managers and workers did not see literacy or numeracy as 'barriers to how workers performed in their existing jobs' and the workers had demonstrated, in these changing work environments, 'the capacity to learn and adapt' (Black, Yasukawa & Brown 2012: 34–35). These findings suggest the crisis is more one of perception than reality. Nevertheless, where employee literacy levels are not commensurate with expanding literacy demands related to workplace change, this could be addressed by governments through a more equitable distribution of literacy and numeracy knowledge and skills in schools, further education contexts, workplaces and communities.

When employees are judged to be inadequate in handling literacy tasks, they are also judged to be not conforming to the new workplace that is seeking to set new goals and new relationships. For those whose work has always involved reading and writing, these changes have been easier than for those who have been used to working through a spoken chain of command. Many workplace research projects into literacy practices have shown that this too easily adopted deficit view of employees' literacy and numeracy skills masks a much more complex picture. For example, in many workplaces, not conforming to literacy practices can be the only form of resistance open to workers when the pace and characteristics of change become overwhelming.

In an extensive ethnographic project undertaken by Belfiore et al. (2004 and reported in Chapter 7 of this book) over a period of six to eight months, four Canadian organisations were studied: a food processing plant, a textile factory, an urban tourist hotel and a high-tech metal parts manufacturer. The study revealed that many so-called workplace literacy problems had other underlying causes that could have been dealt with more effectively through changes in work practices. One example in the textile factory was the mismatch between supervisors wanting employees to complete forms more fully and the pressure to respond quickly to customer requirements, with workers reporting to the researcher that 'there are subtle and not-so-subtle messages that getting the product done and out the door is more important than paperwork' (Belfiore et al. 2004: 75).

Socially oriented research into the literacy practices of workplaces reveals a complex picture, and a more critical orientation to the discourse of crisis and deficit is required. There is a need, for example, to question the 'popular discourse on the role of literacy at work' that workers' low levels of literacy skills are 'a prevailing cause of [the] nations' poor economic performance' (Castleton 2003: 9). The discourse around workplace literacy emphasising the skills, or lack of skills, of individual workers ignores 'the reality of workplaces as communities of workers who possess a diverse range of skills that they use in complementary ways' and contradicts changes in workplace cultures that emphasise teamwork and shared responsibilities (Castleton 2003: 10).

All workplace literacy teachers are ethnographic and literacy researchers who explore the structures and relationships in workplaces in order to assist the employees in their classes. This research effort should include a focus on understanding the ways the texts within the workplace are part of workplace practices and, as in all literacy learning contexts, it should also seek to hear 'workers' understandings (or voices) of work or of literacy at work', which are largely absent from official policy documents and strategy statements (Castleton 2003: 12).

Quotes

To be literate in a workplace means being a master of a complex set of rules and strategies which govern who uses texts, and how, and for what purposes ... [it means knowing] when to speak, when to be quiet, when to write, when to reveal what was written, and when and whether and how to respond to texts already written ...

(Hull 1995: 19)

... secondary education can be thought of as a device for directing members of the society towards specialised economic roles. These specialisations are both horizontal, most generally between production of goods, services and information, and vertical, most generally between professional, vocational, and unqualified labour. It is assumed that students specialise according to their ability or their interest in a field. However, from a socioeconomic perspective, specialisation depends more on social factors such as class, ethnicity and gender.

In considering language and literacy in relation to school and work, secondary education distributes access to *discursive resources*, in differing proportions to different groups in the society. This is a deliberate analogy with the way that economic production distributes *material resources* in differing proportions to different groups. Tertiary-trained workers are generally paid more than vocationally-trained workers, who are paid more than unqualified workers. Tertiary education involves a great deal more reading and writing than vocational training, where unqualified labouring has in the past required very little.

(Korner, McInnes & Rose 2007: 10)

The literacy demands of professional work has not been a major focus of literacy research, perhaps because it is assumed that professional employees have high levels of literacy skills as university graduates. The research that has been undertaken is a response to the increasing numbers of English as an additional language professionals practising in English-speaking contexts or needing to use English in international contexts. One example is in the field of accountancy, where Forey and Nunan (2002) interviewed members of the Hong Kong Society of Accountants and collected texts, which showed 'that 55% of the working week involve written communication' in English (Moore & Burns 2008: 48).

Literacy as lifelong learning in a plurilingual world

Quote

It is clearly possible to go through life using only one language; but it is scarcely possible to go through life using only one register. Typically all adults are multilingual in the 'register' sense: they use language in a variety of different ways, for a variety of different purposes, and hence they are constantly changing their speech styles. This ability to control different registers is a natural human ability; it is built up in adolescence, and school plays a significant part in it. It also seems to be a natural human ability to control different languages, given the right conditions for doing so. Not all adults, obviously, are multilingual in this other sense, of controlling different languages. But

> if we extend the notion of variation in language to include variation in dialect, we shall find that very many more adults are multilingual in this sense: they may not switch among different languages, but they do switch among different dialects of the same language.
>
> (Halliday 2007/1979: 241)

In an interconnected world in which employment and study are increasingly internationalised, changing academic contexts or employment routinely means moving into a new cultural and linguistic terrain. For people displaced for reasons to do with conflict, poverty and environmental change, managing unfamiliar cultural and linguistic domains becomes a matter of survival. An intercultural orientation and a plurilingual mindset are rapidly becoming an essential component of literacy education in the 21st century 'as a societal asset not only to elites but also to linguistic minority populations' (Ortega 2013: 6).

Quotes

... at this historical moment, people around the world engage daily in the complicated social, political, cultural, and psychological work of learning and using literacies in multiple languages and scripts that are enmeshed within other channels or modes of communication and diverse semiotic systems.

(Garcia, Bartlett & Kliefgen 2007: 207)

Intercultural language learning involves developing with learners an understanding of their own language(s) and culture(s) in relation to an additional language and culture. It is a dialogue that allows for reaching a common ground for negotiation to take place, and where variable points of view are recognised, mediated and accepted.

(Liddicoat, Papademetre, Scarino & Kohler 2003: 46 – cited in Scarino & Liddicoat 2009: 33)

Most of the world's population is *plurilingual*, that is, either bilingual or multilingual.[11] Most people, therefore, take part in literacy practices in a plurilingual environment. Nevertheless, studies of literacy, literacy development and literacy education are routinely undertaken from the perspective of separate languages, as if 'language is perceived as a closed and limited entity, governed by fixed boundaries' (Shohamy 2006: 2). This tendency has been identified as a consequence of the 'monolingual mindset', a world view that sees 'everything in terms of a single language' (Clyne 2008: 348), a mindset particularly prevalent where English is the dominant language, even if, in reality, the community is multilingual. A prevailing view that monolingualism is the normal state of affairs, contra the reality, and that plurilingualism is unnecessary or even undesirable, results in a failure to exploit the substantial cultural, social, economic and educational advantages of plurilingualism (Clyne 2005, Ellis 2006, Meakins 2014).

In recent decades researchers have begun to reconceptualise second and foreign language education, in particular the teaching of English to speakers of other languages (TESOL), from a plurilingual point of view. Instead of studying how individual languages are learned and used in isolation, there is a shift towards investigating the interaction and interdependence of languages used in plurilingual settings. Research undertaken from the plurilingual point of view accounts for Indigenous, migrant, heritage and foreign languages as valuable linguistic resources, too often wasted when language and language education policy is based on a monolingual mindset. In particular, a plurilingual perspective emphasises the value of bilingualism and multilingualism, not just to those who are already educationally advantaged, but also as means for advancing more equitable educational outcomes among those whose first languages have not been traditionally recognised as an asset worth developing and building on.

Quote

We argue that government antipathy to bilingual programs for Indigenous students is based on a monolingual worldview that prevents understanding the experiences of multilinguals among individual bureaucrats and politicians, and also renders them willing to disregard the substantial evidence that education in the first language is crucial to later educational achievement in a second language.

(Ellis, Gogolin & Clyne 2010: 449)

The notion of the 'multilingual turn' has been proposed by Ortega (2013: 3) as the most productive approach available to the field of language and literacy education research into the future, and a logical development from the 'social turn' of the previous two decades, which had supplanted earlier 'quantitative, cognitive, positivist epistemologies'. With the 'social turn', researchers explored the relation between variation in language use and the learning of an additional language, reconceptualising as social the role of phenomena such as cognition, grammar, interaction, learning and identity (Ortega 2013: 3–4). The 'multilingual turn' has resulted in researchers identifying learners of an additional language as *emergent bilinguals*, who continue to function in their first language as they learn an additional language (Garcia, 2014, Garcia, Kleifgen & Falchi 2008, Menken 2013).

Quotes

The term EMERGENT BILINGUAL ... refers to students, typically immigrants, children of immigrants, or indigenous peoples, who are adding the dominant state language taught in school to their home language, and becoming bilingual in the process.

(Menken 2013: 438)

Globalisation and increasing language contact have engendered reactions by scholars against traditional, rigid conceptualisations of language with territorial links, galvanising a paradigm shift in applied linguistics. Specifically, a new line of research has emerged that is attentive to issues of language and power, and that seeks to break away from static language constructs. Scholarship aligned to this view offers more complex and fluid understandings of language ... and carrying important implications for the education of emergent bilinguals.

(Menken 2013: 445)

A plurilingual view has led to the recognition that bilinguals and multilinguals use their languages in dynamic and interdependent ways, with the result that the language, and literacy, practices of bilinguals are best described 'along a continuum of language rather than as a binary between first and second language' and the dynamic and flexible use by bilinguals of 'their linguistic resources ... to create meaning' (Menken 2013: 446) is called *translanguaging*.

Multiple terms have emerged to describe literacy practices that involve translanguaging, including *pluriliteracies* (Garcia et al. 2007) and *biliteracy continua* (Hornberger 2013). Translanguaging in literacy is also one aspect of the variability in meaning making covered by the term *multiliteracies* (Cope & Kalantzis 2000). The concepts represented by these terms open up a new, inclusive, and exciting terrain for scholars studying literacy and literacy education.

Quotes

Translanguaging is the act performed by bilinguals of accessing different linguistic features or various modes of what are described as autonomous languages, in order to maximise communicative potential. It is an approach to bilingualism that is centered, not on languages as has often been the case, but on the practices of bilinguals that are readily observable in order to make sense of their multilingual worlds. Translanguaging, therefore, goes beyond what has been termed code-switching, although it includes it.

(Garcia 2014: 140)

Due to opportunities presented by communications technology, there is no need for migrants to give up their heritage languages and cultural bonds – while at the same time happily integrating themselves functionally into the new society. We assume that bi- or multilingual everyday lives become more and more actual practice in future.

At the same time, foreign language learning should serve as a bridge to developing reflexivity about one's own language, and provide metalinguistic awareness as an element of command of the 'mother tongue'.

(Ellis et al. 2010: 456)

Conclusion

This chapter has skimmed across the complex and intricate terrain of the contexts in which adults practise literacy and numeracy skills. It has viewed all these environments from a social perspective as a way of understanding their distinctive features and their interconnections. It is in the field of adult literacy teaching, whether it is a workplace, a community education setting or a tertiary educational institution that the role of literacy in enabling people to live fulfilling and productive lives becomes clear. This chapter has drawn attention to literacies associated with different domains of adult life. Moving from one domain to another, for example, from an educational context to a workplace, can be compared to moving into a new culture and being required to learn a new language. This then brings us to the end of the exploration of literacy cross the lifespan and we move on to the final section of the book which reviews the research frameworks through which researchers explore the wide terrain of literacy and we hear directly from researchers who have followed various pathways through this terrain.

Part III
Literacy Research: A Continuing Project

Introduction

This part begins, in Chapter 6, with a map of socially oriented research methodologies that have been applied to investigate literacy in social contexts, literacy development and literacy teaching practice. Examples of specific projects illustrate the ways in which these different methodologies have been used to respond to theoretical shifts within different disciplines, to examine the development of literacy skills across the lifespan, and to examine the effectiveness of different programming and teaching approaches. This chapter also lists references and resources related to the different research approaches in order to assist readers to identify significant research projects and findings and to read more widely about literacy research.

Chapter 7 rounds off the book with the voices of original researchers, who responded to a number of questions about literacy research projects they have undertaken. This provides a more immediate insight into the diversity of research in this field and strengthens the idea that research is contestable and open to further investigation and developments in thinking. These accounts also illustrate the interconnectedness of much research where one study might question or extend the findings of another. Originally we had thought that this chapter would take the form of summaries of the research projects with comments by the researchers; however, as the researchers responded to the questions in their own distinctive ways, we thought it was better to leave the researchers' own voices to explain and reflect on their work.

We hope this book will encourage readers to be open to the findings of socially oriented literacy research as a means of understanding the complexities around literacy and of reconciling why there are variations in how literacy is viewed and how literacy is taught. It is important that researchers and educators make reasoned, informed contributions to the recurring debates about literacy in order to help others to understand its complexity, the different ways it can be developed and the different ways people use literacy across social contexts. Otherwise the literacy agenda, promoted through the media and through policy, will not reflect the needs of the less powerful and the disadvantaged nor the needs of an open society, but will be controlled by those who want to use their own literacy skills to maintain their authority and to promote their self-interests. For as James Gee, in his points about research listed in Chapter 7, notes 'the point is not for you or me to be *right*, it is for us all together to make things better'.

The best result for this book would be that it encourages students, educators and others, to begin their own research in teaching and other social contexts, even if the research is small-scale and localised. To this end, the explanations and examples of research in this chapter will provide a range of possible models for practitioners and researchers. In Chapter 7, the researchers, who have described their own research projects, in response to the question about what further research they think still needs to be done, have identified possible future areas for research which readers might consider. Indeed as Debra Myhill states, 'the most robust evidence comes from an accumulation of studies, preferably including replication studies conducted by others'. While at the same time, as James Gee suggests, 'young scholars also need to create real innovation and need to feel the need – and right – to engage in theory building', particularly, 'in areas like learning, literacy, diversity, and schooling'.

The chapter concludes with a discussion of what might constitute a continuing broad literacy research project as the 21st century unfolds. As stated in Chapter 1, considering what it means to be literate, how literacy is defined and the best way to teach literacy is difficult because the answers to these questions have shifted through history, are currently shifting and will continue to shift. The concept of literacy will remain a complex one, and the valuable 'set of behaviours' (Wignell n.d: 5) which constitute reading, writing, viewing, composing and numeracy, and which enable people to participate in cultural and social practices, cannot remain fixed, as they must shift in response to changing technologies and aspirations.

6
Researching Literacy:
A Methodological Map

Literacy has been researched using many research methodologies and from within many disciplines including history, linguistics, education, philosophy, semiotics, sociology and anthropology. This chapter presents a map of applied research methodologies that have been used to explore the field of literacy, primarily from social perspectives. It does not claim to be a comprehensive map covering all the forms of socially oriented research that can be applied to literacy, but throughout the chapter references are listed to extend the map in various ways. We have chosen to focus on those approaches which practitioner-researchers would find easier to work with in their local contexts. These approaches include action research, case study research, design-based research, discourse analysis, multimodal research, ethnographic research and verbal protocols. In addition, as shown in Chapter 2, historical research into literacy reveals how measures of what it means to be literate have changed over time. We finish this chapter with a brief explanation of meta-analysis because this statistical approach is now being used in educational fields to summarise findings from past studies in order to generalise about the size and nature of positive or negative effects of particular interventions on student achievement (for example, Hattie 2009). The final section of this chapter looks at what might constitute a continuing broad literacy research project into the 21st century, in which we hope our readers will participate.

In this book we have argued that researching the ways reading and writing have been taught in the past provides literacy researchers and educators with insights into the origin of the perspectives, debates and issues which shape the ways we view literacy and practise literacy education in our own time. An historical perspective also helps researchers and educators evaluate their own contribution in terms of the way it responds to changing demands and contexts. Historical research, like literacy research, can be undertaken on the basis of different theories, models and conceptual frameworks but it can only ever reconstruct and interpret the past on the basis of incomplete evidence obtained through both primary and secondary sources. Primary sources are documents, artefacts or eyewitness accounts of the era under investigation, while secondary sources are descriptions or interpretations of events composed at a later time by those who were not present. Both types of sources need to be evaluated, analysed and interpreted. The techniques of historical research enable literacy researchers to identify constants, changes and trends in literate practices and literacy education, to record the contribution of individuals and institutions, and to evaluate these against the historical record as well as claims made by those defending traditional practices and those proposing new approaches or directions.

Historical research references

Fischer, S. R. (2003) *A history of reading.* Clerkenwell, UK: Reaktion Press.

Fischer, S. R. (2001) *A history of writing.* Clerkenwell, UK: Reaktion Press.

Limage, L. (2005) The growth of literacy in historic perspective: clarifying the role of formal schooling and adult learning opportunities. Paper commissioned for the *EFA Global Monitoring Report 2006, Literacy for Life.* Available at: http://unesdoc.unesco.org/images/0014/001460/146061e.pdf

Murphy, J. J. (Ed). (2012) *A short history of writing instruction: From Ancient Greece to contemporary America.* New York: Routledge.

Stahl, N. A. and Hartman, D. K. (2004) Doing historical research in literacy. In N. K. Duke and M. H. Malette (Eds). *Literacy research methodologies.* New York and London: The Guilford Press, 170–196.

Types of research

A first general question to ask is 'What is research?'; a straightforward answer is that it 'simply means trying to find answers to questions' (Dornyei 2007: 15). Finding answers to questions can be done in two ways. The first is to look at what other people have said through secondary research, for example, in a literature review (Brown 1988). This is an important step in any research project because it can provide a springboard for further inquiry, while at the same time it saves the researcher from going over old ground if, for example, someone else has already answered some of the questions you want to explore. The second way to answer research questions is to gather data through original investigations, which means undertaking primary research (Brown 1988). In this chapter we distinguish between three types of primary research, while acknowledging that there are other types:

1. [1]**Pure basic research** is research undertaken through experimentation or theoretical enquiry to acquire new knowledge without looking for long-term benefits other than the advancement of knowledge.
2. **Strategic basic research** is experimental and theoretical work undertaken to acquire new knowledge necessary for the solution of recognised practical problems.
3. **Applied research** is original work undertaken primarily to acquire new knowledge with a specific application in view, that is, to determine possible uses for the findings of basic research or to determine new ways of achieving some specific and predetermined objectives.

Most literacy and numeracy research is concerned with identifying how people use literacy and numeracy skills in social contexts or with making a difference in the literacy and/or numeracy outcomes of students in educational contexts. Consequently the bulk of literacy research falls within the category of applied research. Nevertheless, many researchers, including those who describe their research in Chapter 7, underpin their applied research with insights from psychology, linguistics or semiotics, insights that have been developed through more theoretical enquiries, and call on the findings of pure basic research to inform their research projects. Research is one means for bringing theoretical considerations to the task of teaching literacy and numeracy.

Quote

Unless teaching is informed by principled pragmatism ... it can make no claim to be a serious professional activity. It becomes hack work ... teachers who reject theory as being irrelevant to practice not only misunderstand the nature of their work, but at the same time undermine the profession. Furthermore they lend support in this way to the enemies of education and so ultimately act against their own interests.

(Widdowson 1990: xi)

A further distinction to make is between quantitative research, which is concerned with gathering measurable data, and qualitative research, which focuses on gathering data through what people say or do. Generally speaking quantitative research is said to be more objective, as it is about numbers, measurement and statistics, whereas qualitative research is said to be more subjective, as it is about interpretation. Quantitative methods for data collection are used in studies based on experimental design. Experimental or quasi-experimental design is 'the method of choice for establishing causal relationships' that can be generalised across contexts (Vellutino & Schatschneider 2004: 145).

Quote

In experimentation, one or more independent variables are manipulated by the researcher and their impact is monitored using one or more dependent variables.

(Cooksey & McDonald 2011: 337)

Experimental methods have their origin in the natural sciences and in studies undertaken under laboratory conditions, where variables are more easily controlled. Even when undertaken under laboratory conditions, experimental findings must be replicated to confirm a causal relationship. In social sciences, such as linguistics and education, it is much more difficult to control the experience of human participants, so techniques such as random assignment to interventions or statistical controls are used instead. If, for example, random assignment is not possible because it is being conducted in one particular classroom or workplace, the study is considered quasi-experimental, and the findings less generalisable. Quantitative methods in the social sciences are also used to measure and compare statistical data gathered, for example, through survey responses and test results. The challenge for researchers using quantitative methods is to ensure that claims about the statistical significance of findings can be defended. In contrast, data collected using qualitative methods are analysed on the basis of frameworks used, for example, to code spoken language transcripts, written texts or images according to a system of concepts or categories. The results are then interpreted.

In the past, these two approaches have been seen by some as in opposition to each other, but obviously more than one research approach can be used and 'applied linguists have by and large steered clear of such extreme positions' (Dornyei 2007: 10). Indeed, combining quantitative and qualitative approaches is often seen as a way of strengthening a research project. When quantitative and qualitative approaches are combined in mixed or multi-method studies, often one approach is dominant. In sequential designs, the non-dominant approach might be used in preliminary studies to refine the research design or in follow-up studies to confirm or explain findings. Dornyei (2007:10) describes a 'good enough' researcher as one who must 'master some knowledge of both qualitative and quantitative research, as well as ways of combining them' because, as he explains, 'the most important thing about doing research is that we get down to it, *get our feet wet* and as a result get *hooked* on what is a very exciting activity.

Quantitative literacy research may involve, for example, collecting reading and writing test scores prior to and after a particular literacy teaching intervention in the classroom, as in Table 6.1 which shows examples of miscues identified and counted as adult students read a text prior to and after a specific reading intervention in their classrooms.

Many research projects use quantitative data as a way of identifying a research focus or a research group. Examples include using statistical population data or national testing data to identify particular groups. Other researchers refer to statistical data in their research findings. Two examples are found in the research projects described in Chapter 7

Table 6.1 Miscue scores prior to and after reading intervention

Beginning of course	End of course
M	No miscues
On Sunday morning I took my daughter ^children to a birthday party. While she was at the party, I did the shopping at the supermarket. In the afternoon I took the children to a ^a park and they rode their bikes. I was very tired on Sunday night and went to bed early.	On Sunday morning I took my daughter to a birthday party. While she was at the party, I did the shopping at the supermarket. In the afternoon I took the children to a park and they rode their bikes. I was very tired on Sunday night and went to bed early.
A	On Friday evening I went to dinner at a friend's house. We ate lots of good food and drank a bit of wine ^wb. On Saturday morning I got up early ^w and went to the market. I bought fruit, vegetables, fish and meat. In the afternoon I did some ^some housework then played with the children. On Saturday night I watched a video with my husband.
On Friday evening I went to dinner at a friend's house ^home. We ate lots of good food and drank a bit of / wine. On Saturday morning I got ^w up early and went to the market. I bought fruit, vegetables, fish and meat. In the afternoon I did / some housework then played with the children. On Saturday night I watched a video with my husband.	
L	No miscues
On Sunday morning I took my daughter to a birthday party. While she was at the party, I did the shopping at the supermarket. In the afternoon I took the children to a / park and they rode their bikes ^took them bikes. I was very tired on Sunday night and went to bed early	On Sunday morning I took my daughter to a birthday party. While she was at the party, I did the shopping at the supermarket. In the afternoon I took the children to a park and they rode their bikes. I was very tired on Sunday night and went to bed early.
Codes: daughter ^children = substitution good = omission	a / park = hesitation market = repetition

Source: de Silva Joyce, Hood & Rose (2008: 18)

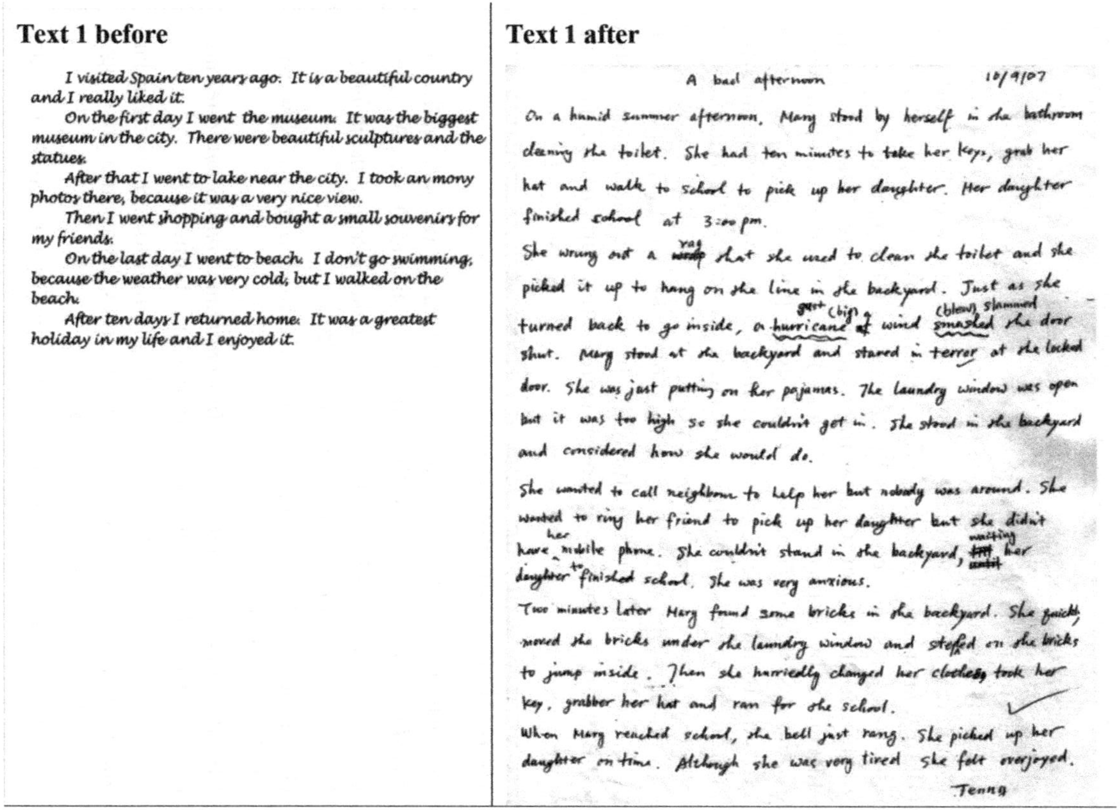

Text 1 before

I visited Spain ten years ago. It is a beautiful country and I really liked it.

On the first day I went the museum. It was the biggest museum in the city. There were beautiful sculptures and the statues.

After that I went to lake near the city. I took an mony photos there, because it was a very nice view.

Then I went shopping and bought a small souvenirs for my friends.

On the last day I went to beach. I don't go swimming, because the weather was very cold, but I walked on the beach.

After ten days I returned home. It was a greatest holiday in my life and I enjoyed it.

Text 1 after

A bad afternoon 10/9/07

On a humid summer afternoon, Mary stood by herself in the bathroom cleaning the toilet. She had ten minutes to take her keys, grab her hat and walk to school to pick up her daughter. Her daughter finished school at 3:00 pm.

She wrung out a ~~mop~~ rag that she used to clean the toilet and she picked it up to hang on the line in the backyard. Just as she turned back to go inside, a hurricane (big) gust of wind smashed (blew) slammed the door shut. Mary stood at the backyard and stared in terror at the locked door. She was just putting on her pajamas. The laundry window was open but it was too high so she couldn't get in. She stood in the backyard and considered how she would do.

She wanted to call neighbour to help her but nobody was around. She wanted to ring her friend to pick up her daughter but she didn't have her mobile phone. She couldn't stand in the backyard, ~~till~~ ~~until~~ waiting her daughter to finished school. She was very anxious.

Two minutes later Mary found some bricks in the backyard. She quickly moved the bricks under the laundry window and stepped on the bricks to jump inside. Then she hurriedly changed her clothes, took her key, grabber her hat and ran for the school.

When Mary reached school, the bell just rang. She picked up her daughter on time. Although she was very tired she felt overjoyed.

Tenna

Figure 6.1 Comparison of student texts before and after a specific reading intervention
Source: de Silva Joyce et al. (2008: 22–23)

below. Brian Byrne states '[o]ur studies have shown that in the Australian National Assessment Program – Literacy and Numeracy (NAPLAN) genetic variability accounts for at least 80% of reading scores – although there are a lot of qualifications. Writing has less variability (50%)'. Maria Estela Brisk refers to quantitative data when she explains the results after a planned pedagogical intervention as follows: '[t]he school advanced from one of the ten worst performing schools in the city to Level 1, the highest level of performance'.

Qualitative literacy research often involves recording and transcribing classroom interactions or gathering students' written texts in order to analyse for changes in the texts after a particular intervention in the classroom. One example from Chapter 7 is the research undertaken by Frances Christie and Beverly Derewianka, in which they used Systemic Functional Linguistics (SFL) as a tool to analyse texts and to look for development in students' writing. In a further example, the two sample texts in Figure 6.1 were collected in a study designed to compare the standard of writing in adult student texts prior to and following the reading intervention in Table 6.1. The texts were evaluated quantitatively, by awarding each one a score against features such as genre, language and formatting, as shown in Table 6.2.

General research references

Creswell, J. W. (2014) *Research design: Qualitative, quantitative and mixed methods approaches* (4th Edition). Thousand Oaks, CA: Sage.

Duke, N. K. and Mallette, M. H. (2004) *Literacy research methodologies*. New York and London: The Guildford Press.

Gomm, R. (2009) *Key concepts in social research methods*. New York: Palgrave Macmillan.

Paltridge, B. and Phakiti, A. (2010) *Continuum companion to research methods in applied linguistics*. London: Continuum.

Riazi, A. M. and Candlin, C. (2014) Mixed-methods research in language teaching and learning: Opportunities, issues and challenges. *Language Teaching*, 47(2), 135–173.

Winkle-Wagner, R., Hunter, C. A. and Hunderliter Ortloff, D. (Eds). (2013) *Bridging the gap between theory and practice in educational research*. New York: Palgrave Macmillan.

Table 6.2   Scoring as a comparison across texts

Table 3   Comparative analysis of student story text performances

	CSWE II sample recount		Student sample	
Purpose	simple personal recount	2	successful narrative, resolving complicating events	3
Staging	orientation, record of events	2	orientation, complication, resolution	3
Field	events and places in personal travel experience	2	imaginative, intricate plot	3
Tenor	some feelings and appreciation of places	1	engages with series of problems and reactions	3
Mode	simple spoken English, few written features	2	more written features, elaborations, variety of sentence structures	3
Phases	series of episodes in tour	2	series of problems within complication——building tension	3
Lexis	common lexis of places—Spain, country, museum, city, sculptures, statues, lake, view	2	rich lexis building field—humid summer afternoon, wrung-out rag, turned back to go inside ...	3
Conjunction	simple succession—on the first day, after that, then, on the last day plus cause because	2	variety of time resources—ten minutes, just as, two minutes later, quickly, on time	3
Reference	simple reference to self and preceding things—I, it	1	variety of reference to people and things	2
Appraisal	common feelings and appreciation—beautiful, liked, biggest, very nice, greatest	1	appraisal used to build problems and reactions—stared in terror, very anxious, hurriedly, overjoyed	2
Grammar	problems with number and tense—an mony photos, small souvenirs, I don't go swimming	2	few problems, variety of sentence structures used creatively	3
Spelling	one error, many	2	accurate spelling of infrequent words	3
Punctuation	accurate sentence punctuation	2	accurate sentence punctuation	2
Presentation	uses paragraphs for each episode	2	uses paragraphs for stages, title, fair handwriting	2
Total	25		38	

Source: de Silva Joyce et al. (2008: 24).

Research methods

Quote

Conceptualising the object of study and what can be known about it is thus a worldview issue, which depends on the researcher's explicit or implicit reference to the principles of a particular paradigm. 'Methodology', in our view, is the conceptual framework that helps researchers to design their study. In such a framework, responses to the question of the nature of reality and what can be known about it as informed by a particular paradigm will be framed at different

> levels and stages of the research process, from formulating research questions to using appropriate data and conducting analyses from which to draw relevant inferences.
>
> (Riazi & Candlin 2014: 136)

The term *method* has been defined as 'a way of doing something, especially in accordance with a definite plan'.[2] Researchers have adopted many methods for undertaking research within the field of literacy. This section will outline seven methods that are most frequently used within applied literacy research. Again this is not to deny that there are many more methods with many variations; however, the purpose here is to explore those methods that have, over recent decades, helped researchers to investigate the complexity of what it is to be literate in a diverse and changing world and of how literacy teaching can be improved and can 'make things better' (see Gee Chapter 7 in this volume). By examining how research in which the methods outlined below are used has contributed to and continues to contribute to our understandings of how people use literacy and numeracy in social and work contexts and how different approaches to teaching literacy and numeracy meet the needs of different students, we hope readers will be inspired to undertake their own research if they have not already done so, perhaps starting with a small-scale and localised project.

Some studies are based on a single approach selected from those described below and others are based on a combination of different methods. While exploring these methods, and the studies in which they have been used, it is important to see all literacy research as 'an accumulation of studies' (Myhill Chapter 7 in this volume) that build on one another or, in some cases, challenge one another. If research is to be a way of furthering our understanding of literacy and numeracy and their implications, then it is important to consider seriously research that might not support nor agree with our particular view. This would mean entering into dialogue and arguing, on the basis of evidence, against the conservative trend towards 'literacy reductivism' which is emerging at a time 'when, ironically, the whole notion of what it means to be literate has become increasingly complex' (Ewing 2006: 2), an approach which, of course, relies on other researchers taking the same open approach to debate.

Action research

> ### Quote
>
> Action research involves a self-reflective, systematic and critical approach to enquiry by participants who are at the same time members of the research community. The aim is to identify problematic situations or issues considered by the participants to be worthy of investigation in order to bring about critically informed changes in practice. Action research is underpinned by democratic principles in that ownership of change is invested in those who conduct the research.
>
> (Burns in Cornwell 1999)

Action research is not a new approach to research. According to Burns (1999: 26) [t]he seeds of action research are to be found as early as the late nineteenth century'. It developed from the work of a range of early educators who were involved in reforming educational practice, such as John Dewey who sought to democratise educational practice and research (Burns 1999). It has also been used widely across different fields such as health, psychology and business but, for some time, it has been accorded a lower status than research considered to be more academically rigorous, particularly quantitative research. However, the growing acceptance of action research as a legitimate way of understanding how, for example, teachers, students, nurses, doctors and employees operate in their work contexts, and how their work impacts on others, has accompanied a growing acceptance of other qualitative forms of research. Action research has become 'part of the trend towards socially constructed and contextualised research' (Burns 2005: 20).

> ### Quote
>
> The process usually begins by participants [...] perceiving a critical gap or dilemma between current practice and their more ideal view of practice. The gap or dilemma may relate to something they have been puzzled, uncertain or dissatisfied with for a while, a 'burning question' or issue they have always wanted to experiment with, a change they would like to see happening in themselves or their learners, or a desire to make a difference in the way things are generally organized in their classrooms or schools.
>
> (Burns 2010a: 3)

Action research can be undertaken by a single researcher, who wants to investigate a particular issue or problem in their work environment, and how the problem might be addressed. Action research can also be a collaborative activity involving groups of practitioners working together or with an experienced action research leader. This was the approach adopted in a unique ten-year project in the Australian Adult Migrant English Program (AMEP) where collaborative action research brought groups of teachers across the country together to work with experienced researchers. Over the ten years, the teachers and researchers investigated a range of issues around curriculum planning and classroom practice, which led to the following publications that demonstrate how action research can be used to investigate both broader and more detailed issues in education.

- *Teachers' Voices: Exploring course design in a changing curriculum*
- *Teachers' Voices 2: Teaching disparate learner groups*
- *Teachers' Voices 3: Teaching critical literacy*
- *Teachers' Voices 4: Staying learner-centred in a competency-based curriculum*
- *Teachers' Voices 5: A new look at reading practices (see Anne Burns contribution in Chapter 7)*
- *Teachers' Voices 6: Teaching casual conversation*
- *Teachers' Voices 7: Teaching vocabulary*
- *Teachers' Voices 8: Explicitly supporting reading and writing in the classroom*

Quote

… working collaboratively with others in an action research process means that teachers can simultaneously draw on and distance themselves from their established approaches to classroom action which may often be undertaken implicitly or intuitively. This process helps to build, in a collective and usable way, generalisable and realistic models for wider use by other teachers.

(Burns in Burns & Hood 1995: 5)

Kemmis and McTaggart (1988) promoted a four-step action research process – planning, action, observation and reflection (see Figure 6.2 which focuses on these action research steps in relation to science teaching). These four steps have remained the basis of action research over the

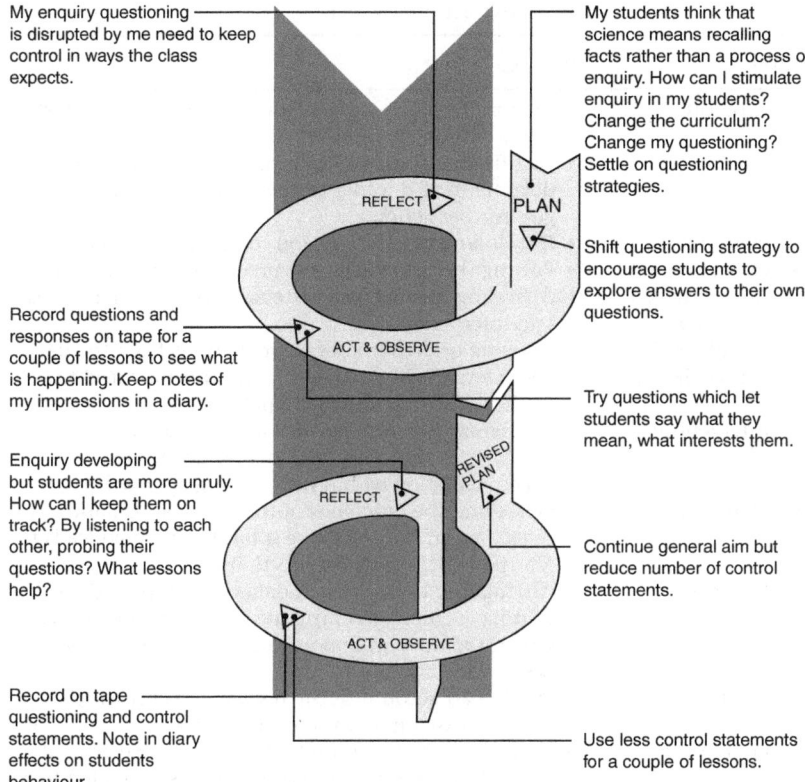

Figure 6.2 Steps in action research cycle
Source: Kemmis & McTaggart (1988 in Burns 1999: 33)

years, with some criticism and modifications coming from writers who want to build in greater rigour or more flexibility in order to respond to particular contexts or from others who want to extend the model (for example, Ebbutt 1985, McNiff 1988, McNiff & Whitehead 2011, Elliott 1991).

Burns (1999) extends the Kemmis and McTaggart model into a collaborative framework of eleven phases, outlined in Table 6.3. Burns emphasises that these phases represent a general framework from which teachers may choose different processes. It aims to guide researchers in action research, which should be flexible and adaptive, as the phases and the processes within the phases need to respond to issues or insights that arise during the research process.

Table 6.3   Phases in collaborative action research

Phases	Processes
1 Exploring	• Identifying a general issue or idea which is the starting point for the research
2 Identifying	• Fact finding through, for example, recording and documenting in order to clarify the issue and to suggest further action
3 Planning	• Developing a plan of action for gathering data
4 Collecting data	• Putting the data collection procedures into action
5 Analysing & reflecting	• Analysing data using a systematic process of analysis and interpretation
6 Hypothesising & speculating	• Drawing up hypotheses or predictions from the data about what is likely to occur and this may lead to further action to test the hypotheses
7 Intervening	• Changing classroom practice in response to the hypotheses which may involve deliberate experimentation with other teaching approaches
8 Observing	• Observing the outcomes of the intervention and reflecting on how effective it has been which leads to a further cycle of data collection
9 Reporting	• Articulating the activities, data collection, and results that have emerged during the action research process which provides an opportunity to critique the processes with others
10 Writing	• Writing an account of the research project which ensures dissemination of project findings
11 Presenting	• Giving a formal presentation to ensure that the research processes and findings are disseminated to a wider audience

Source: Adapted from Burns (1999: 36–42)

Action research is primarily concerned with reflecting on and improving practice at the local level and involves members of the local context. Its appeal to many teachers is its practical significance in dealing with their own problems and the fact that it can be integrated into their daily teaching practice. Action research, whether undertaken individually or in collaboration with colleagues and/or researchers, has the following characteristics (adapted from NSW Department of Education and Training 2010: 2):

• It is integrated in that it is conducted as part of a teacher's normal daily practice.
• It is reflective in that it is a process which alternates between implementation and critical reflection.

- It is flexible in that its methods, data collection and interpretation are refined in the light of the understanding gained during the research process.
- It is active in that it is a process designed to generate change in small steps.
- It is relevant in that it meets the needs of teachers and/or their students.
- It is cyclical in that it involves a number of cycles with each clarifying issue leading to a deeper understanding and more meaningful outcomes.
- It is focused on a single issue of improvement.
- It is collaborative in that teachers, leaders and/or researchers can work together to improve outcomes.
- It is planned in that it adopts an organised approach to answering a question.
- It involves learning through the simultaneous construction of new knowledge by researchers about own their practice.

An example of a funded literacy focused action research project in adult English as second-language (ESL) classes is outlined in the box below (de Silva Joyce et al. 2008). This example illustrates the variety of processes that can be incorporated into action research.

Action research project example

Investigating the impact of intensive reading pedagogy in adult literacy

Reading is a crucial skill for participation in adult life. However, teaching those who cannot read or who have very poor reading skills is a complex process. This is particularly true for adults from a non-English speaking background, and when classes consist of learners with different reading abilities, sporadic attendance patterns, and study, the authors introduced six adult literacy tutors to a particular reading methodology, known as Reading-to-Learn (Rose 2007), and examined how this approach could help adult learners from non-English speaking backgrounds become efficient and independent readers.

Six teachers in adult literacy classrooms located at two adult and community education (ACE) colleges and one technical and further education (TAFE) college participated in the project. The study comprised a professional development component to introduce teachers to the methodology, and to cover the principles and techniques underpinning the approach. The teachers also used 'action research', which involved implementing the new approach in the classroom and participating in workshop discussions to review and analyse classroom data.

The teachers involved in the project reported a number of positive outcomes, largely in the context of changed teaching practices:

- Their professional knowledge was strengthened and they developed a greater awareness of language. This enabled them to improve their ability to select appropriate well-constructed texts, identify key phases of texts, prepare texts for reading, and to manage the process that helped students to make connections between meanings and words.
- The more conscious planning processes demanded by the new approach meant they managed their time more effectively.
- They paid more attention to all students in the class, especially those for whom reading was most challenging, and found they praised students more frequently.

In terms of the students, teachers reported the following gains:

- Students' writing and reading greatly improved, as did their grasp of grammatical structures. The method also increased their enthusiasm for discussing the language of the texts they were reading.
- Although this method focuses on reading, it is also the basis for learning to write. Teachers reported widespread improvement in writing ability, attributing this to a developing awareness of text structure, an expanded vocabulary and a growing understanding of grammar, gained through the detailed reading, and the joint emotional impediments, such as a fear of failure or ridicule. In this rewriting stages. Students were able to write texts across a much wider range of genres.
- The reliance by ESL students on electronic dictionaries (for translations into their own languages) was greatly reduced as they became familiar with the approach. In some cases students gave up their dictionaries entirely as they were introduced to more effective ways of understanding texts.
- Attendance patterns were significantly improved which also improved the potential for success.

An action research project is often seen as a way of engaging teachers in professional development, as professional development sessions are often integrated into the overall project design. This was one of the aims of a project involving researchers from the School of Education at Murdoch University and teachers at Waikiki Primary School in Perth, Western Australia (Murcia & Powell n.d.). The focus of the project was to explore innovative teaching strategies to improve student numeracy outcomes across the whole school and, interestingly, to incorporate partnerships with parents.

> This project demonstrated the valuable role action research could take in the professional development of teachers. The process supported a constructivist approach to professional learning and facilitated real, practical action based on the numeracy learning needs of students in the school. Learning through action research conducted as a part of, not separate from, daily classroom practice provided a real, meaningful context in which teachers were motivated by their own students' needs and could observe improvements in their progress.
>
> (Murcia & Powell n.d.: 3–4)

The *Teacher learning for European literacy education (TeL4ELE) project* (Acevedo, Coffin, Gouveia, Lövstedt & Whittaker reported in Chapter 7) drew on principles of action research (Kemmis & McTaggart 1988) to promote a learning-through-doing approach, with teacher reflection on self and student learning becoming a source of data. The study provided an evidence-based approach to professional development and classroom learning, an approach which made 'a significant difference to the developing awareness, understanding and practice' of the research participants.

Action research projects can easily be undertaken as localised studies. It can be a way of bringing colleagues together to solve common on-site issues and it, therefore, offers a valuable entry point into the fields of literacy and numeracy research for would-be teacher researchers. The action research projects outlined above illustrate different orientations to this research approach.

Action research references

Action Research Journal (Editor in Chief – Hilary Bradbury) Sage publications – http://www.sagepub.com

Burns A. (1999) *Collaborative action research for English language teachers*. Cambridge: Cambridge University Press.

Burns A. (2005) Understanding action research. In A. Burns and H. de Silva Joyce (Eds). *Teachers' Voices 8: Explicitly supporting reading and writing in the classroom.* Sydney: Macquarie University, 17–25.

Burns, A. (2010b) *Doing action research in English language teaching. A guide for practitioners.* New York: Routledge.

Coghlan, D. and Brannick, T. (2014) *Doing action research in your own organisation.* London: Sage Publications.

Kemmis, S. and McTaggart, R. (Eds). (1981) *The action research planner.* Geelong: Deakin University Press.

Kemmis, S., McTaggart, R. and Nixon, R. (2014) *The action research planner: Doing critical participatory action research.* New York and London: Springer.

Klein, S. R. (2012) *Action research methods: Plain and simple.* London: Palgrave Macmillan.

McNiff, J. and Whitehead, J. (2011) *All you need to know about action research* (2nd edition). London: Sage Publications.

NSW Department of Education and Training. 2010. *Action research in education: Guidelines* (2nd Edition). Sydney: NSW Department of Education and Training – available at https://www.det.nsw.edu.au/proflearn/docs/pdf/actreguide.pdf

Sager, R. (2000) *Guiding school improvement with action research.* Association for Supervision and Curriculum Development (ASCD) – available at http://www.ascd.org

Stringer, E. T. (2013) *Action research* (4th Edition). London: Sage Publications.

Taylor, C., Wilkie, M. and Baser, J. (2006) *Doing action research: A guide for school support staff.* London: Paul Chapman Publishing Ltd.

Teacher's voices series Volumes 1 to 8. Search for Teachers voices at http://www.ameprc.mq.edu.au

Case studies

Quote

Case study refers to the collection and presentation of detailed information about a particular participant or small group, frequently including the accounts of subjects themselves. A form of qualitative descriptive research, the case study looks intensely at an individual or small participant pool, drawing conclusions only about that participant or group and only in that specific context. Researchers do not focus on the discovery of a universal, generalisable truth, nor do they typically look for cause-effect relationships; instead, emphasis is placed on exploration and description.

(Colorado State University – http://writing.colostate.edu/guides – accessed 9.3.2015)

Case study research is closely aligned to ethnographic research and is a form of qualitative research. It has, at times, been dismissed as 'a weak sibling among social science methods' (Yin 1994 in Barone 2004), particularly when large-scale experimental studies were seen as more rigorous. Case study is a descriptive form of research that focuses on a specific individual or a small group of people. Barone (2004 following Stake 2000) outlines three types of case studies. These are *intrinsic case studies* that seek to understand a particular case simply because it is interesting; *instrumental case studies* that focus on particular cases to provide insights into a broader theory or research agenda, and *collective or multiple case studies* that seek to study a phenomenon with multiple cases, thus building a stronger base for understanding the phenomenon. These case study categories[3] can be expanded to illustrate how this method can be adapted for different purposes:

1. **Illustrative case studies** are descriptive studies focusing on one or two instances of an event or one or two subjects. They aim to demonstrate elements in order to familiarise the researcher and readers with the situation or subject and to develop a common language about the topic in question.
2. **Exploratory (or pilot) case studies** are concentrated case studies undertaken before implementing a large-scale investigation in order to identify questions and select types of measurement prior to the main investigation.
3. **Cumulative case studies** seek to aggregate information from several sites collected at different times to enable greater generalisation.
4. **Critical instance case studies** examine one or more sites in order to investigate a situation of unique interest or to question or challenge generalisations or universal assertions.

In literacy and language research there have been many instances of intrinsic case studies of single children that focus on their developing language skills (for example, Halliday 1975, Painter 1999) and case studies of single children focusing on their developing literacy skills (for example, Bissex 1980, Butler 1975, White 1956).

Although the 1950s saw case studies being used in academic study to enable students to 'formulate their own questions' and to learn from actual situations (Writing @CSU Guide), in the 1980s and 1990s case study research began to expand as people were inspired by the work of researchers such as Shirley Brice Heath and her seminal publication *Ways with words: Language, life and work in communities and classrooms* (1983). Heath's work can be seen as crossing between case study research and ethnography as it 'was conducted over 10 years and looked at the home, community and school' (Barone 2004) through families in those communities. This was one of the first research studies to draw a clear link between home and community language and literacy practices, and school achievement.

An interesting research project, although not literacy or numeracy focused, is that of Rose (2004) in which he uses a multiple case study approach in studying competent workers in occupations that are classified as unskilled, semi-skilled and skilled trades, including waitressing, hairdressing, plumbing, carpentry, construction, electrical and welding. His aim in studying these multiple cases was to identify the intellectual processes required by the day-to-day work tasks that competent workers undertake. Rose's focus was on cognition and the link between hand and brain, but his case studies reveal complex contextualised uses of literacy and numeracy skills, which only become clear through case study research involving close observation and follow-up questioning with those being observed.

Quote

One of the findings of this research is that a wide range of mathematical concepts and operations is embodied in carpentry's artifacts and routines of practice, and ways suited to the properties of materials and the demands of production. The carpenter's math[s] is tangible and efficient. Take, for example, measurement. The ruler and the framing square provide measurements, but so do objects created in the shop, like the layout stick, and one piece of wood, precisely cut, then functions as the measure for another. Tools are also used as measuring devices. A sixteen-inch claw hammer laid sideways on a wall provides a quick measure for the location of studs in a wall frame. And carpenters use their hands and fingers to measure and compare. They develop an eye for length and dimensions, but also for relations and correspondences. Disciplined perception. Working in the shop, the young carpenter learns a range of other mathematical concepts: symmetry, proportion, congruence, the properties of angles. Planing straight the edge of a board, cutting angles on the mitre box, laying out the pieces of a cabinet's face frame to check for an even fit – through these activities [the young carpenters] see mathematical ideas manifested, and feel them, too, gaining a sense of trueness and error.

(Rose 2004: 97)

Case study research is strengthened by the researcher spending extended periods of time in the field. This time is spent collecting multiple sources of information, through multiple observations and/or interviews or the collection of documents, which develops a chain of evidence leading to a conclusion which is reviewed by the informants (Yin 1994 in Barone 2004). Yin (1991) proposes that, from the outset, case study research needs to adopt a theoretical perspective, for example, observing a child's reading practices across multiple formats could be informed by a socio-linguistic theoretical approach which is concerned with not only what the child reads but what uses they make of the texts they read in books or on screen. The following are eight components of case study design (adapted from Yin 1991) that need to be considered:

1. The question(s) being asked
2. The proposition being put forward
3. The data to be collected
4. The method for collecting the data
5. The method for analysing the data
6. The way the data is linked to the proposition
7. The criteria for interpreting the findings
8. The way the findings will be communicated to others

The case study method offers the researcher a flexibility that many other methods do not offer, with the possibility of more questions arising or questions becoming more focused, as the situation is explored. In choosing the case study method, researchers need to be aware that, while this method offers the opportunity to gather intense data around a situation or subject, it runs the risks of being too subjective and inferring too much from a relatively small sample.

Case studies usually require the researcher to spend a great deal of time in the field, leading to the collection of large amounts of data that may be difficult to manage. As case studies generally focus on particular people in particular locations, ethical considerations need to be carefully addressed, which include ensuring there are no conflicts of interest or personal biases that may affect the findings. Merriam (1985 following Owens 1982) offers six techniques for improving the credibility of case study research:

1. Prolonged data gathering on site
2. Triangulation using a variety of data sources, which means using more than one method to gather data as a way to validate the data and the research findings

3. Corroboration of interpretation of the data with the informants who provide the raw data
4. Collection of referential materials from the site that relate to findings and interpretation
5. Development of thick descriptions, which in case study research means not just describing the informants and what they say but the research context
6. Consultation with peers

Quote

Even though case study methodology suffers from definitional problems and is not always clearly distinguishable from other qualitative research, it nevertheless offers a means of investigating questions important to education. The growing interest in using case study in educational research reflects the need on the part of practitioners and researchers alike to deal with questions of meaning and process that can best be answered by understanding the context in which they exist.

(Merriam 1985: 214)

A review of literacy research over the past four decades shows that case study research is 'important in our understandings of literacy' (Barone 2004: 25). It can be a complex process to set up case study research in terms of seeking permission from informants, eliminating bias and ensuring that the data collection processes provide enough variety of information to be triangulated and interpreted in order to answer the research questions. 'However for those who engage in this form of research, the rewards are many' as it applies to real life and 'facilitates understanding of complex situations, understandings that cannot be made explicit in most other research designs' (Barone 2004: 25).

Case study research references

Adult Literacy Agency (NALA). (2013) *Adult literacy and numeracy in action: Six case studies of practice work in Ireland.* Dublin: National Adult Literacy Agency.

Barone, D. M. (2004) Case study research. In N. K. Duke and M. H. Mallette (Eds). *Literacy research methodologies.* New York and London: The Guildford Press National.

Baxter, P. and Jack, S. (2008) Qualitative case study methodology: Study design and implementation for novice researchers. *The Qualitative Report* Vol. 13 No. 4 December 2008, 544–559. Available at: http://www.nova.edu

Colorado State University. Writing @ CSU Guide–Case Studies – available at http://writing.colostate.edu/guides – accessed 9.3.2015.

Merriam, S. B. (1985) The case study in educational research: A review of selected literature. *Journal of Educational Thought* Vol. 19 No. 3, 204–217. Available at: http://www.jstor.org

Mills, A. J., Durepos, G. and Wiebe, E. (Eds). (2010) *Encyclopedia of case study research*. Thousand Oaks, CA: Sage Publications.

Yin, R. K. (2013) *Case study research: Design and methods* (5th Edition). Thousand Oaks CA: Sage.

Design-based research

Design-based research (DBR) is a more recent approach to literacy research that employs 'small, pragmatic, planned and classroom data-informed interventions, designed with the intention of developing theory about and demonstrating evidence of effective literacy pedagogic practice' (Comber, Freebody, Nixon, Carrington & Morgan in Chapter 7).

This approach to research is increasingly being applied in literacy teaching contexts and in fact six of the projects described by researchers in Chapter 7 can be described as design-based research. For example, in Chapter 7 Comber, Freebody, Nixon, Carrington and Morgan describe a four-year design-based research project that involved teacher-researchers working with university researchers. The *New literacy demands in the middle years: learning from design experiments project* aimed to document and improve student literacy in the middle years (Years five to nine) using design experiments. The project was collaborative in that the teachers participated in the design and implementation of the classroom interventions.

Quote

... design-based research, which blends empirical educational research with the theory-driven design of learning environments, is an important methodology for understanding how, when and why educational innovations work in practice. Design-based researchers' innovations embody specific theoretical claims about teaching and learning, and help us understand the relationships among

> educational theory, designed artefact and practice. Design is central in efforts to foster learning, create usable knowledge, and advance theories of learning and teaching in complex settings. Design-based research also may contribute to the growth of human capacity for subsequent educational reform.
>
> (The Design-based Research Collective 2003: 5)

The increased use of this research method can be seen as an attempt to bring theory and research closer to practice and to counter what some see as a credibility gap between practitioners and researchers. The issues around this type of research include assessing the success of a particular intervention in terms of learning and, if researchers want to claim that the intervention could be successful in other settings, then they need to 'study the effects across a variety of settings in order to generalise' (The Design-based Research Collective 2003: 5).[4]

Design-based research 'views a successful innovation as a joint product of the designed intervention and the context' and is not concerned with simply 'perfecting a particular product' but with inquiring 'into the nature of learning in a complex system' and refining 'generative or predictive theories of learning' (The Design-based Research Collective 2003: 7). This research approach 'relies on techniques used in other research paradigms, like thick descriptive datasets, systematic analysis of data with carefully defined measures, and consensus building within the field around interpretations of data' (The Design-based Research Collective 2003: 7). Design research is an iterative and lengthy process comprising four connected phases as shown in Figure 6.3. The following explanation of these phases has been adapted from Herrington, Reeves and Oliver (2010: 6–14).

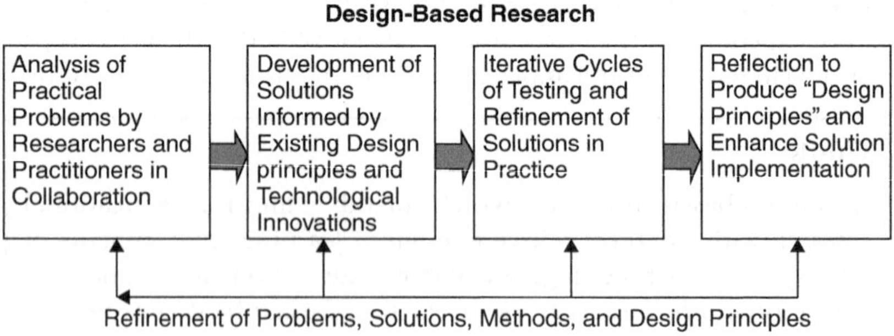

Design-Based Research

| Analysis of Practical Problems by Researchers and Practitioners in Collaboration | Development of Solutions Informed by Existing Design principles and Technological Innovations | Iterative Cycles of Testing and Refinement of Solutions in Practice | Reflection to Produce "Design Principles" and Enhance Solution Implementation |

Refinement of Problems, Solutions, Methods, and Design Principles

Figure 6.3 Steps in design-based research
Source: From Amiel & Reeves (2008: 34)

Phase 1 Analysis of practical problems by researchers and practitioners

A significant educational problem is identified and explored as a crucial first step in creating a purpose and focus for the research. This phase can also involve the researchers thinking of a solution, for example, a technology tool, a pedagogic strategy or an explicit teaching cycle.

Phase 2 Development of solutions informed by existing design principles and technological innovations

A solution to the problem (or an intervention) is proposed that can be implemented in the educational setting. This may be found in the literature, in a relevant theory that can guide thinking or in an existing design principle that has addressed a similar problem.

Phase 3 Iterative cycles of testing and refinement of solutions in practice

The learning solution or intervention designed and developed in Phase 2 is implemented and evaluated in practice. Qualitative and quantitative methods can be used in these processes.

Phase 4 Reflection to produce design principles and enhance solution implementation

Following implementation, evaluation and refinement through cycles, the entire process is reviewed with reflection on how the design principles can inform future development and implementation decisions.

Quote

By trying to promote objectivity while attempting to facilitate the intervention, design-based researchers regularly find themselves in the dual intellectual roles of advocate and critic. Although there are no simple solutions to what we see as a necessary tension arising from the coupling of empirical research to design, it is possible to employ specific research methods to question the designer-researcher's tacitly held assumptions. In particular, design-based research typically triangulates multiple sources and kinds of data to connect intended and unintended outcomes to processes of enactment. In our view, methods that document processes of enactment provide critical evidence to establish warrants for claims about why outcomes occurred.

(The Design-based Research Collective 2003: 7)

Design-based research can provide three useful outcomes – improved design principles, a product that can be shared more widely and enhancement of professional development for those involved in the research (Herrington, Reeves & Oliver 2010). The overall aims of this approach can be understood as improving educational practice in context, exploring ways of creating new and innovative learning and teaching environments, and developing contextually based theories of teaching and learning. It provides 'a lens for understanding how theoretical claims about teaching and learning can be transformed into effective learning in educational settings' (The Design-based Research Collective 2003: 7).

Design-based research references

Anderson, T. and Shattuck, J. (2012) Design-based research: A decade of progress in educational research? *Educational Researcher* Vol. 41 No. 1, 16–25.

Herrington, J., Reeves, T. C. and Oliver, R. (2010) *A guide to authentic e-learning*. London and New York: Routledge.

Herrington, J., McKenney, S., Reeves, T. and Oliver, R. (2007) *Design-based research and doctoral students: Guidelines for preparing a dissertation proposal* – Edith Cowan University Research Online. Available at: http://ro.ecu.edu.au

Reinking, D. and Bradley, B. A. (2004) Connecting research and practice using formative and design experiments. In N. K. Duke and M. H. Mallette (Eds.), *Literacy research methodologies*. New York and London: The Guildford Press, 149–169.

The Design-based Research Collective. (2003) Design-based research: An emerging paradigm for educational inquiry. *Educational Research*, Vol. 32 No. 1, 5–8. Available at: http://www.designbasedresearch.org

Discourse analysis

The questions a section on discourse analysis must first address relate to what is meant by the term *discourse,* how it can be analysed, why people analyse it, and how discourse analysis relates to the literacy and numeracy classroom. To begin, *discourse* has been defined in many ways, but all definitions agree that the term refers to language 'above the sentence or above the clause' (Stubbs 1983: 1). Brown and Yule (1983: 1) define it as 'language in use', while Fairclough (1992a: 28) identifies it as 'language use, whether speech or writing, seen as a type of social action'. It is this perspective of language as social action or practice that is most relevant to research into literacy. and numeracy, and one that has been applied, for example, in investigations of parent-child interactions in relation to reading and classroom discourse.

In some non-linguistic fields, analysts may only be concerned with 'the *content* of the language being used, the themes or issues being discussed in a conversation or a newspaper article, for example' (Gee 2011a: 8). Discourse analysis within the broad field of linguistics is concerned with how stretches of language fulfil different social purposes through the way the discourse is structured and through the components that make up the discourse. Linguistic approaches 'pay more attention to the structure of the language (*grammar*) and how this structure functions to make meanings in specific contexts' (Gee 2011a: 8).

From a linguistic perspective, Gee (2011a) identifies two categories of discourse analysis . The first is descriptive analysis, used to describe how language works in order to understand it. Although the work of descriptive discourse analysts 'may have practical applications in the world, these discourse analysts are not motivated by those applications' (Gee 2011a: 9). The second is critical discourse analysis in which the goal is 'not just to describe how language works', but also to apply the analysis and 'to speak to or even intervene in social or political issues, problems and controversies in the world' (Gee 2011a: 9).

Quote

My view ... is that all discourse analysis needs to be critical, not because discourse analysts are or need to be political, but because language itself is ... political ... any use of language gains its meanings from the 'game' or practice of which it is a part and which it is enacting ... such 'games' or practices inherently involve potential social goods and the distribution of social goods, which I have defined as central to the realm of 'politics'. Thus, any full description of any use of language would have to deal with 'politics'. Beyond this general point, language is the key way we humans make and break our world, our institutions and our relationships through how we deal with social goods. Thus, discourse analysis can illuminate problems and controversies in the world. It can illuminate issues about the distribution of social goods, who gets helped and who gets harmed.

(Gee 2011a: 9–10)

While Fairclough also distinguishes between two categories of discourse analysis, which he labels 'non-critical' and 'critical', he does not see this division as absolute (Fairclough 1992b: 12). For Fairclough, critical discourse analysis is concerned with 'how discourse is shaped by relations of power and ideologies and the constructive effects discourse has upon social identities, social relations and systems of knowledge and belief, neither of which is normally apparent to discourse participants' (Fairclough 1992b: 12). This distinction is particularly relevant for researchers who want to investigate discourse as it relates to literacy development.

Analysis of classroom discourse

Early analysis of classroom discourse, for example, by Sinclair and Coulthard (1975), was concerned with developing a descriptive framework through which classroom talk could be coded from the level of the lesson to the individual utterances of teachers and students as they engaged in exchanges. Sinclair and Coulthard adopted a rank scale approach, reflective of systemic functional grammar (Halliday 2002/1961: 43), whereby 'going from the top (largest) to the bottom (smallest), each consists of one, or of more than one, of the unit next below (next smaller). The scale on which the units are in fact ranged ... may be called *rank*'. The ranks in the scale adopted by Sinclair and Coulthard in their analysis of classroom discourse were identified as lessons, transactions, exchanges, moves and acts (See also Coulthard 1985).

Sinclair and Coulthard 'made it clear that their interest was primarily to take an identified field of discourse and subject it to study in order to understand more about the nature of discourse' (Christie 2002: 1). This is not to say, however, that their analytical framework has not influenced subsequent more critically or socially oriented studies of classroom discourse, as their pioneering work generated a system of units that could be used to study exchanges in the classroom while also promoting the classroom as a legitimate site for the study of discourse.

On the basis of their study of classroom discourse, Sinclair and Coulthard revealed how classroom exchanges inform, direct and elicit student responses. They also described the now familiar IRF classroom exchange, a type of exchange used in situations where parents and teachers ask questions to which they already know the answer. An IRF exchange is made up of three turns. In the first turn the teacher initiates the exchange by posing a question (I), which is answered in the second

Table 6.4 IRF: three examples

IRF example 1 Feedback	IRF example 2 Follow-up	ERF example 3 Evaluation
T: How many clauses are there in this sentence?	T: How many clauses are there in this sentence?	T: How many clauses are there in this sentence?
S: Three	S: Three	S: Two
T: Good, three.	T: Tell me what they are?	T: Two, are you sure?

turn by the student(s) (R) before in the third turn the teacher gives feedback, a follow-up or an evaluation (F), as illustrated in Table 6.4.

According to Fairclough (1992b), Sinclair and Coulthard developed a framework that enabled a systematic description of dialogic discourse but they were limited because they lacked a social orientation to the data, their data collection was restricted to traditional teacher-centred classrooms, and they did not pay attention to interpretation.

An equally seminal study of classroom discourse, this time from a more critical perspective, was undertaken by Cazden (1988). Cazden (1988: 2) argues that 'while other institutions such as hospitals serve their clients in non-linguistic ways, the basic purpose of school is achieved through communication'. She characterises classrooms as places where speech is the medium through which 'much teaching takes place' and students demonstrate 'much of what they have learned' and as crowded places where the teacher controls the talk to monitor behaviour and 'to enhance the purposes of education' (Cazden 1988: 2–3). Cazden was one of the first analysts of classroom discourse to recognise the growing diversity within classroom populations and to point out that the classroom communication system could not be dismissed as transparent because such an approach could 'seriously impair effective learning and accurate evaluation' (Cazden 1988: 3).

On the basis of her analysis of classroom discourse, Cazden identified a range of interaction types used in classrooms. She applied the concept of scaffolding to these interactions. The term *scaffolding* was first used by Wood, Bruner and Ross (1976) to explain the way adults use discourse to support children's language learning. Parents, for example, model language for their children, divide language tasks into manageable components, and direct children's attention to the essential or most relevant components of each task. Using a model developed by Campione (1981), and expanded by Pearson and Gallagher (1983),

Cazden showed how scaffolding is implemented in the classroom, as illustrated in Figure 6.4.

The analysis of classroom discourse undertaken by Cazden (following work by French & MacLure 1981) revealed how scaffolding works at the micro-level as teachers guide the students towards required answers. For example, her analysis showed how teachers preformulate, or preface, each question with guiding information, as in the example: *Can you see what the elephant's got at the end of his trunk?* [preformulator] *What is it?* [nuclear question]. Teachers also reformulate the question when an answer is wrong, as in this example: *What colour have you used?* [original question] *It's a brown, isn't it?* [reformulation] (Cazden 1983: 109).

Over the intervening decades, Cazden's approach to classroom discourse analysis has been repeated in many studies, including those which have both focused on scaffolding and applied a critical orientation to classroom discourse. These include studies in classrooms where students are learning English as a second language, for example, Gibbons (2006), or the studies described by Jenny Hammond, by Mary Schleppegrell and Annemarie Palincsar, and by Anna-Vera Meidell Sigsgaard in Chapter 7 of this volume.

Many studies of classroom discourse undertaken using a critical discourse approach have been inspired by the work of Basil Bernstein, a British sociologist who was interested in the general principles underlying the transformation of knowledge into pedagogic communication (Bernstein 1996). Bernstein sought to understand why students from different sociocultural groups respond to education in different ways

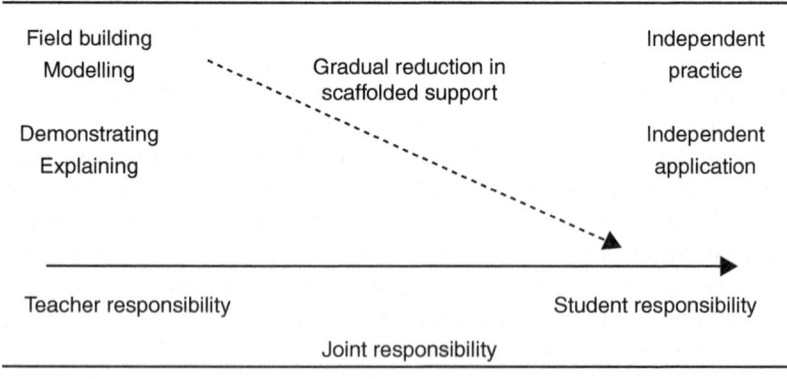

SHIFTING CLASSROOM RESPONSIBILITY

Field building		Independent
Modelling	Gradual reduction in	practice
	scaffolded support	
Demonstrating		Independent
Explaining		application

Teacher responsibility   Student responsibility

Joint responsibility

Figure 6.4 Basic structure of scaffolded learning

and why educational experience leads to different achievement levels across these groups. On the basis of his research, Bernstein developed two concepts to describe the arrangement of the pedagogic space. The concept of *classification* refers to the relative strength of boundaries between categories or contexts within educational settings, for example, the boundaries between educational disciplines. Bernstein suggests that strong classification keeps categories apart by maintaining the boundaries between them, and weak classification brings categories together, by weakening the boundaries between them. The second concept, *framing*, refers to the way in which knowledge is transmitted in classrooms through the roles adopted by teachers and the learners. Bernstein (1996: 27) proposes that where framing is strong the teacher controls the selection of what is learned and how it is learned, for example, sequencing and pacing; where framing is weak, the distinctions between the roles of teachers and learners is less strictly maintained.

The experiences students bring with them to a classroom, for example, from their homes or previous educational settings, will prepare them in different ways for the pedagogy of that classroom. Some students will be better prepared for a visible pedagogy in which the educational disciplines are strongly classified and teacher-student roles are strongly framed, in other words, where the knowledge, and the way it is delivered in terms of sequencing and pacing, as well as the rules of classroom interaction, are explicit to both the teacher and learners. When pedagogy is 'visible', students have a clearer idea of what they are learning, of the purposes and goals of classroom activities and of what is expected of them. Some students, on the other hand, will respond more effectively in classrooms where the pedagogy is less visible, in other words, where both the teacher's decisions and instructions and what is expected of students are more implicit (see Bourne 2004, Sadovnik 2001).

Another conceptual framework useful in classroom discourse analysis is the distinction made by Bernstein (1996) between two types of classroom discourse: *instructional* and *regulative*. Instructional discourse relates to the knowledge being taught, and regulative discourse relates to the social order of the classroom through which the knowledge is delivered (Arnot & Reay 2004: 135).

Quote

Basil Bernstein's early work as a sociologist grew out of his experience as a teacher in London schools in the 1950s, and his profound concern for the many students of working-class background who failed in schools. He wanted to find an explanation for the apparent differences in school performance of students of different social classes. His efforts to explain why middle-class children were more successful in schools caused him to focus on aspects of language use ... The explanation he was to propose would lead him in time to mount a major sociological theory, addressing questions of school structure, power relations, the differential ways in which power and knowledge are distributed to various social groups, and the mechanisms by which such distribution occurs.

(Christie 1999: 1)

Bernstein's concepts of classification and framing were used by Burns and de Silva Joyce (2008) to explore explicit teaching in adult English as a second language (ESL) classrooms. Burns and de Silva Joyce were interested in how, for example, classification in classrooms affected the teaching of the macroskills of reading, writing, speaking and listening. In some classrooms the macroskills were found to be differentiated through strong classification and were specifically addressed by the teachers. In other classrooms the macroskills were conflated through weak classification in which each macroskill was embedded with other macroskills. The difficulty for the ESL students, when the macroskills were conflated, was in recognising which macroskill was the focus of learning. The research findings suggested the following strategies for making the teaching-learning process more transparent to adult ESL learners, especially those unused to the Western classroom or from backgrounds with little formal schooling:

- Learning is more effective when the roles of the teacher and learners in the classroom are explicit and made clear.
- Explicit teaching involves clarifying the skills that are the focus of teaching and learning and making explicit to the learners the purpose of activities and the anticipated learning outcomes.
- Language is embedded in social contexts and is fundamental to cognitive development as it is a tool for thinking and doing.
- Learners can achieve more learning with the support of skilled others than they can achieve alone.
- Learners move towards greater independence as their knowledge and skills increase.
- Teachers can gradually withdraw support as skills and knowledge are acquired and learners achieve success.

- Effective pedagogy is tuned to the needs of learners and constantly adjusted in response to what they are able to do.
- Learners are more likely to be successful when tasks are broken down into manageable and achievable steps.
- Demonstration and modelling are crucial aspects of scaffolded learning.
- Focusing towards the whole task and the goals to be achieved is central to effective scaffolding.
- Learners gain success in new tasks when they are located within formats and routines that are already familiar.

These findings about the value of explicit teaching align with conclusions drawn by many researchers who have applied critical discourse analysis to the study of the achievement of disadvantaged students in classroom settings.

Analysis of written texts

The analysis of written texts is an essential element of studies which explore what it means to be literate, literacy development and literacy teaching, 'because the ability to read and understand [written texts] is definitional to literacy' (Goldman & Wiley 2004: 62). However, the concept of literacy, once concerned only with reading and writing monomodal written texts, has now been expanded to include viewing and composing visual and multimodal texts. Becoming and being *literate* in the contemporary world means being multiliterate, the ability to engage as a receiver and producer of multimodal texts that integrate written language, spoken language, visual images, moving pictures and mathematical information.

We will begin this section by looking at how analysis of written texts has added to our understandings of literacy in social contexts, before moving on to studies of multimodal texts and multiliteracy. In literacy research written texts are analysed for two reasons: first, to determine the structure and language features of texts that occur in various contexts and, second, to assess the impact of a particular pedagogic intervention on students' writing.

In the 1970s and 1980s, the dominant writing pedagogy was process writing. This approach was based on the view that

> language is more learned than taught; that while some things about writing need to be taught, many more need to be learned *by discovery* in action, in frequent use, across a range of situations that are full of

meaning for the learner. So the dictum LET THEM WRITE will safe-guard the main need of primary children in learning to write.

(Walshe 1981: 9)

The basis of process writing in schools, and later in adult literacy class-rooms, was that students would learn to write by writing after a few *teachables* were taught. These included the mechanics of writing (alpha-bet, handwriting, punctuation and spelling), half a dozen grammar items (including the concept of sentence versus clause versus phrase, subject-verb agreement, present and past simple tense, and the subject and object forms of personal pronouns), and craft issues which relate to formalities of usage, for example, *affect* versus *effect* (Walshe 1981). The main roles of the teacher were to teach the few teachables and to build a writing community where students could discover writing through writing, that is, the novice writer could 'discover his or her own *process* of moving from rather messy drafting *(first thoughts)* through revision to the polished form' (Walshe 1981: 11).

This *laissez-faire* approach to writing pedagogy was challenged by findings emerging from sociolinguistic, sociological and ethnographic studies. Bernstein's sociological concern with how differences in school achievement aligned with social class alongside sociolinguistic research which applied theoretical frameworks such as Systemic Functional Linguistics (SFL), began to identify the written texts students needed to control in order to succeed in educational contexts. As well as iden-tifying those texts that students need to control for school success (see Martin's description of the *Write it Right Disadvantaged Schools Project* in Chapter 7), sociolinguistic studies identified texts that adults needed to control if they were to participate effectively in community and work contexts and on the links between these texts and reading and writing in schools (for example, Christie & Martin 1997, Crowther, Hamilton & Tett 2001, Joyce 1992, Korner, McInnes & Rose 2007).

Quote

Enterprises are organised as communication systems and it is pos-sible to describe the contextual background of specific worksites and the language used. It is also possible to analyse and compare the texts and language used in these contexts with the language used in the secondary science classroom ... The different kinds of reading and writing skills that workers need in each context are of particular interest in relating industry sectors to the secondary curriculum.

(Korner, McInnes & Rose 2007: 6)

Texts critical to success in academic contexts were also identified, along-side the specific reading and writing requirements of educational disciplines (for example, Coffin 2006, Ghadessy 1988, Halliday 2004/1988, Hood 2010, Hyland 2009, Korner et al. 2007, Veel 1997 and 1999).

Quotes

The term 'scientific English' is a useful label for a generalised functional variety, or register, of the modern English language. To label it in this way is not to imply that it is either stationary or homogeneous. The term can be taken to denote a semiotic space within which there is a great deal of variability at any one time, as well as continuing diachronic evolution.

(Halliday 2004/1988: 140)

Academic discourse refers to the ways of thinking and using language which exist in the academy. Its significance, in large part, lies in the fact that complex social activities like educating students, demonstrating learning, disseminating ideas and constructing knowledge, rely on language to accomplish ... But academic discourse does more than enable universities to get on with the business of teaching and research, it simultaneously constructs the social roles and relationships which create academics and students and which sustain universities, the disciplines, and the creation of knowledge itself. Individuals use language to write, frame problems and understand issues in ways specific to particular social groups and in doing these things they form social realities, personal identities and professional institutions.

(Hyland 2009: 1)

The level of technicality and abstraction associated with representations of academic knowledge can often present challenges for those who are novices in the register. While this is to some extent at least acknowledged and accounted for in the pedagogic design of learning of the content in a field, there is another area of challenge that is typically less overtly addressed, that of managing what we can refer to as the 'subjective' or interpersonal meanings of academic discourse, that is, how we position ourselves in interaction with knowledge.

(Hood 2010: 1)

Analysis of written texts has been undertaken from the perspective of New Rhetoric in an effort to reinstate classical rhetoric and to consider how it might be expanded and 'employed in the twenty-first century' (Thomas 2007: 1). The analysis of written texts has also included the analysis of genre, a fine-grained investigation of the text structures and language features of written texts within different contexts and disciplines, which has been undertaken from the perspectives of both English for Specific Purposes (ESP) and Systemic Functional Linguistics (SFL). Genre analysis 'is a broad term embracing a range of tools and attitudes to texts, from detailed qualitative analyses of a single text to more quantitative counts of language features' and the examination of 'the actions of individuals as they created particular texts' and 'the distribution of different genre features to see how they cluster in complementary distributions across a range of texts' (Hyland 2099: 25–26).

Over the past three decades or so, the concept of genre has been applied systematically to the analysis of written and spoken texts. Genres have been defined as 'staged, goal-oriented social processes' (Rose and Martin 2012: 54). Many genres, the recognisable structural patterns or configurations of meaning that recur in texts used in English-speaking cultures, particularly in educational contexts, have been identified, and similar studies of texts used in other languages are also being undertaken (for example, Caffarel, Martin & Matthiessen 2004, Thomson, Sano & de Silva Joyce in publication). Educators concerned with addressing disadvantage in education, community or work contexts often advocate genre-based approaches to literacy pedagogy, in contrast, for example, to process writing. This is because genre pedagogy is based on explicit teaching about the purpose, structure and language features of the texts which people need to control in order to access social power and opportunity. The analysis of genres and their role in educational contexts provides an essential basis for this approach to literacy education.

Genre-based approaches to literacy education have at times been criticised for being formulaic and for limiting the creativity for students. When texts are analysed in context, however, they can be viewed from an historical perspective to draw attention to how text patterns change over time as the culture itself changes. A comparison of the news reports below illustrates how the structure of news stories has changed over time. News story 1 lacks a headline and is written as a recount with all the events presented in a temporal sequence, while News story 2 has an attention-seeking headline and a nucleus-satellite structure in which each paragraph relates back to the headline and lead.

News story 1 – Published in *The Sydney Morning Herald* on 9th May 1831

On Tuesday evening, about the hour of eight o'clock, a puncheon of rum in the bonded store at the back of the Gazette Office burst, and the intoxicating stream found its way through the drain into St George Street, the invigorating cry of 'grog ahoy' was immediately raised, and pots, pans, buckets, &c were put into instant requisition for saving the precious liquid, which by this time had obtained the consistency of pea soup; some who had not the convenience of utensils stretched themselves on mother earth and lapped up the beverage, until they became incapable of rising; others were staggering off in various directions scarcely capable of maintaining their equilibrium, and even a batch of children were seen quaffing the beverage with much gout. A bacchanalian scene ensued, and the conservators of the peace were required to put it down.

(In Feez, Iedema & White 2008: 76)

News story 2 – Published in *The Australian* on Thursday 5th April 1999

NUCLEUS = HEADLINE AND LEAD	**CITY BATTERED BY GIANT HAILSTONES** By Georgina Safe and Matt Price Hailstones the size of tennis balls smashed roofs, battered cars and injured people across Sydney in a freak storm last night.
SATELLITE 1 CONSEQUENCES OF STORM FOR MOTORISTS	Thirty motorists were stranded in the Royal National Park at Sutherland and cars taking shelter in the Sydney airport tunnel caused major traffic problems. Some 30 sets of traffic lights went out after the hailstorm hit at 8pm.
SATELLITE 2 DESCRIPTION OF HAILSTORM BY POLICE	Roofs were torn off houses in Caringbah, in Sydney's south, roads were flooded in North Manly, and cars were 'floating away' in the eastern suburb of Edgecliff in the aftermath of the 20-minute pummelling, a police spokesperson said.
SATELLITE 3 CONSEQUENCES FOR AMBULANCE AND HOSPITALS	Ambulance crews were flat-out attending to people with head injuries and severe lacerations from huge chunks of ice, and a driver was taken to Royal Prince Alfred Hospital after blinding hail caused him to swerve off the road and into a power pole at Marrickville, in Sydney's inner west.

SATELLITE 4 CONSEQUENCES FOR SUBURBS	The storm caused a power failure in Collaroy and along Oxford St, in the eastern suburb of Paddington. Many motorists sought refuge by parking under eaves on the footpath.
SATELLITE 5 CONSEQUENCES FOR AN INDIVIDUAL	Chris Chambers suffered mild concussion when he was hit by a giant hailstone while walking 12m from his car into a Paddington hotel. The front and back windscreens on his $65,000 new model Alfa Romeo were smashed. 'It was just huge,' he said, blood pouring down his face as hotel staff provided medical treatment.
SATELLITE 6 EFFECT ON NUMBER OF PEOPLE	Hundreds of people emptied restaurants and cafes to witness the hailstorm, many gathering giant samples from the streets and footpaths.
SATELLITE 6 DESCRIPTION OF STORM BY EYE WITNESS	'It sounded like a plane was about to crash,' Robyn Bradfield said. 'Then stones the size of golf balls – no, cricket balls – started bouncing into the restaurant.' Ms Bradfield's partner, a doctor, was busy treating the injured.

Source: de Silva Joyce & Feez (2012: 16–17)

The analysis of written texts can also be used to study writing development. While studies of writing development tend to concentrate on a single age range or on particular language elements, a study by Christie and Derewianka (2008), and also reported by Christie in Chapter 7, based on a database of 2 000 texts, set out to describe 'what development in writing actually looks like' from early childhood to late adolescence 'in a range of curriculum areas across a variety of genres' (Christie & Derewianka 2008: 1 and 5). Using Systemic Functional Linguistics (SFL) as their conceptual framework, these researchers were 'interested in the increasing range of contexts within which children are likely to participate as they grow older, the kinds of linguistic demands which these contexts make on children and the types of linguistic resources the learners need to develop if they are to operate successfully in these contexts' (Christie & Derewianka 2008: 6).

> **Quote**
>
> The ability to write is prized in English-speaking cultures, bringing considerable advantage to those who can do it well in many sites,

personal, occupational, political and communal. Many children do not succeed in their writing, for it is in fact quite difficult to learn to write well. All children deserve the opportunity to learn to write ... where teachers are possessed of appropriate knowledge of the ontogenesis of writing ability, of the kind the functional grammar provides, they can the more effectively guide their students as they learn to write.

(Christie & Derewianka 2008: 244)

The study by Christie and Derewianka revealed four broad developmental phases progressing from common-sense knowledge to uncommonsense knowledge, as shown in Figure 6.5.

Common-sense knowledge is local everyday knowledge learned at home, in the community and in peer groups, while uncommonsense knowledge, in contrast, is 'freed from the particular, the local, through the various

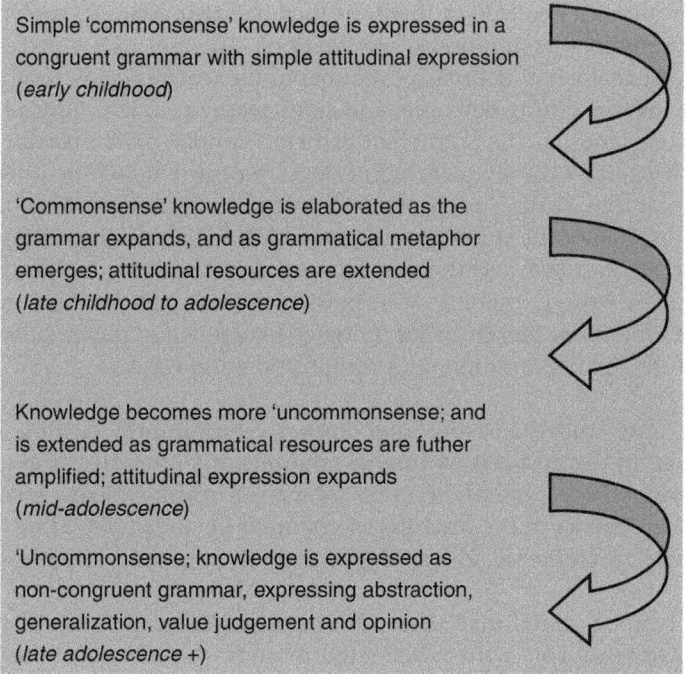

Figure 6.5 Developmental phases in learning to write
Source: Christie & Derewianka (2008: 218).

languages of the sciences or forms of reflexiveness of the arts which make possible either the creation or the discovery of new realities' (Bernstein 1975: 99, cited in Christie & Derewianka 2008: 218). In their study, Christie and Derewianka outlined the major linguistic developmental steps from early childhood to late adolescence students needed to accomplish if they were to gain control of the writing required for success in school and beyond. The findings from the study emphasise the important role played by the teacher in literacy development and provide a blueprint for the development of writing curricula across the phases of schooling.

Many researchers have used and continue to use the analysis of written texts to assess the impact of particular pedagogic interventions on students' writing, as in the sample adult texts in Figure 6.1. A significant large-scale research project was conducted in the United Kingdom (Myhill, Jones, Lines & Watson 2012 and reported in Chapter 7 by Debra Myhill) with 744 students in 31 schools chosen randomly in the southwest and the Midlands of England.[5] The project adopted a mixed-method research design involving a randomised controlled trial with some classes chosen for the grammar intervention and other classes used as a control group. Data collection methods included text analysis, student and teacher interviews and lesson observations. The aim of the project was to investigate whether linking grammar to the teaching of writing would lead to better writing outcomes and an increase in students' metalinguistic understanding. The researchers gathered samples of first-person narratives written by the students before and after introducing the integrated grammar intervention as pre-test and post-test assessments. To avoid task bias, one half of the students were given Task 1 as a pre-test task and Task 2 as a post-test task and this was reversed with the other half of the students. The written responses were marked by three independent markers, and a final mark was given for sentence structure and punctuation, text structure and organisation, and composition and effect.

> '[T]hose students in the intervention group improved their attainment in the post-test writing test significantly more than the control group. This represents the first robust statistical evidence for a beneficial impact of the teaching of grammar in students' writing attainment' (Myhill et al. 2012: 151).

More fine-grained analysis of the data arising from this project showed that the more able writers benefited more from the intervention. The researchers feel that further research is necessary 'to establish whether using the same pedagogic strategy of embedded grammar teaching but addressing different aspects of writing more relevant to lower attaining writers needs would be more successful' (Myhill et al. 2012: 152).

Discourse analysis references

Cazden, C. B. (1988) *Classroom discourse: The language of teaching and learning*. Portsmouth, NH: Heinemann.

Christie, F. (2002) *Classroom discourse: A functional perspective*. London and New York: Continuum.

Christie, F. and Derewianka, B. (2008) *School discourse*. London and New York: Continuum.

Fairclough, N. (1992b). *Discourse and social change*. Cambridge: Polity Press

Gee, J. P. (2011a) *An introduction to discourse analysis: Theory and method* (3rd Edition). New York and London: Routledge.

Gee, J. P. (2011b) *How to do discourse analysis: A toolkit*. New York and London: Routledge.

Gee, J. P. and Handford, M. (2012) *The Routledge handbook of discourse analysis*. Oxford: Routledge.

Gibbons, P. (2006) *Bridging discourse in the ESL classroom*. London and New York: Continuum.

Hyland, K. and Paltridge, B. (2011) *The Bloomsbury companion to discourse analysis*. London and New York: Bloomsbury.

Jaworski, A. & Coupland, N. (Eds). (2006) *The discourse reader (2nd edition)*. London and New York: Routledge.

Myhill, D. A., Jones, S. M., Lines, H. and Watson, A. (2012) Re-thinking grammar: The impact of embedded grammar teaching on students' writing and student's metalinguistic understanding. *Research Papers in Education* Vol. 27 No. 2 April 2012, 139–166.

Sinclair, J. M. and Coulthard, M. (1975) *Towards an analysis of discourse: The English used by teachers and pupils*. Oxford: Oxford University Press.

van Leeuwen, T. (2008). Discourse and practice: New tools for critical discourse analysis. Oxford: Oxford University Press.

Multimodal text analysis

The study of visual texts in different contexts, and for different purposes, is not a new pursuit and has been a feature for some time of disciplines such as art history, art criticism, cognitive science, psychology, neurology and media studies. However, over recent years the focus of text analysis has shifted to include multimodal texts in which verbal and visual texts are combined, and these texts have been analysed using visual and multimodal grammars (for example, Bateman 2008, Kress 2003, Kress & van Leeuwen 1996, Lemke 1998, Marion & Crowder 2013, O'Halloran 2006, O'Toole 2011).

Multimodal texts are not a recent phenomenon. Texts that combine words and pictures date back as far as the creation of wall carvings in Ancient Egypt and sculptural friezes in Ancient Greece. Written texts in medieval illuminated manuscripts were enhanced with decorations and illustrations. In the late 18th century illustrated books were published for children, and multimodal picture books continue to be the way children are introduced to reading (de Silva Joyce & Gaudin 2011). In contemporary social contexts it is now unusual to find texts that use only one semiotic system to communicate with their audiences. Most use a combination of semiotic systems to fulfil their social purposes.

Quote

Experience is the basis for understanding and creating new ways with words and images and, thus, too, multimodal texts. Thus, it is not surprising that, in a world where innovation, creativity, design and the creation of new experiences are crucial for economic success, multimodal texts have proliferated ... What we are looking at, in reality, is the proliferation of representations of all sorts – re-presentations of ever more aspects of ever more realities, virtual and 'real'.

(Gee & Hayes 2011: 119)

Visual literacy is the ability to interpret the elements within images that an image-maker has used to make meaning as well as the ability to produce images for social purposes, for example, to create a diagram. The combination of images with other semiotic systems, including spoken and written language sound and gesture create multimodal texts, as illustrated in Figure 6.6,

> the words EMPTY BOTTLES make no sense in this context without the liquid pouring from the bottle and the recycling symbol. The whole sign can then be interpreted as *Empty bottles for recycling* with the words acting as an imperative/command to empty bottles before

recycling or *Empty bottles can be recycled* with the words acting as a noun group. Either way, it is only through the words and visual elements working together that the overall meaning is made.

(de Silva Joyce 2014: 43)

Being able to engage with visual and multimodal texts is an aspect of being multiliterate which, according to Unsworth (2001: 10), means understanding 'how different modalities separately and interactively construct different dimensions of meaning' in texts. The analysis of visual and multimodal texts is a feature of studies into the use of these texts in educational contexts and in educational resources (for example, Anstey and Bull 2010, Callow 2013 and 1999, Gee & Hayes 2011, Serafini 2012, Unsworth 2001, Walsh 2010). As multimodal texts are now ever present in contemporary contexts, students need to develop the skills and understandings needed to approach these texts critically in order to understand the features of these texts that prompt specific responses in viewers. Students also need to expand their critical literacy skills by understanding the motivations behind the choices made by creators of images and multimodal texts from the wide range of resources available to them.

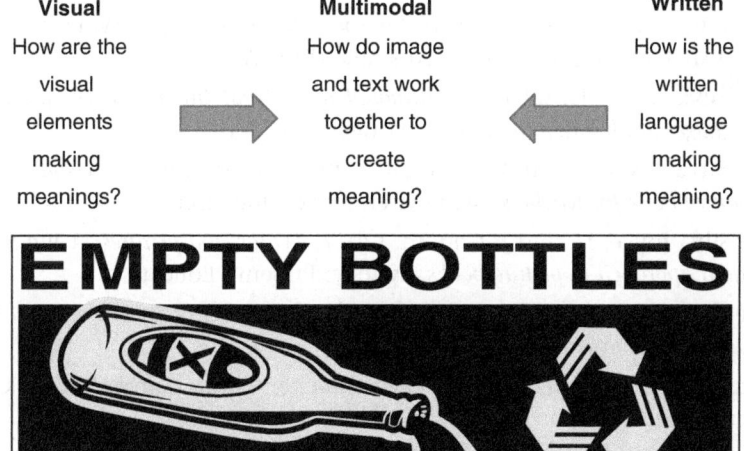

From NSW EPA – http://www.epa.nsw.gov.au

Figure 6.6 Visual and written elements in multimodal text
Source: From de Silva Joyce (2014: 43).

The field of literacy research is continuing to expand. Valuable directions for future research include ethnographic research into the social practices around the use of multimodal texts in different sociocultural contexts across different delivery modes, longitudinal studies of how children develop their ability to read/view multimodal texts, as well as studies to establish how to integrate multimodal texts effectively into classroom programming and which interventions are most effective in enabling students to use multimodal texts successfully and critically.

Multimodal analysis references

Anstey, M. and Bull, G. (2010) Helping teachers to explore multimodal texts. *Curriculum and Leadership Journal* Vol. 8 No. 16. Available at: http://www.curriculum.edu.au/leader/helping_teachers_to_explore_multimodal_texts,31522.html?issueID=12141 – accessed 30.11.13.

Bateman, J. A. (2008) *Multimodality and genre: A foundation for the systematic analysis of multimodal documents.* Basingstoke: Hampshire: Palgrave Macmillan.

Callow, J. (1999) *Image matters: Visual texts in the classroom.* Marrickville, NSW: Primary English Teaching Association Australia (PETAA).

Callow, J. (2013) *The shape of text to come.* Marrickville, NSW: Primary English Teaching Association Australia (PETAA).

de Silva Joyce, H. (2014) *Multimodal and visual literacy in the adult language and literacy classroom.* Sydney: NSW AMES.

de Silva Joyce, H. and J. Gaudin. (2007) *Interpreting the visual: A resource book for teachers.* Sydney: Phoenix Education.

de Silva Joyce, H. and J. Gaudin. (2011) *Words and pictures: A multimodal approach to picture books.* Sydney: Phoenix Education.

Gee, J. P. and E. R. Hayes. (2011) *Language and learning in the digital age.* London and New York: Routledge.

Kress, G. (2003) *Literacy in the new media age.* London and New York: Routledge.

Kress, G. and T. van Leeuwen. (1996) *Reading images: The grammar of visual design.* London and New York: Routledge.

Lemke, J (1998) Multiplying meaning: Visual and verbal semiotics in scientific text. In J. R. Martin and R. Veel (Eds). *Reading science:*

Critical and functional perspectives on discourses of science. London: Routledge, 87–113.

Marion, J. S. and J. W. Crowder. (2013) *Visual research: A concise Introduction to thinking visually*. London and New York: Bloomsbury.

O'Halloran, K. (Ed). (2006) *Multimodal discourse analysis: Systemic functional perspectives*. London and New York: Continuum.

O'Toole, M. (1994) *The language of displayed art*. London: Leicester University Press.

O'Toole, M. (2011) *The language of displayed art* (2nd edition). London and New York: Routledge.

Painter, C., Martin, J. R., and Unsworth, L. (2013) *Reading visual narratives: Image analysis of children's picture books*. Sheffield UK: Equinox.

Serafini, F. (2012) *Expanding the four resources model: Reading visual and multi-modal texts* in *Pedagogies: An International Journal* Vol. 7 No. 2, 150–164.

Unsworth, L. (2001) *Teaching multiliteracies across the curriculum: Changing contexts of text and image on classroom practice*. Buckingham, UK: Open University Press.

Walsh, M. (2010) *Multimodal literacy: Researching classroom practice*. Marrickville, NSW: Primary English Teaching Association Australia (PETAA).

Ethnographic research

Various forms of ethnographic research have helped to broaden the concepts of literacy and what it means to be literate. Literacy can no longer be viewed, by any reasonable person, as merely a set of skills developed in school. Following, for example, Shirley Brice Heath's (1983) formative work, ethnographic approaches have been used to research literacy development, literacy teaching and learning and how literacy is used as part of sociocultural practice. Literacy researchers using ethnographic methods have found 'patterns and themes' (Purcell-Gates 2004: 92) which have enhanced the work of other researchers and educators.

Quote

Ethnography is not for researchers who already know what they are seeking or for those who have strong hypotheses to test. Rather, it

> is for those researchers who are truly wondering, seeking, curious
> about some aspect of literacy as it occurs naturally in sociocultural
> contexts. These contexts can be schools, classrooms, homes, commu-
> nities, workplaces – any naturally occurring context for literacy use.
>
> (Purcell-Gates 2004: 94)

Literacy researchers who use ethnography as a research method conduct
their research by choosing from a variety of approaches, as outlined in
Table 6.5 (adapted from Purcell-Gates 2004: 96–97).

Scribner and Cole (1981) were perhaps the first to question the view
of literacy as simply a set of skills. Instead, they defined literacy as 'a
set of socially organised practices which make use of a symbol system
and a technology for producing and disseminating it' with the 'nature
of these practices, including of course their technological practices'
determining 'the kinds of skills (*consequences*) associated with literacy'
(Scribner & Cole 1981: 236). Subsequent influential ethnographic literacy studies (for example, Heath 1983, Street 1984) undertaken in a
variety of sociocultural contexts have further broadened this view of
literacy and its practice in different societies and communities.

Table 6.5 Ethnographic approaches to literacy research

Approaches	Characteristics
Phenomenological	The researcher seeks to understand the world from the participants' perspectives and must live in the participants' world, interact with group members, observe and interview.
Ecological	The researcher studies how social structures such as family, peers, school, work, community and society define individuals and groups and remains more detached and objective. The goal is to observe behaviour and elicit participants' perspectives.
Critical	The researcher focuses on inequality, oppression, and marginalisation that result from unequal power relations. The goal is to uncover and describe ine-qualities and oppressive structures in order to bring about change.
Network	The researcher studies literacy as it is influenced and occurs within social networks within specific cul-tural domains. This approach is particularly relevant at times when technological and social changes are occurring.

Findings from ethnographic studies have resulted in a social view of literacy practices (see, for example, Barton 2007, Barton & Ivanič 1991, Christie 1990, Christie & Martin 1997, Graff 1987, Hasan & Williams 1996). As a result of these studies literacy has come to be understood as 'a social activity and can best be described in terms of people's literacy practices which they draw upon in literacy events' (Barton 2007: 35). Literacy events are the 'occasions in everyday life where the written word has a role' (Barton 2007: 35).

A social practices view of literacy rejects the idea of literacy as a set of generic reading and writing skills used in the same way across different contexts, but instead is concerned with how readers and writers use their literacy skills to be participating members of specific social contexts. This social focus adopts a multidimensional view of literacies 'as plural and as complex, multifaceted social and cultural practices' (Belfiore, Defoe, Folinsbee, Hunter & Jackson 2004: 4–5) and enables researchers to look behind and beyond assessments of people's literacy skills based on deficits. For example, ethnographic research undertaken by the In-Sites Research Group (Belfiore et al. 2004) into four Canadian workplaces – a food processing plant, a textile factory, an urban tourist hotel and a high-tech metal parts manufacturer – revealed over-simplified analyses by managers of employee skills, resistance to literacy practices that masked employee abilities, as well as inabilities to deal with workplace documents. One illustrative example from the study were mixed messages about paperwork where on the one hand managers claimed they wanted better completion of the forms that employees had to fill out when something went wrong, while at the same time they were pressing employees to respond quickly to customer requirements. The employees reported to the researcher that 'there are subtle and not-so-subtle messages that getting the product done and out the door is more important than paperwork' (Belfiore et al. 2004: 75).

The expansion of literacy research from the perspective of a variety of disciplines including linguistics, history, anthropology, rhetoric and composition studies, cultural psychology and education led Gee (1990/2012) to coin the term *New Literacy Studies*. It appeared to Gee (2009: 2) that these researchers 'were converging on a coherent and shared view about literacy, though they never did come to share a common language out of which they wrote'. The motivation of researchers in the field of New Literacy Studies has been to understand how literacy relates to social inequalities and 'to challenge the way *literacy* is socially distributed to different groups', particularly at a time when 'in an information-rich world there is an increasing gap between those with access to information and those denied it' (Crowther et al. 2001: 3).

Quote

... the demands of a *knowledge economy* and an *information society* cannot simply be constrained within the traditional conventions of literacy understanding. Its development exposes the inadequacy of current thinking that constitutes literacy as externally defined rungs on a ladder that has been designed as an extension of initial schooling, rather than in terms of the real shape of literacy practices and goals in adult life. Rather than seeing literacy as a tool for organising our knowledge that is consistent with the economic vision of the global economy, we need other ways of conceptualising literacy that can embody more democratic visions ... Literacy that obscures the power relations inscribed in its construction ultimately disempowers. It treats as technical what is in fact socially and politically constructed and is therefore misleading.

(Crowther et al. 2001: 3)

Ethnographic research references

Barton, D. (2007) *Literacy: An introduction to the ecology of written language*. Oxford: Blackwell Publishing.

Heath, S. B. (1983) *Ways with words: Language, life and work in communities and classrooms*. Cambridge: Cambridge University Press.

Purcell-Gates, V. (2004) Ethnographic research. In N. K. Duke and M. H. Mallette (Eds). *Literacy research methodologies*. New York and London: The Guildford Press.

Rose, M. (2004) *The mind at work: Valuing the intelligence of the American worker*. New York and London: Penguin Group.

Street, B. (2001a) *Literacy and development: Ethnographic perspectives*. London and New York: Routledge.

Verbal protocols

Verbal protocols, also referred to as *think-aloud protocols*, are a research method used across various disciplines. They are an attempt to understand the cognitive or thinking processes that people go through when they are undertaking a task. Verbal protocols have been used by online content designers, as an evaluation tool, to gain some insights into how users respond to different elements in the online environment and to make adjustments to content and navigation based on users' responses. They have also commonly been used in reading research, 'as reading is normally a silent, hidden process and researchers are unable to determine processes by simple observation or by a product-based assessment' (Giridharan & Conlan 2012: 139). There are two main types of verbal protocols – retrospective and concurrent. As the terms imply, in retrospective protocols the participants are asked to recall what they were thinking as they undertook the task, for example, reading a text, while in concurrent protocols the participants are asked to think aloud as they compete a task, for example, how readers infer the meaning of unknown words while reading (Giridharan & Conlan 2012).

Trickett and Trafton (2009: 333–334) outline six main issues to consider when adopting this research method. The first is that when participating in a retrospective protocol the participant 'may not have access either to what they did or why', and the second is to differentiate between a participant thinking aloud while problem solving, and having them describe, explain or rationalise, which removes them from the process. The third issue is the potential for subjective interpretation, particularly when a researcher assumes that they know what a participant has meant by, for example, an incomplete statement. The final three issues relate to confidentiality and to resources, for example, the need for good quality recording equipment and transcription and the time commitment demanded of both researchers and participants to complete this type of research.

Quotes

Briefly put, verbal protocol analysis involves having participants perform a task or set of tasks and verbalising their thoughts ('talking aloud') while doing so. The basic assumption of verbal protocol analysis, to which we subscribe, is that when people talk aloud while performing a task, the verbal stream functions effectively as a 'dump' of the contents of working memory ... the verbal stream can thus be taken as a reflection of the cognitive processes in use

and, after analysis, provides the researcher with valuable information about not only those processes, but also the representations
on which they operate. In addition, verbal protocols can reveal
information about misconceptions and conceptual change, strategy
acquisition, use and mastery, task performance, affective response
and the like.

(Trickett & Trafton 2009: 332)

The strength of concurrent verbal protocols is that they can be considered a reflection of the actual processes people use as they perform
a task. Properly done, verbal protocol analysis can provide insights
into aspects of performance that might otherwise remain inside a
'black box' accessible only by speculation. Although they are time
consuming to collect, process and analyse, we believe that the richness of the data provided by verbal protocols far outweighs the costs.
Ultimately, as with all research, the purpose of the research and the
resources available to the researcher will determine the most appropriate method: however, the addition of verbal protocol analysis
to a researcher's repertoire will open the door to a potentially very
productive source of data that invariably yield interesting and often
surprising results.

(Trickett & Trafton 2009: 345–346)

Swain (2006: 1–2) argues 'for alternative interpretations of verbal protocol data based on sociocultural research and theory' by contrasting 'two
different theories of human cognition' – information processing theory
and a sociocultural theory of mind – which view 'the relationship
between language and thought' in different ways. For those researchers
who accept a sociocultural theory of mind '[l]anguage is not simply a
vehicle for communication, but plays critical roles in creating, transforming, and augmenting higher mental processes', a view influenced
by the work of Vygotsky (1978) and his colleagues. In relation to verbal
protocols, this means that thinking aloud processes 'not only potentially transform thinking, focussing it in highly specific ways, but also
are the sources of changes in cognition' (Swain 2006: 7). This means
that verbal protocols are not neutral data collection procedures but processes whereby the participant comprehends and reshapes experience
and this 'needs to be taken account of in any study which makes use of
verbal protocols' (Swain 2006: 18–19).

> ## Quote
>
> In a sociocultural theory of mind, verbalisation is conceived of as a tool that enables *changes* in cognition. Speech serves to mediate cognition. Initially an exterior source of physical and mental regulation, speech takes on these regulatory functions for the self. One's own speech (through a process of internalisation) comes to regulate, organise and focus an individual's own mental activities (e.g. Luria 1959 and 1973, Sokolov 1972) ... Another way in which language intersects with the activities of the mind is that it allows ideas to be retained and held up for inspection by the self and others; it allows ideas to move between people. Such movement allows for 'the communal construction of extremely delicate and difficult intellectual trajectories and progressions ... moreover, the sheer number of intellectual niches available within a linguistically linked community provides a stunning matrix of possible inter-agent trajectories' (Clark 1998: 172).
>
> (Swain 2006: 6)

Verbal protocols can be the sole approach adopted in a research design or they can become one means of data collection alongside other methods. They can also be used from within different theoretical frameworks such as critical discourse theory. Critical discourse theory is the framework within which Fawns used verbal protocols to examine the practices used by six university students, with high levels of literacy, to complete a health costs claim form and how the form restricted the way the students could represent themselves to the funding organisation (Fawns & Ivanič 2001). '[W]hat people do, think and feel when required to fill in forms reveals that literacy is not just a matter of decoding and spelling, but a complex social practice through which bureaucratic documents can strip people of their identities' (Fawns & Ivanič 2001: 80).

As form filling is so much a part of the institutional organisation of modern life and an 'institutionally imposed literacy practice', Fawns was also interested in 'the ways in which users can take more power into their own hands when faced with forms to fill in' (Fawns & Ivanič 2001: 80). Data collection included concurrent verbal protocols, enabling the researcher to examine the strategies adopted by the form fillers, whether they read or ignored section headings and whether they read and followed all the routing instructions. This enabled the researcher 'to focus on the places where the participants were experiencing a clash between their own sense of self and the identities made available by the form, and where they were submitting to or challenging the power exercised by the form' (Fawns & Ivanič 2001: 84). The findings revealed that even highly literate people can experience difficulties when participating in literacy practices such as completing complex forms but that it is possible to take more control of these practices when completing a form, for example, by choosing assertively to put N/A rather than feeling obliged to answer a question.

Verbal protocol references

Fawns, M. and Ivanič, R. (2001) Form-filling as a social practice: Taking power into our own hands. In J. Crowther, M. Hamilton, and L. Tett (Eds). *Powerful literacies*. Leicester: National Institute of Adult Continuing Education (NIACE).

Hilden, K. and Pressley, M. (2004) Verbal protocols of reading. In N. K. Duke and M. H. Mallette (2004) *Literacy research methodologies*. New York and London: The Guildford Press.

Trickett, S. and Trafton, J. G. (2009) A primer on verbal protocol analysis. In D. Schmorrow, J. Cohn, and D. Nicholson (Eds). *The PSI handbook of virtual environments for training and education* Vol.1. Westport, CT: Praeger Security International, 332–346.

Meta-analysis

Meta-analysis is a process of reviewing the results of multiple research studies in a particular field to look for contrasts, similarities, patterns or disagreements. The aim of meta-analysis is to look for recurring evidence of statistical significance in order to draw generalisable conclusions.

Quote

In the 1970s there was a major change in the manner that we reviewed the research literature. This approach offered a way to tame the massive amount of research evidence so that it could offer useful information for teachers. The predominant method had always been to write a synthesis of many published studies in the form of an integrated literature review. However, in 1976 Gene Glass introduced the notion of meta-analysis – whereby the effects in each study, where appropriate, are converted to a common measure (an effect size), such that the overall effects could be quantified, interpreted and compared, and the various moderators of this overall effect could be uncovered and followed up in more detail ... The method soon became popular and by the mid 1980s more than 100 meta-analyses in education were available.

(Hattie 2009: 3)

An example of this approach used in education is Hattie's (2009) meta-analysis of influences on student learning, which he refers to as a *meta* meta-analysis as he reviewed and attempted to synthesise 800 meta-analyses that had previously been undertaken in relation to the features of educational contexts which influence student outcomes. His aim was to 'develop an explanatory story about the key influences on student learning' and 'to generate a model of successful teaching and learning based on the many thousands of studies in 800 and more meta-analyses' (Hattie 2009: 6 and 235). He concludes that visible teaching and visible learning are key to student achievement and acknowledges that the teacher who is 'directive, influential, caring and actively engaged in the passion of teaching and learning' is one of 'the most powerful influences in learning' (Hattie 2009: 238).

Meta-analysis is not for the faint hearted and is not something that individual researchers are likely to undertake as a way of exploring specific aspects of literacy and numeracy teaching and learning. This method has also been criticised, from within education and in other fields, as obscuring 'important qualitative information by averaging simple numerical representations across studies' and some critics think that meta-analysis should only be undertaken by 'a reflective expert who can sift kernels of insight from the confusing argumentation of the field' (Bangert-Drowns & Rudner 1991). However, literature reviews are usually part of any research project and being aware that there may be previous meta-analyses in the same or similar research area can provide information and ideas and can inform the process of research design.

Meta-analysis references

Glass, G. V. (1976) Primary, secondary and meta-analysis of research. *Educational Researcher* Vol 5. No. 10, 3–8.

Hattie, J. (2009) *Visible learning: A synthesis of over 800 met-analyses relating to achievement.* London and New York: Routledge.

Hattie, J. H., Rogers, J., and Swaminathan, H. (2014) The role of meta-analysis in educational research. In A. D. Reid, E. P. Hart, and M. A. Peters (Eds). *A companion to research in education.* New York and London: Springer.

Conclusion

This chapter has reviewed research methods that have been used to investigate multiple aspects of literacy across the domains of literacy learning and practice. Some of these methods have been used by the researchers who have added their voices to the book in Chapter 7. These include distinguished researchers who have, over the years, expanded our understandings of what it means to be literate and numerate and what it means to teach and learn literacy and numeracy. Other contributors to Chapter 7 are just beginning their research careers and have drawn inspiration from those who have charted new pathways across the literacy terrain or who have made new discoveries by retracing earlier research pathways.

7
Researcher Voices

One important motivation for writing this book has been to widen the view of literacy and literacy education by examining theory, research and practice across a broad range of contexts. Rather than providing second-hand descriptions of exemplary recent studies, this chapter offers the reader the opportunity to hear directly from researchers who have studied various aspects of literacy and literacy development, including language, numeracy, cognition and community issues. It includes exemplary studies in which a range of methodological approaches have been applied, including participatory research, studies of community and family literacy, and text analysis.

   We are very grateful to the researchers who took the time to respond to our questions and we hope that hearing directly from the researchers themselves enhances the sense of immediacy, and of being in the field with the researcher, while also revealing that research is contestable and researchers are always open to further insights and developments in thinking. The contributions from the researchers were gathered by asking them to respond to the following eight questions:

1. Based on your research in the field of literacy in society and literacy development, can you briefly describe the research project, study or investigation you think provided the most significant insights into the nature of literacy and/or literacy development? What were these insights? What impact/s did the project have?
2. What prompted you to research in this context/area of literacy, for example, a previous study you found inspiring, or a particular social concern or problem?
3. What approach, conceptual framework and/or methodology did you adopt for the project and why?

4. Why do you think this project provided such insights?
5. In retrospect, what would you do differently? To address the same or a similar problem now, would you use the same or a different approach?
6. What do you think other researchers could learn from this project and its approach?
7. What further research do you think still needs to be done in this area?
8. Are there any other comments you would like to make about the project, and this or other areas of literacy research?

For the reader who wishes to join the community of literacy and numeracy researchers these accounts of research provide ways of approaching the field through guiding principles, considerations and perspectives. James Gee begins this important chapter with a recount of his research journey and the lessons and insights he has learned along the way.

James Gee: a literacy research journey

James Gee of Arizona State University discusses how research done by others into school literacy practices prompted his life-long academic research interest in literacy. He discusses how his research has shifted in focus over the years, building on the past but incorporating new perspectives. He ends his discussion with advice to other researchers in the form of ten things his research journey has taught him.

I need to answer the first two questions together, because, for me, they really cannot be disentangled. I will take as my example my first paper on literacy, a paper called *What is Literacy?* The paper was delivered as a talk at a very small Mailman Foundation Conference on Families and Literacy at the Harvard Graduate School of Education in March 1987. After I had presented it, I got a request to publish it in a journal I had never heard of and which I think went out of business soon after it started. The journal was *Teaching and Learning* (2: 3–11, 1987) and the paper has since been republished a great many times in many different forms. It was foundational to my first book *Social linguistics and literacies: Ideology in discourses* (1st Edition 1990; 5th Edition 2015), a book which has been continuously in print for 25 years and which was one of the foundations of the New Literacy Studies (NLS) and, in fact, helped name that field.

Here is the story behind the paper. I began my academic career 40 years ago as a linguist studying the structure of language (*grammar*). At that time, thanks to the seminal work of Noam Chomsky, the fashionable thing to study was the basic design properties of language, the core grammatical properties that all human languages shared (Chomsky 1957 and 1986). There was much less interest in meaning and in language in use. The study of language was then a pretty abstract affair.

Thanks to the *accidents* of life – mistakes made, lessons learned – years later I found myself employed in an applied linguistics programme. The programme happened to be in a School of Education at Boston University (later the programme moved out of the School of Education – had that happened before I went, I would not now be me as an academic). I knew absolutely nothing about education then. Early in my time there, the Dean of the School of Education came up to me and asked me to attend a meeting about applying for a grant to research adult literacy. As a generative (Chomskian) linguist I believed that only oral language was real language. Literacy was only a derivative and relatively trivial *code*. After all, oral language arose in humans long ago (Pinker 1994). It is a good part of what separated humans from their primate relatives. On the other hand, literacy is a relatively recent cultural invention (Olson 1994). Writing has been invented independently only a few times in history. All human groups have had oral language, but not all cultures have had literacy and not all have it today. In the not too distant past, in fact, literacy was rare within societies and across the world.

When I attended the meeting, I was surprised to find out that there were adults in the United States who were *illiterate*, let alone the supposed millions I was told were close to it. Since everyone in the United States went to school, how could this have happened? I assumed schools gave everyone an equal chance and at least ensured that everyone learned to read and write. When I attended the meeting, I was as naïve as I could be. I thought that surely literacy would be a simple, straightforward topic of little depth (I should have known better, since many languages in the world do not even have a word for *literacy*). Surely, literacy was just a practical matter of no theoretical interest. It was not something real academics would study,

As I studied literacy, the whole topic seemed stranger and stranger. Simplicity turned to complexity. Paradoxes abounded. Because I had been *coerced* to work on literacy and was trying to get any help I could, I ended up meeting Sarah Michaels, then working at Harvard and now at Clark University. My colleague David Dickinson (now at Vanderbilt) introduced me to Sarah. Sarah showed me data she and others had collected on first-grade *sharing-time* sessions in schools. Sharing-time is something teachers of very young children tend to do to start off the school day. It is sometimes called *rug time* or *show and tell*. At the time I could not have imagined anything seemingly less important. Sarah and her colleagues had found that some African-American children gave sharing-time turns that were different from those of the white children in the classrooms (Cazden 2001, Michaels 1981, Michaels & Cazden 1986, Michaels & Cook-Gumperz 1979, Michaels & Collins 1984). These African-American children told what Sarah called 'topic-associating' stories, while the Anglo children (and some of the other African-American children) told 'topic-centred' stories. Topic-associating stories were ones that appeared to move from topic to topic with no overt theme. The unifying theme had to be supplied by the listener. Topic-centred stories were ones that focused on and developed one unitary explicit topic. These were usually, in fact, not really stories, but reports, such as an *event cast* of a trip to a swimming pool, or procedures, such as the steps involved in making a candle. The African-American children's sharing-time turns were not well received by their teachers. The teachers thought the children were rambling on and not making sense. The teachers in these classrooms had instituted a rule that each turn had to be about *one important thing* and felt the African-American children often violated this rule.

The teachers, it turns out, could seamlessly interrupt and interact with the white children and the African-American children who told topic-focused stories, though not with the topic-associating African-American children. In a sort of interactive dance, the teachers helped the topic-focused children produce a piece of language that, while spoken, was explicit and topic-focused in the way we later expect school-based writing to be. Sarah and her colleagues argued that these sharing-time sessions were early practice at literacy or literate language for children who could not yet read and write very well. This was not necessarily the teachers' conscious plan, but it seemed to be the underlying goal in their practice.

When I looked at the sharing-time data, a number of the African-American stories stood out. They were long, robust, well-organised poetic stories. Unfortunately, the researchers had thrown these stories out of their data, concentrating on the shorter ones told by the African-American children. They did this in order to *control for length*, since the white children's sharing-time turns, in particular, were relatively short (because they were so concise). It appeared to me that some of the shorter African-American turns were cases where children had been stopped by the teacher and told to sit down (for not talking about one important thing). Or they were cases where the child had started a story, but for one reason or another did not choose to finish it. The stories that were clearly finished seemed thematically based, but not loosely structured. While they were not like early versions of the sort of explicit, concise language we later expect in reports and essays, they were *literate* in the sense of being early versions of the literary language we expect in poetry and other forms of literary art.

In my early work I showed that some of the African-American children in the sharing-time research were giving the teacher a quite recognisable linguistic performance (*oral literature*). Their performances were rooted in a long history of African-Americans going back to Africa. They are a type of performance once prevalent in many other cultures, though done in somewhat different ways in each. They are also a type of performance that, via figures like Homer and Chaucer, is the foundation of Western written literature. Of course, these were young children and, thus, early in their apprenticeships to this cultural verbal style, though obviously well on their way.

One thing that went on in these classrooms was that some of the African-American children were misled by the ways in which teachers (and many academics) use the word *story* to cover both narrative verbal texts with plots and oral texts more akin to reports or the news (e.g. going swimming or making candles). In fact, following the original sharing-time terminology I have continued this unfortunate tradition here.

Some of the African-American children thought the teacher really wanted a story and gave her a culturally-embedded version of one. But the teacher was actually after a news-like report through which she could scaffold early school-based literate language in the *expository* style (i.e. linear, sequenced, concise, explicit, non-poetic, non-literary, expository language). All children need practice in many different styles, of course, but such a lack of clarity about goals, practice, and what language means creates a fundamental unfairness.

These children were being seen as deficient when they were enacting a culturally known, important, and impressive way of being, making meaning and using language. They were not being seen as African-American storytellers. Furthermore, they were not being helped to recognise the ways with words the teacher expected. The teachers assumed all the children already knew what they, the teachers, wanted – what *the rules of the game* were – and, thus, did not tell them. Many of the *mainstream* children (white and black) in the classrooms had engaged in sharing-time like reports with their parents at dinner-time, another now well-studied phenomenon.

A deep problem here is that these were very young children. They were being told by an authority figure, as part of their early socialisation into schooling, that they did not make sense. This is not because the teachers were bad people. It was because they did not know that these African-American children were using ways with words that had come from their early socialisation into their own home-based culture, a culture tied to the historical legacy of oral literature. This sort of *cultural misunderstanding* (misrecognition, missed opportunities for recognition) can and often does alienate children from school and school-based language and literacy. It can force such young children to choose between family and school in terms of who makes sense.

All these issues were in my mind as I remembered in a busy day that I was due, in a few hours, to go over from Boston University to Harvard to give my talk. I realised, with a panic, that I had not really prepared the talk and so sat down to write it out (by hand, in those days). All the confusions, discussions and interactions that I had been having over literacy with colleagues and texts (outside of and far from theoretical linguistics) all of sudden jelled. The paper just poured out of me with no revision. When I delivered it, the respondent got up and said, *All I can do is ask him to read it again*, he liked it so much. During questions after the talk, a Harvard graduate student said, with trepidation, *I liked the talk, but Jeanne is here, and I would guess she would not have liked it.* She was referring to Jeanne Chall, perhaps the greatest reading scholar of the 20th century, and a woman feared by some (OK, many). Jeanne thought for a minute and said, with a sound of surprise, *I can't think of anything I disagree with in the paper.*

This was how my (second) career as a literacy scholar in education – and no longer a syntactician in linguistics – started in earnest. Though I have long hoped it would happen again, no paper ever again leapt so effortlessly from pen (or keyboard) to paper (or screen) as did the first. I think my work in this area has had impact, but that is not for me to say.

The paper was almost entirely theory building with examples from the research I was doing on the sharing-time data. I adopted this approach because of my training in generative linguistics. Generative linguistics is based on taking the word *language* and giving it a specific definition in terms of a theory about what its core properties are taken to be. The theory does not cover all aspects of language, nor does it cover the everyday meaning of the term. The theory singles out one core meaning of the word and uses the theory to explicate and explain the properties that language has in that core sense. The proof, then, becomes whether interesting results and discoveries follow from the theory. I approached *literacy* in the same spirit.

Timing. At the time (in the 1980s) educational research was really changing. Lots of people from different disciplines, but not necessarily with degrees in Education, were beginning to find educational problems highly significant and ripe for new approaches. Such people – like myself, with a degree in linguistics but never having taken a course in education – were, in fact, usually welcomed warmly by Schools of Education and educators, at least in my experience. As I argued in *Social linguistics and literacies*, lots of people in the 1980s were beginning to work on literacy from all different disciplinary angles, but converging on a sociocultural approach (e.g. Brian Street, Shirley Brice Heath, Harvey Graff, Michael Cole, Sylvia Scribner, Ron Scollon, Suzanne Scollon, Gunther Kress, Alan Luke, Jay Lemke, Colin Lankshear, Peter Freebody, Bill Cope, Mary Kalantzis, Sarah Michaels, Courtney Cazden, David Barton, Mary Hamilton and others). My work saw and caught a wave.

I have continued to work in the area and have repeatedly done things differently to improve the earlier work, I hope. In *The Social Mind* (1992), I sought to deal with the ways in which the mind is social and, thus, to think about how work on learning in situated/embodied cognition could be added to the New Literacy Studies work. In *What video games have to teach us about learning and literacy* (2003) I sought to relate newer digital literacies and digital media to literacy more traditionally conceived. In *The Anti-education era* (2013), I sought to embed literacy in the larger framework of today's global crises and the need for collective intelligence before we put the human species out of business.

There is a deep reason though why I would not have done *What is Literacy?* differently. I have never been able to write well about what I know too much about. When I know a great deal about an area, I find I can offer nothing very much other than cautious tales and quite limited and deeply hedged claims. The work might be factually *truer*, but it is not very motivating for readers and does not lead to much real impact. When I know *too much*, I move on.

What I have always thought fuelled my work, and whatever contributions I have made or impact I have had, was that I was always on the lookout for how melding a new area of interest with an old one could give rise to new ideas, even if the two areas seemed quite unconnected. It was relating new interests in distributed parallel processing (*connectionism*) in psychology to old work on literacy that gave rise to *The Social Mind*. It was relating new interests in so-called *fast capitalism* in the business world to old work on literacy that gave rise to *The new work order* (1993). It was playing video games with my then six-year-old son that gave rise to *What video games have to teach us about learning and literacy.* My recent book, *Unified discourse analysis: Language, reality, virtual worlds and video games* (2014) was an attempt to relate my interest in discourse analysis in linguistics to my interest in video games and both to my interest in literacy, an interest which was itself now moving to an interest in multimodality. The same sort of thing has been true of most of my books.

Some of what I thought should be done, I did. Right now, in a world where the nature of diversity, inequality, risk, institutions, media, economies and the global world is deeply changed from the 1960s, the world in which baby-boomers like myself (born in 1948) came of age, what I think we need most is new theories based on that changed world and all the new ideas that have recently proliferated in fields outside of Education. Young scholars today sometimes follow the lead of old ones and their theories and methods too slavishly. We need young scholars to create real innovation, albeit in a very high-risk academic world these days. This is beginning to happen in some areas where the tech-savvy nature of younger scholars is leading them to innovate, but it is not really happening in areas like learning, literacy, diversity and schooling. In my view, more young scholars need to feel the need – and right – to engage in theory building.

Here are ten things my journey from *What is Literacy?* to video games has taught me:

1. If something seems trivial, it probably isn't (study it).
2. If two things don't seem connected, they probably are (search for the connection).
3. Don't wait until you know all you need to know to join the discussion.
4. From time to time, revisit long settled matters and reopen the *black box* and ask *Why did we all agree on this?*
5. Never wait until a piece of work is *perfect* – that just stunts the conversation.
6. The point is not for you or me to be *right*, it is for us all together to make things better.
7. The point of academics is ideas, ideas which we hope will help.
8. Learn something deeply and then find something new that you don't know much about and seek connections.
9. There is no way to engage in any empirical work without a theory, so always ask yourself what your theory is and then work to make it better and clearer.
10. Write to be read by others – make your writing as accessible as you can while still being fair to the content.

References

Cazden, C. (2001) *Classroom discourse: The language of teaching and learning* (2nd Edition). Portsmouth, NH: Heinemann.

Chomsky, N. (1957) *Syntactic structures*. The Hague: Mouton.

Chomsky, N. (1986) *Knowledge of language: Its nature, origin, and use*. New York: Praeger.

Gee, J. P. (1987) What is literacy? *Teaching and Learning* Vol. 2 No. 1, 3–11.

Gee, J. P. (1990) *Social linguistics and literacies: Ideology in Discourses* (5th Edition, 2015). London: Taylor & Francis.

Gee, J. P. (1992) *The social mind: Language, ideology, and social practice*. New York: Bergin & Garvey. Reprinted 2014: Champaign-Urbana: Common Ground.

Gee, J. P. (2001) *Unified discourse analysis: Language, reality, visual worlds, and video games*. London: Routledge.

Gee, J. P. (2003) *What video games have to teach us about learning and literacy* (2nd Edition, 2007). New York: Palgrave/Macmillan.

Gee, J. P. (2013) *The anti-education era: Creating smarter students through digital learning*. New York: Palgrave/Macmillan.Michaels, S. (1981) 'Sharing time': Children's narrative styles and differential access to literacy. *Language in Society* Vol. 10, 423–442.

Michaels, S. and Cazden, C. (1986) Teacher/child collaboration as oral preparation for literacy. In B. Schieffelin (Ed). *Acquisition of literacy: Ethnographic perspectives*. Norwood, NJ: Ablex, 132–154.

Michaels, S. and Cook-Gumperz, J. (1979) A study of sharing time with first-grade students: Discourse narratives in the classroom. In *Proceedings of the Fifth Annual Meetings of the Berkeley Linguistics Society*, 647–660.

Michaels, S. and Collins, J. (1984) Oral discourse styles: Classroom interaction and the acquisition of literacy. In D. Tannen (Ed). *Coherence in spoken and written discourse*. Norwood, NJ: Ablex: 219–244.

Olson, D. R. (1994) *The world on paper: The conceptual and cognitive implications of writing and reading*. Cambridge: Cambridge University Press.

Pinker, S. (1994) *The language instinct: How the mind creates language*. New York: William Morrow.

Literacy in primary school contexts

Maria Estela Brisk: 'Genres in writing' – a collaborative research project

Maria Estela Brisk (Boston College) describes a research project through which a team of university academics collaborated with teachers to implement an approach to teaching writing informed by Systemic Functional Linguistics (SFL). The project focused on developing and implementing a curriculum for the teaching of writing while researching the impact of using a genre-based approach on students' writing development.

In 2007, the mayor of Boston asked private universities to support struggling schools. Boston College (BC) was assigned two schools, one of which was interested in improving writing instruction. The Russell is a small elementary school with a population comprising 58% Latino, 26% Black, 10% Asian and 6% White. With respect to language proficiency, 51% of the students are considered English-language learners, while an additional 15% are bilingual, fully fluent in English and 34% are monolingual English speakers.

I met a group of fourth and fifth grade teachers, and briefly explained Systemic Functional Linguistics (SFL) and genre-based pedagogy to them. The teachers were enthusiastic and the project started in the last week of August 2008 with a three-day whole school meeting before classes started. The Collaborative Fellows Grant from the Lynch School of Education at Boston College funded the first three years of this project. I continued the work with the school and the team received an additional three-year grant to study the impact of this project on second-language (L2) learners.

The goal of this project was to develop and implement a curriculum for the teaching of writing and to research the impact of using a genre-based approach on students' writing. Specifically, teachers collaborated with the university team on implementing an approach to teaching writing informed by SFL. During the first year of the project, the Boston College team worked with third, fourth and fifth grade teachers and specialists. For six years thereafter, the BC team worked with all of the teachers from pre-kindergarten to fifth grade. Currently, the BC team is observing three to five grade classrooms, focusing specifically on students who are considered English-language learners from beginners to advanced.

Every year, during the week before classes start, the BC team meets with the whole school to present the genres, new ideas, and decide on the writing calendar for the whole school, making sure that over the years the children experience different genres. The teachers also connect the genres of writing with the disciplinary topics demanded of their grade level.

Based on observations over the year, new content is suggested at these annual meetings. For example, after noticing that there was very limited teaching of explanations, as team leader, I proposed that all grades teach scientific explanations. In collaboration with the science specialist, each grade explored topics covered at that grade level and decided what type of explanation would be appropriate. For example, pre-K through to Grade 1 chose cyclical explanations to teach the life cycle of plants and animals and weather cycles. Teachers were shown how to use puzzles and diagrams for the early grades, and posters with captions for third grade, while fourth and fifth grades would practise writing full explanations. A former member of the BC team who had become an instructor at another university took over the research of just this part of the project (see Hodgson-Drysdale & Rosa, 2015).

During the academic year, the BC team leader meets monthly with grade-level groups of teachers. The principal, Tamara Blake-Canty, has attended every meeting and has provided full support for the project from the start. In the first year, teachers were encouraged just to implement two genres. During the meetings, the features of the genres were presented and together the group discussed possible ways of teaching. The principles of the teaching and learning cycle (TLC) were also introduced. Over time, teachers increased the number of genres they taught. Currently, Pre-K through to Grade 1 teach procedures, personal recounts and reports, repeating them so that children get a chance to try them again as they rapidly progress in their writing skills. Grades 3–5 teach between four and five genres a year, taking between four to eight weeks per genre. The length depends on the specific genre and the amount of content they need to teach. The science specialists became enthusiasts of the project, excelling in integrating writing with science instruction (Hodgson-Drysdale 2014, Hodgson-Drysdale & Ballard 2011). After the third year of the project, when teachers had gained sufficient confidence with the genres, the focus of the meetings turned to student work and specific language demands of register. Student work was analysed using SFL inspired forms developed by the BC team leader (Brisk 2015). These forms focus on purpose, stages of the genre and specific language features essential for that genre. Initially, all aspects of language were included, but it turned out to be overwhelming for teachers. Thus in reviewing the theory and student work, the areas covered by the forms were narrowed down to those essential for a particular genre. For example, processes, expressed by verbs and verb groups, are important in writing recounts. They carry a lot of information about participants, while noun groups contain much of the information of reports. Arguments (exposition) depend heavily on language choices based on tenor.

This work has significantly impacted the two collaborating institutions and the field in general. Before the project started, writing was not a priority at this school and it was left to the discretion of the teachers as to what to do. Currently, all teachers use genre-based pedagogy to teach writing on a daily basis in connection with a variety of disciplines using the genre-based pedagogy. They plan the writing calendar as a whole school and work cooperatively within each grade level and in some cases across grade levels (Daniello 2014). The school advanced from one of the ten worst performing schools in the city to Level 1, the highest level of performance. Students have steadily advanced in the English Language Arts (ELA) state tests with some peaks and valleys over the years. Most of the L2 learners in Grades 3–5 have advanced in all skills, especially speaking and writing. These data led to the current study, which is investigating how the genre-based pedagogy is helping L2 students when instructed in mainstream classrooms with limited or no support from an ESL specialist.

The project also had an impact on the university by providing faculty and graduate students with an opportunity to carry out research, which has been disseminated through conference presentations and papers (Brisk 2012, Brisk & De Rosa 2014, Daniello, Turgut, & Brisk 2014). In addition, the curriculum for the Teaching Language Arts course at the graduate and undergraduate levels was completely changed to reflect a genre-based SFL informed content. Teachers at the school have been participating each semester as co-instructors in the course. This practice has further solidified these teachers' knowledge of the theory.

This project has provided rich information with respect to writing instruction and the writing development of elementary students. The BC team, in collaboration with the teachers, has developed ways to implement instruction defining strategies and materials that support implementation. Classrooms were visited weekly to document instruction and analyse the content of writing instruction to determine the features of the theory that the teachers were applying in their instruction. In addition, a picture of the various aspects of children's writing development has emerged from a review of students' work. For the early grades, the work students produced, as a result of instruction, was collected and analysed. In Grades 3–5, students wrote an uncoached piece at the start of a genre unit. The analysis of this writing informed instruction and provided a comparison with writing that emerged at the end of the unit. Much of this work is documented in Brisk (2015). These data became material for monthly professional development meetings, providing continuous feedback to teachers.

There are a number of factors that have made this programme possible and successful. Perhaps the most important is the full support of an enlightened principal who was new in 2008, when the project started. She consistently attended the meetings to become familiar with the theory and learn what she should expect when visiting classrooms. The work with teachers was fully collaborative. Teachers' ideas were always welcomed, became part of the practice, and were documented in published research (Brisk, Hodgson-Drysdale, & O'Connor 2011, Pavlak 2013). Teachers were introduced to the theory in stages, with the purpose and stages of genres first and the language demands of register later. Concepts of language, which are harder and newer for teachers, were presented slowly over the years, mainly through discussion of student work. Having funding initially to provide the school with books and technology for the classrooms, as well as to support graduate students who weekly observed and assisted the teachers with the implementation, was essential in giving the programme a strong start.

A genre-based pedagogy can be transformative by not only improving writing instruction, perhaps the most neglected language skill in schools (Graham & Harris 2013), but also by making teachers expert language teachers. With an increasing number of students in schools who come from homes where English is not the daily language of interaction, it is essential that all teachers in English-medium schools become expert language teachers.

Making teachers knowledgeable in the theory makes instruction sustainable. No matter what curricular demands the system makes in the school, these teachers know about writing in the English-speaking cultural context and can teach it within any constraints imposed by the district administration.

References

Brisk, M. E. (2012) Young bilingual writers' control of grammatical person in different genres. *Elementary Education Journal* Vol. 112, 445–468.

Brisk, M. (2015) *Engaging students in academic literacies: Genre-based pedagogy for K-5 classrooms*. New York: Routledge.

Brisk, M. E., Hodgson-Drysdale, T. and O'Connor, C. (2011) A study of a collaborative instructional project informed by Systemic Functional Linguistic theory: Report writing in elementary grades. *Journal of Education* Vol. 191, 1–12.

Brisk, M. E. and De Rosa, M. (2014) Young writers' attempts at making meaning through complex sentence structures while writing a variety of genres. In L. de Oliveira and J. Iddings (Eds). *Genre pedagogy across the curriculum: Theory and application in US classrooms and contexts*. London: Equinox, 8–24.

Daniello, F. (2014) Elementary grade teachers using Systemic Functional Linguistics to inform genre-based writing instruction. In L. Oliveira and J. Iddings (Eds). *Genre pedagogy across the curriculum: Theory and application in US classrooms and contexts*. Bristol, CT: Equinox Publishing, 41–56.

Daniello, F., Turgut, G. and Brisk, M. E. (2014) Applying systemic functional linguistics to build educators' knowledge of academic English for the teaching of writing. In A. Mahboob and L. Barret. (Eds). *Englishes in multilingual contexts*. London: Springer, 183–204.

Graham, S. and Harris, K. R. (2013) Designing an effective writing program. In S. Graham, C. A. MacArthur and J. Fitzgerald (Eds). *Best practices in writing instruction*. New York: Guilford Press, 3–25.

Hodgson-Drysdale, T. (2014) Concepts and language: Developing knowledge in science. *Linguistics and Education* Vol. 27, 54–67.

Hodgson-Drysdale, T. and Ballard, E. 2011. Explaining electrical circuits. *Science and Children* Vol. 48 No. 8, 37–41.

Hodgson-Drysdale, T. and Rosa, H. (2015). Go with the flow: Energy in ecosystems. *Science and Children*.

Pavlak, C. M. (2013) 'It is hard fun': Scaffolded biography writing with English learners. *The Reading Teacher* Vol. 66 No. 5, 405–414.

Mary Schleppegrell and Annemarie Palincsar: the iterative development of modules to support teachers' engagement in exploring language and meaning in text with English-language learners

Mary Schleppegrell and **Annemarie Palincsar** (University of Michigan) describe a project to develop materials to support the use of functional grammar, informed by Systemic Functional Linguistics (SFL), in elementary school classrooms where the majority of students were learning English as an additional language. They worked in six schools with about 30 teachers and resource teachers to engage in design-based research. The project aimed to develop curriculum and teaching practices and propose ways of organising instruction to optimise the opportunities for children to use language during instruction. It also provided professional development to teachers that was close to practice, learning from teachers' enactment of the curriculum, as well as from children's responses to the instruction, and then engaging in further cycles of development.

We conducted a study together from 2010 to 2014 – a project we called *The iterative development of modules to support teachers' engagement in exploring language and meaning in text with English language learners.* This was a project to develop materials to support the use of functional grammar, informed by Systemic Functional Linguistics (SFL), in elementary school classrooms with a majority of students who were learning English as an additional language. We worked in six schools with about 30 teachers and resource teachers to engage in design-based research – developing curriculum and teaching practices, proposing ways of organising instruction to optimise the opportunities for children to use language during instruction, providing professional development to teachers that was close to practice, learning from teachers' enactment of the curriculum, as well as from children's responses to the instruction, and then engaging in further cycles of development.

We identified many ways that functional grammar can serve as a valuable resource for focusing on meaning during text-based discussions and in supporting children's writing. Furthermore, we learned:

1. that the curriculum had to be aligned with the subject-matter learning goals of the teachers
2. the importance of focusing our collective attention on the idea that knowledge about language is learned through the use of language
3. that extant texts available to elementary-aged students are not designed to support teachers to reach the ambitious instructional goals that young children are most capable of achieving

The project is in its final stages, and so it is somewhat premature to talk about impact. As we disseminate findings from our study, we hope to support others who are investigating the affordances of functional grammar for supporting students learning language and school subjects, as well as to inform research seeking ways of providing explicit information about language to English-language learners. The teachers who participated in the project reported that the approach helped them support their English learners in learning language and content and that the functional grammar offered them support in teaching writing. Furthermore, teachers reported that students used the tools provided by functional grammar in a broad range of academic contexts. We have published some of our findings.

We were prompted by the calls for teachers to talk about language with English learners and the absence of robust preparation for them to do this in pre-service and in-service professional development contexts. Our previous research enabled us to bring together a focus on talk about text in new ways. Annemarie brought her research on text-based discussions to the project (e.g. Kucan & Palincsar 2013, Palincsar 2003). This research revealed the kinds of teacher-student interactions that support knowledge-building with text. Mary's work with the California History Project (e.g. Schleppegrell 2011, Schleppegrell, Greer, & Taylor 2008) and other work with teachers had helped her understand how to make the functional grammar constructs useful to and usable by teachers. Her more recent work with elementary teachers (e.g. Schleppegrell 2010) had shown her the need for more scaffolded writing instruction for English learners. We brought these interests and experiences together in this project.

Our conceptual frameworks come from Vygotskyan and Hallidayan perspectives on language and learning. Our research methodology for this development project was design-based research (DBR) (Design-based

Research Collective 2003). Vygotsky and Halliday provide theories that are commensurate and that offer complementary contributions to the study of language and learning (Wells 1993) and DBR offers a research methodology that enabled us to engage in iterative design and development of our approach and intervention.

The project provided insights because it was situated in an authentic context where our teacher-collaborators worked closely with us and enabled us to explore and develop our approach in relation to the goals the teachers had for literacy instruction. We partnered with the teachers in virtually every aspect of the research including curriculum development, co-teaching and gathering of ongoing feedback from the teachers, as well as evidence from the students. We were therefore able to study teacher implementation and student engagement in the kinds of classroom activity to which our efforts aimed to contribute.

Based on what we learned, we would begin work of this type at a higher level of understanding about the need to connect with teachers' current practice and use disciplinary and linguistic metalanguage to support both language and content goals. In our first attempts in the *Language and Meaning* project, we focused on developing teachers' linguistic knowledge as a first step. Through our design-based research approach, we came to understand that for in-service teachers, the linguistic knowledge can be developed as they engage children in discussion and activities that use the functional grammar metalanguage in meaningful ways to talk about texts and writing.

Those adopting genre-based approaches could gain insights into how this approach can be situated in new contexts (Schleppegrell, Moore, Al-Adeimi, O'Hallaron, Palincsar, & Symons 2014). For practising teachers and teacher educators, the specific tools we developed, using SFL metalanguage, could provide ways to begin talking explicitly about language and meaning with their students (see, for example, Moore & Schleppegrell 2014, Palincsar & Schleppegrell 2014, Schleppegrell 2013).

The exploration of how best to engage teachers in talk about language with children is still in its early stages and much more needs to be done across different age levels and content areas. There are few studies that provide detailed insights into what this work looks like in classroom interaction.

We found it valuable to collaborate and bring our different histories and approaches to this study. We think more collaboration between applied linguists and literacy researchers is needed so that approaches to language development are firmly grounded in the disciplinary literacy classroom where they also support content learning.

References

Design-Based Research Collective (2003) Design-based research: An emerging paradigm for educational inquiry. *Educational Researcher* Vol. 32 No. 1, 5–8, 35–37.

Kucan, L. and Palincsar, A. S. (2013) *Comprehension instruction through text-based discussion.* Newark, DE: International Reading Association.

Moore, J. and Schleppegrell, M. J. (2014) Using a functional linguistics metalanguage to support academic language development in the English Language Arts. *Linguistics and Education* Vol. 26, 92–105.

Palincsar, A. S. (2003) Collaborative approaches to reading comprehension. In A. Sweet and C. Snow (Eds). *Rethinking reading comprehension.* New York: Guilford Press, 99–115.

Palincsar, A. and Schleppegrell, M. J. (2014) Focusing on language and meaning while learning with text. *TESOL Quarterly* Vol. 48 No. 3, 616–623.

Schleppegrell, M. J. (2010) Supporting a 'reading to write' pedagogy with functional grammar. *NALDIC Quarterly* Vol. 8 No. 1, 26–31.

Schleppegrell, M. J. (2011) Supporting disciplinary learning through language analysis: Developing historical literacy. In F. Christie and K. Maton (Eds). *Disciplinarity: Functional linguistic and sociological perspectives.* London: Continuum, 197–216.

Schleppegrell, M. J. (2013) The role of metalanguage in supporting academic language development. *Language Learning* Vol. 63 No. Suppl 1, 153–170.

Schleppegrell, M. J., Greer, S. and Taylor, S. (2008) Literacy in history: Language and meaning. *Australian Journal of Language and Literacy* Vol. 31 No. 2, 174–187.

Schleppegrell, M., Moore, J., Al-Adeimi, S., O'Hallaron, C., Palincsar, A. and Symons, C. (2014) Tackling a genre: Situating SFL genre pedagogy in a new context. In L. de Oliveira and J. Iddings (Eds). *Genre pedagogy across the curriculum: Theory and application in US classrooms and contexts.* Sheffield, UK: Equinox, 26–40.

Geoff Williams and Ruth French: teaching and learning grammatics

> **Geoff Williams** and **Ruth French** (University of Sydney) describe a project that examined the value of teaching primary school children to use selected grammatical concepts for literacy work throughout the curriculum. The research addressed two main questions – Are the selected concepts accessible to primary-aged children? Is learning about the concepts efficacious for literacy development?

The purpose of our studies was to examine the value of teaching primary school children to use selected grammatical concepts drawn from Systemic Functional Linguistics for literacy work throughout the curriculum. Following Halliday (2002/1998), we thought of this as the study of grammatics rather than grammar, in order to distinguish it from questions about children's language development, which obviously involves the development of knowledge of grammar. 'Since the study of language is called *linguistics*, I have been calling the study of grammar *grammatics* in order to make the distinction clear. A grammatics is thus a theory for explaining the grammar' (Halliday 2002/1998: 369). No prior research into these questions had been conducted before we began in 1994. The research addressed two main questions – Are the selected grammatical concepts accessible to primary-aged children? / Is learning about the grammatical concepts efficacious for literacy development?

Children of six, eight and 11 were involved in the first studies. It was also possible to study the development of one of the 11-year-old groups, when the children moved from primary to secondary school. This was because they spontaneously expressed interest in continuing to learn about systemic functional grammar (SFG) and so formed an after-school Grammar Club at the beginning of the next year. They participated in the club once a week after school, returning from their various secondary schools.

We found strong evidence that the concepts were both accessible and efficacious in relation to a range of literacy development factors, including understanding text-type differences, increased reading fluency, thematic structure in writing and the effects of linguistic patterning on characterisation in fiction.

Historical research on the teaching of grammar had not examined the potential of SFG as a resource for helping students to think about language, especially language in use. Most research in the field had considered the value of teaching *traditional school grammar* – an approach that focuses on word classes (form, syntax) and *rules of usage* – grammar for accuracy. There had also been a smaller degree of interest in teaching transformational grammar – again here there was an emphasis on form and rules, albeit *rules* defined in terms of hypothesised cognitive transformations rather than *rules* of usage – grammar as cognition.

Neither of these approaches to teaching grammar had foregrounded the relationship between grammar, meaning and contexts of use, which systemic functional grammar was designed to address. Systemic Functional Linguistics (SFL), from which SFG derives, maintains that it is the social uses of language that drive the ways in which we speak and write, that language is essentially about making meaning in the various social contexts of life. The approach to language description adopted by SFG is therefore one that seeks to explain how choices in wordings relate to differences in meaning. That is, SFG is a meaning-oriented language description as given by its design principles.

To us it seemed that there was potential to explore how we might use SFG to help school students comprehend how texts are organised to make meaning, and also to help students make purposeful applications of grammar for composing rhetorically successful texts – grammar for meaning and a grammar about making effective choices rather than following rules. We were also interested in exploring effective pedagogy for teaching grammatics because the quality of teaching had been elided in most of the historical literature. We derived our approach from Vygotsky's theory, noting that in *Thought and language* (1987) he had foregrounded the importance of children learning about grammar. The main Vygotskian concepts we worked with were semiotic mediation, the structuring of attention through verbal signs, relations between signs and activities and the importance of play in children's development.

A case study approach has been a productive methodology for us to explore the possibilities of innovation, while also examining in some depth the responses of children and the pedagogical strategies that could support effective learning. This approach was adopted in order to give the broadly qualitative approach a clear focus and manageable scope. The case study has a robust and established place in present-day educational research. It is 'an empirical enquiry that investigates a contemporary phenomenon in depth and within its real-life context' (Yin 2009: 18) and is defined by both design features – the macro unit of analysis is 'the case', a bounded entity – and approaches to data collection, particularly the use of multiple sources of evidence.

A further, related advantage of the case study is its ability to accommodate and elucidate the dynamic and complex practices of the classroom, including tracing the detailed pathways in which teaching-learning develops, a process the importance of which Vygotsky had underscored. If the historical research on learning grammar tended to elide teaching practice, in the present work the emphasis was on what has historically been under-scrutinised, that is, actual observations of classroom interactions in teaching and learning grammatics. Thus the main aim of the case study design in the present project was 'the generation of rich knowledge of a given phenomenon', whereas the well-known historical grammar teaching studies followed traditional scientific methodology aimed at 'less rich but generalisable knowledge of that phenomenon' (Moriceau 2010: 422).

An important consideration in adopting a case study design was the fact that this research was such an emergent field of inquiry. Exploratory work with different groups of learners was needed in order to expand understandings about the possibilities and challenges in teaching and learning a functional grammatics.

We think there are three key reasons why this project provided insights into the teaching and learning of grammatics:

1. Children have a natural interest in language in use, as indicated in their spontaneous observations about language (for example, their consciousness of language variation, awareness of adult language patterns, their use of others' wordings in playground and sibling arguments) and their enjoyment of language play.
2. Primary concepts in the SFG description are close to children's everyday experience, for example, different types of processes and the associated Participants, clauses as structural units of both speech and writing, interpersonal effects of modality expressions and logical relations in natural language.
3. The pedagogy we derived from Vygotsky's theory provided the basis for a new approach to the teaching of grammatics.

We would probably use a broadly similar approach, if we were to do the project again, though, with greater time and financial resources, we would build in work in contrasting socioeconomic locations. We would also now foreground register as a point-of-departure for the research, to complement our use of genre or text-type. A longer timespan, over at least three years, would be valuable because we still do not have any clear evidence about the potential for young children's learning over time.

The most basic point is that Halliday's introduction of SFG re-opens questions about the value of children learning grammatics, because this learning can now be situated within a broader literacy learning perspective, that is, developing knowledge about real uses of language.

Further research in grammatics teaching and learning might explore how best to sequence the teaching of grammatical knowledge so as to facilitate logical and cumulative knowledge-building, for example, which concepts are most significant and in what order. We have preliminary suggestions here but more should be done to both detail and expand our ideas. A key component of such research should be a focus on how and when to develop understanding of relations between grammatical classes such as nouns and verbs and systemic functional grammatical concepts. Other aspects of teaching systemic functional grammar, which have been hitherto under-researched, such as relations between mood selection and speech functions in different contexts, could become the focus of future research. Longitudinal studies are urgently needed to trace the development of knowledge of grammatics over longer periods of schooling. This could lead to the further development, documentation, and analysis of effective pedagogies for teaching functional grammatics, including, as a key component, the development of digital resources for pedagogy, probably including web-based resources to support international collaboration.

References

Halliday, M. A. K. (2002) *On grammar*. Edited by J. Webster. London and New York: Continuum.

Halliday, M. A. K. (1998) Grammar and daily life: Concurrence and complementarity. In Moriceau, J. L. (2010) Generalisability. In A. J. Mills, G. Durepos and E. Wiebe (Eds). *Encyclopedia of case study research* Vol. 1. Thousand Oaks, CA: Sage Publications, 420–423.

Vygotsky, L. (1987 translation by A. Kozulin) *Thought and language*. Cambridge, MA: MIT Press.

Yin, R. (2009) *Case study research: Design and methods* (4th Edition). Thousand Oaks CA: Sage.

Literacy in middle school contexts

Len Unsworth and Angela Thomas: teaching effective 3D authoring in the middle school years – multimedia grammatical design and multimedia authoring pedagogy[1]

Len Unsworth (Australian Catholic University, Sydney) and **Angela Thomas** (University of Tasmania) describe a three-year project through which a research team engaged with 44 teachers from 18 schools and over 1 100 students to develop resources for, and insights into, helping middle years students become effective 3D multimodal authors.

As is now emphasised in the Australian English curriculum, *writing* is no longer about *words* alone, but effective communication using a range of modes, including linguistic, visual, spatial, gestural and audio. For example, the work of *multimodal* authors such as the aural storyteller, the picture book illustrator or the 2D animator involves harnessing the resources of more than one mode to richly communicate meaning. Three-dimensional multimodal texts are those which involve an author/creator using computer software to produce the same kind of text as can be produced using live-action work with a video camera. That is, they must *construct* and *film* in a virtual space which involves considerations of length, breadth, depth and the passage of time to develop a visual product, which may be combined with the audio mode including narrative, dialogue, sound effects and music.

The wide availability of the 3D multimodal authoring software *Kahootz* in several Australian educational jurisdictions provided an opportunity to develop approaches to teaching and learning that fostered students as effective 3D multimodal authors and, in particular, as authors of narrative texts. From 2009 to 2011, a research team including Professor Len Unsworth, Dr Angela Thomas, Dr Paul Chandler, and Ms Annemaree O'Brien engaged with 44 teachers from 18 schools and over 1 100 students to develop resources for, and insights into, helping middle years students become effective 3D multimodal authors. Whilst *Kahootz* itself is discontinued software, the resources from the project may be applied to software of the same type (for example, MovieStorm, muvizu, Alice) and the findings illuminate issues of multimodal authoring more generally.

The following insights were gained from the project:

Knowledge and experience – From our interviews with both teachers and students, along with the questionnaire returns, it is clear that both teachers and students have very limited knowledge of multimodal authoring. They are modestly confident at the more general levels of knowledge about text and production processes, but knowledge of specific semiotic devices is quite weak (that is, camera angles and point of view are less well understood than location and setting). It is clearly the case that whilst students live in a multimodal world they do not implicitly either understand the communicative subtleties of visual communication or develop a metalanguage for communicating with others how meanings are constructed. One of the participating teachers put it like this – *It's like they're Year 6 with words, but Preps with multimodal texts.*

Because of their background, we assumed that both teachers and students would benefit from explicit teaching of multimodal authoring, and the curriculum resource was devised accordingly, balancing an experiential and *play-based* approach with explicit instruction. A long-term exposure seems quite important in this regard so that concepts are understood, rehearsed and incorporated into students' thinking. The survey indicated some general characteristics of the students. The results indicated moderate to low knowledge of computers in general and, overall, quite low levels of pre-existing knowledge of *Kahootz*. A fairly *ordinary* cohort, all in all, and in no sense did the survey results suggest that they should be presumed to be *gifted* or capable of learning high-level literacy concepts unaided.

Quality multimodal texts – If it is true that the students are *like Preps with multimodal texts*, then even a highly intensive programme will be unlikely to accelerate students to an extraordinarily high level of quality. Notions of *quality* need to be interpreted somewhat relatively. Even so, a number of high quality student-created 3D multimodal narrative texts have been identified – texts which have been given the very highest rating on all aspects of the evaluation rubric. Therefore, it is clear that upper primary children are capable of producing multimodal texts of extremely high quality. Indeed, some children have been able to respond in some quite innovative ways to the instruction they received. Furthermore, high quality work can be identified in a range of classroom environments – in high and low socioeconomic status schools, individual teacher and team-taught environments, year level 5 and 6 and 5/6 mixed.

What of those texts that are *not* rated at the very highest levels of proficiency? Is there something that they are consistently *missing out* on, which could be the focus for improving teaching and learning? In fact, any trends are most unclear. It can certainly be said that students find the more specific semiotic devices more difficult to work with (as above) and that a strong representation of, say, point of view is either the mark of an extraordinary student or an extraordinary teacher. A thoroughly integrated sense of multimodality – where the modes collaborate to make meaning synergistically – is not found frequently and can thus be presumed to be quite difficult. More generally, it seems more accurate to say that students find it challenging to sustain attention to the full range of semiotic devices. So, for example, some fall marginally short on atmosphere and mood, others on characterisation, and yet others on effective use of the 3D space, even though these are amongst the more straightforward of semiotic devices to attend to. We have not studied cognitive load, but this may be a productive line of investigation in relation to a programme's *intensity* and its placement within an overall scope-and-sequence.

Characteristics of high-achieving classrooms – It is important to acknowledge the nature of the program, which was both highly intensive and long-term. In any learning activity, there are always issues of constrained time and limited opportunity. The effort and commitment of the 44 participating teachers to navigate around those realities cannot be underestimated. It is probably the case that consistently higher quality work was produced where teachers had greater commitment **and** found ways to work around the constraints. That being said, there is a range of considerations that interact with both of these factors.

From the corpus of texts analysed, it has been possible to identify both *high-achieving* and *low achieving* classes. This is somewhat approximate and based only on visual inspection of student outcomes, as the number of texts from each class is insufficient to justify any statistical technique. Nevertheless, combined with case study data, this gives a basis for hypothesising optimal pedagogic contexts.

To the extent of data analysis to date, the high-achieving classrooms are Year 6 classes, and the majority of high-achieving student texts are also Year 6 students (though not exclusively from those classes). Questionnaire items (*prior experience* and *perceived competence*) reveal no statistically significant difference between any of the participating classes, so it is possible that general intellectual maturity (Year 5 to Year 6) is an important influence. It is also possible that teachers who exhibited particularly effective pedagogical practices just happened to be teaching Year 6 classes.

In most classes, students worked independently to create texts, but in 14 classes the work was undertaken in pairs, which was a response to limited access to technology. Pair-constructed texts are under-represented amongst those rated as very high quality. This is not to suggest that students working together is a bad thing, but it may be that a genuinely shared *vision* for a text is hard to achieve, as is finding ways to share the production task. It may also be that where there is better access to equipment this leads to more time-on-task and a greater commitment to the task.

It is tempting to teach *about* the software and follow this with *application*. The curriculum materials were carefully constructed to teach both in a simultaneous learning act, so as to both deepen learning and make it more efficient. Despite this, the higher-achieving classes had at least several sessions specifically learning the software. Whether this is a necessary condition for success, a practical response in how to manage what is an intensive programme or something deeper to be understood about each teacher's approach is something which requires further investigation.

Where multimodal authoring is embraced as an integral part of classroom practice (viewing/reading along with writing/creating), and embedded throughout the year in various aspects of work, there seems to be higher levels of student achievement than when it is included as an *extra*. The ability of the teacher to help students to produce a manageable outcome is important. There was a range of technical challenges with using *Kahootz* to the extent that we did. The better work was completed in classes where teachers were able to provide technical assistance to their students along with *conceptual* help in rethinking what they tried to achieve so that it would be more manageable. It can also be asserted that a classroom culture of persistence and completion of long-term project work does not hurt, when it comes to projects such as this. Perhaps surprisingly, these are not routine features of all participating classrooms. Long-term exposure from a project such as this seems to be quite an important influence.

Strong literacy practices, including the engagement of the teacher in the work of students, are vital. In the classes where the higher quality texts were produced, there was a strong culture of focused and immediate feedback and established processes for review by peers and by teachers. The teachers had a sound grasp of how to scaffold students in their construction of narratives and an agenda of *quality*, expecting the best from their students, and actively assisting them to achieve this. Indeed, in the higher-performing classroom, the relationship between the teacher and student is such that a *conversation of equals* may lead to nearly co-authoring the text. Laissez-faire approaches do not seem to result in quality outputs, even though there is sometimes a view that, because the work involves the use of a computer, students will be naturally good at it. It is clear that this does not happen *naturally*, and students benefit from explicit scaffolding and instruction. It could be argued than any weakness in teachers' literacy practices becomes magnified (as lower quality texts) in a longitudinal project that has a layer of technical complexity which must be navigated.

High-achieving teachers – Regardless of what might have been done for students in many classrooms to provide technical assistance to one another, it is nevertheless the case that classes where teachers were less technically capable or confident were amongst the lower achieving classes. Thus, technological know-how does seem to be important, though in exactly what ways this shapes the teaching and learning is a matter for further investigation.

The experience of the project team has shown that constructing the curriculum resource has been a fairly major intellectual enterprise, and so it is little wonder that teachers, typically time-poor, did not *naturally* know what to do with *Kahootz* or how to approach the creation of multimodal texts. However, when provided with a starting point, and when they believe in the value of multimodal authoring, professional autonomy and exploratory pedagogy seem to emerge more naturally, and student achievement is heightened compared with when teachers are reluctant or follow a recipe-style approach.

In recent decades, the teaching of writing has been increasingly understood as a process (such as pre-writing, drafting and writing, sharing and responding, revising and editing and publishing). The project team assumed that effective writing and literacy practices would already be in place in the classroom, and the construction of multimodal texts would be, in part, a matter of translating such approaches to the new medium. Classes where the teacher had this background knowledge and practice tended to more reliably produce quality texts. It has taken encouragement, on occasion, for teachers to see multimodal text creation as a literacy practice but also a general lack of strong literacy knowledge and practice was evident in some cases.

A final observation is that there seems to be advantages in teachers working together to get excited about the work being done, and to share highlights and disappointments. In other words, the culture of professional learning and collaboration is important.

Jenny Hammond: the needs of English as an additional language (EAL) students in Australian schools

> **Jenny Hammond** (University of Technology, Sydney) describes a project that consisted of two major phases completed over ten years. The project focused on English as an additional language (EAL) students in Australian schools in across-the-curriculum programs and the nature of the conceptual and linguistic support necessary to enable EAL students to engage successfully with high challenge curricula. In implementing the project, researchers worked with teachers across different curriculum areas to design, plan, and implement high challenge, high support programs that also integrated systematic teaching of language and literacy.

The project that I describe consisted of two major phases that were completed over a number of years. Both phases were undertaken with colleagues Pauline Gibbons (University of Technology, Sydney), Michael Michell (then NSW Department of Education and Communities), and Tina Sharpe (independent consultant) and with input from others at various times. The project was jointly funded by the Australian Research Council and by the (then) Multicultural Programs Unit of the NSW Department of Education and Communities.

The project aimed to address the needs of English as an additional language (EAL) students in Australian schools. Our particular focus was on students who were beyond the initial and obvious stages of learning English and who were located in mainstream classes. Our assumption in approaching the research was that equitable education requires all students, including EAL students, to have access to across-the-curriculum programmes that are characterised by high challenge and high support, and, that the needs of EAL students are not well served by a modified or simplified curriculum. Our further assumption was that, with appropriate levels of differentiated and targeted support, all students, including EAL students, can achieve educational success. The focus of the project therefore was on the nature of the conceptual and linguistic support necessary to enable EAL students to engage successfully with high challenge curricula. In implementing the project, researchers worked with teachers across different curriculum areas to design, plan and implement high challenge, high support programmes that also integrated systematic teaching of language and literacy. A major task in the research was to articulate what such programmes looked like in the lived curriculum, as teachers and students engaged in their day-to-day learning.

Insights from the project included better understandings of the nature of high challenge and high support within programmes designed for EAL students. In addressing the dimension of high challenge, researchers and teachers sought to engage students with deep levels of curriculum knowledge, and with 'opportunities to engage in higher-order thinking, transform information, engage in inquiry-oriented activity, and construct their own understandings through participating in substantive conversations with others' (Gibbons 2008: 157). Analysis of lessons highlighted the value of classroom practices in which:

- students engaged with the key ideas and concepts of the discipline
- students transformed what they had learned into a different form, for use in a new context or for a different audience
- students moved between concrete knowledge and abstract theoretical knowledge
- students engaged in substantive conversation (substantive conversation while learning and public demonstration of what had been learned)
- students made connections between the spoken and written language and the semiotic tools and artefacts of the discipline
- students were encouraged to problematise knowledge and question *accepted wisdom*

(See Gibbons 2008 for a more detailed discussion of these practices.)

In addressing the dimension of high support, the research focused extensively on the role of *scaffolding*. The term *scaffolding* has traditionally been defined as the kind of support provided by teachers that enable students to complete tasks and develop understandings that they would not be able to accomplish alone (Gibbons 2002, Hammond & Gibbons 2005, Mercer 1994). Analysis of lessons in the project provided evidence that scaffolding occurred at both the *designed-in* macro level of overall programme planning, as well as the micro level where teachers responded *contingently* to the teachable moment. The analysis also pointed to the importance of *handover*, so that students increasingly took responsibility for their own learning.

A major component of the high support programmes was support for students' academic language and literacy development. Analysis of lessons provided insights into the range of ways in which such support was provided:

- teaching of curriculum content (Science, Maths, Literature) and of the language of that content, so that all students (including EAL students) were able to talk, read and write about the curriculum content they were learning
- ongoing talk about language that focused students' attention on the role of language itself in the learning process, with the result that learning about language, in effect, constituted a second field of study
- an emphasis on language for thinking, language for thinking out loud and language for *exploratory talk*.

Language for thinking (we inferred) was the silent *inner language* that accompanied students' thinking as they focused on new or challenging learning in tasks. Thinking out loud occurred as teachers demonstrated a process or presented a concept, and it occurred when teacher and students engaged in verbal reasoning as they completed a problem-solving task. Exploratory talk occurred particularly in student group work or when students led discussion on a topic or issue.

The project led to a significant ongoing collaboration between researchers and the NSW Department of Education and Communities, which in turn had a considerable impact on EAL education in NSW schools. The collaboration resulted in the development of an EAL professional support programme that involved teachers from eight to ten schools each year for a period of ten years (from 2003 to 2013). This programme was based on the model of research developed during the project and it incorporated the principles of high challenge and high support proposed in the research. Following the model of the research, teachers from participating schools were involved in cycles of professional input and action research. These cycles involved teachers working with consultants to plan and implement programmes that targeted the specific needs of their EAL students. Outcomes from both phases of the research have been taken up in other states in Australia and elsewhere. Professional presentations and publications from the research have contributed to educational debates in and beyond Australia regarding education for EAL students (Gibbons 2008, Hammond 2014).

The research arose from a concern with the ways in which EAL students were being positioned in schools. Across the total Australian school population, 25% of students are from non-English-speaking backgrounds. NSW schools have over 50% of Australia's EAL students, of whom 96% are enrolled in schools in the Sydney metropolitan region – primarily in large urban schools where there is an intersection between ethnicity, poverty and social class. In such schools, teachers' expectations of students' academic abilities are often low (Johnston & Hayes 2008).

In NSW there had long been broad acknowledgment of the need for equality of access to learning for EAL students. However, there had rarely been an explicit emphasis on developing students' critically oriented and higher-order thinking skills. A more typical response to addressing the needs of EAL learners in mainstream classes was to simplify the curriculum. Our concern was that a reduced curriculum results in a reductive diet of non-challenging and low-level activities that focus on the development and/or remediation of basic skills, and that emphasise rote learning and the reproduction of facts. Our research was based on the assumption that all students, including all EAL students, needed to be engaged in intellectual challenge. We felt this was especially important in the middle years of secondary schooling where groups of EAL students are most likely to disengage with academic work and drop out of school. Our research, with its emphasis on the centrality of intellectual quality, and on the nature of high support attempted to provide a positive alternative to pedagogy for EAL students.

The research design in both phases of the project was qualitative in nature. In both phases we sought to gain insights and understandings, rather than to provide 'proof' of anything. In addition, both phases of the research were primarily interventionist in that they involved researchers working with teachers in schools to plan and implement programmes that were designed to meet the needs of EAL students. Specifically, we invited experienced classroom and specialist EAL teachers in the middle years of schooling (Years 5 to 8) in six schools to participate in the research in each of the two phases. Researchers and teachers then worked together to plan and implement programmes that were characterised by dimensions of high challenge and high support.

The research itself involved cycles of professional and theoretical input, collaborative programme planning, documentation and analysis of the impact of programmes and shared reflection on teaching practices. Documentation of programmes involved video recording of sequences of lessons, collection of students' written texts, and collection of key curriculum and teaching resources.

A key issue in this research (as with any large-scale research) was our approach to analysis of data. In order to do justice to the complexity of classroom interactions, we focused on complete units of classroom work, that is the teaching of a complete topic, specific goals for that topic, and sequences of relevant lessons. In Christie's (2002) terms, our unit of analysis was the curriculum *macrogenre*. The macrogenre provided the context for a closer analysis of lessons, tasks and specific interactions. Our aim was to produce *thick* descriptions of classroom interactions in order to gain insights into the nature of intellectual practices and of the role of scaffolding within those practices. Video recordings of classroom lessons constituted our major source of data, and our starting point in analysis was with these recordings, and with transcripts of the recordings. Our methods consisted of analysis at two levels – initial content analysis to identify major recurring themes and issues and a more detailed linguistic analysis to provide insights into ways in which teachers planned their programmes and supported their students in classroom interactions (Hammond 2011).

There were a number of reasons for the kinds of insights that resulted from the research. First the research was located within a specific educational context and it addressed clearly defined aims. Second, it was large in scale and took place over a number of years. The scale of the research enabled ongoing and intensive analyses of complete units of work in a number of schools, thereby making it possible to balance breadth (across schools) and depth of analysis of classroom patterns within specific lessons and interactions. The scale also made it possible to identify recurring classroom practices and to address their significance for the education of EAL students.

Additionally, the research team consisted of researchers and teachers who worked together. While researchers designed the project, provided theoretical input, and took the major role in analysis of data, the *voices* of all participants contributed to the research process. Thus teachers, whose classrooms were the focus of research, were also active participants in the research process (Wells 1999: xiv). This partnership contributed to the theoretical strength, as well as the practically grounded nature, of the research outcomes.

Overall, the research was successfully planned and implemented – it was completed on time and on budget. In addition, the approach to research and the collaborative model that involved researchers and teachers were appropriate to the research purposes. All participants reported very positive professional learning outcomes. Consequently, I believe there is little that we should have done differently. However, the scale of the research meant it was a huge commitment of time and energy. Without funding from a major research organisation, this scale of research is not possible. A key issue in any research design is to balance worthwhile research aims and design with existing practical constraints of time and money.

There were a number of lessons that the project can offer other researchers:

1. **The importance of clear research design** – research design involves understanding the context of the research, clarifying aims, choosing an appropriate approach, planning methods of data collection, and working with appropriate methods for analysis of data. It also involves taking account of the ethics of the research, and the logistical and practical challenges associated with implementation of research. Having said that, qualitative research is often *messy* and a good research design needs to be able to respond to specific challenges if and when they arise. I think our research provided a good model of a carefully planned project, but one that was sufficiently flexible to be able to adjust to the needs of working in schools with teachers and students.

2. **Ethics in classroom research** – any research project must take questions of ethics seriously. Indeed, most universities require ethics approval before projects can proceed. It is therefore necessary to have approval and agreement from school, teachers and students to conduct research, and this means meeting the ethics requirements of explaining research purposes and procedures to participants, ensuring anonymity and reducing risk of harm. However, research in classrooms raises particular ethical challenges. In many cases, research in classrooms involves external researchers going into classrooms to investigate and analyse what is going on in the classrooms. This may focus on programme planning, teacher-student interactions, teacher or student talk, the role of multimodality in literacy development, and so on. As a researcher what do you do if you find yourself critical of the practices that you are investigating? How can you respect the

professional integrity of those who have given permission for you to undertake the research, while also doing justice to your research findings? There are a number of ways of addressing such issues – one is by ensuring that outcomes are genuinely anonymous. However, if the research is small scale that can be difficult, especially if the participants can identify themselves in the outcomes. Our research team addressed the challenges of ethics in two ways. We invited teachers to participate in the research on the grounds that they were already doing *good things*. Thus our focus was on positive models and on practices that were effective in meeting the needs of students. We also worked collaboratively with teachers. This meant that teachers were active participants in the research process, and the collaborative analysis of teachers' own practices contributed to the overall outcomes of the project. While this approach may not be relevant or useful in all classroom-based research, it may serve to highlight the complex ethical issues that are likely to arise in classroom-based research, and to emphasise the importance of thinking-through, as part of the research planning process, how such issues will be addressed.

3. **Analysis of large quantities of data** – most qualitative research, by its nature, generates extensive amounts of data. This is especially true of classroom-based research. A major challenge therefore is how to do justice to the complexity of what goes on in any classroom, including the progression from one lesson to the next (and the extensive amount of data generated by recordings of sequences of lessons), while at the same time undertaking analysis that is of sufficient depth to be able to say something of interest. This was one of the biggest challenges that we faced in our research project (Hammond 2011). The approach taken in our research may prove useful to other researchers, although the issue of dealing systematically with large quantities of data is one that must be resolved in response to the purposes of research within any specific project.

More research of a similar nature is required to address the nature and implications of high challenge, high support pedagogies in different contexts and for different groups of students. Research of a different nature is required that evaluates the impact over time of pedagogies that are characterised by high challenge and high support. As educational researchers (at least in Australia), we tend to be good at qualitative research, but less proficient at quantitative research. We need large-scale research that can draw on both quantitative and qualitative approaches to provide evidence of impact. I am aware of only one such study – the *Successful Language Learners'*

Project (Commonwealth of Australia 2011a and b) – that has managed to do this. Its significance lies in the nature of educational intervention outlined in the project and in the evidence it provides of positive impact on young students' educational outcomes.

References

Christie, F. (2002) *Classroom discourse analysis: A functional perspective.* London: Continuum.

Commonwealth of Australia, (2011a) *Literacy and numeracy pilots: Final report. Report of successful language learners' project.* Australian Government, Department of Education, Employment and Workplace Relations, Commonwealth of Australia.

Commonwealth of Australia. (2011b) *Successful language learners' project.* Available at: http://www.lowsesschools.nsw.edu.au/Portals/8/Documents/TLS_22_Successful_language_3[2].pdf

Gibbons, P. (2002) *Scaffolding language, scaffolding learning: Teaching ESL children in the mainstream classroom.* Portsmouth, NH: Heinemann.

Gibbons, P. (2008) 'It was taught good and I learned a lot': Intellectual practices and ESL learners in the middle years. *Australian Journal of Language and Literacy* Vol. 31 No. 2, 155–173.

Hammond, J. (2011) Classroom discourse. In K. Hyland and B. Paltridge (Eds). *Continuum companion to discourse analysis.* London: Continuum, 291–305.

Hammond, J. (2014) An Australian perspective on standards-based education, Teacher knowledge and English as an additional language students. *TESOL Quarterly* Vol. 48 No. 3, 507–532.

Hammond, J. and Gibbons, P. (2005) Putting scaffolding to work: The contribution of scaffolding in articulating ESL education. *Prospect* Vol. 20 No. 1, 6–30.

Johnston, K. and Hayes, D. (2008) 'This is as good as it gets': Classroom lessons and learning in challenging circumstances. *Australian Journal of Language and Literacy* Vol. 31 No. 2, 109–127.

Mercer, N. (1994) Neo-Vygotskian theory and classroom education. In B. Steiner and J. Maybin (Eds). *Language, literacy and learning in educational practice.* Clevedon: Multilingual Matters, 92–110.

Wells, G. (1999) *Dialogic inquiry: Towards a sociocultural practice and theory of education.* Cambridge: Cambridge University Press.

Anne-Vera Meidell Sigsgaard: classroom interactions in a Danish history classroom

Anna-Vera Meidell Sigsgaard (Aarhus University and the University of Copenhagen) describes a project that used linguistic and sociological tools to analyse interactions between teachers and students during a fifth grade history unit. Most of the students in the class had a second-language background and were offered Danish as a second-language instruction.

The project described here looked at linguistic interactions between teachers and students during a fifth grade history unit – a study of Denmark in the early 1900s – where most of the students in the class have a second-language background. I was particularly interested in looking at how communication between teachers and students negotiated the knowledge students were expected to learn throughout the unit, while also observing if and how the language needed to develop this knowledge was focused on.

The main finding is that teachers have difficulty incorporating Danish as a Second Language into content classes, resulting in lessons where both the subject-matter and language learning are downplayed to the point of near absence, leaving students to fend for themselves in terms of what they are expected to learn (Meidell Sigsgaard 2013).

The findings provide insights into the importance and complexity of classroom discourse for shaping students' understandings of the content being learned and ultimately the shaping of their consciousness, in terms of what is and is not considered legitimate knowledge in the classroom. They point to the importance of spoken language interactions within the classroom context to students' development of understandings of the complex and abstract knowledge alluded to in the teaching materials chosen for the unit. In Denmark, this is not particularly well documented in modern classroom research. At the same time, questions arose concerning why teachers seem unwilling to provide clear answers to students' queries regarding the correctness of their work. The project findings have strong implications for practice, including potential changes to Danish curriculum guidelines, teacher training, and the dynamics of teaching and learning, in order to improve the educational performance of all students, including minority students.

The overarching aim of the project was to investigate why minority students, who are offered instruction in *Danish as a Second Language,* as a means of academic support, nonetheless seem to have more difficulty attaining school success than their majority peers. This is a common and often heated topic of discussion in local politics and the media, since these so-called bilingual children are said to end up in gangs and as social misfits.

Based on a theoretically informed position that classroom discourse plays an important role in both student learning and the shaping of their consciousness (Bernstein 2000, Christie 2002, Maton 2010), the project investigated the implementation of the school subject Danish as a Second Language within the school subject of History. The teacher-student interactions of three teachers involved in the teaching of the unit were analysed at various points as the unit of study progressed.

The research explored connections between learning, language, knowledge and knowers in the observed classroom practice. The analytical tools included the linguistic tool of analysis known as *exchange structure analysis* (Martin 1992, Martin & Rose 2007) that is based on Hallidayan Systemic Functional Linguistics, sociological tools of analysis based on Bernstein's code theory, namely *Legitimation Code Theory* (Maton 2014) and particular dimensions of semantics and specialisation for analysis.

The methodology was inspired by Gibbons (2006), in so far as the type of data collected and in following a complete unit of study. Video observations of teacher-student interactions were collected which, after transcription, served as the main source of data, supplemented by screen shots of the multimedia teaching materials used for the unit and teacher interviews.

The combination of linguistic and sociological tools was important in developing a nuanced perspective on what was going on in the classroom. If I conducted similar research in the future, I would use a similar approach. However, I would add more time for teacher and student interviews alongside the observations (not only after), in order to gain further insight through the teachers' reflections, as well as to add the dimension of the students' perspectives. These students were not expected to do any significant writing during this unit of work, so I would also choose an older grade level next time, where students' written products could provide another source of data.

The project has contributed to a growing body of research that is exploring connections between learning, language, knowledge and knowers in classroom practice. Its outcomes contribute to theory and practice by bringing together linguistic and sociological approaches in educational contexts and applying and refining these tools for analysing classroom discourse. It has contributed to a growing field of research that is developing methodologies for analysing knowledge-building in classroom practices and student work (for example, Chen, Maton & Bennett 2011, Dreyfus, Macnaught & Humphrey 2011, Freebody, Martin & Maton 2008, Hood 2010, Howard & Maton 2011, Matruglio, Maton & Martin 2013). It is also contributing to links between the disciplinary boundaries of educational linguistics and educational sociology and introduces and encourages this interdisciplinarity in the Danish context.

Resources in this project did not allow for working with teachers to develop their understandings of the role played by language in their ability to help students build language and knowledge. This, along

with a focus on the teaching potential of common classroom interactions and negotiations, remains to be explored within the Danish
context.

References

Bernstein, B. (2000) *Pedagogy, symbolic control, and identity: Theory, research, critique.* New York: Rowman & Littlefield.
Christie, F. and Maton, K. (Eds). (2011) *Disciplinarity: Functional linguistic and sociological perspectives.* London: Continuum.
Chen, R. T., Maton, K. and Bennett, S. (2011) Absenting discipline: Constructivist approaches in online learning. In F. Christie and K. Maton (Eds). *Disciplinarity: functional linguistic and sociological perspectives.* London: Continuum, 129–150.
Dreyfus, S. J., Macnaught, L. and Humphrey, S. (2011) Understanding joint construction in the tertiary context. *Linguistics and the Human Sciences* Vol. 4 No. 2, 135–160.
Freebody, P., Martin, J. R. and Maton, K. (2008) Talk, text and knowledge in cumulative, integrated learning: A response to 'intellectual challenge'. *Australian Journal of Language and Literacy* Vol. 31, 188–201.
Gibbons, P. (2006) *Bridging discourses in the ESL classroom: Students, teachers and researchers.* London: Continuum.
Halliday, M. A. K. and Matthiessen, C. (2004) *An introduction to functional grammar.* London: Routledge.
Hasan, R. (1996) *Ways of saying: Ways of meaning – selected papers of Ruqaiya Hasan.* London: Cassell.
Hood, S. (2010) Writing discipline: Comparing inscriptions of knowledge and knowers in academic writing theorizing knowledge-construction. In F. Christie and K. Maton (Eds). *Disciplinarity: Systemic functional and sociological perspectives* London: Continuum, 106–128.
Howard, S. and Maton, K. (2011) Theorising knowledge practices: A missing piece of the educational technology puzzle. *Research in Learning Technology* Vol. 19 No. 3, 191–206.
Martin, J. (1992) *English text: System and structure.* Philadelphia and Amsterdam: John Benjamins Publishing Company.
Martin, J. R. (1999) Mentoring semogenesis: 'genre-based' literacy pedagogy. In F. Christie (Ed). *Pedagogy and the shaping of consciousness.* London: Continuum, 123–155.
Martin, J. R. and Rose, D. (2007) *Working with discourse: Meaning beyond the clause* (2nd Edition). London: Continuum.
Maton, K. (2010) Analysing knowledge claims and practices: Languages of legitimation. In K. Maton and R. Moore (Eds). *Social realism, knowledge and the sociology of education – coalitions of the mind.* London: Continuum, 35–59.
Maton, K. (2014) *Knowledge and knowers – towards a realist sociology of education.* Abingdon: Routledge.
Matruglio, E., Maton, K. and Martin, J. R. (2013) Time travel: The role of temporality in enabling semantic waves in secondary school teaching. *Linguistics and Education* Vol. 24 No. 1, 38–49.
Meidell Sigsgaard, A.-V. (2012) Who has the knowledge if not the primary knower? – Using exchange structure analysis to cast light on particular

pedagogic practices in teaching Danish as a second language and history. In J. S. Knox (Ed). *To boldly proceed: Papers from the 39th International Systemic Functional Congress*. 39th ISFC Organising Committee – Sydney.

Meidell Sigsgaard, A.-V. (2013) *Who knows what? The teaching of knowledge and knowers in a fifth grade Danish as a second language classroom*. University of Aarhus. Available at: http://www.legitimationcodetheory.com/publications.html

Barbara Comber, Peter Freebody, Helen Nixon, Victoria Carrington and Anne-Marie Morgan: new literacy demands in the middle years – learning from design experiments

Barbara Comber (Queensland University of Technology), Peter Freebody (University of Sydney), Helen Nixon (Queensland University of Technology), Victoria Carrington (University of East Anglia), and Anne-Marie Morgan (University of South Australia), describe a four-year design-based research project that involved teacher researchers working with university researchers. The *New literacy demands in the middle years: Learning from design experiments* project aimed to document and improve student literacy in the middle years (Years 5 to 9) using design experiments, and to place issues of sustainability and the wellbeing of the classroom teacher at the centre of debates about teachers' professional identities and practice.

The project presented here was titled *New literacy demands in the middle years: Learning from design experiments* and was conducted from 2009 to 2013. The chief investigators included Barbara Comber, Helen Nixon and Peter Freebody. Anne-Marie Morgan was a Research Fellow and Victoria Carrington was a partner investigator. It was funded through the Australian Research Council Linkage Program and the Industry Partners were the South Australian Department of Education and Child Development (DECS) and the South Australian Branch of the Australian Education Union (AEU).

The project aimed to document and improve student literacy in the middle years (Years 5 to 9) using design experiments, and to place issues of sustainability and wellbeing of the classroom teacher at the centre of debates about teachers' professional identities and practice. The project focused on four key and interrelated areas of relevance to the middle years:

1. Curriculum literacies
2. Youth cultures and digital literacies
3. Place-based pedagogies
4. Teachers' work and professional knowledge

The researchers collaborated with seven *change ready* teachers of Years 5 to 7 in 2010 and six teachers of Years 8 to 9 in 2011. The teachers participated in the design and implementation of classroom interventions based on one or more of the focus areas. The intervention model used was Design Based Research (DBR) – utilising small, pragmatic, planned and classroom data-informed interventions, designed with the intention of developing theory about and demonstrating evidence of effective literacy pedagogic practice.

The project provided the following insights:

- It reinforced the complexity and the contingency of the demands of literate practices in the middle years.
- The literate demands of students' assignments, including the processes of reading, researching and writing are not always understood by teachers, particularly middle years subject specialists, for example, the language of Mathematics and the discourses of Science.
- Students need explicit teaching about the literate practices of each curriculum area and opportunities to practise and to discuss and reflect on these practices.
- Students need explicit teaching and support in learning to orchestrate tasks that are largely completed online.
- Some *literacy* learning processes and practices, such as research or inquiry, continue to change with the affordances and limits of digital technologies, and both students and teachers need opportunities to explore and understand such changes.
- Sustained pedagogical innovation is difficult in secondary school contexts, where prescribed curricula demands are seen by many teachers to preclude innovation and experimentation.
- It identified the importance of building teacher subject knowledge in primary contexts and teacher curriculum literacies knowledge and an awareness of the need for explicit teaching of these.
- It reinforced the value of collaboration between teacher researchers and university researchers in conducting classroom-based inquiry.
- It reinforced the appropriateness of DBR as a methodology to support teacher inquiry of this nature.
- It reinforced the importance of opportunities for teacher inquiry to support teacher wellbeing and sustainability of the profession.

It is often hard to know the final impacts of research but during the study the participating teachers learned more about the literacy and learning demands that their curriculum designs required, and trialled different approaches to enhance student understandings. The teachers were able to experience the potential of learning from and with their peers, and of working in collaborative partnerships with university researchers. They presented to their colleagues in school, at conferences, online and in a book.

We have limited knowledge of whether other teachers took up insights from this work, although there is, at the time of writing, a follow-up project in an education sector in one state, based on the examples in the book that was published from the project. Education jurisdictions are also inviting project researchers to present on the outcomes of the project to a wider teacher and school leader audience. The book from the project is being used by at least one university as a required text for literacy units in teacher education programmes.

Given the focus on literacy in the media, and in NSW particularly, in response to the NSW Board of Studies Teaching and Educational Standards (BOSTES) review of teacher education, the insights from the project and from publications and presentations provide guidance on ways forward to improving literacy education and teacher preparation for teaching literacy.

Several things provided the impetus for the study. These include:

- requests and invitations from our industry partners to engage in collaborative research on literacy in the middle years
- specific interest that grew from the previous research and experience of the group members – Peter Freebody's previous research on the four resources model and curriculum literacies, Victoria Carrington's expertise in digital literacies and Barbara Comber's interests in teachers' work and place-conscious pedagogies
- interest in exploring teacher wellbeing and innovation together
- the previous consultancy and research work that Peter Freebody and Barbara Comber had done for the industry partners
- methodologically, there was also growing evidence of the value of Design-Based Research as an inquiry methodology for teacher researchers

Our conceptualisation of literacy was informed by Freebody and Luke's heuristic, Freebody's work in curriculum literacies and Carrington's work on digital literacies and youth cultures. We were also influenced by Comber and Nixon's model of collaborative research with teachers conducted over the long-term, especially in relation to place-based pedagogies, and with regard to the sustainability of teachers' work.

The research framework adopted for the project was Design-Based Research. This involves using designed pedagogical experiments and implementing interventions in iterative cycles, based on the collection and analysis of evidence and the modification of pedagogies and interventions in subsequent intervention iterations. As a research methodology, it sits between more open-ended action research and formal experimental research, the latter of which would not normally utilise modifications to interventions during the course of the experiment. Modification of the intervention design, in the progress of the research, allows for close attention to the current needs of the students and the teacher, and for relevant, timely adaptation. DBR in an education context frequently involves collaborative approaches, involving teacher researchers and university researchers, to allow the research to be teacher-driven and to promote teacher agency, with additional design and theory input, and critical feedback, from university researchers. It is always site (classroom)-based, responding to the needs identified by the teacher-researcher. DBR aims to generate new theory, of both pedagogies and student learning, based on the data collected during experiments, as well as to provide practical examples of teacher inquiry and teaching approaches.

DBR is appropriate as a literacies education research methodology, as it offers a means to collect evidenced findings in sequential and consequential ways, under experimental conditions that allow for the range and complexity of *variables* present in any classroom setting (e.g. diversity of learners, learner language and culture backgrounds, learning and behaviour challenges, teacher experience and knowledge, SES and other status or particularities of the context of the school, previous learning, etc.). Such variability makes it near impossible to gather meaningful (valid and reliable) outcomes from more formal experimental approaches (such as replicable, control-based, quantitative experiments), aimed at understanding the complexities of literacy learning. DBR can support data collected in more formal approaches (such as the National Assessment Program – Literacy and Numeracy (NAPLAN) and test data), and include quantitative elements relevant to the teacher and students involved, and to the focus of the teacher's inquiry interest. Finally, as a collaborative research approach, teacher-researcher and joint teacher-university researcher publications in the academic literature are frequent outcomes of projects. The book from this project, and teacher presentations at conferences are examples of such outcomes, with support provided by university researchers to teachers to publish in these forums.

The project provided insights into teacher work and literacy learning in the middle years through close collaboration throughout the design and implementation of the teacher DBR experiments, based on the previous work, partner connections, and conceptual framings of the project (for example, Freebody's work on curriculum literacies, Carrington's on digital literacies, Comber and Nixon's on place-based pedagogies and approaches from project partners who had worked with the researchers previously). Working closely with project partners, and teachers in schools, on projects relevant to their needs and contexts, allowed for focused attention on the challenges teachers and students face, on teachers' knowledge needs, and on the complexity of literacy requirements across the curriculum for students beyond the early years. Changing literacy needs in relation to new technologies and classroom practices related to these (for example, working in an online environment) also became clear through the close collaboration and in-school work.

Design Based Research provided experimental evidence of both needs and learning, and also allowed experiments to be developed to address specific contextual requirements, and to illustrate and document literacy teaching and learning practice. A focus on teacher wellbeing alongside teacher knowledge also allowed insights into teachers' professional practice and into what sustains teachers.

In the future, longer research periods with teachers would be useful. Some teacher researchers involved voluntarily extended their time working on their projects, and this was beneficial for them and for the broader project goals, in generating more data for analysis, and also for allowing teachers to see the benefits of working in this way for improving pedagogies, and their sense of wellbeing and satisfaction. To address the same or a similar problem now, we would use the same approach, but we would build in longer timeframes for participation.

The value of DBR for teacher researchers working collaboratively with university researchers for genuine and valuable changes to occur in approaches to literacy teaching and learning and teachers' knowledge growth were clear. Others might usefully take up this model.

The importance of literacies in the middle years remains an under-researched area, especially for teachers researching their own work in situ, and in relation to disseminating their learning. Other researchers could take from this project valuable insights into the ongoing need to address the middle years literacy demands. Middle years literacy, its demands for teachers and students, and the knowledge, understanding and agency teachers working in this area needs considerably more work. Analysing the logics and demands of assignments is urgently needed, especially where schools are adopting state-designed curricula based on the Australian National Curriculum. Teachers need to see if curricula designed elsewhere are suitable .for the needs of their student cohorts and to plan for the necessary pedagogical supports to be in place to ensure all children can participate and be successful.

References

Carrington, V. (2012) Barbies & Chimps: Text and childhood in virtual worlds. In G. Merchant, J. Gillen and J. Marsh (Eds). *Virtual literacies: Interactive spaces for children and young people.* London: Routledge, 41–53.
Comber, B. (2005) Making use of theories about literacy and justice: Teachers researching practice. In *Educational Action Research*, 43–56.
Freebody, P., Chan, E. and Barton, G. (2014) Curriculum as literate practice: Language and knowledge in the classroom. In K. Hall, T. Cremin, B. Comber and L. Moll (Eds). *International Handbook of research on children's literacy, learning, and culture.* Oxford: Wiley-Blackwell, 304–318.
Luke, A. and Freebody, P. (1990) Literacies programs: Debates and demands in cultural context. *Prospect: Australian Journal of TESOL* Vol. 5 No. 7, 7–16.
Morgan, A-M., Comber, B., Freebody, P. and Nixon, H. (2014) *Literacy in the middle years: Learning from collaborative classroom research.* Sydney: Primary English Teachers' Association of Australia.

Literacy in secondary school contexts

Debra Myhill: grammar for writing

Debra Myhill (University of Exeter) describes an Economic and Social Research Council funded study – *Grammar for Writing* – which has been significant in offering new ways of thinking about the grammar-writing relationship. The study was not concerned with eradicating grammatical errors, nor with teaching students grammatical terminology. Instead, the focus was on writing and learning about writing, explicitly drawing attention to grammar, where it was relevant to the writing.

Our Economic and Social Research Council funded study, *Grammar for Writing*, has been significant in offering new ways of thinking about the grammar-writing relationship. For the first time, it provided evidence that addressing grammatical concerns could improve student outcomes in writing. But what is critically important about this is that the study adopted a view of grammar informed by Halliday's (1994) functionally oriented perspectives in exploring the grammar-meaning relationships in writing. The study was not concerned with eradicating grammatical errors, nor with teaching students grammatical terminology – the focus was on writing and learning about writing, drawing explicit attention to grammar, where it was relevant to the writing.

The key insights from the study were:

- A meaning-focused attention to grammar in the context of writing can have a significant positive impact on student attainment in writing.
- Teachers' subject knowledge of grammar mediated the effect of this approach.
- Teachers' subject knowledge of grammar includes both declarative knowledge of grammar and more applied knowledge of how to recognise what grammatical constructions in a text or in students' writing to draw attention to.

The study has had considerable impact in the United Kingdom, with high demand for professional development courses for teachers across the country, and adoption of the pedagogical approach by Pearson Education for their secondary writing materials. The research won the ESRC *Outstanding Impact in Society* Award in 2014.

We had undertaken a previous study investigating patterns of linguistic development in writing that led us to wonder whether explicit attention to teaching these structures at an appropriate time might be helpful. At the same time, we were critical of previous research that dismissed grammar as having no effect because it was evident that none of these studies had contextualised the teaching of grammar within the teaching of writing.

We adopted a mixed-methods approach, combining a randomised controlled trial (RCT) with qualitative data collection. This was a very conscious choice. We felt an RCT was needed because the topic of grammar was so contentious and a research design regarded as the *gold standard* might be necessary to secure credibility for any results. In addition, we observed teachers using the approach and interviewed students about their writing. The qualitative data was crucially important because we were less interested in testing a hypothesis or proving the effectiveness of an approach, and more interested in understanding how it worked, the factors which seemed to enable success, and the barriers which mitigated against success.

We think the fact that this study built on our earlier work, and was well theorised at the point of design meant that it was effective in exploring the issue. In particular, we were very pleased that we had chosen a mixed-methods design as the statistical data and qualitative data proved highly complementary, and provided a rich understanding of the topic. We think it is also important to note that we do not think one study alone is sufficient to draw wide-ranging conclusions in a context as complex as the classroom. We have continued to work on this topic, with several further small-scale studies since then, and increasingly now we are connecting up with other researchers internationally.

Every time we finish a research project, we know how we should have done it! As noted above, the combination of the RCT and qualitative data was particularly helpful. If we were doing this again, and were not limited by funding, we would build in more lesson observations, teacher interviews and student interviews, perhaps including some sub-sampling and following some classes in more depth. We would also have liked to conduct a detailed linguistic analysis of the pre-test and post-test writing, and the pieces of writing produced in each unit of work.

We are sure other researchers could teach us a lot about how we approached this research. Perhaps other researchers might learn from our mixed-methods approach, and their complementarity. As noted earlier, we believe the most robust evidence comes from an accumulation of studies, preferably including replication studies conducted by others. But we think there is still significant research to be done, including:

- more detailed investigation of the ways in which teachers' grammatical subject knowledge influences how they embed grammar within the teaching of writing
- investigation of the precise role grammatical metalanguage plays and when it is helpful and when it acts as a barrier
- investigation of how the teaching of explicit grammatical points is revealed, or not, in the writing of students
- how students develop the facility to make meaning-related reflections on the grammar of their own and others' writing
- the role of talk in developing grammatical thinking and reflection on writing

We are always keen to hear from people interested in this research, or doing similar research.

References

Halliday, M. A. K. (1994) *An introduction to Functional Grammar.* London: Edward Arnold.

Literacy across school contexts

James Martin: language and social power – *Write It Right Disadvantaged Schools Projects*

> **James Martin** (University of Sydney) describes the insights and impacts arising from two long-term projects that led to the development of the genre-based approach to teaching writing. The first project investigated writing in primary school classrooms and the second focused on the literacy demands within and across industrial sectors to relate these findings to literacy demands in the secondary curriculum key learning areas.

The long-term *Write it Right Disadvantaged Schools Project* led to the development of the genre-based approach to teaching writing. Stage 1 of the project identified the written text requirements of primary school classrooms and how best to teach these texts. Stage 2 of the project focused on the literacy demands within and across industrial sectors and how these related to the literacy demands in the secondary school curriculum key learning areas.

The projects were prompted by the important influence of two colleagues – Joan Rothery and Frances Christie – and I was concerned to try and practise linguistics as an ideologically committed form of social action and to try to do something with it in the world. I adopted two conceptual frameworks – Systemic Functional Linguistics (SFL) as the richest description we have of meaning-making and the work of Basil Bernstein for his insights into pedagogic discourse and social relations.

Insights from the projects included:

- the need for a genre-based approach to literacy teaching and learning
- the need to develop curriculum genres (teaching and learning cycles) as a pedagogy for such interventions
- the relation of types of pedagogy to the struggle between factions of the middle class (old and new) and others
- the need to use our principle of guidance through interaction in the context with teachers we are in-servicing, as well as with the kids they are teaching

These insights arose from the fact that there was a need, recognised by some committed teachers, as far as literacy for disadvantaged groups was concerned. A language-based theory of learning underpinned the pedagogy and led to its success.

The impacts of the projects included:

- a reorientation of primary literacy curriculum and pedagogy in Australia and other sites around the world and pockets of work here and there in tertiary and adult sectors but there was little impact on secondary education
- the main goal of redistributing cultural capital was achieved for some individuals, but not for whole sectors of disadvantaged citizens.

In retrospect, I would use the same SFL model, which is now much richer in terms of addressing multimodality and appraisal in language, etc. I would try more successfully to get my colleagues to work down from genre through register to discourse semantics and not try and get into functional grammar too soon. I would also attend more carefully to the institutional politics of universities and state education departments. I would also not underestimate the conniving power of the new middle-class progressivist/constructivist educators and their instinctive reaction to a pedagogy that is able to redistribute cultural capital and which they see as taking away their children's inheritance. I would put more emphasis on field alongside genre, to help get content teachers involved and demonstrate to them how much more efficient our teaching/learning cycles are compared with their time-wasting inefficient guess what's in my head teaching routines.

The main lessons these projects offer other researchers are:

- the need for a language-based theory of learning informed by a rich model of social semiosis
- the need to design curriculum genres and not leave teachers to teach the way they were taught and have been teaching – from the level of the macrogenre (teaching/learning cycle) right down to exchange structure

As a consequence of these projects, I will always dream of having a school or two, with stable teaching staff, using a genre-based approach, over a 13-year study, tracking kids from Kindergarten to Year 12, and seeing what they are in fact capable of. We currently have no idea and sell them so short.

The lack of resources, diminishing resources in fact, for in-service training make systemic change very difficult. The irresponsible conservatism of education faculties is a problem we never overcame. It is naïve to think the best approach can win the day as the new middle-class agendas get in the way, even unholy alliances of new and old middle-class agendas.

Frances Christie and Beverly Derewianka: literacy development across the years of schooling

> **Frances Christie** (University of Sydney) and **Beverly Derewianka** (University of Wollongong) describe a project that sought to provide evidence of the developmental stages or processes that children go through in mastering control of writing, at least for school purposes. They emphasise the importance of using a sound linguistic theory that enables fine-grained analyses of texts, when looking for development in writing.

The project we describe sought to provide evidence of the developmental stages or processes that children go through in mastering control of writing, at least for school purposes. The previous research of Halliday (for example, 1978, 1985, 1993 and 1994) was of paramount importance, since he gave us the Systemic Functional Linguistic (SFL) theory we used. The work of Martin (for example, 1984, 1986 and 1999), Rothery (for example, 2000) and others into genres and genre-based pedagogy was the influential base on which we proceeded, though Painter's (1999) research on the emergence of spoken language was also significant.

What were these insights? One important insight was that we can use the metafunctions (as described by Halliday 1994) to trace development across children's ages and across the years of schooling. The functional grammar is a very reliable tool to trace growth. In fact, we would suggest that if one was trained in the use of the grammar for parsing and analysis, then that person would reach similar conclusions. In other words, such conclusions would rest on more than impressions, as some work in the past has done. The insights we gained were based on SFL theory and, as noted above, we were reassured at the strength of the functional grammar as it permits a fine-grained analysis.

What impact/s did the project have? Well, the previous research (Martin 1984, 1986, 1999 and 2000) has had a very important impact, as it is found in use in language education (or sometimes in debate) in most parts of the world today. As indicated above, the study built on well-established work in the SFL and genre-based research of Martin, Rothery and others. A few older non-SFL developmental studies of writing had been undertaken in the past, but this was different in its use of SFL. There are still very few longitudinal studies of developmental growth in writing and ours was not longitudinal either, since we did not follow the same group of students but sampled across the school years.

We sought to collect examples of students' texts from low and high socioeconomic backgrounds and we also sought to sample texts across the secondary school years in English, History and Science. The method of analysis used genre and SFL theory. However, we did not succeed in gathering texts from lower socioeconomic schools because, although some said they would let us have texts, in practice they were not forthcoming. The book we eventually wrote used primary texts that we had acquired in earlier studies and drew heavily on the secondary data we acquired. The book makes evident our debt to the earlier work of Martin, Rothery, and others that prompted us, we think.

If we were to address the same or a similar problem now, we would use the same approach, though probably make more of appraisal than we did. We would also try to gather more texts from students from low socioeconomic backgrounds. I think the project demonstrates the rigour and strength of the functional grammar for such work. We need more such studies, not least because we need larger samples of texts. We also need someone willing to start longitudinal studies, though that requires stamina, given it could take at least 12 years!

References

Halliday, M. A. K. (1978) *Language as social semiotic.* London: Edward Arnold.

Halliday, M. A. K. (1985) *Spoken and written language.* Geelong, Victoria: Deakin University Press.

Halliday, M. A. K. (1993) Towards a language-based theory of learning. In *Linguistics and Education* 5, 93–116.

Halliday, M. A. K. (1994) *An introduction to Functional Grammar.* London: Edward Arnold.

Halliday, M. A. K. (2009) (1994) A language development approach to education. In M. A. K. Halliday (Ed). *Language and education: Collected works of M. A. K. Halliday.* Vol. 9. London and New York: Continuum (Edited by Jonathan Webster), 368–382.

Martin, J. R. (1984) Types of writing in infants and primary school. In L. Unsworth (Ed). *Reading, writing, spelling.* (Proceedings of the Fifth Macarthur Reading/Language Symposium), Sydney: Macarthur Institute of Higher Education.

Martin, J. R. (1986) Intervening in the process of writing development. In C. Painter and J. R. Martin (Eds). *Writing to mean: Teaching genres across the curriculum.* Applied Linguistics Association of Australia (Occasional Papers 9), 11–43.

Martin, J. R. (1999) Mentoring semogenesis: genre-based literacy pedagogy. In F. Christie (Ed). *Pedagogy and the shaping of consciousness: Linguistic and social processes.* London and New York: Cassell, 123–155.

Martin, J. R. (2000) Close reading: Functional linguistics as a tool for critical discourse analysis. In L. Unsworth (Ed). *Researching language in schools and communities: Functional linguistics perspectives.* London: Cassell, 275–304.

Painter, C. (1999) *Learning through language in early childhood*. London and New York: Continuum.

Rothery, J. and Stenglin, M. (2000) Interpreting literature: The role of appraisal. In L. Unsworth (Ed). *Researching language in schools and communities: Functional linguistics perspectives*. London: Cassell, 275–304.

Claire Acevedo, Caroline Coffin, Carlos Gouveia, Ann-Christin Lövstedt and Rachel Whittaker: Teacher Learning for European Literacy Education (TeL4ELE) 2011–2013 Project

Claire Acevedo (Reading for Life, UK), **Caroline Coffin** (Open University, UK), **Carlos Gouveia** (University of Lisbon), **Ann-Christin Lövstedt** (Reading for Life, Sweden) and **Rachel Whittaker** (Universidad Autónoma de Madrid) describe the *Teacher Learning for European Literacy Education (TeL4ELE) 2011–2013 Project* which supported the development of literacy educators in five European countries (Sweden, Denmark, Spain, Portugal and Scotland) to become experts in a genre-based literacy pedagogy entitled *Reading to Learn* with support from the non-European partner, Australia. The aims of the projects were for the teachers to implement literacy pedagogy in their classrooms to improve the learning outcomes for all students especially those who were educationally disadvantaged.

The *Teacher Learning for European Literacy Education (TeL4ELE) 2011–2013 Project* – http://tel4ele.eu) was a Comenius Multilateral Project funded by the Lifelong Learning Project of the European Union (EU). 'Comenius Multilateral Projects are undertaken by consortia working together to improve the initial or in-service training of teachers and other categories of personnel working in the school education sector to develop strategies or exchange experiences to improve the quality of teaching and learning in the classroom'.[2] The overall aim of the Teacher Learning for European Literacy Education Project was to support the development of literacy educators in five European countries (Sweden, Denmark, Spain, Portugal and Scotland) to become experts in a genre-based literacy pedagogy, specifically *Reading to Learn* (Rose 2015), with support from the non-European partner, Australia. The educators were to use their expertise to lead and support the development of teachers as they implemented the literacy pedagogy in their classrooms to improve the learning outcomes for all students, especially those who were educationally disadvantaged. The project was carried out in the five different educational contexts in each national language as well as the Basque language (Euskera) in the north of Spain. Inherent in the overall aim of the project was the notion that, with some local adaptations and expert leadership, a robust pedagogy based on the Systemic Functional model of language would be capable of transcending international educational and linguistic boundaries to improve learning outcomes for even the most educationally disadvantaged learners.

A range of data on the classroom implementation was collected – teacher learning data, recordings of implementation and reflective teacher responses, student learning data, classroom recordings and student response data, pre-intervention and post-intervention analysed writing samples and pre-reading and post-reading comprehension tests. The external evaluation of the project [3] determined that the overall aim of the project was achieved. Survey and interview data showed high levels of engagement with the pedagogy on the part of both educators and classroom teachers. Ninety-seven per cent stated that, in their view, the pedagogy offered a completely different approach to reading and writing compared to those that are generally used in schools. Moreover almost all teachers perceived that the pedagogy had had an impact on their students' understanding of how language operates in different texts to make meaning and on their students' reading and writing. Ninety-two per cent wished to continue with the approach citing the following reasons as motivation – improvement in student learning, the empowering nature of the pedagogy and the fact that they enjoyed working with the approach. Most significantly students' assessment scores, based on their pre-reading and post-reading and writing scores, showed that all students (drawn from the 97 participating classes) had improved by an average of 14.3% on their writing and 9% on their reading (in almost half of all cases in less than five weeks). It is significant that, across the student cohort as a whole, the educationally disadvantaged and lower scoring students showed the greatest gains (in line with previous studies e.g. Culican 2005).

What these findings point to is that an approach to literacy which makes language visible and brings into sharp relief its relationship with learning amounts to a paradigm shift for many educators, classroom teachers and students but one they were motivated to work with. Prior to participating in the TeL4ELE project, many participants had a relatively narrow view of language and even where there was recognition of its relationship with meaning-making and with reading, writing and learning, there was an absence of practical strategies for harnessing its power. For many educators and teachers learning to enact a meaning-oriented theory of language and learning, rather than a form-oriented one, in the classroom, was challenging. However, the carefully worked out strategies and techniques that are integral to the *Reading to Learn* program enabled them to bring about a major change to their classroom practice (see the project website at www.tel4ele.eu for sample materials produced during the project).

Education as the base on which to build social cohesion and economic development has been on the EU list of priorities for many years. However, still in 2010, Europe only had 24% of its adult population with tertiary level education, far behind the USA and Japan at 40% (European Union 2010). Literacy has always been recognised as vital for access at all educational levels, and language skills (mother tongue and foreign languages) have long been identified as key competences for European citizens (European Union 2006: 10). However, the 2010 document reported no progress, but, instead, a worrying regression – 'The growing number of people with low levels of reading literacy provides the greatest cause for concern' (European Union 2010: 6), leading to calls for action to develop teachers' competence to support literacy, especially through in-service training. Such a call resonated with the European partners in this project:

- the Multilingual Research Institute in Stockholm, Sweden
- the National Centre for Reading in Copenhagen, Denmark
- the Universidad Autónoma de Madrid, Spain
- the Institute of Theoretical and Computational Linguistics, Lisbon, Portugal
- Strathclyde University, Scotland, United Kingdom.

For many years these partners had been working in educational linguistics and teacher training, and had the skills, experience, and evidence from research to propose the development and trialling of a functional, language-based approach to the teaching of literacy to improve literacy and learning outcomes, particularly for disadvantaged learners.

Research has shown that language, and particularly academic language, is central in the achievement of school outcomes in all subjects and throughout all school grades (Christie & Derewianka 2008, Schleppegrell 2004). It is this growing recognition of the relationship between language and learning that underpins the European Core Curriculum for Mainstreamed Second Language – Teacher Education, a framework developed as part of the Comenius funded project EUCIM-TE (European Union 2011a) and which is currently informing pre-service and in-service teacher education through the European network of Teacher Education Partnerships (established as part of the project). In the EUCIM-TE project there was a strong focus on the development of language as a meaning-making resource and the need to see language development as both learning language and learning through language. The TeL4ELE project thus extended the foundational work of EUCIM-TE by further raising the awareness of educators and teachers of the interconnectedness of language competence and educational achievement. With teachers trained to address language and literacy needs in a focused and sustained way students are more likely to have the linguistic resources to pursue their studies and achieve higher educational certificates.

The idea of a project that would build on and extend this earlier work was thus very motivating. Partners felt that the exchange of knowledge and experience across the five nations and the input from the non-European partner (University of Sydney, Australia) would place them in a strong position to learn more about, test and evaluate the appropriateness and effectiveness of the latest genre-based pedagogy – *Reading to Learn* (Rose 2015, Rose & Martin 2012) in their own local context. The notion of social justice was also a strong motivating force in that the partners wanted to evaluate the effectiveness of the *Reading to Learn* pedagogy in targeting the educational improvement of pupils with a migrant background, and those with poor literacy levels and therefore limited access to the entire curriculum.

TeL4ELE was designed as a two-year teacher professional development project drawing on the principles of action research (Kemmis & McTaggart 1988), which allows for an innovative 'learning through doing' approach. To this end it incorporated as far as possible elements that brought about success in Australian *Reading to Learn* projects (see Culican 2005, Koop & Rose 2008) and the Stockholm project in Sweden (Acevedo 2011). In those projects, for example, it was shown that the degree of support that teachers receive through partnering with teacher educators greatly increased the likelihood of the future sustainability and success of the pedagogy beyond the life of the project.

The project design was thus based on the premise that, if transformed classroom learning is to be achieved, the learning needs of teacher educators and teachers must be viewed as similar to those of students, requiring opportunities for supported practice. The *Reading to Learn* (R2L) programme for educators and teachers that formed the core input in the first year of the project provided those opportunities. Through supported practice and reflection teacher educators were able to experiment with the R2L approach and then lead teachers to successfully implement the approach in the classroom.

The reciprocal learning approach to professional development, combined with the robust model of a genre-based literacy pedagogy (informed by the Systemic Functional model of language), provided a dynamic framework to successfully achieve the aims of the project. The difference between an action learning style project and the more common professional development courses or workshops is that in the latter there is data collection for reflection on action, which includes teacher reflection on self and student learning. It is an evidence-based approach to professional development and classroom learning and we found this made a significant difference to the developing awareness, understanding and practice of the participants.

In retrospect, as this was an international project which brought together such a diverse group of educators from different contexts and language groups, there was insufficient time for the group to develop a shared identity either before or during the project implementation. The consequence was that it took more time than the project allowed for the teacher educators, the teachers and the students to work through the learning cycles and to become completely fluent in the pedagogy. As a result, almost half of the teachers in the project only implemented the pedagogy in the classroom for five weeks or less. In a future project, the same design could be used but in order to have a greater impact in the classroom, either more time would need to be provided or previously trained teacher educators could work directly with teachers and provide more support to them as they implemented the pedagogy in the classroom as is usually the case in *Reading to Learn* projects. This presupposes however that such a group of expert educators is available to train teachers and the goal of this project was to create such a group of experts.

A key learning from this project is that despite the international diversity, a robust pedagogy based on the Systemic Functional model of language (Halliday 1994) has the capacity, with some local adaptations, to transcend international educational and linguistic boundaries to improve learning outcomes for even the most educationally disadvantaged learners. It is also clear that teacher professional development needs to be designed to include ongoing support for teachers and their educators in order to sustain changes in their thinking and practice.

Further research is needed on how the teacher training programme, the pedagogy and the genre theory might be adapted for different national education and linguistic contexts. An exploration of how different types of communication media could be used to support a dispersed group would be beneficial e.g. video linked training sessions. Further research on assessment would also be timely.

Despite the challenging nature of this project, we would encourage more cross-national and cross-linguistic projects on literacy. It was a rewarding experience for all the teams, and led to many insights into literacy and teacher professional development. The work initiated by this project is being sustained and further developed by many of the teachers and teacher educators in classrooms and training centres in the partner countries.

References

Acevedo, C. (2011) *Will the implementation of reading to learn in Stockholm schools accelerate literacy learning for disadvantaged students and close the achievement gap? A report on school-based action research.* Stockholm, Sweden: Multilingual Research Institute [online]. Available at: http://www.pedagogstockholm.se/kunskapsbanken/ – accessed 10.1.2012.

Christie, F. and Derewianka, B. (2008) *School discourse: Learning to write across the years of schooling.* London: Continuum.

Coffin, C. Acevedo, C. and Lövstedt A-C. (2013) *Teacher learning for European literacy education (TeL4ELE) Final Report, Public Part* – available from: http://tel4ele.eu/ – accessed 16.9.2014.

Culican, S. J. (2005) *Learning to read: Reading to learn: A middle years literacy intervention research project, final report 2003–4* [online] Catholic Education Office: Melbourne – available from: http://www.ceomelb.catholic.edu.au. Available at: http://www.readingto learn.com.au – accessed 20.11.2009.

European Union. Audiovisual and Culture Executive Agency (2011a) *European core curriculum for mainstreamed second language teacher education end of project report* [online] Brussels. Available at: http://www.eucim-te.eu/32341 – accessed 14.7.2011.

European Union. Audiovisual and Culture Executive Agency (2011b) *Teaching reading in Europe: Contexts, policies and practices.* Eurydice, [online] Brussels. Available at: http://www.indire.it/lucabas/lkmw_file/eurydice/reading_literacy_EN.pdf – accessed 15.11.2013.

European Union (2006) Recommendation of the European Parliament and of the Council of 18 December 2006 on key competences for lifelong learning, L 394, *Official Journal of the European Union.* Available at: http://eur-lex.europa.eu/LexUriServ/LexUriServ.do?uri=OJ:L:2006:394:0010:0018:en:PDF – accessed 4.12.2008.

European Union (2010) 2010 joint progress report of the Council and the Commission on the implementation of the Education and Training 2010 work programme May 2010: 117/5 *Official Journal of the European Union IV.* available at: http://www.ecvet-team.eu/en/system/files/documents/74/key-competences-vet-2020.pdf – accessed 8.2.2011.

Halliday, M. A. K. (1994) *An introduction to functional grammar.* London: Edward Arnold.

Kemmis, S. and McTaggart, R. (1988) *The action research planner.* Victoria: Deakin University Press.

Koop, C. and Rose, D. (2008) Reading to learn in Murdi Paaki: Changing outcomes for Indigenous students, *Literacy Learning: the Middle Years* Vol. 16 No. 1, 41–46.

Rose, D. (2015) *Reading to Learn: Accelerating learning and closing the gap* – Sydney: Reading to Learn. Available at: http://www.readingtolearn.com.au – accessed 15.1.2015.

Rose, D. and Martin, J. R. (2012) *Learning to write, reading to learn: Genre, knowledge and pedagogy in the Sydney School*. London: Equinox.

Schleppegrell, M. J. (2004) *The language of schooling: A functional linguistics perspective*. Mahwah, NJ: Erlbaum.

Literacy development

Brian Byrne: behaviour-genetic studies of literacy development

Brian Byrne (University of New England) has completed small and large-scale twin studies in Australia, the United States and Scandinavia into the relation between genetics and literacy development – the genetics of reading ability. Educators are uncomfortable that genes can be a marker of literacy development but his research shows that genetic endowment is a big player in the development of literacy.

Our behaviour-genetic studies of literacy development, undertaken on an international scale (across Australia, the United States and Scandinavia), have shown that a child's genetic endowment is the single most influential factor in early literacy development in societies that have mandatory, universal education (Byrne, Olson, Samuelsson, Wadsworth, Corley, DeFries, & Wilcutt 2006, 2009 and 2012, Christopher et al. 2013). The impact of this kind of finding, which other groups have also observed, has been limited owing to a degree of reluctance on the part of educational professionals to acknowledge the influence of genes on school achievement.

Our studies have shown that in the Australian *National Assessment Program – Literacy and Numeracy* (NAPLAN) genetic variability accounts for at least 80% of reading scores – although there are a lot of qualifications. Writing has less variability (50%). The question is what are the implications of this and one answer is that educators need to know about this dimension of literacy development.

Knowing about genetic variability has the potential to diminish blame and stigma but it also increases pessimism, that is, it's a two-edged sword. Teachers and parents are scared of this. Although genes may only be part of the story, this knowledge means it is easy to be gloomy about the child's prospects. However, genes are only one of the variables. Environment amplifies the genetic effect and management can include changes in the environment, for example, diet, attendance at school, good teaching practice, including more cues from the teacher. Those with a severe reading disability are more influenced by the environment than those without.

In the United States there are bigger environmental effects than in Australia, they think because of greater social inequality in the United States. In Sweden, the variability in reading is about half of what it is in Australia because of the effect of teaching. In Swaziland, where there is no free education, there are low genetic effects because the largest effect is whether children go to school or not.

It has been known for over 100 years that reading disabilities tend to run in families, and discovering whether this was due to shared genes or shared environments presented itself as an important issue to resolve. We used the Classic Twin Model (CTM), whereby the relative degrees of similarity between monozygotic and dizygotic twin pairs is used to estimate genetic and environmental influences on human characteristics and traits. The CTM is a well-proven methodology for addressing the so-called Nature-Nurture questions. The methodology is an efficient and important tool for studying differential achievement in many domains, including literacy and other academic subjects and I'd stick to the same approach if starting the research again.

We need to discover *how* genes exert their influence on literacy development, and which aspects of a child's environment are the most important as well – because genes are only part of the story. The finding of a substantial genetic influence on academic achievement needs to be taken seriously by educational professionals so the implications of this observation can be considered and thereby kept in perspective. Do we accept that some children will find learning to read tougher, and then forget in the classroom that this is the case? Such children need more time and more support and money should go to individual children, for example, tutoring.

While there is a difference between children in terms of reading, you don't want teachers to be part of that. Teacher effects are small in the differences between children in early literacy and NAPLAN. There are no simple solutions but in interactions with children having problems with reading they need to be encouraged to build on their strengths.

References

Byrne, B., Olson, R. K., Samuelsson, S., Wadsworth, S., Corley, R., DeFries, J. C. and Wilcutt, E. (2006) Genetic and environmental influences on early literacy. *Journal of Research in Reading* Vol. 29 No. 1, 33–49.

Byrne, B., Coventry, W. L., Olson, R. K., Samuelsson, S., Corley, R., Wilcutt, E., Wadsworth, S. and DeFries, J. C. (2009) Genetic and environmental influences on aspects of literacy and language in early childhood: Continuity and change from preschool to Grade 2. *Journal of Neurolinguistics* Vol. 22, 219–236.

Byrne, B., Wadsworth, S., Boehme, K., Talk, A. C., Coventry, W. L., Olson, R. K., Samuelsson, S. and Corley, R. (2012) Multivariate genetic analysis of learning and early reading development. *Scientific Studies of Reading* Vol. 17 No. 3, 224–242.

Christopher, M. E., Hulslander, J., Byrne, B. Samuelsson, S., Keenan, J. M., Pennington, B., DeFries, J. C., Wadsworth, S. J., Willcutt, E. G. and Olson, R. K. (2013) Modeling the etiology of individual differences in early reading development: Evidence for strong genetic influences. *Scientific Studies of Reading* Vol. 17 No. 5, 350–368.

Literacy and numeracy in adult learning contexts

Anne Burns: action research

Anne Burns (University of New South Wales, Sydney) describes an action research project in which she worked collaboratively with a group of teachers to investigate their students' reading practices outside the classroom and what could be learned from this about classroom literacy instruction.

Over the years I've worked with teachers extensively in Australia and elsewhere who have been interested in conducting action research in their workplaces. Many of these projects have focused in one way or another on aspects of literacy use, literacy development in relation to students' needs, encouraging reading in the students' new language or developing writing skills. I've chosen to focus on one project (Burns & de Silva Joyce 2000), which I found particularly interesting. My colleague Helen de Silva Joyce and I worked collaboratively with a group of three teachers from New South Wales, South Australia and Tasmania respectively, who were all interested in knowing more about their adult immigrant students' literacy practices. Specifically, they wanted to focus on their students' reading practices outside the classroom and what could be learned from this research about classroom literacy instruction. The project had three aims:

- to identify how students from three different cultural backgrounds employed reading in their daily lives, both individually and in relation to other family members

- to investigate the same students' perceptions of their experiences of reading in formal classroom situations
- to draw out implications for reading instruction.

The teachers, one of whom was an Arabic speaker, chose to work with students in their classes from different language backgrounds. The students were members of three-generation families who had emigrated to Australia from the Lebanon, China, and El Salvador respectively. They also interviewed other students from the same language backgrounds who were currently enrolled in their classes, to extend the investigation of current and previous reading practices. They also asked them to keep reading diaries over seven days.

Among the numerous insights our research group gained were that reading practices were plurilingual with both (or additional) languages being used translinguistically according to needs, relevance and understanding. Practices were also highly diverse within and across the families, and interacted both with personal interests (for example, sport, religion, fashion) and community needs (for example, work-related, university preparation, club or church membership).

Reading was frequently a collaborative practice, for example, with younger family members providing extensive support to older relatives with less developed skills in literacy, or in the second language. A wide variety of literacy modes were used including the Internet and print media. It was noticeable that reading practices depended too on a trajectory of literacy development, with skills and interests in reading in the second language emerging over time, and often mediated in their development by intervening life events (for example, marriage, pregnancy, family loss, work opportunities, financial circumstances). Evident in some people's experiences was that migration had led to a loss of a *reader self*, where previous avenues for reading were now shut off because of less availability of reading material, or lack of knowledge about sources of material. For some readers this situation had a considerable impact on their ability to connect with the local community, the country and even the world.

A major impact of the project was that the teachers gained a much greater appreciation of the need to avoid making assumptions about students' literacy abilities and interests and to spend more time finding out about their literacy histories. They also realised they needed to become cross-cultural literacy *coaches* or *guides* who engaged their students in discussions of their social purposes and preferred modes of literacy in their new environment. They saw the need to introduce students to the types of genres and materials they could gain access to in the community, where to find them, and how to use them critically, rather than to take a more traditional focus on primarily developing basic reading skills and strategies.

Turning to the students' point of view, it became obvious that students were not always aware that what they were doing in class was in fact a reading activity. Many felt that teachers should be more explicit in naming the skill focus of the activities they were being asked to do and explaining why they were doing it. Perhaps one of the most surprising findings, however, was that students from all three backgrounds exhibited strong enthusiasm for having teachers read aloud to them in class, especially if they could read along simultaneously. They valued opportunities to hear a text being read fluently, to practise their listening skills, and to have a means to hear and develop English pronunciation.

My interest in the literacy needs and practices of adult immigrant students stemmed from my own experiences over several years of working as a teacher with refugees and immigrants in a community-based English as a second language (ESL) class. Many came from limited educational backgrounds and their literacy skills were not well developed. I was struck by the immense challenges they faced in learning English, particularly in a society that demands very high levels of literacy in daily life, and in education in particular. At the same time, I was undertaking postgraduate studies and reading the work of Paulo Freire, Shirley Brice Heath, Brian Street and David Barton and his colleagues, at a time when the New Literacy Studies movement was emerging. My doctoral work explored literacy teaching practices in adult immigrant ESL classrooms, in a period when strong versions of communicative language teaching were very much in vogue. My research revealed that little explicit attention was being paid at that time to the development of students' literacy. It was assumed that students would simply be able to handle the large amount of written material they were presented with in classrooms. The focus seemed to be very much on speaking and oral interaction, which was not unreasonable, but completely overlooked the need to develop literacy skills explicitly, and to prepare students for participation in a literacy-focused society.

The studies that were influencing literacy research at this time in Australia were those that adopted an ethnographic and socially contextualised perspective. These studies, by researchers such as those mentioned above, see literacy as culturally and socially purposeful, or 'ideological' to use Street's (1984) term. In contrast with the concept that reading is a neutral 'autonomous' (Street 1984) cognitive skill, reading practices are seen as embedded in contexts of history, power and culture and mediated by societal and personal imperatives. Another powerful influence on the project was Freebody and Luke's (1990) conceptualisation of four reader roles: code breaker (learning to crack the code), text participant (gaining literal and figurative textual meaning), text user (interacting with and using texts for social purposes), and text analyst (understanding how readers are positioned by writers and how to critically deconstruct text).

Action research was adopted because it enabled ESL teachers we were working with nationally to be directly involved as co-investigators in the project and to explore their own students' lives. This form of research was familiar and attractive to many teachers in the national adult ESL programme, through the work of colleagues such as David Nunan and Geoff Brindley. It had gained credibility among ESL teachers nationally, who reported that they benefited considerably from reading their colleagues' research insights into teaching challenges they themselves were constantly facing. My book (Burns 1999) was based on the experiences of working collaboratively in this way with ESL teachers nationally.

Because many adult ESL language programmes are intensive and driven by accountability requirements of testing and assessment, teachers rarely get opportunities to explore reading practices in such in-depth ways. The structured nature of the action research programme, the regular meetings involved and the fact that the teachers were able to work collaboratively to share and analyse their insights, provided the means to discover much more about students' experiences so that more appropriate courses could be designed to meet their literacy development needs. Because the project adopted an ethnographically oriented approach it could incorporate social, cultural and historical perspectives that went much further than many curriculum-focused needs analysis procedures.

This research was very small scale and, as is typical of action research, was highly localised. It would be valuable to repeat the research with a larger number of teachers undertaking this kind of action research approach and using principles of ethnography, and with students of different cultural backgrounds, especially more recent immigrant groups. It would also be very valuable to see in what ways the literacy histories and practices of refugee families might differ from those of the students and families in this research, who had chosen to migrate to Australia.

Recently there has been a growing interest in learning beyond the classroom (for example, Nunan & Richards 2015) and narrative enquiry (Barkhuizen, Benson & Chick 2014), both of which align with the purposes and focus of this action research study. These research trends highlight the need to bring the lived experiences of second-language students into the classroom for several reasons. By investigating the narratives of students' lives, researchers will learn more about their authentic language histories and what these might mean for classroom learning. We can also begin to identify new roles for students and teachers in incorporating these experiences, in order to overcome the limitations of classroom instruction. This kind of research can also contribute to identifying what motivates (or demotivates) student development of more effective literacy practices in the classroom. Pursuing this line of research can also help us to understand more about students' investment in learning during their daily lives and what can be done pedagogically to support autonomous learning outside the classroom.

There's a huge lack of research on adult immigrant learners in general, and on their literacy and reading practices in particular. We still know very little about this group of English learners, although Bonny Norton Pierce's work began to cast more light in this area in the 1990s and has continued in her subsequent work on learner identity. Recent studies by Roberts, Baynham (for example, 2006) in the UK and Tarone, Bigelow and Hansen (2009) in the United States have provided further insights, as did the special issue of *TESOL Quarterly* I co-edited with Celia Roberts (2010), which contained articles on adult immigrant students' experiences both within and outside the classroom. There is a pressing need for many more studies, qualitative, quantitative, and those employing action research so that we can learn more about the needs of these students and the teaching practices that would assist them. Classroom-based case studies, such as that carried out by my former PhD student and colleague, Susan Ollerhead (2012), would tell us much more about the literacy experiences and aspirations of this group of students and whether their needs in literacy classrooms are being met.

References

Barkhuizen, G., Benson, P., and Chick, A. (2014) *Narrative inquiry in language teaching and learning research*. New York: Routledge.

Burns, A. (1999) *Collaborative action research for English language teachers*. Cambridge: Cambridge University Press.

Burns, A. and de Silva Joyce, H. (Eds). (2000) *Teachers' voices 5: A new look at reading practices*. Sydney: NCELTR. Available at: http://www.ameprc.mq.edu.au/docs/research_reports/teachers_voices/Teachers_Voices_5.pdf

340 *Exploring Literacies*

Burns, A. and Roberts, C. (Eds). (2010) Special topic issue on: Migration and language learning. *TESOL Quarterly* Vol. 44 No. 3. 409–419.

Freebody, P. and Luke, A. (1990) Literacies programs: Debates and demands in cultural context. *Prospect: Australian Journal of TESOL* Vol. 5 NO. 3, 7–16.

Freire, P. (1970) *Pedagogy of the oppressed*. New York: Herder & Herder.

Norton, B. (2013) *Identity and language learning* (2nd Edition). Bristol: Multilingual Matters.

Nunan, D. C. and Richards, J. C. (Eds). (2015) *Language learning beyond the classroom*. New York: Routledge.

Ollerhead, S. (2012) 'Passivity' or 'potential'?: Teacher responses to learner identity in the low-level ESL classroom. *Literacy and Numeracy Studies* Vol. 20 No. 1, 63–83. Available at: http://epress.lib.uts.edu.au/journals/index.php/lnj/article/view/2620/2841

Roberts, C. and Baynham, M. (Eds). (2006) Special issue: Where talk is work: The social contexts of adult ESOL classrooms. *Linguistics and Education* Vol. 17 No. 1. 1–5.

Street, B. (1984) *Literacy in theory and practice*. Cambridge: Cambridge University Press.

Tarone, E., Bigelow, M. and Hansen, K. (2009) *Literacy and second language oracy*. Oxford: Oxford University Press.

Dave Tout: adult numeracy teaching – making meaning in mathematics

> **Dave Tout** (Australian Council for Educational Research – ACER) describes an action research project to develop a national training programme for teaching numeracy to adult students in the vocational education and training sector across Australia.

The project I conducted with Betty Johnston (Tout & Johnston 1995) was a nationally funded project to develop a national training programme for teaching numeracy to adult students in the vocational education and training (VET) sector across Australia.

As an experienced practitioner (and the joint author/researcher) it gave me a number of insights, including:

- how theory and practice were much more strongly connected than I thought or expected, and that they often matched what I believed to be best practice
- how wide a range of theories were relevant to the field of adult numeracy education – from school maths education through to adult education; from transmission through to constructivism; from theories of language and literacy education and more
- what these theories were and how they applied to the teaching and learning of maths to adults

- the value of writing – documenting your thoughts and ideas certainly makes you more aware of what you are doing and why, and increases your understanding and knowledge of both theory and practice.

The impact of the programme was substantial across Australia – all states and territories ran the programme for a number of years and it was instrumental in developing a core number of well-trained adult numeracy personnel. Not only did it train many personnel in Australia but it was viewed and considered in key documentation about pedagogical content knowledge and understanding of teaching adult numeracy, not only in Australia but also internationally. Some of the key lessons and impacts from the *Adult numeracy teaching: Making meaning in mathematics* project were:

- It put adult numeracy on the map.
- It had a theoretical and pedagogical basis – at that time we believed it was unique in the world.
- It had a strong critical literacy/numeracy focus.
- It also addressed the content knowledge of the practitioners to be trained, many of whom would not have been trained in teaching any maths or numeracy.
- It was recognised and given credit at a number of universities in Australia as being equivalent to a number of postgraduate subjects.

It has been the basis of many adult numeracy units in adult language, literacy and numeracy (LLN) training programmes since that time. For example, there have been two key vocational education and training (VET) qualifications that have been based around the original Adult Numeracy Teaching (ANT) course. The most recent was the unit *Analyse and apply adult numeracy teaching practices* in the nationally accredited TAE80113 Graduate Diploma in Adult Language, Literacy and Numeracy Practice.

There was a developing awareness, in the late 1980s and early1990s, that numeracy was an important skill in its own right and that it needed to be addressed and supported separately from literacy and English as a second language (ESL). But numeracy was only a very minor part of the adult education sector that encompassed a range of adult literacy and ESL programmes. These had grown and expanded in the late 1970s and into the 1980s as the Technical and Further Education (TAFE) and VET sectors grew and became more established. Adult numeracy, by comparison, was a very small field with little published research and with only a small number of teaching and professional development opportunities available.

As part of a roll-out across Australia of a comprehensive set of training programmes by the National Staff Development Committee for Vocational Education and Training, adult numeracy was eventually nominated as an area to be addressed. A joint application by Betty Johnston from the University of Technology, Sydney (UTS) and Language Australia (the National Languages and Literacy Institute of Australia), where I was based, won the project. UTS had been running a postgraduate course in teaching adult numeracy under Betty's guidance and in Victoria I had been involved in a number of state and national projects around adult numeracy. Some interstate collaboration had begun between Victoria and New South Wales (NSW) and this project was able to pull in the expertise from both institutions and from across both states. In the Introduction to the programme we wrote:

> The primary purpose of *Adult Numeracy Teaching* is to blend theory and practice about teaching and learning adult numeracy within a context of doing and investigating some mathematics, whilst developing a critical appreciation of the place of mathematics in society.

This statement sums up some of the unique characteristics of the programme – the explicit aim to connect theory and practice and also to address the content and pedagogical knowledge of the participants. Up to the time of the development and writing of *Adult Numeracy Teaching*, there was little research or analysis about the teaching and learning of numeracy for adults. Underpinning the project, especially from UTS and Betty's perspective, was a social, critical literacy/numeracy philosophical and pedagogical base.

We worked in a cooperative manner – both in how Betty and I worked as the lead workers/researchers and also with the broader group of experienced practitioners, rather than by working individually and in isolation. In essence, it was an action research project, even though we were *only* developing a professional development programme. The course was piloted in two states, NSW and Victoria, in 1994 and 1995. A train-the-trainers programme was held in early 1995 for representatives from all states and territories.

I believe that the project was important and valuable in providing the insights it did because, first, it involved the collaboration of an academic (Betty Johnston) and myself as an experienced practitioner and, second, because we took a collaborative, action research approach in working with a team of adult numeracy practitioners. The lead Betty took was crucial – her theoretical knowledge influenced the structure and content of the course – whilst the role of the practitioners was to make sure the course and pedagogical approach was embedded in the world of practice. The connections I was able to make as the leading practitioner between the theoretical knowledge and the practice was also quite important in the development and documentation of the final programme.

Would I do anything differently? No – I think it was extremely successful in how it worked and what it achieved.

I believe the original *Adult Numeracy Teaching* programme still stands up as pedagogically sound, especially in its structure and purpose, that is, to connect theory and practice and also to address the content and pedagogical knowledge of the participants. It has been instrumental and is still relevant today for the teaching of adult numeracy. As mentioned above, in essence it has been the basis of recent adult numeracy training programmes.

As well, the methodology used is a good model to follow, as I said above, the collaborative model of an academic working with an experienced practitioner and utilising an action research approach in working with a team of practitioners was critical to its success.

Numeracy in adult education and VET is still the poor cousin – often overlooked and forgotten. I believe research is required to learn more about the connections between the world of maths and the worlds of practice – whether that be in workplaces or in the community. More research is required into the connections between numeracy and literacy and language – and how these impact on teaching and learning.

References

Tout, D. and Johnston, B. (1995) *Adult numeracy teaching: Making meaning in mathematics*. Melbourne: National Staff Development Committee for Vocational Education and Training.

Stephen Black and Jo Balatti: adult literacy and social capital

Stephen Black (University of Technology, Sydney) and **Jo Balatti** (James Cook University, Townsville) describe research that examined the social capital outcomes of adult literacy and numeracy programmes. This project was the first Australian study to focus on the social capital related to adult literacy and numeracy, and it found that the great majority of adult literacy and numeracy students (almost 80% in this study) experienced social capital outcomes from participating in an accredited adult literacy and numeracy course.

In 2004, three researchers, Stephen Black, Jo Balatti, and Ian Falk, were funded by the Australian National Centre for Vocational Education Research (NCVER), to examine the social capital outcomes of adult literacy and numeracy programmes. The final report of the project was entitled *Reframing adult literacy and numeracy course outcomes: A social capital perspective* (Balatti, Black & Falk 2006). This project was the first Australian study to focus on the social capital related to adult literacy and numeracy, and it found that the great majority of adult literacy and numeracy students (almost 80% in this study) experienced social capital outcomes from participating in an accredited adult literacy and numeracy course. Furthermore, these outcomes were related to students' socioeconomic wellbeing.

By *social capital* we meant the 'networks, together with shared norms, values and understandings which facilitate cooperation within or amongst groups' (Australian Bureau of Statistics 2004: 5). Thus, social capital outcomes from courses referred to changes in the nature of the connections that students had in existing or new social networks that led to more involvement in society. In addition to students experiencing social capital outcomes, it was found that acquiring the technical skills of reading and writing, and the application of these skills in domains such as workplaces (as human capital), often required social capital as a prerequisite or corequisite.

These findings were (and remain) important because adult literacy and numeracy courses have been promoted and valued, and their outcomes to date have been expressed, primarily as the measured technical skills of reading, writing and numeracy, using for example, national assessment tools such as the National Reporting System (now the Australian Core Skills Framework). This project indicated there was another important dimension, social capital, that while related to human capital, was unrecognised in the official promotion of adult literacy and numeracy programmes and in existing reporting frameworks. A number of qualitative, situated examples were provided in the main research report that demonstrated the importance of social capital outcomes derived through network interactions in the adult literacy classroom, and the interrelationship of social and human capital. For example, one young (formerly rebellious) student with no improvements reported in literacy skills (human capital), nevertheless learned through the classroom network involving teachers (social capital) how to work with *authority figures*, thus leading directly to employment outcomes.

In another example, a student, a mother from a non-English speaking background, improved her literacy skills in a course (human capital) that enabled her to write letters to her son's school and to negotiate with teachers (social capital) so that her son could receive English as a second-language assistance. This was the first time a study had examined the inter-relationships of human and social capital in the adult literacy classroom and the subsequent impact on socioeconomic wellbeing. From the perspective of the funding body, the National Centre for Vocational Education Research (NCVER), the research was clearly seen to have an impact insofar as the NCVER funded a follow-up study by the same authors to produce guidelines on how to deliver adult literacy and numeracy education and training using a social capital approach (Balatti, Black & Falk 2009).

The overall impact of the study is a little difficult to gauge. At an academic level according to a *Google Scholar* search, the study has been well received, and to date (excluding references by the authors themselves) the study has been cited in close to 50 studies worldwide, including those by leading adult literacy researchers. At a policy level, however, there is little evidence that the study has had an impact. The Australian *National Foundation Skills Strategy* (NFSS) for example, made only a single reference to foundation skills having a positive effect on both human *and* social capital (SCOTESE 2012: 7), though the study was referenced in some of the publications that influenced the formation of the NFSS (e.g. Perkins 2009: 9–15; Skills Australia 2010: 37). Predominantly the adult literacy policy focus to date has been on human capital skills and economic outcomes, expressed primarily in terms of people getting jobs, and not social capital.

There were a number of factors that led us to seek funding for this project. First, social capital in the early 2000s was a major contemporary research topic with a proliferation of studies, and significantly in the area of adult and community education (e.g. Balatti & Falk 2002). Falk (2001) had also recently started to analyse the role of social capital in adult literacy programmes and how it might influence how people obtain jobs. This project involved two researchers (Jo Balatti and Ian Falk) who had recent experience in conducting social capital research. It also involved the active participation of a head teacher of adult literacy at the time in technical and further education (Stephen Black), who could provide an additional *coalface* perspective.

In addition to this alignment of researcher interests, it was apparent to the researchers that the field of adult literacy and numeracy might be receptive to and benefit from a focus on social capital. Since the beginnings of adult literacy as a distinct field of practice in the 1970s, researchers had sought to describe the outcomes of adult literacy programmes, which involved in the early stages mainly volunteers working one-to-one with students. In a seminal British study by Charnley and Jones (1980), adult literacy provision was found to increase the self-confidence and esteem of students (expressed mainly as 'affective personal achievements' and 'affective social achievements'), which for the students seemed to outweigh in importance the acquisition of the technical skills of reading and writing ('cognitive achievements') and how they used these skills ('enactive achievements').

For a couple of decades in the 1980s and 1990s researchers continued to report adult literacy programme outcomes largely in terms of students' increased 'confidence' (e.g., Black & Sim 1990, Grant 1987), and for adult literacy/numeracy teachers it became well entrenched as their mantra. Rarely, however, did these social/affective outcomes seem to gain resonance with policymakers. A focus on social capital appeared to offer an additional conceptual framework that incorporated self-confidence within the network of elements such as trustworthiness and self-efficacy and how people related with others in social networks. It seemed to have the potential to gain some traction in adult literacy policy. A study of social capital and literacy also represented for the researchers another element of the 'social turn' (Gee 2000) that had recently been reflected in the growth of the New Literacy Studies (e.g. Barton & Hamilton 1998).

Our methodology was primarily qualitative, involving semi-structured interviews with a total of 75 respondents, mainly adult literacy students. A qualitative approach was seen as appropriate for exploring and then building new knowledge and theory. Following Marshall and Rossman (1999:15), the qualitative research design was deemed ideal for:

- identifying and uncovering the complexities of multiple inputs and outcomes
- identifying unexplained outcomes
- understanding *how* outcomes and inter-relationships occur.

One of the limitations of our study was that we were directed by the funding organisation, the NCVER, to work within the conceptual framework of social capital developed by the Australian Bureau of Statistics (ABS 2004). Social capital was, and remains, a contested concept and the use of the ABS framework eliminated the problematic issue of which model of social capital to apply in the study. The ABS framework was designed primarily for large-scale quantitative and survey-style research work. Thus, with very little detail provided to describe activities and interactions at the micro social level, the researchers had to make value judgements as to where these activities should be located within the ABS framework.

To a large extent it was the use of semi-structured interviews undertaken in a relatively informal research context (usually while the students were attending classes) that enabled the rich qualitative insights that the researchers documented in their report. An additional key element was trust, itself an important component of social capital. For example, one of the target adult literacy groups was young people, often disaffected with formal education. Semi-structured interviews with young people were potentially problematic, and especially if the interviews probed aspects of their relationships and networks. But it was largely the trust and support of their technical and further education teachers that enabled a researcher (also a technical and further education teacher) to gain access to these students in a relatively informal way that encouraged them to be forthcoming and honest in their interview responses. Similarly, trust in the researcher (also being a teacher) was a necessary component of interviews in the Northern Territory that involved Indigenous students. Often these interviews with Indigenous students were undertaken in the form of small focus groups rather than one to one, to encourage student responses.

This project represented an initial foray into the issues of adult literacy and numeracy courses and social capital. In the early stages of the research project we had no clear idea whether we would in fact find social capital outcomes, but the methodology proved appropriate, revealing social capital played a significant role in such courses. Faced with the same circumstances, with little other research in the field to guide us, we would undertake the research in a very similar way. However, having now determined the extent and role of social capital outcomes, we would target further research more specifically. Rather than focus on a broad range of student groups, as we did with our project (including Indigenous, mature-aged, non-English speaking background and young people across three Australian states), it would be useful to examine, for example, the role of social capital in different sites/contexts, including workplaces. To date, literacy and numeracy in workplaces have been examined primarily as human capital skills, with no studies focusing on social capital outcomes and how both forms of capital relate to each other. Further, in the area of health literacy, our follow-up study (Balatti et al. 2009) examined the role of social capital and how some pedagogical approaches encourage social capital outcomes, but health literacy and numeracy remain largely unexplored areas in need of further research on social capital.

Apart from the above more focused contexts, in-depth ethnographic-type studies of educational sites – classrooms or training rooms or community centres (see for example Grenfell et al. 2011) – would enable additional insights into the processes of social capital and how interactions within networks develop over time. Our use of semi-structured interviews was limited in so far as they were based on the reflections of students and teachers, rather than the researchers observing first hand (through ethnographic approaches) the dynamics of social networks.

In recent years, Australian adult literacy and numeracy policy and research have been framed very much in *economic crisis* terms, and the recent NFSS (SCOTESE 2012) is a clear demonstration of this. The research that counts in this policy work has been primarily quantitative, based on international survey data (e.g. ABS 2007). The focus was and is almost exclusively on literacy and numeracy as human capital measured statistically (for example, Productivity Commission 2010). What our research demonstrated was that social capital plays a part in adult literacy and numeracy courses and that it is often interrelated with human capital. In some cases, for example, social capital outcomes, including changes in network qualities such as trust levels and self-efficacy, were found to precede human capital outcomes, and in other cases the reverse was found to be true. Thus even for those stakeholders in adult literacy and numeracy contexts, who are primarily concerned with economic development, exploring social capital may have some benefits, but to do this will require qualitative in addition to quantitative research methodologies.

References

Australian Bureau of Statistics (ABS). (2004) *Measuring social capital: An Australian framework and indicators*. Canberra: ABS.

Australian Bureau of Statistics. (2007) *Adult literacy and life skills survey: Summary results, Australia*. Canberra: ABS.

Balatti, J. and Falk, I. (2002) Socioeconomic contributions of adult learning to community: A social capital perspective. *Adult Education Quarterly* Vol. 52 No. 4, 281–298.

Balatti, J., Black, S. and Falk, I. (2006) *Reframing adult literacy and numeracy course outcomes: A social capital perspective*. Adelaide: National Centre for Vocational Education Research.

Balatti, J., Black, S. and Falk, I. (2009) *A new social capital paradigm for adult literacy: Partnerships, policy and pedagogy.* Adelaide: National Centre for Vocational Education Research.

Barton, D. and Hamilton, M. (1998) *Local literacies: Reading and writing in one community.* London: Routledge.

Black, S. and Sim, S. (1990) *The learning experience: Perspectives of former students from two adult literacy programmes.* Sydney: Adult Literacy Information Office.

Charnley, A. and Jones, H. (1980) *The concept of success in adult literacy.* London: Adult Literacy and Basic Skills Unit.

Falk, I. (2001) Sleight of hand: Job myths, literacy and social capital. In J. Lo Bianco and R. Wickert (Eds). *Australian policy activism in language and literacy.* Melbourne: Language Australia. 203–220.

Gee, J. (2000) The new literacy studies: From 'socially situated' to the work of the social. In D. Barton, M. Hamilton, and R. Ivanič (Eds). *Situated literacies: Reading and writing in context.* London: Routledge.

Grant, A. (1987) *Opportunity to do brilliantly: TAFE and the challenge of adult literacy provision in Australia.* Canberra: AGPS.

Grenfell, M., Bloome, D., Hardy, C., Pahl, K., Rowsell, J. and Street, B. (2011) *Language, ethnography and education: Bridging new literacy studies and Bourdieu.* London: Routledge.

Halliday, M. A. K. (1975) Language as social semiotic: Towards a general sociolinguistic theory in A. Makkai and V. Mecker Makkai (Eds). *The first LACUS forum,* Columbia SC: Hornbeam Press, 17–46.

Halliday, M. A. K. (1984) Language as code and language as behaviour. In R. Fawcett, M. A. K. Halliday, S. Lamb and A. Makkai (Eds). *The semiotics of language and culture,* Vol. 1: Language as social semiotic. London: Pinter, 3–35.

Kress, G. and Van Leeuwen, T. (1996) *Reading images: The grammar of visual design.* Oxford and New York: Routledge.

Marshall, C. and Rossman, G. (1999) *Designing qualitative research.* Thousand Oaks, CA: Sage.

Maton, K. (2014) *Knowledge and knowers: Towards a social realist sociology of education.* London and New York: Routledge.

Perkins, K. (2009) *Adult literacy and numeracy: Research and future strategy.* Adelaide: National Centre for Vocational Education Research.

Productivity Commission. (2010) *Links between literacy and numeracy skills and labour outcomes.* Canberra: Productivity Commission.

Ravelli, L. (1996) Making language accessible: Successful text writing for museum visitors. *Linguistics and Education,* Vol. 8, 367–387.

Ravelli, L. (1998) The consequence of choice: Discursive positioning in an art institution in A. Sánchez-Macarro and R. Carter (Eds). *Linguistic choice across genres: Variation in spoken and written English.* Amsterdam/Philadelphia: John Benjamin.

Ravelli, L. (2006) *Museum texts: Communication frameworks.* London: Routledge.

Rose, D. and Martin, J. R. (2012) *Learning to write, reading to learn: Genre, knowledge and pedagogy in the Sydney School.* Sheffield: Equinox.

Skills Australia. (2010) *Australian workforce futures: A national workforce development strategy.* Canberra: Commonwealth of Australia.

Standing Council on Tertiary Education, Skills & Employment (SCOTESE) (2012) *National foundations skills strategy for adults.* Canberra: SCOTESE.

Brian Paltridge, Sue Starfield and Louise Ravelli: doctoral writing in visual and performing arts

Brian Paltridge (University of Sydney), **Sue Starfield**, and **Louise Ravelli** (University of New South Wales) describe a research project that investigated doctoral writing in the visual and performing arts. In this field a key feature of doctorates is that they comprise two components – a visual or performance component and a written text that accompanies it, which in some ways is similar to but in others quite different from a traditional doctoral dissertation. They explain why they adopted a textography approach that explicitly draws together textual and ethnographic perspectives into one overarching framework for approaching the analysis of texts.

The study (Paltridge, Starfield, Ravelli & Tuckwell 2012, Paltridge, Starfield, Ravelli, Tuckwell & Nicholson 2014, Ravelli, Paltridge, Starfield & Tuckwell 2013, Starfield, Paltridge & Ravelli 2012) investigated doctoral writing in the visual and performing arts. A key feature of doctorates in these areas is that they comprise two components – a visual or performance component and a written text that accompanies it, which in some ways is similar to but in others quite different from a traditional doctoral dissertation. The study was motivated by the reported difficulties experienced by students and their supervisors with the written component.

The study found that there was a range of possibilities for the students' texts, each at different points on a continuum. In some cases, the text and the creative component were separate products in which one did not reference the other. In other cases, the two were more closely combined where the text reported on the creative process and each component contextualised the other. The organisation of the texts was also found to be on a continuum, from those that contained the same organisational structures and in the same order as conventional doctoral dissertations, through to texts that were much more dispersed and would not, at first sight, be recognised as typical examples of the doctoral dissertation genre.

The study found that there is a range of options for how students might write their texts. They still need, however, to meet the criteria set by universities for the examination of doctoral dissertations and these criteria have to be met, at least in part, through the texts that students submit for examination. The study showed how innovative texts can be related to, but not necessarily conform to, conventional writing practices and that students writing in these areas do not necessarily have to fit with preconceived patterns or typical expectations for writing at this particular level of study. It also revealed the influence of key figures and institutions in terms of how students might present their texts as well as how this impacted on the choices the students had for their writing. The field as a whole, however, was found to recognise and accommodate the variation we found in the students' texts and was not resistant to it in the examination process.

The study had its origins in our teaching of doctoral writing and our observation of the ways in which texts that are submitted for examination in the visual and performing arts vary, in sometimes quite substantive ways, from texts submitted in other areas of study, yet still meet the same overarching requirements for the award of doctoral degrees. A study that we found especially inspiring for our project was Swales's (1998a) *Other Floors, Other Voices* in which he carried out an examination of the kinds of writing that people, who worked on three different floors of his building at the University of Michigan, were engaged in, the kinds of texts they wrote and the reasons they wrote the texts that they did.

The study was a textography (Starfield, Paltridge & Ravelli 2014, Swales 1998b), an approach to genre analysis that combines elements of text analysis with elements of ethnography. A textography, then, is something more than a traditional piece of discourse analysis, while at the same time less than a full-blown ethnography. A textography might include the examination of language and discourse features of texts, together with ethnographic techniques such as interviews, surveys, field notes and observations, as well as an analysis of texts that surround and have an impact on the texts, in order to get a view of the world in which the texts are written. Our study employed this approach in order to examine what the students' texts were like and why they were written as they were.

The project was carried out over a number of stages. The first stage was a nation-wide survey to establish a database of institutions, their doctoral programmes, assessment regimes, and numbers of recent graduates, to determine the extent of practice-based doctoral submissions taking place in Australia in the visual and performing arts. The second stage of the project involved the collection of doctoral texts selected on the advice of supervisors working in the schools and faculties identified in the first part of the study. Thirty-six doctoral texts were collected for the study and these became the focus of our analysis. Thirty-two supervisors completed surveys and 15 students and 15 supervisors were interviewed, who were paired as much as possible around the students' doctoral work. Some of these supervisors had been examiners of some of the doctoral works that were collected, adding a further dimension to the data. University handbooks and prospectuses were also examined, as was information given to students in relation to their candidature. Published research into visual arts PhDs was taken into account, as well as books and journals that discussed visual and performing arts research more generally. In-house art school publications and discussion papers on doctoral studies in the visual and performing arts were also examined and the researchers attended roundtable discussions on the topic and went to doctoral students' exhibition openings.

The third stage of the study involved a textual analysis of the students' texts, including an analysis of the macrostructures of the texts, multi-modal relations between the text and the related creative component, and how these relations were expressed in language. A theme-based analysis of the ethnographic data was also carried out. The textual and ethnographic data were then considered in relation to each other as the process of analysis and interpretation of the data proceeded.

The strength of textography lies in its explicit drawing together of textual and ethnographic perspectives into the one overarching framework for approaching the analysis of texts. The ethnographic component gave us insights into the students' texts that we could not have gained from looking at the texts alone. Equally, the text analysis provided details of the texts that an ethnographic examination, on its own, would not have given. The data that were collected thus contributed to the building of a rich description of the context of the students' texts that was drawn on for interpreting the results of the study.

If we undertook the project again, we would address the problem in the same way. We would like, however, to complement it with a number of longitudinal collective case studies that would give us greater insights into the issues that students face with their writing and how they deal with them.

Our study supports arguments for the importance of contextualising genre studies, which have been put forward by researchers such as Swales and others, so that we produce not only descriptions of genres, but also explanations for why they are written as they are and what this means for student writing. We would argue for greater contextualisation of genre studies to complement the body of textually-oriented research that has been carried out, in order to explore the socially situated nature of academic writing, that is, what it does, how and why it does it and what this means for student writers (see Paltridge, Starfield & Tardy 2016 where this argument is developed further).

The study revealed centripetal forces for unification interacting with centrifugal forces for change (Bakhtin 1981) that play out through the academy, as communities and their members position themselves within new and emerging contexts of doctoral research. The main centripetal force, in the case of the visual and performing arts texts, was the underlying functions of a doctoral thesis, such as the need to contextualise the research, the need to engage with theory, the need to place the research within a broader field, and the need to demonstrate the way/s in which the doctoral project moves the field forward. Centrifugal forces were also seen, however, in the influence of particular supervisors, academics with high standing in the field, and institutions where particular views of doctoral research and, concomitantly, doctoral writing are held.

An important outcome of the study was an end-of-project symposium that brought together people with an interest in doctoral writing in the visual and performing arts. At this symposium presenters discussed the challenges they faced with writing and with supervising writing, in these areas of study. The symposium resulted in a book titled *Doctoral writing in the creative and performing arts* (Ravelli, Paltridge & Starfield 2014) with contributions by presenters at the symposium and other researchers with an interest in this field.

References

Bakhtin, M. M. (1981) *The dialogic imagination: Four essays*. Edited by M. Holquist, trans by C. Emerson, and M. Holquist. Austin, TX: University of Texas Press.

Paltridge, B., Starfield, S., Ravelli, L. and Tuckwell, K. (2012) Change and stability: Examining the macrostructures of doctoral theses in the visual and performing arts. *Journal of English for Academic Purposes* Vol. 11, 332–334.

Paltridge, B., Starfield, S., Ravelli, L., Tuckwell, K. and Nicholson, S. (2014) Genre in the creative-practice doctoral thesis: Diversity and unity. In G. Garzone and C. Ilie (Eds). *Evolving genres and genre theory: Specialised communication across contexts and media*, Boca Raton, FL: Brown Walker Press, 89–106.

Paltridge, B., Starfield, S. and Tardy, C. M. (2016) *Ethnographic perspectives on academic writing*. Oxford: Oxford University Press.

Ravelli, L., Paltridge, B., Starfield, S. and Tuckwell, K. (2013) Extending the notion of text: The creative arts doctoral thesis. *Visual Communication* Vol. 12 No. 4, 395–422.

Ravelli, L., Paltridge, B. and Starfield, S. (Eds). (2014) *Doctoral writing in the creative and performing arts*. Faringdon, UK: Libri.

Starfield, S., Paltridge, B. and Ravelli, L. (2012) 'Why do we have to write?': Practice-based theses in the visual and performing arts and the place of writing. In V. K. Bhatia, C. Berkenkotter and M. Gotti (Eds). *Insights into academic genres*. Bern: Peter Lang, 169–190.

Starfield, S., Paltridge, B. and Ravelli, L. (2014) Researching academic writing: What textography affords. In J. Huisman and M. Tight (Eds). *Theory and method in higher education research II*. Oxford: Emerald, 103–120.

Swales, J. M. (1998a) *Other floors, other voices: A textography of a small university building*. Mahwah, NJ: Laurence Erlbaum.

Swales, J. M. (1998b) Textography: Toward a contextualisation of written academic discourse. *Research on Language and Social Interaction* Vol. 31 No. 1, 109–121.

Susan Hood: multiple modes and modalities of communication

> **Susan Hood** (University of Technology, Sydney) describes a study that aims to contribute a stronger theoretical and empirical base to understanding the potential for meaning-making across multiple modes and modalities of communication in the teaching and learning of uncommonsense knowledge in higher education.

The study described here aims to contribute a stronger theoretical and empirical base to understanding the potential for meaning-making across multiple modes and modalities of communication in the teaching and learning of uncommonsense knowledge in higher education. It explores ways in which lecturers manage the interplay of a complex set of social semiotic resources in teaching in live, face-to-face lectures as they teach the disciplinary knowledge of their fields. Attention is paid to the semiotics of visual images and visual written text on presentation slides, spoken language and the body language of the lecturers, and to the ways in which these different semiotic modes cooperate in meaning-making. Of particular interest are the ways in which the lecturers mediate between the here-and-now of the shared presence with students in the lecture theatre, and the reflective written discourses in which the disciplinary knowledge resides, and which students need to be supported to access.

There is a strong trend amongst institutions of higher education globally to move away from face-to-face lecturing to online modes in the presentation of new knowledge for undergraduate students. Online modes may engage a range of technologies of communication affording different kinds of interaction, supporting different kinds of pedagogic encounters. In many contexts the change is being implemented at high speed with a relatively weak research base informing the shift in practice. Notably missing is research into the kinds of meaning-making that are afforded or constrained by the different modes, and what the implications might be for the learning of disciplinary knowledge. The study reported here aims to contribute to this project by strengthening a base understanding of the complex multimodal curriculum genre of lectures. Of particular interest is the potential of the live lecture to mediate between the here-and-now of the shared presence in the lecture theatre, to the reflective written discourses in which the disciplinary knowledge resides.

The study draws on Systemic Functional Semiotics to encompass an exploration of meaning-making across the modes of language and the semiotics of body language and of image. The focus is on the interplay of these systems of meaning, and how they cooperate in the staging and phasing of the curriculum genre of lectures. As such, the approach to analysis is a logogenetic one, looking closely at a small number of instances from diverse disciplinary contexts with a focus on the detailed interplay of multimodal meaning choices.

Insights gained in the project are a consequence of the power of the theory that was applied, most significantly the potential to consider the different semiotic systems within an overriding social semiotic perspective. The theorisation of genre within Systemic Functional Linguistics (SFL), as an abstracted stratum of context, has also been significant as a means for exploring the coordinated patterning of meanings not only metafunctionally but also across semiotic modes.

The approach to the analysis of discourse undertaken in this study has generated some specific insights that can be taken up for narrower attention within corpus-based studies of larger data sets. There are advantages to both approaches, but for me the detailed analysis of the unfolding interaction of meanings in individual texts needs always to be the precursor.

The exploration of body language as part of this study can inform the broader field of discourse analytic work on spoken interactions. It might also encourage and support researchers working in more loosely framed ethnographic orientations, who might for example be analysing interview data transcribed only for language, to supplement that work with attention to the accompanying body language, as intrinsic to the meaning-making of participants.

From a theoretical perspective there is much work to be done in further developing system networks within the systems of body language. There are complementary studies to be undertaken in contexts where live lectures have been replaced with other modes of interaction, to consider the gains and losses in terms of the ways we can mean to each other in support of building uncommonsense knowledge.

Literacy in social contexts

Jennifer Blunden: word work – linguistic perspectives on meaning, accessibility and knowledge-building in museum exhibitions

Jennifer Blunden (University of Technology, Sydney) describes a research project concerned with the role played by language in museums in shaping the experience and understanding of public audiences and the role that museum texts play as a bridge between everyday and specialised knowledge, both in terms of making this knowledge accessible to audiences outside the field and in terms of building literacies which can then enable these audiences to reach further into the field. In exploring this role of language, the project also touches on issues around student audiences and literacies, and the role museums might play in developing programming that explicitly supports the literacy demands of school curricula.

Rather than an individual project, the research that for me has provided the greatest insights into the nature of and obstacles to literacy has been the genre pedagogy work developed initially by the Sydney School linguists (see Rose & Martin 2012 for a good overview). Framed within a social semiotic (systemic functional) model, over several decades, this body of research and practice has shown the value of *explicit knowledge about language* as a tool for developing the subject-specific literacies of students from the earliest school years through to tertiary levels.

Central to this approach is a detailed and systematic focus on texts themselves, and how they act to make meaning within particular social and disciplinary contexts. Equally central is the principle that making the structures and processes inherent in these texts visible, and then teaching them in an explicit and systematic way, can enable students of all abilities and backgrounds to master the literacy demands of a given subject. Another key insight I have gained from this work is the importance of shared metalanguage, a shared language for talking about language, in developing literacy skills and in understanding and negotiating meaning.

Similarly, I think the work of Kress and van Leeuwen (for example, *Reading images* 1996) in extending the systemic functional model to other semiotic modes has been, and continues to be, enormously significant to literacy research and practice. In offering a unified conception of how language, image, and other modalities work together to make meaning, their work and the work of more recent scholars in multi-modal semiotics has allowed the principles of genre pedagogy to be used across the full range of modalities and texts we encounter today.

The impact of this work on my own research has been to inspire me to explore the value of this framework to the museum context, in terms of both student and public audiences, and as a methodology for developing the communication skills of the museum professionals who work with them.

My initial inspiration has come from working as a writer and editor within the museum field. Particularly in recent years, the expanding range of media used in and by museums to interpret collections, exhibitions and programmes has dramatically increased the role played by verbal texts in both the visitor experience and the work of museum professionals. Yet the methodologies typically used to evaluate these texts and inform their development have been limited in their delicacy and analytical power. Even as a person who has worked with language for many years, I found that with my existing knowledge and understanding of language I did not have the tools or insights to resolve many of the questions and issues around language that we faced over and over again.

I then encountered Louise Ravelli's work on museum texts (for example,1996 and 2006), and particularly her study of texts at the Museum of Contemporary Art in Sydney (1998). This work showed me the value of linguistics in providing both a structure and metalanguage that allowed even the most subtle differences in wordings and meanings to be brought into view, so the meaning-making work of these texts could be understood and evaluated. Her 1998 study also highlighted the presence and strength of values and attitudes around language that may be in conflict with both individual and institutional aspirations concerning accessibility and literacy, and the need also to bring these into view so that they can be better understood.

My research is underpinned by two conceptual frameworks and related methodologies. The first is Systemic Functional Semiotics, pioneered in terms of language by Michael Halliday (1975 onwards) and beyond language by Kress and van Leeuwen (1996 onwards). This framework has been valuable for a number of reasons. The first is its delicacy in enabling the detailed and systematic description of text. The second is its unified conception of semiosis across modalities, including the range of modes used in and by museums – spoken and written language, objects, still and moving images, sound, gesture, built form and physical space. The third is its track record in investigating language and communication issues in a diverse range of social contexts, with a particularly extensive track record within educational contexts. As argued by Halliday some 30 years ago, and from my experience still holding true today, the systemic functional model 'make[s] it possible to say sensible and useful things about any text' (Halliday 1984: xv).

But while Systemic Functional Semiotics makes possible the detailed description and analysis of language and other semiotics, it does not fully explain *why* particular choices are made; what is it that makes certain choices more desirable or legitimate than others? For this reason, my research also draws on Legitimation Code Theory (LCT). Developed by Karl Maton in the 1990s (see Maton 2014), LCT is a multidimensional framework for the study of knowledge and knowledge practices that builds particularly on the work of the educational sociologist Basil Bernstein (for example, 1974 and 2000). From its earliest days, the theory has developed in close association with Systemic Functional Semiotics and, in recent years, the two approaches, in collaboration, have proved valuable in providing fresh insights into the nature and interplay of language, knowledge and literacy within and across different disciplinary fields and social contexts.

My current research project is concerned with the role played by language in museums in shaping visitor experience and understanding. My primary interest is with public audiences, and the role museum texts play as a bridge between everyday and specialised knowledge, both in terms of making this knowledge accessible to audiences outside the field and in terms of building literacies which can then enable these audiences to reach further into the field. In exploring this role of language, the project also touches on issues around student audiences and literacies, and the role museums might play in developing programming that explicitly supports the literacy demands of the curriculum.

One of the key insights I have gained from this project is that museums do a great deal of work in this area already, but there is enormous potential for them to do more. In order for this to happen, however, museums need to apply frameworks that more explicitly consider literacy and are delicate enough to show the pedagogy at work in their various exhibitions, projects and programmes. A second key insight has been the value of these two conceptual frameworks in addressing this need.

This is still an ongoing project, but if I were starting again with the benefit of hindsight, I would definitely use these same frameworks again. To date they have proved to be as useful and valuable as I had hoped. Both frameworks, however, are expansive and complex as theories and as methodologies, and both were unfamiliar to me before I began this project. This has meant a huge and, at times, almost overwhelming burden in terms of developing sufficient knowledge of the frameworks to apply them to my data. But now having done that, I feel it has been a good investment, and will prove increasingly valuable in the future to me personally and to the museum and broader literacy research fields.

First, for the museum field, I hope this project shows how we can look at the range of texts that museums produce with greater delicacy than has occurred to date, so that we have a firmer basis for making claims and negotiating meanings. In museum research in recent years, there has been an increasing focus on the visitor – their behaviour, their motivations, their needs and interests, their *personae* – while the messages produced by museums have been pushed to the margins and rarely considered. Both, of course, are central to communication and meaning-making, and I hope this research helps show how we can bring *the message* back into focus, and into view in new ways.

Beyond the museum field, this project applies recent theoretical work in language, literacy, and multimodal studies in new analytical contexts. It thus offers some fresh approaches to a number of methodological issues, particularly concerning relations across semiotic modes. And through the empirical application of emerging theory, the project also hopes to contribute to the theoretical development of the two frameworks that underpin the study.

I think there is huge potential and opportunity for further research in the area of museums and literacy, but particularly in terms of the value of a *knowledge about language* (KAL) approach in three key areas. The first is in understanding the role played by language in the museum experience and accounting for that across the range of modalities and disciplines that make up the 21st century museum. The second is in school programming and how museums can work with students and teachers to support the literacy demands of the curriculum. What potential is there for museums to develop programmes that explicitly embed literacy outcomes? The third is in the professional development of museum staff. How might a KAL approach be of value in developing the communication and writing skills of museum professionals and others involved in creating and delivering interpretive programmes and materials? These are all important issues for museums today and into the future.

References

Bernstein, B. (1974) *Class, codes and control: Theoretical studies towards a sociology of education* Vol. 1 (2nd Edition). London, Henley and Boston: Routledge & Kegan Paul.

Bernstein, B. (2000) *Pedagogy, symbolic control and identity: Theory, research, critique*, Lanham, MD: Rowman & Littlefield.

Halliday, M. A. K. (1975) Language as social semiotic: Towards a general sociolinguistic theory. In A. Makkai and V. Mecker Makkai (Eds). *The first LACUS forum.* Columbia SC: Hornbeam Press, 17–46.

Halliday, M. A. K. (1984) Language as code and language as behaviour. In R. Fawcett, M. A. K. Halliday, S. Lamb and A. Makkai (Eds). *The semiotics of language and culture* Vol. 1: *Language as social semiotic.* London: Pinter, 3–35.

Kress, G. and Van Leeuwen, T. (1996) *Reading images: The grammar of visual design.* London and New York: Routledge.

Maton, K. (2014) *Knowledge and knowers: Towards a social realist sociology of education.* London and New York: Routledge.

Ravelli, L. (1996) Making language accessible: Successful text writing for museum visitors. *Linguistics and Education* Vol. 8, 367–387.

Ravelli, L. (1998) The consequence of choice: Discursive positioning in an art institution. In A. Sánchez-Macarro and R. Carter (Eds). *Linguistic choice across genres.* Amsterdam and Philadelphia: John Benjamins.

Ravelli, L. (2006) *Museum texts: Communication frameworks.* London: Routledge.

Rose, D. and Martin, J. R. (2012) *Learning to write, reading to learn: genre, knowledge and pedagogy in the Sydney School.* Sheffield: Equinox.

Helen Whitty: researching museums and their relationships to families and literacy

> **Helen Whitty** describes research undertaken as a doctoral student at the University of Technology, Sydney. The research was designed to critically review the interaction between families and museum collections through identifying literacies, existing or provoked by this interaction.

The research being undertaken for a Doctorate at University of Technology Sydney was designed to critically review the interaction between families and museum collections through identifying literacies, existing or provoked by this interaction. The study setting is the geographically remote Australian island state of Tasmania and the museums are new or have recently undergone refurbishment. The participants were recruited from community agencies that assist marginalised or vulnerable groups that tend to be under-represented in museum studies, especially with respect to engagement with the collections.

The research was supported by nine families who came together as research participants in a multicase study extending across two museum sites. Further support was provided by a small grant from 26TEN, a Tasmanian Government initiative to support literacy research and practices, and a working party from the museum sites and nongovernment agencies supporting marginalised groups. Each family member exhibited considerable sophistication and complexity in their responses to the museums and, whether first time museum visitors or not, managed to secure the help they needed to leap the void between the known and the unknown with dignity and relative ease.

Preliminary findings were that:

a. family engagement with museum objects is multidimensional and dynamic
b. emotion and physicality contribute to the literacy events provoked by museum objects
c. the child was the primary catalyst for engagement with museum objects, their display and interpretation
d. humans and non-humans (Fenwick 2010, Latour 2005, Law 1999) acted as literacy mediators in the research

It is hoped that this research, once finalised and disseminated, can forge new partnerships between literacy providers and museums. A contribution to the broader discussion of participatory museum cultures and new literate identities for visitors also inhabits this research space.

Museums matter to the public. The investment in museums, expenditure and visitation to them is considerable and yet they have reached a certain hiatus in their trajectory as public monies grow scarce and increasingly they need to justify expenditure. Change is in the air and direction required. Families are an important visiting group for museums, despite observations that family programming rarely contributes to a museum's scholarly reputation. Nor is it mined as a way to rethink, enliven or even inform engagement with the collection for other types of visitors. An understanding of how child and adult visitors, with different strengths, abilities, and range of literacies, access and utilise museum collections as learning objects is a positive step.

As a practitioner turned academic, I believe that a better understanding of this key audience could yield the required fresh perspective for change. Learning in museums has been extensively studied and theorised and possibly because of this level of familiarity did not stand as the most effective change agent. Literacy however loomed as a giant orb travelling in a parallel trajectory and, if it could be pulled closer, would offer a different and meaningful way to illuminate key relationships in the museum context and opportunities for new partnerships.

This research built on readings from the New Literacy Studies (Street, Pahl & Rowsell 2009) and, by extension, multiliteracies, artefactual critical literacies (Pahl & Rowsell 2010, Pahl & Rowsell 2011, Street et al. 2009) and material semiotics (Callon 1986, Law 2009) and combined critical literacy with materiality via the stories that objects can hold and generate. Drawing on the researcher's own museum programming experience, the study investigated the literacy affordances of collection objects within the multimodal museum environment and how children and adults, with varying literacy abilities, understand and respond to them.

It is assumed that visitors put their personal literacies to work within museums and galleries to engage with collection objects. Most consideration of these types of literacies are binary based and predicated on print literacies. Museums worry that their content is either too easy and therefore *dumbed down* or too difficult and therefore inaccessible. The *just right* level seems always out of reach. This research disputes this basic assumption believing that a plurality of literacies, each socially and materially assembled, are provoked and productively used in a range of localities, situations and communities. This perspective could be put to use within museums to both dispose of the binary understanding of the problem and to consider the possibility that museums as performative spaces where families, as productive assemblages, provoke literacies that are of value.

The key findings were obtained from 17 in-depth interviews with the nine participant families, two visits each by the nine families to one of two museums and materials generated by the researcher and each member of the nine families (including drawing, making activities and photographs). The data was then reviewed through thematic analysis within a material semiotics framework used to generate a series of theoretically based heuristics, positioning literacy events as a unit of analysis.

The project introduces a novel perspective and methodology into the field of museum studies. As a practitioner, the museum visitor studies I had been most familiar with, and which were generally accepted by the industry, use very different methodology based on questionnaires and focus groups conducted with adults. Sample size was reinforced as the most suitable and often best benchmark. This study deployed in-depth observation and multiple data sets to better understand an underutilised visitor demographic in visitor research (as families) and a new way to frame communication (as literacies) and indeed the museum environment (as multimodal). The research reinforces and extends the few studies that use literacy as a measurement or indication of engagement in a holistic way rather than a critique of written text.

The connection between objects and literacy and the way families and young children can contribute to scholarship in the museum field beyond public programming or family only projects can be theorised. Whilst literacy is sociocultural, it is also material. It simultaneously presents as living and technological and therefore a material semiotic theoretical perspective is a suitable and potentially productive match. Matter does matter in museums and never more so than when activated by people and their engagement with it.

The link between museums and literacy is very fertile. Learning in museums has long been studied and to a certain extent theorised. Museums as knowledge agents containing a range of text-rich resources and a mandate to use these for educational purposes should establish a position in relation to literacy and be able to use appropriate language to describe literacy practices and processes within the institution. The use of literacy as a lens is a novel way to approach the content, context, and display of objects and one that potentially reflects greater community concern and therefore appeal.

References

Callon, M. (1986) Some elements of a sociology of translation: Domestication of the scallops and the fishermen of St Brieuc Bay. In J. Law (Ed). *Power, action and belief: A new sociology of knowledge?* London: Routledge.

Fenwick, T. (2010) Re-thinking the 'thing': Sociomaterial approaches to understanding and researching learning in work. *Journal of Workplace Learning* Vol. 22 No. 1/2, 104–116.

Latour, B. (2005) *Reassembling the social: An introduction to actor-network-theory.* Oxford: Oxford University Press.

Law, J. (2009) Actor network theory and material semiotic. *The new Blackwell companion to social theory*, 141–158.

Law, J. (1999) After ANT: Complexity, naming and topology. *The Sociological Review* Vol. 47 No. S1, West Sussex: Blackwell Publishing, 1–14.

Pahl, K. and Rowsell, J. (2010) *Artifactual literacies: Every object tells a story.* New York: Teachers College Press.

Pahl, K. H. and Rowsell, J. (2011) Artifactual critical literacy: A new perspective for literacy education. *Berkeley Review of Education* Vol. 2 No. 2, 129–151.

Street, B., Pahl, K. and Rowsell, J. (2009) Multimodality and new literacy studies. In C. Jewitt (Ed). *The Routledge handbook of multimodal analysis.* London and New York: Routledge.

Nancy Jackson: reading work – Literacies in the new workplace

> **Nancy Jackson**, formerly of the Ontario Institute for Studies in Education at the University of Toronto, describes a workplace literacy project undertaken by the In-Sites Research Group. This project consisted of ethnographic studies of literacy practices in four Canadian workplaces and was based on a social practice understanding of literacy. Nancy emphasises the strength of research involving partnerships between practitioners and researchers but also expresses regret that this type of research is no longer readily funded.

In Canada, a good deal of early interest in the *social practice* approach to literacy can be traced back to the work of Brian Street, writing in the early 1980s around literacy in cross-cultural and international development contexts. He used the notion of an 'ideological' approach to literacy to draw attention to the context-dependent and power-laden nature of literacy, in contrast to the more traditional emphasis on linguistics. James Gee and Colin Lankshear were also influential in North America, combining theories of language and power in various ways in studies of literacy, including at and about work. The workplace collection edited by Hull (1997) also had a big impact in terms of broadening the focus of study from reading and writing per se to the social context of work. Mary Hamilton and David Barton were very influential, particularly amongst practitioners in Canada, in popularising the use of ethnography to understand the nature of literacy. And in more recent years, the research of Stephen Reder has become very important in developing useful ways to respond to the labyrinth of statistical models being used to reshape and govern literacy policy and practice across the world.

The In Sites group was prompted to do our own research by all of the above developments plus many of our own observations about the changing conversations around us in the world of workplace education. Employers everywhere were being told that in order to stay competitive, or possibly even survive, they needed to have a learning culture and that literacy needed to be part of that. Some employers known to us were interested in developing a learning culture to enhance their business objectives. They knew they needed to create more learning and training opportunities but did not have a good understanding of literacy and where it would fit on the learning continuum. We felt that ethnographic research could help answer some of those questions.

We were also motivated, like many others internationally, by watching the widening gap between literacy policies and developments in the realm of theory (see for example Hammond 2001). Despite the growing acceptance of *social practice theories* of literacy, increasingly *formulaic* and reductionist curricular and assessment frameworks were being imposed internationally on literacy practitioners (in schools, communities and workplace settings) throughout the 1990s. This trend seemed to be driven by the desires of policy makers to show more *clear results* for dollars spent, and compliance was commonly achieved by making such approaches a condition of funding. Meanwhile, people closer to the ground were whispering to one another about how poorly most of these approaches fitted the complex needs and circumstances of learners of all ages, and thus how likely they were to fail to produce meaningful learning.

By the mid-1990s in North America, research using a social practice approach to adult literacy had mostly been done in community contexts, with less attention paid to workplaces. Two important exceptions were Sheryl Gowen's (1992) study of hospital workers and the collection of diverse articles edited by Glynda Hull in 1997 – *Changing work, changing workers*. Our research group used both of these sources as starting points for our own internal discussions and as ongoing reference points as our work unfolded. We were also influenced by the seminal work of Geraldine Castleton (2000) focusing on the role of discourse, per se, in shaping the public understanding of literacy issues at work.

Our common conceptual starting point was an interest in a social practice understanding of literacy. Our methodological common ground was a belief that ethnography could show what a social practice approach to literacy means in a workplace setting. But we were a mixed group of three very experienced workplace literacy practitioners and two academics, one with a background in English as a second language (ESL) and sociolinguistic theory and the other in the social organisation of work and skill. So we needed a dialogue that would bring us closer to a common understanding of what a social practice approach to literacy might actually mean in an analysis of specific workplace settings. Forging a workable common ground was an ongoing process throughout an approximate five-year period.

The resulting publication from our workplace research – *Reading work: Literacies in the new workplace* (2004) – does seem to have been well received and indeed is still selling in modest numbers a decade later. Why? Well, we have been told that the narrative approach to reporting our findings did help *show* as well as *tell* readers with different backgrounds about the complexity of these workplace settings, and why/how literacy actually matters in those contexts. We wanted to counter the dominant media myth that the so-called *literacy crisis* was simply the fault of poorly educated workers who lacked basic skills. Rather, what was changing was the new and expanding ways that the use of print was being required at work, setting up new relationships that made the use of even limited literacy skills much more *risky* for workers. Non-compliance did not always mean lack of skill, but was sometimes a way to avoid blame. So indeed the growing problem was, and still is, exactly embedded in the meanings of literacy as a social practice.

I think we have continued to be happy with the general approach of this work. As always, it was a challenge to write for multiple audiences. And, as with many pursuits in life, I am not sure we would have started if we really knew what we were getting into!! The project took a lot longer at every stage than we had hoped. It took a lot of time and effort to set up the *hosting* arrangements for our government grant at the university at which one member of our team worked. It took time, persistence, and flexibility to get final access in so many different research sites. We were most surprised that it took several years (!) of writing and talking together about our data to come to common understandings of what these stories *were about*. Fortunately, the members of our group were strong writers and lively storytellers, so that carried us along when our spirits were flagging.

In terms of doing it again, truthfully in today's *lean* policy environment in Canada, we would be unlikely to get the kind of generous government funding that supported this work. So it would only be feasible with an academic research grant, and those are also becoming more competitive. An academic grant today would make it harder to assemble a research team composed primarily of such experienced practitioners, who need a reasonable wage for their time. Without their seasoned perspective on the constraints and pressures of actually *doing* literacy work as consultants in workplace settings, it would have been a very different book.

We wrote the book at a time of much interest and optimism about the promise of practitioner research, and indeed of collaboration between academics and practitioners. Thus, we tried to demystify some of the process of doing ethnography by *telling stories* to show some of the daily challenges and skills involved and the importance of our own learning along the way. Indeed, we would still advocate for practitioner research in theory, but in practice in Canada, nobody is funding it. So projects are more rare, much smaller and done on a shoestring. Today, a similar but smaller project might be done on the combined resources of funded graduate students working with practitioners who have access to some small-scale project funding to pay for some of their own time. This combination would provide the theoretical and methodological confidence that it often takes to sustain a project from start to finish, and would match this confidence with the vital knowledge and hands-on experience of practitioners. But still, such university-community collaborations are famously fraught with power struggles, misunderstandings, and conflicting interests, and should be undertaken with great care and honest communication.

In terms of further research on workplace literacy, a sense of what is important keeps shifting with the changing policy climate. These days, research funding opportunities seem to be more narrowly tied to government priorities, like monitoring short-term training outcomes as measured by national standardised literacy and numeracy tests. A common mantra is *measurable value for taxpayer money.* Such a focus on measurement leaves untouched many pressing concerns of workers, workplace trainers, and even employers, all of whom would benefit from research that is focused on issues closer to the ground. It might explore how investment in literacy at work can contribute to the long-term development of more effective workplace cultures, or how successful programmes and cultures of learning can benefit from consultation with workers themselves. Close-up research on workplace culture could also help to reduce barriers by showing how literacy issues are commonly misrecognised in everyday workplace life; how text is embedded in power relations at work; how documents are routinely used to ensure that people at the bottom of the hierarchy can be held responsible for mistakes or how racism often means that even well-educated people, speaking or writing non-standard English, are often blamed as a *literacy problem*

References

Barton, D. (1994) *Literacy: An introduction to the ecology of written language.* Oxford: Blackwell.

Barton, D. and Hamilton, M. (1998) *Local literacies: Reading and writing in one community.* London: Routledge.

Belfiore, M. E., Defoe, T. A., Folinsbee, S., Hunter, J. and Jackson, N. S. (The In-Sites Research Group). (2004) *Reading work: Literacies in the new workplace.* Mahwah, NJ: Lawrence Erlbaum Associates.

Castleton, G. (2000) Workplace literacy: Examining the virtual and virtuous realities in (e)merging discourses on work. *Discourse: Studies in the Cultural Politics of Education* Vol. 21 No. 1, 91–104.

Freire, P. (1970) *Pedagogy of the oppressed.* New York: Herder & Herder.

Gee, J. P. (1990) *Social linguistics and literacies: Ideology in discourses.* London: Falmer Press.

Gee, J. P., Hull, G. and Lankshear, C. (1996) *The new work order: Behind the language of the new capitalism.* Boulder, CO: Westview Press.

Gowen, S. G. (1992) *The politics of workplace literacy*. New York: Teachers College Press.

Hamilton, M. (2000) Sustainable literacies and the ecology of lifelong learning. *A Global Colloquium Supporting Lifelong Learning Presented by the Open University*. Available at: http://www.open.ac.uk/lifelong-learning/index.html.

Hammond, J. (2001) Literacies in school education in Australia: Disjunctions between policy and research. *Language and Education* Vol. 15 No. 2–3, 162–177.

Hull, G. (1997) *Changing work, changing workers: Critical perspectives on language, literacy and skills*. Albany, NY: State University of New York Press.

Hull, G. (1995) Controlling literacy: The place of skills in 'high performance' work. *Critical Forum* Vol. 3 No. 2/3, 3–26.

Lankshear, C. (1987) Language and the new capitalism. *The International Journal of Inclusive Education* Vol. 1 No. 4, 309–321.

Lave, J. and Wenger, E. (1991) *Situated learning: Legitimate peripheral participation*. Cambridge: Cambridge University Press.

Redder, S. (2012) *The longitudinal study of adult learning: Challenging assumptions* (Research Brief). Montreal Quebec: The Centre for Literacy.

Street, B. (1984) *Literacy in theory and practice*. Cambridge: Cambridge University Press.

Literacy research: the onwards journey

Gazing into a crystal ball to see what lies in the future for literacy research and practice is not possible but we can make some forecasts about the social, environmental, economic and political changes that lie ahead because they are already beginning to happen. We also know that 20th century inequalities in terms of participation in education, work and the broader society still persist and, if anything, are becoming more widespread. Transnational corporations wield enormous power globally and the drive for private profit on an individual and organisational level has contributed to the dismantling of public infrastructure and services, many of which were established in the 19th and 20th centuries to meet the needs of the disadvantaged in society.

In the past, many literacy educators who sought 'to make things better' (James Gee in Chapter 7) believed that education, 'particularly state sponsored compulsory education' (Christie 2010a: 9), would lead to 'positive, long-term civic consequences that arise from the distribution of literacy capabilities via strong educational programs' (Freebody 2010: 41). However, the world continues to change rapidly, and this change brings into sharp focus the literacy capabilities of different groups in society. For example, over the past three decades, in Western countries, '[t]he loss of low-skilled jobs has forced less able school leavers to compete for jobs higher up the employment ladder' and more students are expected to enrol in university so it is 'hardly surprising that the average achievement levels of this much larger group are going to be lower' (Bonner & Caro 2007: 58–59).

Some respond to these changes in limited economic terms and assume the only role of literacy research and education is to ensure participation in the workforce. They seek simple answers to what they see as a simple problem which can be solved by pulling 'literacy back to a simpler form' as a 'nostalgic retreat' to an apparently 'more literate society of the past' where literacy could be achieved through drilling a basic set of skills (Morgan, Comber & Nixon 2014: 4). However, as Resnick and Resnick (1977: 385 in Freebody et al. 2014) state:

> ... there is little to go back to in terms of pedagogical method, curriculum, or school organisation. The old tried and true approaches, which nostalgia prompts us to believe might solve current problems, were designed neither to achieve the literacy standard sought today, nor to assure successful literacy for everyone.

For others, socially responsible literacy research and education should address 'responsibilities that arise from our past neglect or imagined futures' (Freebody 2010: 40) and should be concerned with the role of literacy in 'learning, in promoting personal development, in fostering self-expression and self-esteem' as well as 'conferring skills that build employability' (Christie & Simpson 2010: 4).

In these times of rapid change, it is local schools, mostly public schools, that are struggling to make a difference 'in marginalised communities' and governments are assuming 'there is something wrong with these schools: that they must need more accountability, prescribed curriculum, benchmarking, incessant testing and monitoring. In essence the schools are being punished rather than helped' (Bonner & Caro 2007: 60). This perceived failure of state sponsored education justifies the redistribution of funds in some countries, such as Australia, to private schools. This is occurring at a time when local schools, which are dealing with the intersections of disadvantage such as class, unemployment, poverty, ethnicity and children who have missed out on the phase of emergent language and literacy development (Vinson 2010) need more funding and resources.

Quote

Some notion of social responsibility has long been at the heart of Western ideas about schooling. Even a selective scan of dramatic

> moments in that history send us some clear messages that some ver-
> sion of social responsibility is at the heart of why schools are with
> us, and why the contents and processes of schooling remain under
> constant scrutiny, debate and change.
>
> (Freebody 2010: 40)

There still remain enormous gaps in the distribution of literacy capabilities, despite government literacy policies across a wide range of countries over a number of decades. There have been some large-scale and small-scale programmes that have succeeded in meeting the literacy needs of various disadvantaged groups (see, for example, the research projects described in Chapter 7, as well as Culican 2005, Koop & Rose 2008, Parkin 2006, Riley & Randall 2010, Vinson 2010). However, overall 'there remain some enduring problems in literacy education, themselves a legacy of its history and of a time-honoured tendency to create false dichotomies or dualisms where none really exist', for example, 'between *process* and *product* or *form* and *function* in writing' (Christie 2010a: 9).

Part II of this book examined literacy research in early childhood, school and adult contexts and the educational implications of this research. These chapters confirm that literacy is not a simple set of skills that children develop in early schooling and which then enable them to undertake all the myriad literacy tasks they encounter, throughout their lives, in middle and secondary school, tertiary education, and social and work contexts. What we also know is that if children, in their communities and homes, do not develop the emergent literacy skills that prepare them for entry into literacy, then they start off behind their peers. If they are then offered no 'compensatory educational experiences and appropriate forms of social support', then 'today's socially disadvantaged small children are positioned to become tomorrow's frustrated and rejected adults' (Vinson 2010: 71).

Quote

Unless we are reconciled to a future in which some individuals have disadvantage piled upon disadvantage from the beginning of their lives and an ever-increasing number of human disposal institutions to contain the inevitable consequences, we will insist on a high quality and adequately funded approach to the early education of all our children.

(Vinson 2010: 84)

Research has also given us insights into the shifts that occur in literacy demands throughout the lifespan (as discussed in more detail in Part II and represented in Figure 6.5). Christie and Derewianka (2008: 219–237) give a detailed summary of the major linguistic changes that students must control if they are to succeed at the different stages of schooling. As children move from home to school, there is often an expectation, not necessarily based on evidence, they will already know about some features of written texts, how to use some literacy tools such as books, pencils and computers, and that they have rehearsed literate behaviours in their homes. If they cannot meet these expectations, and if they have not engaged in conversations at home in which they have talked about past events, causes and effects, and hypothesised about the future, then they will find it difficult to understand and participate in the decontextualised language of the classroom.

The next move from the early years to the middle years of school brings new literacy demands. Children are expected to independently read more complex, often multimodal, texts across discipline areas such as Science, History and Geography. For those children who entered school already at a disadvantage, this is the period of education where they fall even further behind and, in many cases, start to disengage from education, thus, compounding their disadvantage. The move from middle school to senior school is for many disadvantaged students, who have received no compensatory education, a step too far. They are forced to stay at school but the demands of highly abstracted discipline specific texts and high stakes assessments drive many young people from formal schooling, with too many ending up in what Vinson (2010: 84) calls 'human disposal institutions'. This is despite the fact that in many countries vocational subjects have been brought into the senior school curriculum in an effort to make school relevant to students who want to prepare more directly for work.

This progression is complicated in most educational contexts by the increasing diversity of classrooms with, for example, migrant and refugee students needing assistance to develop the language skills required of the school system in their countries of resettlement. The need to meet the language and literacy needs of children from diverse backgrounds will continue to increase because of transnational migration and refugee resettlement. The United Nations High Commission for Refugees (UNHRC: 2013: 6) estimated that there were 51.2 million people forcibly displaced worldwide at the end of 2013, with 10.7 million newly displaced during that year, and 1.2 million of these people were seeking asylum.[4] Many of these refugees are children, who flee to or settle in

other countries. Many are unaccompanied and with no formal education and consequently enter school systems with additional needs.

Quote

... it is important to be cognisant of the resilience and capacity of
all children in the challenging worlds they meet as refugees. While
being young makes them vulnerable, this can also make them inven-
tive, creative and positive in situations of extreme difficulty. These
children, if supported appropriately, have a history of survival that
is a part of their identity as much as the past trauma is also a part of
their identity. Many children find connections, friendships and an
ability to learn in different ways through times of transition. Many
do achieve very adequate adjustments to life in their schools, and
they go on to make contributions to their new community ...

(Lynch 2010: 125–126)

One of the goals of the development of literacy skills throughout the
years of schooling is to prepare students to go on to tertiary education
and into the workforce.

Quote

It is possible to relate the types of texts written and read, and the types
of language used in school subjects, with corresponding fields of economic production and community life. For example, the secondary science curriculum is significant for a wide range of sectors in the society
such as manufacturing, agriculture, medicine and urban development.

At the most general level, industrial economies are often divided into
sectors concerned with the production of goods, services or information.
The basic distinction is between the production of goods, for example,
consumer goods, heavy manufacturing, agriculture, mining, and the
production of services, for example, retailing, transport, health services,
administration, education. Production of information is generally
classified as part of the services sector. The information sector includes
the media, advertising, the arts, financial services, computing and
education at all levels. The relative proportions of the economy engaged
in each sector (or field of production) have shifted markedly over the
past two decades and these proportions will continue to change with
shifts in the global economy.

(Korner, McInnes & Rose 2007: 4)

Of course, the relationship between school literacy and the workplace is undergoing radical realignment as industrial societies shift to service economies, or restructure workplaces in an attempt to survive against increasing international competitiveness. Changing technologies, changing management structures and ways of operating in workplaces bring new texts into daily work with the predictable political and media moral panic about falling literacy standards and the failure of schools to prepare students for these new circumstances but, we repeat Graff's (2001: 3) continually relevant comment, '[a]s a student of literacy for over two decades, I cannot recall a time when literacy was not in a crisis'.

We know that change will continue to occur, probably at an ever-increasing rate. In these circumstances, the best that schools can do for students is to give them portable literacy skills built on a firm basis of understanding how texts work and how texts relate to contexts, providing them with a way of dealing with new texts analytically, critically, and with confidence. This requires explicit continuous literacy intervention, for all students, at all stages of schooling, with specific compensatory interventions for those who are disadvantaged during their literacy development. These interventions may involve working with a range of agencies and services to provide services such as speech therapy and health, and psychological interventions for those who have suffered trauma or abuse.

What to research

Research is an ongoing human endeavour to understand the world and to add to human knowledge. It is undertaken as new contexts arise, new knowledge challenges old assumptions, and developments in theory provide new perspectives. It involves moving into new fields but it also involves revisiting previous research in order to accumulate or to review understandings.

This ongoing endeavour must include socially responsible literacy research because participation in the contexts of a literate society – school, work and community – requires literacy capabilities that can only be effectively developed through explicit intervention at all stages of schooling and beyond. Those who are disadvantaged need particularised interventions. Continuing literacy research into the 21st century should enhance our understanding of the challenges and opportunities that social and technological change brings and the skills people will need to control new texts emerging alongside new technologies and changing social structures. Socially responsible literacy research also needs to focus on the role of literacy in establishing a critical participating citizenry that can challenge the texts that dominate their lives, feed them with information and seek to influence public opinion. It should explore ways in which people do and can effectively participate in the civic space (see Humphrey 2006 and 2010).

Quote

We are reminded that, 'good-heartedness and power are insufficient for creating a just world. Some modest development of the intellectual virtues seems essential for future human survival and well-being. Whether the energy, the resources, and the insights necessary for this development can be significantly mustered remains open. This is certain: we will never succeed in cultivating traits whose roots we do not understand and whose development we do not foster.'

(Paul 1993: 58 in Frey & Fisher 2015: 1)

Future literacy research will need to be both broad and detailed in design so groups and individuals in different contexts of literacy use can be studied, including longitudinally. It will be innovative in the selection of appropriate methodologies and mixing quantitative and qualitative methods, while being based on principled theories of language and other modes of meaning making. Its aims will include the development of innovative solutions to meet the very diverse needs of literacy students and users in different educational, work and social contexts.

Quote

The discourses of 'futuring' – scenario building, projecting, extrapolating, modelling and the rest – have long formed part of educational debates about curriculum, assessment and policy. Innovations are often described as being pulled along by a future that is known to be both imminent and inevitable. But in fact such 'futuring' is an intervention, for better or worse, durable or transient, in the present activities of teachers and students.

(Freebody 2010: 43)

The researchers whose voices we have heard describing their research projects in this chapter were asked to consider future research possibilities to provide a sense of how future literacy research might traverse educational, community and social sectors. We hope this book has provided some insights into the processes of literacy research and its importance in making things better (Gee in Chapter 7). Most of all, we hope that it will inspire some readers to join the community of literacy researchers around the world who continue to add to our knowledge of this complex and prevailing aspect of human lives.

Quote

Neither acquiescence in scepticism nor acquiescence in dogma is what education [and research] should produce. What it should produce is a belief that knowledge is attainable in a measure, though with difficulty; that much of what passes as knowledge at any given time is likely to be more or less mistaken, but that the mistakes can be rectified by care and industry. ... Knowledge, like other good things, is difficult, but not impossible ...

(Bertrand Russell 1960/1926: 30–31)

Notes

1 Literacy: A Field of Evolving Terms, Definitions and Educational Approaches

1. https://www.macquariedictionary.com.au – accessed 2.4.2015.
2. https://nces.ed.gov/naal/index.asp – accessed 2.4.2015.
3. https://www.educationcounts.govt.nz – accessed 2.4.2015.
4. http://www.unric.org/en/literacy/27791-the-evolving-definition-of-literacy – accessed 2.5.2015.
5. Available at http://www.unesco.org/new/en/education/themes/education-building-blocks/literacy/resources/statistics – accessed 2.4.2015.
6. Available at http://ir2.flife.de – accessed 31.3.2015.
7. Go to http://nalp.edu.au
8. Go to http://learning.wales.gov.uk
9. Go to http://ec.europa.eu/education/policy/school/doc/family-literacy_en.pdf
10. Go to http://www.nap.edu.au
11. Graff at http://newlearningonline.com – accessed 12.4.2015.
12. http://www.socialnumeracy.ca/approach.htm – accessed 5.4.2015.

2 Studies of Literacy over Time and across Disciplines

1. Go to http://www.italklibrary.com/ to view the library site.
2. *Plato's Complete Works* (abridged by Henry L. Drake 1959) Patterson, NJ: Littlefield, Adams & Co 529–533.
3. See Cope & Kalantzis 2000, Unsworth 2001, Kress 2003, Street, & Baker 2006, O'Halloran 2006, Bus & Neuman 2009, de Silva Joyce & Gaudin 2007 and 2011.
4. Languages such as English are expressed in written form using letters of an alphabet, graphemes used to represent sounds. Other languages use graphemes to represent morphemes or even whole words, for example, the characters used for writing Chinese (see, for example, Halliday 1985b: 16–19).
5. http://au.eonline.com – accessed 17.4.2015.
6. Go to these sites for more information on multimodality – http://mode.ioe.ac.uk/2012/02/16/what-is-multimodality/ and https://multimodalityglossary.wordpress.com/mode-2/

3 Literacy from Home to School

1. The Project Gutenberg EBook of The Orbis Pictus – available at: http://www.gutenberg.org/files/28299/28299-h/28299-h.htm.
2. No Child Left Behind Act, 20 USC 6301 (2001) & (2002).

4 Literacy at School

1. See also Freebody and Freiberg (2011).
2. For accounts of the work of this group of linguists, sometimes referred to as the *Sydney School*, see Christie (2012), Hyon (1996), Johns (2002), Martin and Rose (2008), Paltridge (2012), Rose and Martin (2012), Rothery (1996).
3. See also Alderson and Hudson (2013), Hammond and Macken-Horarik (2001), Myhill (2010).
4. See also Hammond and Miller (2015).

5 Literacy in Adult Life: Community, Further Education and Work

1. nces.ed.gov/surveys/all/ – accessed 25.4.2015.
2. http://www.oecd.org/site/piaac/mainelementsofthesurveyofadultskills.htm#DirectAssessment – accessed 25.4.2015.
3. US Dept of Education – http://www2.ed.gov/ – accessed 26.4.2015.
4. http://www.oecd.org/site/piaac/Summary – accessed 25.4.2015.
5. http://www.ielts.org/about_us.aspx – accessed 29.4.2015.
6. http://www.ets.org/toefl – accessed 29.4.2015.
7. http://www.sydneytrains.info/travelling_with/trip_tips/ – accessed 26.4.2015.
8. https://ama.com.au – accessed 27.4.2015.
9. http://www.theguardian.com – accessed 27.4.2015.
10. Reading on the inside – http://americanlibrariesmagazine.org accessed 27.4.2015.
11. See, for example, Kramsch 2009, Ellis, Gogolin & Clyne 2011, Garcia 2014.

6 Researching Literacy: A Methodological Map

1. Definitions adapted from the Australian and New Zealand Standard Research Classification 2008 – available at http://www.abs.gov.au – accessed 8.3.2015.
2. Macquarie Dictionary online at https://www.macquariedictionary.com.au – accessed 8.3.2015.
3. The descriptions of the case study categories are adapted from the Writing@ CSU Case Study Writing Guide – http://writing.colostate.edu/guides – accessed 9.3.2015.
4. The Design-based Research Collective is a small group of researchers who engage in design-based research, often in technology enhanced learning environments – website at http://www.designbasedresearch.org
5. Search YouTube to see an interview with Debra Myhill on this research project.

7 Researcher Voices

1. Australian Research Council – 0883563 – 2008–2011.
2. http://eacea.ec.europa.eu/llp/comenius/comenius_multilateral_projects_en.php – accessed 24.3.2015.
3. This was carried out by Professor Caroline Coffin, the Open University UK.
4. http://www.unhcr.org/54cf99109.html – accessed 26.3.2015.

References

Adlington, R. (2014) Exploiting the distinctiveness of blogs to overcome geographic isolation. *Australian and international journal of rural education* Vol. 24 No. 3, 1–13.

Adoniou, M. (2014) What should teachers know about spelling? *Literacy* Vol. 48 No. 3, 144–154.

Adoniou, M. and Macken-Horarik, M. (2007) Scaffolding literacy meets ESL: Some insights from ACT classrooms. *TESOL in context* Vol. 17 No. 1, 5–14.

Adult Literacy Agency (NALA). (2013) *Adult literacy and numeracy in action: Six case studies of practice work in Ireland.* Dublin: National Adult Literacy Agency. Available at: http://www.takingthelead.com.au/resources

Afflerbach, P., Pearson, P. D. and Paris, S. G. (2008) Clarifying the differences between reading skills and reading strategies. *The reading teacher* Vol. 61 No. 5, 364–373.

Alderson, J. C. and Hudson, R. (2013) The metalinguistic knowledge of undergraduate students of English language or linguistics. *Language Awareness* Vol. 22 No. 4, 320–337.

Amiel, T. and Reeves, T. C. (2008) Design-based research and educational technology: Rethinking technology and the research agenda. *Educational Technology & Society* Vol. 11 No. 4, 29–40.

Anderson, T. and Shattuck, J. (2012) Design-based research: A decade of progress in educational research? *Educational Researcher* Vol. 41, No 1, 16–25

Andrews, R., Torgerson, C., Beverton, S., Freeman, A., Locke, T., Low, G., Robinson, A. and Zhu, D. (2006) The effect of grammar teaching on writing development. *British Educational Research Journal* Vol. 32 No. 1, 39–55.

Anstey, M. and Bull, G. (2010) Helping teachers to explore multimodal texts. *Curriculum and Leadership Journal* Vol. 8 No. 16. Available at: http://www.curriculum.edu.au/leader/helping_teachers_to_explore_multimodal_texts,31522.html?issueID=12141 – accessed 30.11.13.

Archer, D. (2005) *Writing the wrongs. International benchmarks on adult literacy.* Johannesburg: Global Campaign for Education.

Arnot, M. and Reay, D. (2004) The framing of pedagogic discourse: Regulating order in classroom learning. In J. Muller, B. Davies and A. Morais. *Reading Bernstein. Researching Bernstein.* London: Routledge Falmer, 135–150.

Ashton-Warner, S. (1963) *Teacher.* London: Bantam.

Australian Commission on Safety and Quality in Healthcare (2014) *Health literacy: Taking action to improve safety and quality.* Canberra: Commonwealth of Australia.

Australian Curriculum Assessment and Reporting Authority (ACARA) (2015) *The Australian Curriculum: English. Version 7.4.* Sydney: Australian Curriculum Assessment and Reporting Authority. Available at: http://www.australiancurriculum.edu.au/

Australian Curriculum Assessment and Reporting Authority (ACARA) (2009) *The shape of the Australian curriculum: English.* Available at: http://www.acara.edu.au/verve/_resources/australian_curriculum_-_english.pdf – accessed 4.4.2015.

Axford, B, Harders, P. and Wise, F. (2009) *Scaffolding literacy: An integrated and sequential approach to teaching reading, spelling and writing*. Camberwell, Victoria: Australian Centre for Educational Research.

Bangert-Drowns, R. L. and Rudner, L. M. (1991) Meta-analysis in educational research. *Practical Assessment, Research and Evaluation*. Available at: http://pareonline.net – accessed 12.3.2015

Barone, D. M. (2004) Case study research. In N. K. Duke and M. H. Mallette (Eds). *Literacy research methodologies*. New York and London: The Guildford Press, pp. 7–27.

Barthel, A. (2007) Are tertiary students competent in English? *Lingua Franca*. Available at: http://www.abc.net.au/rn/linguafranca/stories/2007/1854124.htm

Barton, D. (2007) *Literacy: An introduction to the ecology of written language*. Oxford: Blackwell Publishing.

Barton, D. and Hamilton, M. (1998) *Local literacies: Reading and writing in one community*. London: Routledge.

Barton, D., Hamilton, M. and Ivanič, R. (2000) *Situated literacies: Reading and writing in context*. Oxford: Psychology Press.

Barton, D. and Ivanič R. (Eds). (1991) *Writing in the community*. London: Sage Publications.

Bateman, J. A. (2008) *Multimodality and genre: A foundation for the systematic analysis of multimodal documents*. Basingstoke: Hampshire: Palgrave Macmillan.

Batstone, R. (1994) *Grammar*. Oxford: Oxford University Press.

Baynham, M. (1995) *Literacy practices*. London: Longman

Baxter, P and Jack, S. (2008) Qualitative case study methodology: Study design and implementation for novice researchers. *The Qualitative Report* Vol. 13 No. 4 December 2008, 544–559. – Available at: http://www.nova.edu

Bazerman, C. (2010) Series editor's preface. In A. S. Bawarshi and M. J. Reiff (Eds). *Genre: An introduction to history, theory, research and pedagogy*. West Lafayette, Indiana: Parlor Press and The WAC Clearinghouse, pp. xi–xii.

Belfiore, M. E., Defoe, T. A., Folinsbee, S., Hunter, J. and Jackson, N. S. (The In-Sites Research Group) (2004) *Reading work: Literacies in the new workplace*. Mahwah, NJ: Lawrence Erlbaum Associates.

Bennett, S., Maton, K and Kervin, L. (2008) The 'digital natives debate: A critical review of the evidence. *British Journal of Educational Technology* Vol. 39 No. 5, 775–786.

Bernstein, B. (2000) *Pedagogy, symbolic control and identity: Theory, research, critique* (Revised Edition). Lanham, MD: Rowman and Littlefield Publishers Inc.

Bernstein, B. (1996) *Pedagogy, symbolic control and identity*. London: Taylor and Francis.

Bernstein, B. (1975) *Class, codes and control Volume 3: Towards a theory of educational transmissions*. London and Boston: Routledge and Kegan Paul.

Bissex, G. (1980) *Gnyx at Wrk*. Cambridge, MA: Harvard University Press.

Black, S. (1989) Contextual issues and the functioning abilities of low literate prisoners. *Australian Journal of Adult Education* Vol. 29 No. 2, 8–15.

Black, S., Wickert, R. and Rouse, R. (1990) *The illiteracy myth: A comparative study of prisoner literacy abilities*. Sydney: University of Technology, Sydney.

Black, S. and Yasukawa, K. (2010) Time for national renewal: Australian adult literacy and numeracy as 'foundation skills'. *Literacy and Numeracy Studies* Vol. 18 No. 2, 43–57.

Black, S., Yasukawa, K. and Brown, T. (2013) *Investigating the 'crisis': Production workers' literacy and numeracy practices.* Adelaide, SA: National Centre for Vocational Education Research (NCVER).

Blommaert, J. (2005) *Discourse: A critical introduction.* Cambridge: Cambridge University Press.

Bloom, L. (1993) *The transition from infancy to language: Acquiring the power of expression.* Cambridge: Cambridge University Press.

Bloomfield, L. (1914, 1933) *Language.* New York: Henry Holt.

Bloomfield, L. (1914) *Introduction to the study of language.* New York: Henry Holt.

Boas, F. (1911) *Handbook of American Indian languages* (Vol. 1). Bureau of American Ethnology, Bulletin 40. Washington, DC: Government Print Office.

Bodrova, E. and Leong, D. (2007) *Tools of the mind: The Vygotskian approach to early childhood education* (2nd Edition). Upper Saddle River, NJ: Pearson.

Bonner, C. and Caro, J. (2007) *The stupid country: How Australia is dismantling public education.* Sydney: University of New South Wales Press.

Boughton, B., Ah Chee, D., Beetson, J., Durnan, D. and Leblanch, J. (2013) An Aboriginal adult literacy campaign pilot study in Australia using Yes I Can. *Literacy and Numeracy Studies* Vol. 2 No. 1, 5–32.

Boughton, B. and Durnan, D. (2014) Cuba's 'Yes, I Can' mass adult literacy campaign model in Timor-Leste and Aboriginal Australia: A comparative study. *International review of education* Vol. 60 No. 4, 559–580.

Bourne, J. (2004) Towards a 'radical visible pedagogy'. In J. Muller, B. Davies and A. Morais. *Reading Bernstein. Researching Bernstein.* London: Routledge Falmer, 61–74.

Bowman, A. K. and Woolf, G. (Eds). (1994) *Literacy and power in the ancient world.* Cambridge: Cambridge University Press.

Bowyer-Crane, C., Snowling, M. J., Duff, F. J., Fieldsend, E., Carroll, J. M., Miles, J., Gotz, K. and Hulme, C. (2007) Improving early language and literacy skills: Differential effects of an oral language versus a phonology with reading intervention. *Journal of child psychology and psychiatry* Vol. 49 No. 4, 422–432.

Breen, M. (1994) *Literacy in its place: Literacy practices in urban and rural communities.* Perth: School of Language Education, Edith Cowan University.

Bright, C. and von Randow, J. (2004). Tracking language test consequences: The student perspective. 18th IDP Australian International Education Conference. 5–8 October 2004, Sydney, Australia.

Brisk, M. E. (2015) *Engaging students in academic literacies: Genre-based pedagogy for K-5 classrooms.* New York and London: Routledge.

Brocklebank, C. (2002) Leaving letters: finding letters: An innovative Indigenous literacy project. *Literacy Link* Vol. 4 No. 5, April 2002, 4–5.

Brooks, G. (2013) *What works for children and young people with literacy difficulties?: The effectiveness of intervention schemes* (4th Edition). The Dyslexia-SpLD Trust. Available at: http://www.interventionsforliteracy.org.uk – accessed 31.3.2015.

Brown, G. and Yule, G. (1983) *Discourse analysis.* Cambridge: Cambridge University Press.

Brown, J. D. (1988) *Understanding research in second language learning.* Cambridge: Cambridge University Press.

Bruner, J. S. (1986) *Actual minds, possible worlds.* Cambridge, MA: Harvard University Press.

Bruner, J. (1983) *Child's talk: Learning to use language.* New York: W. W. Norton.

Buckingham, J., Wheldall, K. and Beaman-Wheldall, R. (2013) Why Jaydon can't read: The triumph of ideology over evidence in teaching reading. *Policy* Vol. 29 No. 3, 21–32.

Burn, A. (2010) Rules of grammar, rules of play computer games, literacy and literature. In T. Locke (Ed). *Beyond the grammar wars: A resource for teachers and students on developing language knowledge in the English/literacy classroom*. New York and London: Routledge, 294–312.

Burns, A. (2010a) Action research: What's in it for teachers and institutions? *International House Journal* Vol. 29, 3–6.

Burns, A. (2010b) *Doing action research in English language teaching. A guide for practitioners*. New York: Routledge.

Burns, A. (2005) Understanding action research. In A. Burns and H. de Silva Joyce (Eds). *Teachers' Voices 8: Explicitly supporting reading and writing in the classroom*. Sydney: Macquarie University, 17–25. Search for Teachers Voices series available at: http://www.ameprc.mq.edu.au

Burns, A. (1999) *Collaborative action research for English language teachers*. Cambridge: Cambridge University Press.

Burns, A. and de Silva Joyce, H. (Eds). (2008) *Clearly teaching: Explicit ESL pedagogy in action*. Sydney: AMEP Research Centre, Macquarie University.

Burns, A. and de Silva Joyce, H. (Eds). (2005) *Teachers' voices 8: Explicitly supporting reading and writing in the classroom*. Sydney: National Centre for English Language Teaching and Research (NCELTR) Macquarie University.

Burns, A. and de Silva Joyce, H. (Eds). (2001) *Teachers' voices 7: Teaching vocabulary*. Sydney: National Centre for English Language Teaching and Research (NCELTR) Macquarie University.

Burns, A. and de Silva Joyce, H. (Eds). (2000a) *Teachers' voices 5: A new look at reading practices*. Sydney: National Centre for English Language Teaching and Research (NCELTR) Macquarie University.

Burns, A. and de Silva Joyce, H. (Eds). (2000b) *Teachers' voices 4: Staying learner centred in a competency-based curriculum*. Sydney: National Centre for English Language Teaching and Research (NCELTR) Macquarie University.

Burns, A. and Hood, S. (Eds). (1998) *Teachers' voices 3: Teaching critical literacy*. Sydney: National Centre for English Language Teaching and Research (NCELTR) Macquarie University.

Burns, A. and Hood, S. (Eds). (1997) *Teachers' voices 2: Teaching disparate learner groups*. Sydney: National Centre for English Language Teaching and Research (NCELTR) Macquarie University.

Burns, A. and Hood, S. (Eds). (1995) *Teachers' voices: Exploring course design in a changing curriculum*. Sydney: National Centre for English Language Teaching and Research (NCELTR) Macquarie University.

Bus, A. G. and Neuman, S. B. (2009) *Multimedia and literacy development: Improving achievement for young learners*. London and New York: Routledge.

Butler, D. (1975) *Cushlas and her books*. Boston: The Horn Book.

Butt, D. (2004) How our meanings change: School contexts and semantic evolution. In G. Williams and A. Lukin (Eds). *The development of language: Functional perspectives on species and individuals*. London and New York: Continuum, 217–240.

Butt, D., Fahey, R., Feez, S. and Spinks, S. (2012) *Using functional grammar: An explorer's guide* (3rd Edition). South Yarra, Victoria: Macmillan Education Australia.

Byrnes, H. (Ed). (2009) Instructed foreign language acquisition as meaning-making: A systemic-functional approach. *Linguistics and Education* Vol. 20, 1–9.

Caffarel, A., Martin, J. R. and Matthiessen, C. M. I. M. (Eds). (2004) *Language typology: A functional perspective.* Amsterdam: John Benjamins.

Callow, J. (2013) *The shape of text to come.* Marrickville, NSW: Primary English Teaching Association Australia (PETAA).

Callow, J. (1999) *Image matters: visual texts in the classroom.* Marrickville, NSW: Primary English Teaching Association Australia (PETAA).

Cambourne, B. (1995) Toward an educationally relevant theory of literacy learning: Twenty years of inquiry. *The Reading Teacher* Vol. 49, No. 3, 182–192.

Cambourne, B. (1984) *Language, learning and literacy.* Adelaide: Rigby.

Cameron, D. (1995) *Verbal hygiene.* London: Routledge.

Campbell, S., Torr, J. and Cologon, K. (2014) Pre-packaging preschool literacy: What drives early childhood teachers to use commercially produced phonics programs in prior to school settings. *Contemporary Issues in Early Childhood* Vol. 15 No. 1, 4–53.

Campione, J. (1981) *Learning, academic achievement and instruction.* Paper delivered at the Second Annual Conference on Reading Research of the Study of Reading, New Orleans, April 1981.

Canadian Association of Chiefs of Police – Literacy and Policing Project (2008) *Literacy awareness resource manual for police.* Ottawa: Canadian Association of Chiefs of Police and Crime Prevention Committee.

Candlin, C and Mercer, N. (2001) *English language teaching in its social context: A reader.* London and New York: Routledge.

Carter, R. (Ed). (1990) *Knowledge about language and the curriculum: The LINC Reader.* London: Hodder.

Castells, M. 1993. The informational economy and the new international division of labor. In M. Carnoy, M. Castells, S. Cohen and F. M. Cardoso (Eds). *The new global economy in the information age: Reflections on our changing world.* University Park, Penn: Pennsylvania State University Press, 15–43.

Castleton, G. (2003) Workplace literacy: A contested area. *Fine print magazine.* Available at: VALBEC -www.valbec.org.au/05/fineprint/archive/2003%20 folder/03-au-lo.pdf – accessed 27.4.2015.

Castleton, G. (2001) The role of literacy in people's lives: A case study of its use amongst the homeless in Australia. In J. Crowther, M. Hamilton and L. Tett (Eds). *Powerful literacies.* Leicester: National Institute of Adult Continuing Education (niace).

Cazden, C. B. (1988) *Classroom discourse: The language of teaching and learning.* Portsmouth, NH: Heinemann.

Chall, J. S. (1967) *Learning to read: The great debate.* New York: McGraw Hill.

Chambers, J. K., Trudgill, P. and Schilling-Estes, N. (2002) *The handbook of language variation and change.* Malden, MA and Oxford: Blackwell.

Chan, E. and Unsworth, L. (2011) Image-language interaction in online reading environments: challenges for students' reading comprehension. *The Australian Educational Researcher* Vol. 38 No. 2, 181–202.

Chapman, S. and Routledge, C. (Eds). (2005) *Key thinkers in linguistics and the philosophy of language.* Edinburgh: Edinburgh University Press.

Cheffy, I. (2007) Local literacies in a Cameroonian village. In C. Gabrielatos, R. SLessor and J. W. Unger (Eds). Lancaster: Department of Linguistics and

English Language, Lancaster University. Available at: http://www.ling.lancs. ac.uk/pgconference/v01/Volume01.pdf.

Chomsky, N. (2006) *Language and mind* (3rd Edition). New York: Cambridge University Press.

Chomsky, N. (1986) *Knowledge of language: Its nature, origin and use.* New York: Praeger.

Chomsky, N. (1957) *Syntactic structures.* London: Mouton.

Christie, F. (2012) *Language education throughout the school years: A functional perspective.* Language learning monograph series. University of Michigan: Wiley-Blackwell.

Christie, F. (2010a) Literacy as a theme in educational theory and policy. In F. Christie and A. Simpson (Eds). (2010) *Literacy and social responsibility: Multiple perspectives.* London and Oakville, CT: Equinox, 9–23.

Christie, F. (2010b). The 'Grammar wars' in Australia. In T. Locke (Ed). *Beyond the grammar wars: A resource for teachers and students on developing language knowledge in the English/literacy classroom.* New York and London: Routledge, 55–72.

Christie, F. (2002) *Classroom discourse: A functional perspective.* London and New York: Continuum.

Christie, F. (1999) (Ed). *Pedagogy and the shaping of consciousness.* London and New York: Continuum.

Christie, F. (1990) (Ed). *Literacy for a changing world.* Hawthorn, Victoria: Australian Council for Educational Research (ACER).

Christie, F. and Derewianka, B. (2008) *School discourse: Learning to write across the years of schooling.* London and New York: Continuum.

Christie, F. and Macken-Horarik, M. (2007) Building verticality in subject English. In Christie, F. and Martin, J. R. (Eds). *Language, knowledge and pedagogy: Functional linguistic and sociological perspectives.* London and New York: Continuum.

Christie, F. and Martin, J. R. (Eds). (2007) *Language, knowledge and pedagogy: Functional linguistics and sociological perspectives.* London: Continuum.

Christie, F. and Martin, J. R. (1997) (Eds). *Genre and institutions: Social processes in the workplace and school.* London and Washington: Cassell.

Christie, F. and Maton, K. (2011) *Disciplinarity: Functional linguistic and sociological perspectives.* London and New York: Continuum.

Christie, F. and Simpson, A. (2010) *Literacy and social responsibility.* In F. Christie and A. Simpson (Eds). *Literacy and social responsibility: Multiple perspectives.* London and Oakville, CT: Equinox, 1–8.

Christie, F. and Unsworth, L. (2005) Developing dimensions of an educational linguistics. In R. Hasan, C. M. M. Matthiessen and J. J. Webster (Eds). *Continuing discourse on language: A functional perspective.* London: Equinox.

Clark, A. (1998) Magic words: How language augments human computation. In P. Carruthers and J. Boucher (Eds). *Language and thought: Interdisciplinary themes.* Cambridge: Cambridge University Press, 162–183.

Clanchy, J. and Ballard, B. 1997. *Essay writing for students (3rd ed.). Melbourne: Longman.*

Clark, R. and Ivanič, R. (1997) *The politics of writing.* London and New York: Routledge.

Clarke, U. (2010) The problematics of prescribing grammatical knowledge. In T. Locke (Ed). *Beyond the grammar wars: A resource for teachers and students on developing language knowledge in the English/literacy classroom.* New York and London: Routledge, 38–54.

Cloran, C. (1999) Context, material situation and text. In M. Ghadessy (Ed). *Text and context in functional linguistics*. Amsterdam: John Benjamins, pp. 177–218.

Clyne, M. (2008) The monolingual mindset as an impediment to the development of plurilingual potential in Australia. *Sociolinguistic studies* Vol. 2 No. 3, 347–365.

Clyne, M. (2005) *Australia's language potential*. Sydney: University of New South Wale Press.

Cochrane, I., Reece, A., Ahearn, K. and Jones, P. (2013) *Grammar in the early years: A games-based approach. PETAA 199.* Marrickville: Primary English Teaching Association Australia.

Coffin, C. (2006) *Historical discourse: The language of time, cause and evaluation.* London and New York: Continuum.

Coghlan, D. and Brannick, T. (2014) *Doing action research in your own organisation.* London: Sage Publications.

Coltheart, M. and Prior, M. (2007) *Learning to read in Australia*. Policy Paper No. 6. Canberra ACT: The Academy of Social Sciences in Australia.

Colorado State University. Writing @ CSU Guide–Case Studies – available http://writing.colostate.edu/guides

Comber, B. and Nichols, S. (2004) Getting the big picture: Regulating knowledge in the early childhood literacy curriculum. *Journal of early childhood literacy* Vol. 4 No. 1, 43–63.

Cook, G. and Seidlhofer, B. (1995) An applied linguist in principle and practice. In G. Cook and B. Seidlhofer (Eds). *Principle and practice in applied linguistics: Studies in Honour of H. G. Widdowson*. Oxford: Oxford University Press, pp. 1–26.

Cooksey, R. and McDonald, G. (2011) *Surviving and thriving in postgraduate research*. Prahran, Victoria: Tilde University Press.

Cooper, H. M. and Tom, D. Y. H. (1984) Teacher expectations research: A review with implications for classroom instruction. *The Elementary School Journal* Vol. 85. No. 1, September 1984, 76–89.

Cope, B. and Kalantzis, M. (2000) *Multiliteracies: Literacy learning and the design of social futures*. Melbourne: Macmillan.

Cornwell, S. (1999) Interview with Anne Burns and Graham Crooks. *The Language Teacher* Vol. 23 No. 12, 5–9, 27.

Coulthard, M. (1985) *An introduction to discourse analysis* (2nd Edition). London and New York: Longman.

Cowey, W. (2005) A brief description of the National Accelerated Literacy Program. *TESOl in Context* Vol. 15 No. 2, 3–14.

Cremin, L. A. (1961) *The transformation of the school: Progressivism in American education, 1876–1957*. New York: Vintage Books.

Creswell, J. W. (2014) *Research design: Qualitative, quantitative and mixed methods approaches* (4th Edition). Thousand Oaks, CA: Sage.

Crowther, J., Hamilton, M. and Tett, L. (Eds). (2001) *Powerful literacies*. Leicester: National Institute of Adult Continuing Education (niace).

Crystal, D. (1995) *The Cambridge encyclopaedia of the English language*. Cambridge: Cambridge University Press.

Culican, S. J. (2005) Troubling teacher talk: The challenge of changing classroom discourse patterns. Paper presented at the Australian Association for Research in Education (AARE) Annual Conference, Parramatta 2005. Available at: http://www.aare.edu.au/data/publications/2005/cul05592.pdf – accessed 28.3.2015.

Cummins, J. (2008) BICS and CALP: Empirical and theoretical status of the distinction. In B. Street and H. H. Hornberger (Eds). *Encyclopedia of language and education, Volume 2: Literacy* (2nd Edition). New York: Springer, 71–83.

Dahl, K. L., Sharer, P. L., Lawson, L. L. and Grogan, P. R. (1999) Phonics instruction and student achievement in whole language first grade classrooms. *Reading Research Quarterly* Vol. 34 No. 3, 312–341.

Davis, M. A. and Poston, D. L. (2008) Research methods in sociology. In W. A. Darity (Ed.) *International Encyclopedia of the Social Sciences* (2nd Edition) Vol 5. Detroit: Macmillan Reference, 113–115.

de Oliveira, L. C. (2010) Nouns in History: Packaging information, expanding explanations and structuring reasoning. *The History Teacher* Vol. 43 No. 2, February 2010, 191–203.

Delpit, L. D. (1988) *The silenced dialogue: Power and pedagogy in educating other people's children. Harvard Educational Review* Vol. 58, 280–298.

Derewianka, B. (2012) Knowledge about language in the Australian Curriculum: English. *Australian Journal of Language and Literacy* Vol. 35 No. 1, 127–146.

Derewianka, B. (2011) *A new grammar companion for teachers.* Newtown, NSW: Primary English Teaching Association of Australia.

Derewianka, B. and Jones, P. (2012) *Teaching language in context.* Melbourne: Oxford University Press.

Derewianka, B. and Jones, P. (2010) From traditional grammar to functional grammar: bridging the divide. In C. Coffin (Ed). *Language support in EAL contexts. Why systemic functional linguistics?* Special Issue of *NALDIC Quarterly.* Reading: UK, pp. 6–17.

de Silva Joyce, H. (2005) *Developing writing skills: Teacher resources book.* Sydney: Phoenix Education

de Silva Joyce, H. (2014) *Multimodal and visual literacy in the adult language and literacy classroom.* Sydney: NSW AMES.

de Silva Joyce, H. (Ed.) (2000) *Teachers' voices 6: Teaching casual conversation.* Sydney: National Centre for English Language Teaching and Research (NCELTR) Macquarie University.

de Silva Joyce, H. and Burns, A. (1999) *Focus on grammar.* Sydney: Macquarie University.

de Silva Joyce, H and Feez, S. (2012) *Text-based language and literacy education: Programming and methodology.* Sydney: Phoenix Education.

de Silva Joyce, H and Feez, S. (2004) *Developing writing skills for middle secondary students.* Sydney: Phoenix Education.

de Silva Joyce, H. and Gaudin, J. (2011) *Words and pictures: A multimodal approach to picture books.* Sydney: Phoenix Education

de Silva Joyce, H. and Gaudin, J. (2007a) *Interpreting the visual: A resource book for teachers.* Sydney: Phoenix Education.

de Silva Joyce, H. and Gaudin, J. (2007b) *Interpreting the visual: A resource book for students.* Sydney: Phoenix Education.

de Silva Joyce, H. and Hood, S. (2009) English for community membership: Planning for actual and potential needs. In D. Belcher (Ed). *English for Specific Purposes in Theory and Practice.* Ann Arbor, MI: University of Michigan, 244–263.

de Silva Joyce, H., Hood, S. and Rose, D. (2008) *Investigating the impact of intensive reading pedagogy in adult literacy.* Adelaide, SA: National Centre for Vocational Education Research. Available at: http://www.ncver.edu.au

Diamond, A. (2014) Understanding executive functions: What helps or hinders them and how executive functions and language development mutually support one another. *Perspectives on language and literacy* Vol. 40 No. 2, 7–11.

Diamond, A. (2012) Activities and programs that improve children's executive functions. *Current Directions in Psychological Science* Vol. 21 No. 5, 335–341.

Diehl, W. A. and Mikulecky, L. (1980) The nature of reading at work. *Journal of Reading* Vol. 24 No. 3, 221–227.

Di Renzo, A. (2000) His master's voice: Tiro and the rise of the roman secretarial class. *Journal of Technical Writing and Communication* Vol. 30 No. 2, 155–168.

Djonov, E. (2008) Children's website structure and navigation. In L. Unsworth (Ed). *Multimodal semiotics: Functional analysis in contexts of education*. London: Continuum, 216–236.

Djonov, E., Knox, J. and Zhao, S. (2015) Interpreting websites in educational contexts: A social-semiotic, multimodal approach. In P. Smeyers, D. Bridges, N. C. Burbules and M. Griffiths (Eds). *International handbook of interpretation in educational research*. New York and London: Springer, 315–346.

Dooey, P. and Oliver, R. (2002) An investigation into the predictive validity of the IELTS test as an indicator of future academic success. *Prospect* Vol. 17 No. 1, April 2002, 36–54.

Dornyei, Z. (2007) *Research methods in applied linguistics: Qualitative, quantitative and mixed methodologies*. Oxford: Oxford University Press.

Dreyfus, S., Hood, S. and Stenglin, M. (Eds). (2011) *Semiotic margins: Meaning in multimodalities*. London and New York: Continuum.

Duff, P. A. and Hornberger, N. H. (Eds) (2008) *Encyclopedia of language and education – Volume 8: Language socialization* (2nd edition). New York: Springer.

Duke, N. K. and Mallette, M. H. (2004) *Literacy research methodologies*. New York and London: The Guildford Press.

Dusek, J. B. and Joseph, G. (1985) The bases of teacher expectancies. In J. B. Dusek (Ed). *Teacher expectancies*. Hillsdale, NJ: Erlbaum, 229–250.

Ebbutt, D. (1985) Educational action research: Some general concerns and specific quibbles. In R. Burgess (Ed). *Issues in educational research*. Lewes: Falmer Press.

Eggins, S. (2004) *An Introduction to Systemic Functional Linguistics*. New York and London: Continuum.

Ehri, L. C., Nunes, S. R., Stahl, S. A. and Willows, D. M. (2001) Systematic phonics instruction helps students learn to read: Evidence from the National Reading Panel's Meta-Analysis. *Review of Educational Research* Vol. 71 No. 3, 393–447.

Ehri, L. C., Nunes, S. R., Willows, D. M., Schuster, B. V., Yahgoub-Zadeh, Z. and Shanahan, T. (2001) Phonemic awareness instruction helps children learn to read: Evidence from the National Reading Panel's meta-analysis. *Reading Research Quarterly*, Vol. 36 No. 3, 250–287.

Elder, C. (2003) The DELNA initiative at the University of Auckland. *TESOLANZ newsletter* Vol. 12 No. 1, 15–16.

Elkind, D. (1974) Montessori and Piaget. In *Children and adolescents: Interpretive essays on Jean Piaget* (2nd Edition). New York: Oxford University Press, 128–138.

Elliott, J. (1991) *Action research for educational change*. Milton Keynes: Open University Press.

Ellis, E. (2006) Monolingualism: The unmarked case. *Estudios de Sociolinguistica* Vol. 7 No. 2, 173–196.

Ellis, E., Gogolin, I. and Clyne, M. (2010) The Janus face of monolingualism: A comparison of German and Australian language education policies. *Current Issues in Language Planning* Vol. 11 No. 4, 439–460.

Ewing, R. (Ed). (2006) *Beyond the reading wars: A balanced approach to helping children to read.* Sydney: Primary English Teachers Association (PETA)

Evans, J. (2000) The transfer of mathematics learning from school to work not straightforward but not impossible either! In A. Bessot and J. Ridway (Eds). *Education for mathematics in the workplace.* Dordrecht: Kluwer, 5–15.

Fairclough, N. (1992a). *Critical language awareness.* London: Longman.

Fairclough, N. (1992b). *Discourse and social change.* Cambridge: Polity Press.

Fang, Z. and Schleppegrell, M. (2010) Disciplinary literacies across content areas: Supporting secondary reading through functional language analysis. *Journal of Adolescent & Adult Literacy* Vol. 53 No. 7, 587–597.

Fang, Z. and Schleppegrell, M. J. (2008) *Reading in secondary content areas: A language-based pedagogy.* Ann Arbor, MI: University of Michigan Press.

Fawns, M. and Ivanič R. (2001) Form-filling as a social practice: Taking power into our own hands. In J. Crowther, M. Hamilton and L. Tett (Eds). *Powerful literacies.* Leicester: National Institute of Adult Continuing Education (niace), pp. 151–171.

Feez, S. (2011) Discipline and freedom in early childhood education. In F. Christie and K. Maton (Eds). *Disciplinarity: Functional linguistics and sociological perspectives.* London and New York: Continuum, pp. 201–215.

Feez, S. (2010) *Montessori and early childhood.* London: Sage.

Feez, S. (2008) Multimodal representation of educational meanings in Montessori pedagogy. In L. Unsworth (Ed). *Multimodal semiotics: Functional analysis in contexts of education.* London and New York: Continuum.

Feez, S., Iedema, R. and White, P. (2008) *Media literacy.* Sydney: NSW AMES.

Fieldhouse, R. 1996. A history of modern British adult education. Leicester, UK: National Institute of Adult Continuing Adult Education (NIACE).

Fischer, S. R. (2003) *A history of reading.* London: Reaktion Press.

Fischer, S. R. (2001) *A history of writing.* London: Reaktion Press.

Fishman, A. R. (1991) Because this is who we are: Writing in the Amish community. In D. Barton and R. Ivanič, (Eds). *Writing in the community.* London: Sage Publications, pp. 14–37.

Fleer, M. and Raban, R. (2007a) Constructing cultural-historical tools for supporting young children's concept formation in early literacy and numeracy. *Early Years: An International Research Journal* Vol. 27 No. 2, 103–111.

Fleer, M. and Raban, R. (2007b). *Early childhood literacy and numeracy: Building good practice.* Canberra: Commonwealth of Australia.

Flesch, R. (1955) *Why Johnny can't read: And what you can do about it.* New York: Harper and Row.

Flint, A. S., Kitson, L. and Lowe, K. (2013) *Literacy in Australia: Pedagogies for engagement.* Milton, Qld: John Wiley and Sons.

Forey, G. and Nunan, D. (2002) The role of language and culture in the workplace. In C. Barron, N. Bruce and D. Nunan (Eds). *Knowledge and discourse: Towards an ecology of language.* Harlow: Longman, pp. 204–220.

Fox, M. (2008) *The folly of jolly old phonics.* Paper presented at conference of Auckland principals April 2008. Available at: http://memfox.com/for-parents/for-parents-the-folly-of-jolly-old-phonics/ accessed 4.4.2015.

Freebody, P. (2010) Socially responsible literacy education: Toward an 'organic relation' to our place and time. In F. Christie and A. Simpson (Eds). *Literacy and social responsibility: Multiple perspectives.* London and Oakville, CT: Equinox, 40–55

Freebody, P. (2007) *Literacy education in school: Research perspectives from the past, for the future.* Camberwell, Victoria: Australian Council for Educational Research.

Freebody, P. (2004) Hindsight and foresight: Putting the Four Roles Model of reading to work in the daily business of teaching. In A. Healy and E. Honan (Eds). *Text next: New resources for literacy learning.* Newtown, NSW: Primary English Teaching Association, 3–17.

Freebody, P., Barton, G. and Chan, E. (2014) Literacy education 'about being in the world'. In C. Leung and B. V. Street (Eds). *The Routledge companion to English studies.* London and New York: Routledge, pp. 419–434.

Freebody, P., Chan, E. and Barton, G. (2013) Literacy and curriculum: Language and knowledge in the classroom. In K. Hall, T. Cremin, B. Comber and L. C. Moll (Eds). *International handbook of research on children's literacy, learning and culture* (1st edition). Maldon, MA: John Wiley & Sons, 304–318.

Freebody, P. and Freiberg, J. (2011) The teaching and learning of critical literacy: Beyond the 'Show of Wisdom'. In M. L. Kamil, P. D. Pearson, E. B. Moje and P. P. Afflerbach (Eds). *Handbook of reading research* (Volume IV). New York and London: Routledge, pp. 432–452.

Freebody, P. and Luke, A. (2003) Literacy as engaging with new forms of life: The Four Roles Model. In G. Bull and M. Anstey (Eds). *The literacy lexicon* (2nd Edition). Frenchs Forest, NSW: Prentice Hall, 51–65.

Freebody, P. and Luke, A. (1990) Literacies programs: Debates and demands in cultural context. *Prospect* Vol. 5, 7–1.

Freebody, P., Maton, K. and Martin, J. (2008) Talk, text and knowledge in cumulative, integrated learning: A response to 'intellectual challenge'. *Australian journal of language and literacy* Vol. 31 No. 2, 188–201.

Freebody, P. and Morgan, A-M. (2014) Curriculum explicit-literacy: Expanding the repertoire. In A.-M. Morgan, B. Comber, P. Freebody and H. Nixon (Eds). *Literacy in the middle years.* Newtown NSW: Primary English Teaching Association, pp. 51–73.

Freebody, P., Morgan, A., Comber, B. and Nixon, H. (2014) *Literacy research: A middle years project: Learning from collaborative classroom research.* Sydney: PETAA.

Freedman, A. and Medway, P. (Eds). (1994) *Learning and teaching genre.* Portsmouth, NH: Heinemann

Freire, P. (1985) *The politics of education.* London: South Hadley: Bergin and Garvey.

Freire, P. (1968) *Pedagogy of the oppressed.* New York: Seabury Press. (30th Anniversary Edition 2000). New York and London: Bloomsbury Academic.

Freire, P. and Macedo, D. P. (1987) The Importance of the act of reading. In P. Freire and D. P. Macedo (Eds). *Literacy: Reading the word and the world.* London: Routledge and Kegan Paul, 29–36.

French, R. (2010). Primary school children learning grammar: Rethinking the possibilities. In T. Locke (Ed). *Beyond the grammar wars: A resource for teachers and students on developing language knowledge in the English/literacy classroom.* New York and London: Routledge, pp. 206–229.

French, P. and MacLure, M. (1981) Teachers' questions, pupils' answers: An investigation of questions and answers in the infant classroom. In M. Stubbs and H. Hillier (Eds). (1983) *Readings on language, schools and classrooms*. London: Methuen, 206–229.

Frey, N. and Fisher, D. (2007) The role of critical literacy in citizenship. In *RHI Magazine*. Random House, pp. 13–17. Available at: http://www.randomhouse.com/highschool/RHI_magazine/pdf/RHI07.pdf – accessed 26.3.2015.

García, O. (2014) Multilingualism and language education. In C. Leung and B. V. Street (Eds). *The Routledge companion to English studies*. New York: Routledge, pp. 222–254.

García, O., Bartlett, L. and Kleifgen, J. (2007) From biliteracy to pluriliteracies. In L. Wei and P Auer (Eds). *Handbook on multilingualism and multilingual communication Volume 5*. Amsterdam: Mouton/de Gruyter, 207–228.

García, O., Kleifgen, A. and Falchi, L. (2008) *From English Language Learners to Emergent Bilinguals* (*Equity Matters:* Research Review No. 1). New York: Teachers' College.

Gaur, A. (2000) *Literacy and the politics of writing*. Bristol: Intellect Books.

Geake, J. (2009) *The brain at school: Educational neuroscience in the classroom*. Berkshire: Open University Press.

Gee, J. P. (2014) *Unified discourse analysis: Language, reality, visual worlds, and video games*. London: Routledge

Gee, J. P. (2013) *The anti-education era: Creating smarter students through digital learning*. New York: Palgrave/Macmillan.

Gee, J. P. (2012a) *Social linguistics and literacies: Ideology in discourses* (4th Edition). Oxford and New York: Routledge.

Gee, J. P. (2012b) The old and the new in the new digital literacies. *The educational forum* Vol. 76, 418–420.

Gee, J. P. (2011a) *An introduction to discourse analysis: Theory and method* (3rd Edition). New York and London: Routledge.

Gee, J. P. (2011b) *How to do discourse analysis: A toolkit*. New York and London: Routledge.

Gee, J. P. (2009) *A situated sociocultural approach to literacy and technology*. Available at: http://www.jamespaulgee.com – accessed 16.3.2015.

Gee, J. P. (2003) *What video games have to teach us about learning and literacy*. New York: Palgrave Macmillan.

Gee, J. P. (1992) *The social mind: Language, ideology, and social practice*. New York: Bergin & Garvey. Reprinted 2014: Champaign-Urbana: Common Ground

Gee, J. P. (1990) *Social linguistics and literacies: Ideology in Discourses* (5th Edition – 2015). London: Taylor & Francis.

Gee, J. P. (1987) What is literacy? *Teaching and Learning* Vol. 2 No. 1: 3–11.

Gee, J. P. and Handford, M. (2012) *The Routledge handbook of discourse analysis*. Oxford and New York: Routledge.

Gee, J. P. and Hayes, E. R. (2011) *Language and learning in the digital age*. London and New York: Routledge.

Gee, J. P., Hull, G. and Lankshear, C. (1996) *The new work order: Behind the language of the new capitalism*. London: Allen and Unwin.

Ghadessy, M. (1988) *Registers of written English*. London and New York: Pinter Publishers.

Gibbons, P. (2014) *Scaffolding language, scaffolding learning: Teaching second language learners in the mainstream classroom* (2nd edition). Portsmouth, NH: Heinemann.

Gibbons, P. (2009) *English learners academic literacy and thinking: Learning in the challenge zone.* Portsmouth, NH: Heinemann.

Gibbons, P. (2006) *Bridging discourse in the ESL classroom.* London and New York: Continuum.

Ginsburg, L. and Gal, I. (1996) *Instructional strategies for teaching adult numeracy skills: NCAL technical report TR96-02 May 1996.* Available at: http://citeseerx.ist.psu.edu/viewdoc/download? doi=10.1.1.29.5676&rep=rep1&type=pdf – accessed 5.4.2015

Giridharan, B. and Conlan, C. (2012) The use of verbal protocol analysis in L2 vocabulary acquisition patterns. In *Proceedings of the 2012 Applied Linguistics Association of Australian Annual* Conference, Perth, Australia, 138–159.

Glass, G. V. (1976) Primary, secondary and meta-analysis of research. *Educational Researcher* Vol. 5 No. 10, 3–8.

Goldman, S. R. and Wiley, J. (2004) Discourse analysis: Written text. In N. K. Duke and M. H. Mallette (Eds). *Literacy research methodologies.* New York and London: The Guildford Press, pp. 104–134.

Gomm, R. (2009) *Key concepts in social research methods.* New York: Palgrave Macmillan

Goodman, K. (1997) Putting theory and research in the context of history. *Language arts* Vol. 74 No. 8, 595–599.

Goodman, K. (1996) *On reading.* Don Mills, ON: Pearson Education Canada

Goodman, K. (1973) Miscues: 'Windows on the reading process'. In F. Gollasch (Ed). *Language and literacy: The selected writings of Kenneth Goodman* Vol. 1. Boston: Routledge and Kegan Paul, 93–102.

Goodman, K. (1969) Analysis of oral reading miscues: Applied psycholinguistics. In F. Gollasch (Ed). *Language and literacy: The selected writings of Kenneth Goodman* Vol. 1. Boston: Routledge and Kegan Paul, 125–134.

Goodman, K. (1967) Reading: A psycholinguistic guessing game. In H. Singer and R. B. Ruddell (Eds). *Language and literacy: The selected writings of Kenneth Goodman* Vol. 1. Boston: Routledge and Kegan Paul, 93–102.

Goswami, U. (2006) Phonological awareness and literacy. *Encyclopedia of language and linguistics* (2nd Edition). Amsterdam: Elsevier, 489–497.

Graff, H. J. (2011) *Literacy myths, legacies and lessons: New studies on literacy.* New Brunswick, NJ: Transaction Publishers.

Graff, H. J. (2010) The literacy myth at thirty. *Journal of Social History*, Vol. 43 No. 3, 635–661.

Graff, H. J. (2001) Literacy's myths and legacies: From lessons from the history of literacy to the question of critical literacy. In P. Freebody, S., Muspratt and B. Dwyer (Eds). *Difference, silence and textual practice: Studies in critical literacy.* Cresskill, NJ: Hampton Press, 1–30.

Graff, Harvey J. (1987) *The Legacies of Literacy: Continuities and Contradictions in Western Culture and Society.* Bloomington IN: Indiana University Press, 260–264.

Graff, H. J. (1987) *The labyrinths of literacy: Reflections on literacy past and present.* Lewes, Sussex: The Falmer Press.

Graham, J. G. (1987) English language proficiency and the prediction of academic success. *TESOL Quarterly* Vol. 21 No. 3, 505–521.

Graham, S. and Perin, D. (2007) A meta-analysis of writing instruction for adolescent students. *Journal of Educational Psychology* Vol. 99 No. 3, 445–476.

Graves, D. (2003) *Writing: Teachers and children at work.* Portsmouth, NH: Heinemann.

Graves, D. (1978) *Balance the basics: Let then write.* New York: The Ford Foundation.

Gray, B. (1987) How natural is 'natural' language teaching: Employing wholistic methodology in the classroom. *Australian Journal of Early Childhood* Vol. 12 No. 4, 3–19.

Greene, K. and Moore, T. (2010) *Archaeology: An introduction* (5th Edition). London: Taylor & Francis.

Gregory, E. and Williams, A. (2004) Living literacies in homes and communities In T. Grainger (Ed). *Language and literacy.* London and New York: Routledge Falmer, 33–51.

Gunn, S. and Wyatt-Smith, C. (2011) Learning difficulties – literacy and numeracy: Conversations across the fields. In C. Wyatt-Smith, J. Elkins and J. Gunn (Eds). *Multiple perspectives on difficulties in learning literacy and numeracy.* New York: Springer, 17–48.

Gutiérrez, K. D. (2008) Developing a sociocritical literacy in the third space. *Reading Research Quarterly* Vol. 43, 148–164.

Gumpert, P. and Gumpert, C. (1968) The teacher as Pygmalion: Comments on the psychology of expectation. *Urban Review* Vol. 3 No. 1, September 1968, 21–25.

Halliday, M. A. K. (2009/1978). Is learning a second language like learning a first language all over again. In J. Webster (Ed.), *Language and education: Volume 9 in the Collected Works of M. A. K. Halliday.* London and New York: Continuum, 174–193.

Halliday, M. A. K. (2007/1979) Some reflections on language education in multilingual societies, as seen from the standpoint of linguistics. In J. Webster (Ed.), *Language and education: Volume 9 in the Collected Works of M. A, K. Halliday.* London and New York: Continuum, 239–253.

Halliday, M. A. K. (2007/2002) Applied linguistics as an evolving theme. In J. Webster (Ed.), *Language and education: Volume 9 in the Collected Works of M. A, K. Halliday.* London and New York: Continuum, 1–19.

Halliday, M. A. K. (2007/1996) Literacy and linguistics: A functional perspective. In J. Webster (Ed.), *Language and education: Volume 9 in the Collected Works of M. A, K. Halliday.* London and New York: Continuum, 97–129.

Halliday, M. A. K. (2007/1991) The notion of 'context' in language education. In J. Webster (Ed). *Language and education: Volume 9 in the Collected Works of M. A. K. Halliday.* London and New York: Continuum, 269–290.

Halliday, M. A. K. (2007/1981) A response to some questions on the language issue. In J. Webster (Ed). *Language and education. Volume 9 in the Collected Works of M. A. K. Halliday.* London and New York: Continuum, 331–340.

Halliday, M. A. K. (2004/1993) Towards a language-based theory of learning. In J. Webster (Ed). *The language of early childhood. Volume 4 in the Collected Works of M. A. K. Halliday.* London: and New York: Continuum, 327–352.

Halliday, M. A. K. (2004/1988) On the language of physical science. In J. Webster (Ed). *The language of science: Volume 5 in the Collected Works of M. A. K. Halliday.* London: and New York: Continuum (Edited by J. Webster), 140–158.

Halliday, M. A. K. (2002/1996) On grammar and grammatics. In J. Webster (Ed). *On Grammar: Volume 1 in the Collected Works of M. A. K. Halliday*. Vol. 1. London and New York: Continuum, 384–417.

Halliday, M. A. K. (2002/1987) Spoken and written modes of meaning. In J. Webster (Ed). *On Grammar: Volume 1 in the Collected Works of M. A. K. Halliday*. London and New York: Continuum, 323–351.

Halliday, M. A. K. (2002/1961) Categories of the theory of grammar. In J. Webster (Ed). *On Grammar: Volume 1 in the Collected Works of M. A. K. Halliday*. London and New York: Continuum, 37–94.

Halliday, M. A. K. (1985a) *Spoken and written language*. Victoria: Deakin University Press.

Halliday, M. A. K. (1985b) *An introduction to functional grammar*. London: Edward Arnold.

Halliday, M. A. K. (1981) Mark these linguists. *The English Magazine*. Summer 1981.

Halliday, M. A. K. (1978) *Language as a social semiotic*. London: Edward Arnold.

Halliday, M. A. K. (1975) *Learning how to mean: Explorations in the development of language*. London: Edward Arnold.

Halliday, M. A. K. (1961) Categories of the theory of grammar. In Halliday, M. A. K. (Ed). (2002) *On grammar*. London: and New York: Continuum (Edited by J. Webster).

Halliday, M. A. K. and Hasan, R. (1989) *Language, context and text: Aspects of language in a social semiotic perspective*. Oxford: Oxford University Press.

Halliday, M. A. K. and Hasan, R. (1985) *Language, context and text: Aspects of language in a social semiotic perspective*. Geelong, Victoria: Deakin University.

Halliday, M. A. K. and Hasan, R. (1976) *Cohesion in English*. London: Longman.

Halliday, M. A. K. and Martin, J. R. (1993) *Writing science: Literacy and discursive power*. London and Washington, DC: The Falmer Press.

Halliday, M. A. K. and Matthiessen, C. M. M. (2014) *Halliday's introduction to functional grammar* (4th edition). London and New York: Routledge.

Halliday, M. A. K. and Matthiessen, C. M. M. (1999a) *Construing experience through meaning: A language based approach to cognition*. London: and New York: Continuum.

Halliday, M. A. K. and Matthiessen, C. M. M. (1999b) *An introduction to functional grammar* (3rd Edition). London: Arnold.

Hamilton, M., Barton, D. and Ivanič, R. (Eds). (1994) *Worlds of literacy*. Clevedon: Multilingual Matters.

Hamilton, M., Macrae, C. and Tett, L. (2001) Powerful literacies: The policy context. In J. Crowther, M. Hamilton and L. Tett (Eds). *Powerful literacies*. Leicester: National Institute of Adult Continuing Education (niace), 23–42.

Hammond, J. (Ed). (2001) *Scaffolding: Teaching and learning in language and literacy education*. Newtown, NSW: Primary English Teaching Association.

Hammond, J. and Gibbons, P. (2005) Putting scaffolding to work: The contribution of scaffolding in articulating ESL education. *Prospect* Vol. 20 No. 1, 6–30.

Hammond, J. and Gibbons, P. (2001) What is scaffolding? In J. Hammond (Ed). *Scaffolding: Teaching and learning in language and literacy education*. Sydney: Primary English Teaching Association, 1–14.

Hammond, J. and Miller, J. (Eds). (2015) *Classrooms of possibility: Supporting at-risk EAL students*. Newtown, NSW: Primary English Teaching Association.

Hancock, C. and Kolln, M. (2010) Blowin' in the wind: English grammar in United States schools. In T' Locke (Ed). *Beyond the grammar wars: A resource for teachers and students on developing language knowledge in the English/literacy classroom.* New York and London: Routledge, 21–37.

Harper, R. (2013) From principles to practice: Implementing an English language proficiency model at UniSA. *Journal of Academic Language and Learning* Vol. 7 No. 2, 150–164.

Harris, M. and Evans, J. (1991) Mathematics and workplace research. In M. Harris (Ed). *Schools, mathematics and work.* London: Falmer, London, 123–131.

Harris, W. V. (1989) *Ancient literacy.* Cambridge, MA: Harvard University Press.

Harris, R. (1986) *The origin of writing.* London: Duckworth.

Harste, J. C. and Short, K. G. (1996) Ken and Yetta Goodman: Exploring the roots of whole language. *Language arts* Vol. 73 No. 7, 508–513.

Hasan, R. (2005/1995) On the social conditions of semiotic mediation: The genesis of mind in society. In J. J. Webster (Ed). *Language, society and consciousness: The collected works of Ruqaiya Hasan Volume 1.* London: Equinox, 106–129.

Hasan, R. (2005a) Bernstein: an exceptional 1924–2000. In J. J. Webster (Ed). *Language, society and consciousness: The collected works of Ruqaiya Hasan Volume 1.* London: Equinox, pp. 21–47.

Hasan, R. (2005b). Semiotic mediation and three exotropic theories: Vygotsky, Halliday and Bernstein. In J. J. Webster (Ed). *Language, society and consciousness: The collected works of Ruqaiya Hasan Volume 1.* London: Equinox, 130–156.

Hasan, R. (2005c) *Language, society and consciousness: The collected works of Ruqaiya Hasan* Volume 1. London: Equinox (Edited by J. J. Webster).

Hasan, R. (2004) The concept of semiotic mediation: Perspectives from Bernstein's sociology. In J. Muller, B. Davies and A. Morais (Eds), *Reading Bernstein Researching Bernstein.* London and New York: RoutledgeFalmer, 30–43.

Hasan, R. (1996a) Literacy, everyday talk and society. In R. Hasan and G. Williams (Eds). *Literacy in society.* London and New York: Longman, 377–424.

Hasan, R. (1996b) The ontogenesis of ideology: An interpretation of mother-child talk. In C. Cloran, D. Butt and G. Williams (Eds). *Ways of saying, ways of meaning.* London: Cassell, 133–151.

Hasan, R. (1996c) *Ways of saying: Ways of meaning: Selected papers of Ruqaiya Hasan.* London and New York: Cassell (Edited by C. Cloran, D. Butt and G. Williams).

Hasan, R. (1985) *Linguistics, language and verbal art.* Burwood, Victoria: Deakin University.

Hasan, R. and Cloran, C. (1990) A sociolinguistic interpretation of everyday talk between mothers and children. In M. A. K. Halliday, J. Gibbons and H. Nicholas (Eds). *Learning, keeping and using language. Vol. 1: Selected papers from the 8th World Congress in Applied Linguistics.* Amsterdam: John Benjamins, 67–100.

Hasan, R. and Williams, G. (Eds). (1996) *Literacy in society.* London and New York: Longman.

Hattie, J. (2009) *Visible learning: a synthesis of over 800 met-analyses relating to achievement.* London and New York: Routledge.

Hattie, J. H., Rogers, J. and Swaminathan, H. (2014) The role of meta-analysis in educational research. In A. D. Reid, E. P. Hart and M. A. Peters (Eds). *A companion to research in education.* New York and London: Springer, pp. 197–207.

Heath, S. B. (1983) *Ways with words: Language, life and work in communities and classrooms*. Cambridge: Cambridge University Press.

Hempenstall, K. (2006) What does evidence-based practice in education mean? *Australian Journal of Learning Disabilities* Vol. 11 No. 2, 83–92.

Hensher, P. (2012) *The missing ink: The lost art of handwriting and why it still matters*. London: Macmillan.

Herrington, M. H. and Macken-Horarik, M. (2015) Linguistically informed teaching of spelling: Toward a relational approach. *Australian Journal of language and literacy.*

Herrington, J., McKenney, S., Reeves, T. and Oliver, R. (2007) *Design-based research and doctoral students: Guidelines for preparing a dissertation proposal* – Edith Cowan University Research Online. Available at: http://ro.ecu.edu.au

Herrington, J., Reeves, T. C. and Oliver, R. (2010) *A guide to authentic e-learning*. London and New York: Routledge.

Hilden, K. and Pressley, M. (2004) Verbal protocols of reading. In N. K. Duke and M. H. Mallette (Eds). *Literacy research methodologies*. New York and London: The Guildford Press, pp. 427–440.

Hill, S., Comber, B., Louden, W., Rivalland, J. and Reid, J. (2002) *100 children turn 10: A longitudinal study of literacy development from the year prior to school to the first four years of school*. Canberra, ACT: Commonwealth of Australia.

Holmes, N. (1993) *The best in diagrammatic graphics*. Switzerland: Rotovision.

Hood, S. (2010) *Appraising research: Evaluation in academic writing*. Basingstoke and New York: Palgrave Macmillan.

Hood, S. and Forey, G. (2005) Introducing a conference paper: Getting interpersonal with your audience. *Journal of English for Academic Purposes* Vol. 4 No. 4, October 2005, 291–306.

Hood, S., Solomon, N. and Burns, A. (1996) *Focus on reading*. Sydney: Macquarie University.

Honan, E. (2004) Using the four resources model as a map of possible practices. In A. Healy and E. Honan (Eds). *Text next: New resources for literacy learning*. Newtown, NSW: Primary English Teaching Association.

Hornberger, N. (2013) Biliteracy continuua. In M. Hawkins (Ed). *Framing languages and literacies: Socially situated views and perspectives*. New York: Routledge, 149–168.

Houston, S. D. (2004) Overture. In Houston, S. D. (Ed). *The first writing: Script invention as history and process*. Cambridge: Cambridge University Press, 3–15.

Howard-Jones, P. (2014) *Neuroscience and education: A review of educational interventions and approaches informed by neuroscience*. Millbank: Education Endowment Foundation (EEF).

Howell, A. (2012) The silent voice in the NAPLAN debate: Exploring children's lived experiences of the tests. Paper presented at the Joint AARE/APERA Conference, Sydney 2012. Available at: http://www.aare.edu.au/data/publications/2012/Howell12.pdf – accessed 1.4.2015.

Huey, E. B. (1908) *The psychology and pedagogy of reading*. New York: Macmillan.

Hull, G. (1995) Controlling literacy: The place of skills in 'high performance' work. *Critical forum* Vol. 3 No. 2/3, 3–26.

Humphrey, S. (2013) And the word became text: A 4x4 toolkit for scaffolding writing in secondary English. *English in Australia* Vol. 48 No. 1, 46–55.

Humphrey, S. (2010) Enacting rhetoric in the civic domain. *English in Australia* Vol. 45 No. 3, 9–20.

Humphrey, S. (2006) 'Getting the reader on side': Exploring adolescent online political discourse. *E-learning* Vol. 3. No. 2, 143–157.

Humphrey, S., Droga, L. and Feez, S. (2012) *Grammar and meaning*. Newtown, NSW: Primary English Teaching Association of Australia.

Humphrey, S. and Robinson, S. (2012) Using a 4 x 4 framework for whole school literacy development. In J. Knox (Ed). *Papers from the 39th International Systemic Functional Congress*, 81–86.

Hyland, K. (2014) English for academic purposes. In C. Leung and B. Street (Eds). *The Routledge Handbook of English Language Studies*. London: Routledge, 392–404.

Hyland, K. (2009) *Academic discourse*. London and New York: Continuum.

Hyland, K. (2002) *Teaching and researching writing*. London and New York: Longman.

Hyland, K. and Paltridge, B. (2011) *The Bloomsbury companion to discourse analysis*. London and New York: Bloomsbury

Hynd-Shanahan, C. (2013) What does it take? The challenge of disciplinary literacy. *Journal of Adolescent & Adult Literacy* Vol. 57 No. 2, 93–98.

Hyon, S. (1996) Genre in three traditions: implications for ESL. *TESOL Quarterly* Vol. 30 No. 4, 693–722.

Itard, J. (1972/1801) On the first developments of the young savage of Averyon (1799, printed 1801). In L. Malson and J. Itard (1972/1964) *Wolf children; The Wild Boy of Aveyron*. London: NLB, 91–140.

James, K. (2012) The effects of handwriting experience on functional brain development in pre-literate children. *Trends in neuroscience and education* Vol. 1 No. 1, December 2012, 32–42.

Janks, H. (2010) 'Language as a system of meaning potential': The reading and design of verbal texts. In T. Locke (Ed). *Beyond the grammar wars: A resource for teachers and students on developing language knowledge in the English/literacy classroom*. New York and London: Routledge, 152–169.

Jaworski, A. & Coupland, N. (Eds). (2006) *The discourse reader (2nd edition)*. London and New York: Routledge.

Jensen, A. R. (1969) Review of Pygmalion in the classroom by R. Rosenthal and Lenore Jacobson. American Scientist, 51, 44A–45A.

Jewitt, C., Kress, G., Ogborn, J. and Tsatsarelis, C. (2001) Exploring learning through visual, actional and linguistic communication: The multimodal environment of a science classroom. *Educational review* Vol. 53 No. 1, 5–18.

Johns, A. M. (Ed). (2002) *Genre in the classroom: Multiple perspectives*. London and New York: Routledge.

Jones, O. (2012) *Chavs: The demonisation of the working class*. London and New York: Verso.

Jones, R. H. and Lock, G. (2011) *Functional grammar in the ESL classroom*. Basingstoke and Hampshire: Palgrave Macmillan.

Jones, S. M., Myhill, D. A. and Bailey, T. C. (2013) Grammar for writing? An investigation into the effect of contextualised grammar teaching on student writing. *Reading and writing online* Vol. 26, 1241–1263.

Joyce, H. (1992) *Workplace texts in the language classroom*. Sydney: NSW AMES.

Jussim, L., Smith, A., Madon, S., and Palumbo, P. (1998) Teacher expectations. In J. E. Brophy (Ed). *Advances in research on teaching: Expectations in the classroom Vol. 7*. Greenwich, CT: JAI Press, 1–48.

Kalantzis, M. and Cope, B. (2012) *Literacies*. New York: Cambridge University Press.

Kemmis, S. and McTaggart, R. (1988) *The action research planner* (3rd Edition). Melbourne: Deakin University Press.

Kemmis, S., McTaggart, R. and Nixon, R. (2014) *The action research planner: Doing critical participatory action research*. New York: Springer.

Kincheloe, J. L. (2003) *Teachers as researchers: Qualitative enquiry as a path to empowerment* (2nd Edition). London: Routledge Falmer.

Klein, S. R. (2012) *Action research methods: Plain and simple*. London: Palgrave Macmillan.

Knight, I. F. (1968) *The geometric spirit: The Abbé de Condillac and the French Enlightenment*. New Haven and London: Yale University Press.

Koop, C. and Rose, D. (2008) Reading to learn in Murdi Paaki: Changing outcomes for Indigenous students. *Literacy Learning: The Middle Years. Journal of the Australian Literacy Educators' Association* Vol. 16 No. 1, 41–46.

Korner, H., McInnes, D. and Rose, D. (2007) *Science literacy*. Sydney: NSW AMES.

Kramsch, C. (2009). The Multilingual Subject. What language learners say about their experience and why it matters. Oxford: Oxford University Press.

Kress, G. (2003) *Literacy in the new media age*. London: Routledge.

Kress, G. and van Leeuwen, T. (1996 – 1st Edition/2006 – 2nd Edition) *Reading images: The grammar of visual design*. London and New York: Routledge.

Labov, W. (1972) *Language in the inner city: Studies in Black English vernacular*. Philadelphia: University of Pennsylvania Press.

Lane, H. (1976) *The wild boy of Aveyron*. Cambridge, MA: Harvard University Press.

Lankshear, C. and Knobel, M. (2011) *New Literacies* (3rd edition). Maidenhead: Open University Press

Lanskshear, C. 1997. Language and the new capitalism. *The International Journal of Inclusive Education* Vol. 1 No. 4, 309–321.

Lave, J. (1988) *Cognition in practice*. Cambridge: Cambridge University Press.

Lemke, J. (1998) Multiplying meaning: Visual and verbal semiotics in scientific text. In J. R. Martin and R. Veel (Eds). *Reading science: Critical and functional perspectives on discourses of science*. London: Routledge, 87–113.

Lenhart, A., Arafeh, S., Smith, A. and Macgill, A. R. (2008) *Writing, technology and teens*. [Report] Washington, DC: PEW Internet and American Life Project & The National Commission on Writing.

Lévi -Strauss, C. (1962) *The savage mind*. London: Weidenfeld and Nicolson.

Liddicoat, A., Papademtre, L., Scarino, A. and Kohler, M. (2003) *Report on intercultural language learning*. Canberra: DEST.

Lightbown, P. M. and Spada, N. (2013) *How languages are learned* (4th edition). Oxford: Oxford University Press.

Lillard, A. S. and Else-Quest, N. (2006) Evaluating Montessori education. *Science* Vol. 313 No. 29, September 2006, 1893–1894.

Limage, L. (2005) The growth of literacy in historic perspective: Clarifying the role of formal schooling and adult learning opportunities. Paper commissioned for the *EFA Global Monitoring Report 2006, Literacy for Life*. Available at: http://unesdoc.unesco.org/images/0014/001460/146061e.pdf

Lo Bianco, J. and Freebody, P. (1997) *Australian literacies: Informing national policy on literacy education*. Canberra: Language Australia.

Locke, T. (Ed). (2010) *Beyond the grammar wars: A resource for teachers and students on developing language knowledge in the English/literacy classroom*. New York and London: Routledge.

Love, K., Sandiford, C., Macken-Horarik, M. and Unsworth, L. (2014) from 'bored witless' to 'rhetorical nous': Teacher orientation to knowledge about language and strengthening student persuasive writing. *English in Australia* Vol. 49 No. 3, 43–56.

Luke, A. (2011) Generalising across borders: Policy and the limits of educational science. *Educational Researcher* Vol. 40 No. 8, 367–377.

Luke, A. (2004) Teaching after the market: From commodity to cosmopolitan. *Teachers College Record* Vol. 106 No. 7, 1422–1443

Luke, A. (1996) Genres of power? Literacy education and the production of capital. In R. Hasan and G. Williams (Eds) *Literacy in Society*. London: Longman, 308–338.

Luke, A., Freebody, P. and Land, R. (2000) *Literate future: Report of the literacy review for Queensland state schools*. Queensland: Department of Education.

Luke, A. and Woods, A. F. (2008) Accountability as testing: Are there lessons about assessment and outcomes to be learnt from No Child Left Behind? *Literacy Learning: The Middle Years* Vol. 16 No. 3, 11–19.

Luria, A. R. (1973) *The working brain*. New York: Basic Books.

Luria, A. R. (1959) The directive function of speech in development and dissolution. *Word* Vol. 15 No. 3 December 1959, pp. 341–464.

Lynch, D. (2010) Enhancing literacy education for refugee children. In F. Christie and A. Simpson (Eds). *Literacy and social responsibility: Multiple perspectives*. London and Oakville, CT: Equinox, 116–129.

Macken-Horarik, M. (2012) Why school English needs a 'good enough' grammatics (and not more grammar). *Changing English: Studies in Culture and Education*, Vol. 19 No. 2, 179–194.

Macken-Horarik, M. (2011) Building a knowledge structure for English: Reflections on the challenge of coherence, cumulative learning, portability and face validity. *Australian journal of education* Vol. 55 No. 3, 197–213.

Macken-Horarik, M. (1996) Literacy and learning across the curriculum: Towards a model of register for secondary school teachers. In R. Hasan and G. Williams (Eds). *Literacy in society*. London and New York: Longman, 232–278.

Macken-Horarik, M. and Adoniou, M. (2008) Genre and register in multiliteracies. In B. Spolsky and F. M. Hult (Eds). *The handbook of educational linguistics*. Oxford: Blackwell Publishing Ltd, pp. 367–382.

Macken-Horarik, M., Love, K. and Unsworth, L. (2011) A grammatics 'good enough' for school English in the 21st century: Four challenges in realising the potential. *Australian journal of language and literacy* Vol. 34 No. 1, 9–23.

MacNaught, L., Maton, K., Martin, J. R. and Matruglio, E. (2013) Jointly constructing semantic waves: Implications for teacher training. *Linguistics and education* Vol. 24, 50–63.

Malinowski, B. (1922) *Argonauts of the Western Pacific: An account of native enterprise and adventure in the Archipelagos of Melanesian New Guinea*. London: Routledge and Kegan Paul.

Marion, J. S. and Crowder, J. W. (2013) *Visual research: A concise introduction to thinking visually*. London and New York: Bloomsbury.

Martin, J. R. (2007) Construing knowledge: A functional linguistic perspective. In Christie, F. and Martin, J. R. (Eds). *Language, knowledge and pedagogy*. London and New York: Continuum, pp. 34–64.

Martin, J. R. (1999) Mentoring semogenesis: 'genre-based' literacy pedagogy. In F. Christie (Ed). *Pedagogy and the shaping of consciousness: Linguistic and social processes*. London and New York: Cassell, 123–155.

Martin, J. R. (1993a) Literacy in science: Learning to handle texts as technology. In Halliday, M. A. K. and Martin, J. R. (Eds). *Writing science: Literacy and discursive power*. London and Washington, DC: The Falmer Press, p. 166–202.

Martin, J. R. (1993b) Life as a noun: Arresting the universe in Science and the Humanities. In Halliday, M. A. K. and Martin, J. R. (Eds). *Writing science: Literacy and discursive power*. London and Washington, DC: The Falmer Press, pp. 221–267.

Martin, J. R. (2001) Language, register and genre. In A. Burns and C. Coffin (Eds). Analysing English in a Global Context: A Reader. London and New York: Routledge, 149–166.

Martin, J. R. and Rose, D. (2008) *Genre relations: Mapping culture*. London: Equinox.

Martin, J. R. and Veel, R. (Eds). (1998) *Reading science: Critical and functional perspectives on discourses of science*. London: Routledge.

Martin, J. R. and White, P. R. R. (2005) *The language of evaluation: Appraisal in English*. New York and London: Palgrave Macmillan.

Marvasti, A. B. (2004) *Qualitative research in sociology: An introduction*. London: Sage Publications.

Maton, K. (2014) *Knowledge and knowers: Towards a realist sociology of education*. London and New York: Routledge.

Matruglio, E. (2015) *Objectivity and critique through ENGAGEMENT: The creation of historical perspectives*. Paper presented at the Appraisal Symposium, February 2015, University of New South Wales.

McArthur, T. (2003) *Concise Oxford dictionary of the English language* (Online version). Oxford University Press.

McDonald, L. (2013) *A literature companion for teachers*. Newtown, NSW: Primary English Teaching Association of Australia.

McNiff, J. (1988) *Action research: Principles and practice*. London: Routledge.

McWhorter, J. (2013) Is texting killing the English language? *Time* April 25 2013. Available at: http://ideas.time.com/2013/04/25/is-texting-killing-the-english-language – accessed 29.3.2015.

Meakins, F. (2014) The monolingual mindset: TEDxSouthBankWomen. Availabe at: https://www.youtube.com/watch?v=ISpQasr4He0

Meek, M. (1991) *On being literate*. London: The Bodley Head, 70.

Meiers, M. and Khoo, S. T. (2006) Literacy in the first three years of school: A longitudinal investigation. *Australian journal of language and literacy* Vol. 29 No. 3, 252–267.

Meisels, S. J. (2007) Accountability in early childhood: No easy answers. In R. C. Pianta, M. J. Cox and K. Snow (Eds). *School readiness, early learning, and the transition to kindergarten*. Baltimore: Paul H. Brookes, 31–48.

Mendelovits, J. (2014) *Adult literacy and numeracy: What's the story?* Available at: http://rd.acer.edu.au/article/adult-literacy-and-numeracy-whats-the-story – accessed 25.4.2015.

Menken, K. (2013) Emergent bilingual students in secondary school: Along the academic language and literacy continuum. *Language Teaching* Vol. 46, 438–476.

Merriam, S. B. (1985) The case study in educational research: A review of selected literature. *Journal of Educational Thought* Vol. 19 No.3, 204–217 – accessed at http://www.jstor.org – 10.3.2015

Michaels, S. (1981) "Sharing time": Children's narrative styles and differential access to literacy. *Language in Society* Vol. 10, 423–442.

Michaels, S. and Cazden, C. (1986) Teacher/child collaboration as oral preparation for literacy. In B. Schieffelin (Ed). *Acquisition of literacy: Ethnographic perspectives.* Norwood, NJ: Ablex, 132–154.

Michaels, S. and Collins, J. (1984) Oral discourse styles: Classroom interaction and the acquisition of literacy. In D. Tannen (Ed). *Coherence in spoken and written discourse.* Norwood, NJ: Ablex, 219–244.

Michaels, S. and Cook-Gumperz, J. (1979) A study of sharing time with first-grade students: Discourse narratives in the classroom. In *Proceedings of the Fifth Annual Meetings of the Berkeley Linguistics Society*, University of California, Berkeley, 647–660.

Miller, J. (2015) Classroom strategies for teachers and EAL learners. In J. Hammond and J. Miller (Eds). *Classrooms of possibility: Supporting at-risk EAL students.* Newtown NSW: Primary English Teaching Association, p. 109–120.

Miller, J. (2006) Clash of language, clash of cultures. In M. Stroinska and V. Cechetto (Eds). *International classroom: Challenging the notion.* Berlin: Peter Lang, 43–51.

Mills, K. (2005) Deconstructing binary oppositions in literacy discourse and pedagogy. *Australian Journal of Language and Literacy* Vol. 28 No. 1, 67–82

Mills, A. J., Durepos, G. and Wiebe, E. (Eds). (2010) *Encyclopedia of case study research.* Thousand Oaks, CA: Sage Publications

Mo, Y, G., Kopke, R. A., Hawkins, L. K., Troia, G. A. and Olinghouse, N. G. (2014) The Neglected 'R' in a time of common core. *Reading Teacher* Vol. 67 No. 6, 445–453.

Moore, S. and Burns, A. (2008) Non-English-speaking background accountants and professional communication. *Prospect* Vol. 23 No. 2, 47–45

More, M. (1859) *Mendip Annals.* London: J. Nisbet and Co.

Morris, D. (2015) Preventing early reading failure: An argument. *The Reading teacher* Vol. 68No. 7, 502–509.

Morris, D., Bloodgood, J. W., Lomax, R. G. and Perney, J. (2003) Developmental steps in learning to read: A longitudinal study in kindergarten and first grade. *Reading Research Quarterly* Vol. 38 No. 3, 302–328.

Morriscoe, J. (2014) *Literacy changes lives 2014: A new perspective on health, employment and crime.* London: National Literacy Trust.

Murcia, K. and Powell, B. (n.d.). Action research and the professional development of teachers: The Waikiki Primary School experience. Available at: http://www.murdoch.edu.au/School-of-Education – accessed 17.3.2015.

Murphy, J. J. (Ed). (2012) *A short history of writing instruction: From Ancient Greece to contemporary America.* New York: Routledge.

Myhill, D. (2012) Editorial. *English in education* (Special Issue: Writing) Vol. 46 No. 1, 1–5.

Myhill, D. (2010) Ways of knowing: Grammar as a tool for developing writing. In T. Locke (Ed). *Beyond the grammar wars: A resource for teachers and students on developing language knowledge in the English/literacy classroom.* New York: Routledge, 129–148.

Myhill, D., Jones, S., Watson, A., and Lines, H. (2013) Playful explicitness with grammar: A pedagogy for writing. *Literacy* Vol. 47 No. 2, 103–111.

Myhill, D. A., Jones, S. M., Lines, H. and Watson, A. (2012) Re-thinking grammar: The impact of embedded grammar teaching on students' writing and student's metalinguistic understanding. *Research Papers in Education* Vol. 27 No. 2, April 2012, 139–166.

Myhill, D. and Watson, A. (2014) The role of grammar in the writing curriculum: A review of the literature. *Child Language Teaching and Therapy* Vol. 30 No. 1, 41–62.

National Commission on Writing for America's Families, Schools, and Colleges (April 2003). *The neglected R: The need for a writing revolution.* New York: College Entrance Examination Board.

National Early Literacy Panel (2008) *Developing early literacy: Report of National Early Literacy Panel.* Washington, DC: National Institute for Literacy.

National Reading Panel (2000) Teaching children to read: An evidence-based assessment of the scientific research literature on reading and its implications for reading instruction. Available at: www.nationalreadingpanel.org

Nesi, H. and Gardener, S. (2012) *Genres across the disciplines: Student writing in higher education.* Cambridge: Cambridge University Press.

Neumann, S. B. and Dickinson, D. K. (2011) *Handbook of early literacy research – Volume 3.* New York and London: The Guilford Press.

New London Group (2000) A pedagogy of multiliteracies: Designing social futures. In B. Cope and M. Kalantzis (Eds). *Multiliteracies: Literacy learning and the design of social futures.* Melbourne: Macmillan, pp. 9–36.

NSW Department of Education and Communities (2013) *Developing numerate students: A guide for early action for success.* Available at: http://www.earlyaction-forsuccess.com.au/mathsblock/MathsblockEAfS.pdf – accessed 5.4.2015

NSW Department of Education and Training (2010) *Action research in education: Guidelines* (2nd Edition). Sydney: NSW Department of Education and Training. Available at: https://www.det.nsw.edu.au/proflearn/docs/pdf/actreguide.pdf

NSW Independent Commission Against Corruption (2015) *Learning the hard way: Managing corruption risks associated with international students at universities in NSW.* Sydney: NSW Independent Commission Against Corruption.

Nunan, D. (2015) *Teaching English to speakers of other languages: An introduction.* Routledge, New York and London.

Nunes, T., Bryant, P., Hurry, J. and Pretzlik, U. (2006) Why morphemes are useful in primary school literacy. *Teaching and learning research programme* Vol. 4. London: Institute of Education.

Nunes, T., Schliemann, A. D. and Carraher, D. W. (1993) *Street mathematics and school mathematics.* Cambridge: Cambridge University Press.

O'Halloran, K. (2006) (Ed). *Multimodal discourse analysis: Systemic functional perspectives.* London and New York: Continuum.

O'Halloran, K. L. (2005) *Mathematical discourse: Language, symbolism and visual images.* London and New York: Continuum (reprinted 2008).

O'Halloran, K. L. & Lim, F. V. (2011) Dimensioner af multimodal Literacy. *Viden om Læsning.* Number 10, September 2011, pp. 14–21. Nationalt Videncenter for Laesning: Denmark

Olson, D. (2009) The history of writing. In R. Beard, D. Myhill, M. Nystrand and J. Riley (Eds). *The Sage handbook of writing development*. London: Sage Publications Ltd, 6–17.

Olson, D. R. (1994) *The world on paper: The conceptual and cognitive implications of writing and reading*. Cambridge: Cambridge University Press.

Olson, R. K., Keenan, J. M., Byrne, B. and Samuelsson, S. (2014) Why do children differ in their development of reading and related skills? *Scientific Studies of Reading* Vol. 18 No. 1, 38–54.

Ortega, L. (2013) SLA for the 21st century: Disciplinary progress, transdisciplinary relevance and the bi/multilingual turn. *Language Learning* Vol. 63, 1–24.

O'Toole, M. (2011) *The language of displayed art* (2nd Edition). London and New York: Routledge.

Owens, R. G. (1982) Methodological rigour in naturalistic inquiry: Some issues and answers. *Education Administration Quarterly* Vol. 18 No. 2, 1–21.

Pahl, K. and Rowsell, J. (2006) *Travel notes from the New Literacy studies: Instances of practice*. Clevedon: Multilingual Matters Ltd.

Painter, C. (2001) Understanding genre and register: Implications for teaching. In A. Burns and C. Coffin (Eds). *Analysing English in a global context: A reader*. London and New York: Routledge, 167–180.

Painter, C. (1999a) *Learning through language in early childhood*. London and New York: Cassell.

Painter, C. (1999b) Preparing for school: Developing a semantic style for educational knowledge. In F. Christie (Ed). *Pedagogy and the shaping of consciousness*. London: Cassell, 66–87.

Painter, C. (1984) *Into the mother tongue*. London: Pinter.

Painter, C., Derewianka, B. and Torr, J. (2007) From microfunction to metaphor: learning language and learning through language. In R. Hasan, C. Matthiessen and J. Webster (Eds). *Continuing discourse on language: A functional perspective, Volume 2*. London: Equinox, 561–586.

Painter, C., Martin, J. R. and Unsworth, L. (2013) *Reading visual narratives: Image analysis of children's picture books*. Sheffield: Equinox.

Palinscar, A. S. and Schleppegrell, M. J. (2014) Focusing on language and meaning while learning with text. *TESOL Quarterly* Vol. 48 No. 3, 616–623.

Palincsar, A. S. and Schutz, K. M. (2011) Reconnecting strategy instruction with its theoretical roots. *Theory into Practice* Vol. 50 No. 2, 85–92.

Paltridge, B. (2013) Genre and English for specific purposes. In B. Paltridge and S. Starfield (Eds). *The Handbook of English for specific purposes*. Oxford: Wiley-Blackwell, pp. 347–366.

Paltridge, B., Harbon, L., Hirsh, D., Phakiti, A., Shen, H., Stevenson, M. and Woodrow, L. (2009) *Teaching academic writing*. Ann Arbor, MI: University of Michigan Press.

Paltridge, B. and Phakiti, A. (2010) *Continuum companion to research methods in applied linguistics*. London: Continuum.

Paltridge, B. and Starfield, S. (Eds). (2013) *The handbook of English for specific purposes*. Oxford: Wiley-Blackwell.

Paris, S. G. (2005) Reinterpreting the development of reading skills. *Reading Research Quarterly* Vol. 40 No. 2, 184–202.

Paris, S. G. and Luo, S. W. (2010) Confounded statistical analyses hinder interpretation of the NELP report. *Educational Researcher* Vol. 39, 316–322.

Parkin, R. W. (2006) Expanding Indigenous identity in the South Australian Accelerated Litercay Program: Participants in academic and literate discourse. *TESOL in Context Series 'S': Special Edition*, 104–116.

Paul, R. W. (1993) *Critical thinking: What every person needs to survive in a rapidly changing world*. Tomales, CA: Foundation for Critical Thinking.

Pearson, D. P. and Gallagher, M. C. (1983) The instruction of reading comprehension. *Contemporary Educational Psychology*, Vol. 8 No. 2, 317–344.

Pegg, J. (2013) Building the realities of working memory and neural functioning into planning instruction and teaching. *How the brain learns: What lessons are there for teaching?* Conference Proceedings. Camberwell, Victoria: Australian Council for Educational Research, 81–87.

Peters, P. (1995) *Australian English Style Guide*. Melbourne: Cambridge University Press.

Piaget, J. (1970) *Science of education and the psychology of the child*. Harmondsworth, Middlesex: Penguin Books.

Pinker, S. (1996) *Language learnability and language development*. Cambridge, MA: Harvard University Press.

Pinker, S. (1994) *The language instinct: How the mind creates language*. New York: William Morrow.

Prensky, M. (2001) Digital natives, digital immigrants. *On the horizon* Vol. 9 No. 5, October 2001. MCB University Press, 1–6.

Pressley, M. (2002) *Reading instruction that works: The case for balanced teaching* (2nd Edition). New York: Guildford Press.

Purcell-Gates, V. (2013) Literacy worlds of children of migrant farmworker communities participating in a Migrant Head Start Program. *Research in the teaching of English* Vol. 48 No. 1, 68–97.

Purcell-Gates, V. (2011) Epistemological tensions in reading research and a vision for the future. *Reading Research Quarterly* Vol. 47 No. 4, 465–471.

Purcell-Gates, V. (2004) Ethnographic research. In Duke, N. K. and Mallette, M. H. (Eds). *Literacy research methodologies*. New York and London: The Guildford Press, pp. 135–154.

Purcell-Gates, V. (1997) *Other people's words: The cycle of low literacy*. Cambridge, MA: Harvard University Press.

Rassool, N. (2002) Literacy: In search of a paradigm. In J. Solar, J. Wearmouth and G. Reid (Eds). *Contextualising difficulties in literacy development: Exploring politics, ethnicity and ethics*. London: Routledge Falmer, pp. 17–46.

Reder, S. (2011) *The longitudinal study of adult learning: Challenging assumptions*. Research brief. MONtreal" The Centre for Literacy.

Reid, I. (Ed). (1987) *The place of genre in learning: current debates*. Geelong, Victoria: Deakin University Press.

Reinking, D. and Bradley, B. A. (2004) Connecting research and practice using formative and design experiments. In Duke, N. K. and Mallette, M. H. (Eds). *Literacy research methodologies*. New York and London: The Guildford Press, 149–169.

Resnick, D. P. and Resnick, L. B. (1977) The nature of literacy: An historical exploration. *Harvard Educational Review* Vol. 47 No. 3, 370–385

Riley, C. and Randall, K. (2010) The experience of Youth off the Streets. In F. Christie and A. Simpson (Eds). *Literacy and social responsibility: Multiple perspectives*. London and Oakville, CT: Equinox, 87–100

Rist, R. C. (1970) Student social class and teacher expectations: The self-fulfilling prophecy in ghetto education. *Harvard Educational Review* Vol. 40, 411–451.

Robb, K. (1994) *Literacy and Paideia in Ancient Greece*. New York and Oxford: Oxford University Press.

Robertson, J. D. (2004) The possibility and actuality of writing. In S. D. Houston (Ed). *The First Writing: Script invention as history and process*. Cambridge: Cambridge University Press, 16–38.

Rogoff, B. (2003) *The cultural nature of human development*. Oxford and New York: Oxford University Press.

Rose, D. (2008) *Reading to learn: Selecting and analysing texts – Book 5*. Current versions available at: https://www.readingtolearn.com.au

Rose, D. (2007) Towards a reading-based theory of teaching. In L. Barbara and T. Berber Sardinha (Eds). *Proceedings of the 33rd International Systemic Functional Congress Sao Paulo*, 36–77. Available at http://www.pucsp.br/isfc/proceedings/list_of_all_articles.htm

Rose, D. and Martin, J. R. (2012) *Learning to write, reading to learn: Genre, knowledge and pedagogy in the Sydney School*. London: Equinox.

Rose, J. (2006) *Independent review of the teaching of early reading: Final report*. Nottingham: Department for Education and Skills.

Rose, M. (2004) *The mind at work: Valuing the intelligence of the American worker*. New York and London: Penguin Group.

Rosen, M. (2013) *Alphabetical: How every letter tells a story*. London: John Murray.

Rosenthal, R. and Jacobson, L. (1968) *Pygmalion in the classroom*. New York: Holt, Rinehart and Winston.

Rothery, J. (1996) Making changes: Developing an educational linguistics. In R. Hasan and G. Williams (Eds). *Literacy in society*. London: Longman, 86–123.

Rousseau, J. J. (1974/1762) *Émile*. London: Dent (Trans by B. Foxley).

Rowe, K. and National Inquiry into the Teaching of Literacy (Australia). (2005) *Teaching reading*. Available at: http://research.acer.edu.au/tll_misc/5

Rubie-Davies, C. (2009) Teacher expectations and labeling. L. J. Saha and A. G. Dworkin (Eds). In *International handbook of research on teachers and teaching – Springer International Handbooks of Education* Vol. 21. New York: Springer, 695–707.

Russell, B. (1960/1926) *On education*. London: George Allen and Unwin.

Sadovnik, A. (2001) Basil Bernstein (1924–2000). In *Prospect: The quarterly review of comparative education* (Volume XXXI No. 4). Paris: UNESCO International Bureau of Education.

Saenger, P. (1987) Books of hours and reading habits of the later Middle Ages. In R. Chartier (Ed) and L. G. Cochrane (Trans). *The culture of print: Power and the uses of print in early modern Europe*. Princeton, NJ: Princeton University Press.

Sager, R. (2000) *Guiding school improvement with action research*. Association for Supervision and Curriculum Development (ASCD). Available at: http://www.ascd.org

Samuels, S. J. and Farstrup, A. E. (2011) *What research has to say about reading instruction* (4th Edition). Newark, DE: International Reading Association.

Sanacore, J. and Palumbo, A. (2009) Understanding the fourth grade slump: Our point of view. *The educational forum* Vol. 73 No. 1, 67–74.

Saunders, P., Naidoo, Y. and Griffiths, M. (2008) Towards new indicators of disadvantage: deprivation and social exclusion in Australia. *Australian Journal of Social Issues* Vol. 4 No. 2, .

Scarino, A. and Liddicoat, A. (2009) *Teaching and learning languages: A guide.* Carlton South, Vic: Curriculum Corporation.

Schantz, P and Zimmer, J. (2005) Why Johnny can't read: 50 years of controversy. *History of reading news* Vol. 28, No. 2, pp. 1–4. Available at: http://www.history-literacy.org/newsletters/histlit.2005.28.2.pdf.

Schleppegrell, M. (2013) Systemic functional linguistics. In J. P. Gee and M. Handford (Eds). *The Routledge handbook of discourse analysis.* London and New York: Routledge, pp. 21–34.

Schleppegrell, M. (2010) Supporting a 'reading to write' pedagogy with functional grammar. In C. Coffin (Ed). *Language support in EAL contexts. Why systemic functional linguistics?* – Special Issue of *NALDIC Quarterly.* Reading: NALDIC, 26–31.

Schleppegrell, M. (2007) The linguistic challenges of mathematics teaching and learning; a research review. *Reading and writing quarterly* Vol. 23, 139–159.

Schleppegrell, M. J. (2004) *The language of schooling: A functional linguistics perspective.* New Jersey: Lawrence Erlbaum Associates.

Schmandt-Besserat, D. (2004) Writing: Introduction. In B. M. Fagan (Ed). *The Oxford companion to archaeology.* New York: Oxford University Press. http://www.oxfordreference.com.ezproxy.une.edu.au/view/10.1093/acref/9780195076189.001.0001/acref-9780195076189-e-0494?rskey=CzUpXH&result=1.

Scollon, R. and Scollon, S. W. (2003) *Discourses in place: Language in the material world.* London and New York: Routledge.

Scollon, R. and Scollon, S. W. (1981) *Narrative, literacy, and face in interethnic communication.* Norwood, NJ: Ablex.

Scribner, S. and Cole, M. (1981) *The psychology of literacy.* Cambridge, MA: Harvard University Press.

Sears, E. (2002) Reading images. In E. Sears and T. K. Thomas (Eds). *Reading medieval images: The art historian and the object.* Ann Arbor, MI: University of Michigan Press, pp. 1–8.

Séguin, E. (1971/1866) *Idiocy and its treatment by the physiological method.* New York: Augustus M. Kelley.

Serafini, F. (2012) Expanding the four resources model: Reading visual and multimodal texts. *Pedagogies: An International Journal* Vol. 7 No. 2, 150–164.

Shanahan, C. and Shanahan, T. (2014a) Does disciplinary literacy have a place in elementary school? *The Reading Teacher* Vol. 67 No. 8, 636–639.

Shanahan, C. and Shanahan, T. (2014b) Teaching disciplinary literacy to adolescents: Rethinking content-area literacy. *Harvard education review* Vol. 78 No. 1, 40–59.

Sharpe, T. (2001) Scaffolding in action: snapshots from the classroom. In J. Hammond (Ed). *Scaffolding: Teaching and learning in language and literacy education.* Sydney: Primary English Teaching Association, pp. 31–48.

Shohamy, E. (2006) *Language policy: Hidden agendas and new approaches.* Abingdon: Routledge.

Shulman, L. (1986) Those who understand: Knowledge growth in teaching. *Educational researcher,* Vol. 15 No. 2, 4–14.

Simpson, A. and White, S. with Freebody, P. and Comber, B. (2013) *Language, literacy and literature.* Melbourne: Oxford University Press.

Sinclair, J. M. and Coulthard, M. (1975) *Towards an analysis of discourse: The English used by teachers and pupils*. Oxord: Oxford University Press.

Skinner, B. F. (1974) *About behaviorism*. New York: Random House.

Skinner, B. F. (1938) *The behavior of organisms*. New York: Appleton-Century-Crofts.

Smith, F. (1990) *Reading*. Cambridge: Cambridge University Press.

Smith, F. (1973) *Psycholinguistics and reading*. Stamford, CT: Thomson Learning.

Smith, M. K. (2002). 'Hannah More: Sunday schools, education and youth work', *the encyclopedia of informal education*. [http://infed.org/mobi/hannah-more-sunday-schools-education-and-youth-work/. Retrieved: 12.4.2015]

Smith, M. L. (1980) Meta-analysis of research on teacher expectations. *Evaluation in Education* Vol. 4. 53–55.

Smith, N. B. (2002/1986/1965/1934) *American reading instruction* (4th Revised Edition 2002). Newark DE: International Reading Association.

Snow, C. E. (2004) What counts as literacy in early childhood? In K. McCartney and D. Phillips (Eds). *Blackwell handbook of early childhood development*. Maldon, MA: Blackwell Publishing, 274–294.

Snow, C. E., Burns, M. S. and Griffin, P. (Eds). (1998) *Preventing reading difficulties in young children*. Washington, DC: National Academy Press.

Snyder, I. (2008) *The literacy wars: Why teaching children to read and write is a battleground in Australia*. Sydney: Allen and Unwin.

Sokolov, A. (1972) *Inner speech and thought*. New York: Plenum Press.

Soler, J., Wearmouth, J. and Reid, G. (Eds). (2002) *Contextualising difficulties in literacy development: Exploring politics, ethnicity and ethics*. London: Routledge Falmer.

Stahl, N. A. and Hartman, D. K. (2004) Doing historical research in literacy. In N. K. Duke and M. H. Malette (Eds). *Literacy research methodologies*. New York and London: The Guilford Press, 170–196.

Stake, R. (2000) Case studies. In N. Denzin and Y. Lincoln (Eds). *Handbook of qualitative research* (2nd Edition). Thousand Oaks CA: Sage.

Stanovich, K. (1986) Matthew effects in reading: Some consequences of individual differences in the acquisition of literacy *Reading Research Quarterly*. Vol. 21, No. 4, 360–406.

Steiner, C. with Perry, P. (1997) *Achieving emotional literacy*. London: Bloomsbury.

Stenglin, M. (2004) *Packaging curiosities: Towards a grammar of three-dimensional space*. PhD Thesis – University of Sydney.

Street, B. V. (2011) Inequalities in theory and practice: The power to name and define. *International Journal of Educational Development* Vol. 31, 580–586.

Street, B. V. (2003) What's new in New Literacy Studies? Critical approaches to literacy in theory and practice. *Current issues in comparative education* Vol. 5 No. 2, 77–91.

Street, B. V. (2001a) *Literacy and development: Ethnographic perspectives*. London and New York: Routledge.

Street, B. V. (2001b) Contexts for literacy work: the 'new orders' and the new literacy studies'. In J. Crowther, M. Hamilton and L. Tett (Eds). *Powerful literacies*. Leicester, UK: National Institute of Adult Continuing Education (NIACE), pp. 13–22.

Street, B. V. (1984) *Literacy in theory and practice*. Cambridge and New York: Cambridge University Press.

Street, B. V. and Baker, D. (2006) So, what about multimodal numeracies? In K. Pahl and J. Rowsell (Eds). *Travel notes from the New Literacy studies: Instances of practice*. Clevedon: Multilingual Matters Ltd, pp. 219–233.

Stringer, E. T. (2013) *Action research* (4th Edition). London: Sage Publications.

Stubbs, M. (1983) *Discourse analysis*. Chicago: University of Chicago Press.

Swain. M. (2006) Verbal protocols: What does it mean for research to use speaking as a data collection tool? In Chalhoub-Deville, M., Chapelle, C. and Duff, P. (Eds). *Inference and generalisability in applied linguistics: Multiple research perspectives*. Amsterdam: John Benjamins, pp. 97–113.

Swales, J. M. (1990) *Genre analysis*. Cambridge: Cambridge University Press.

Tardy, C. M. (2011) The history and future of genre in second language writing. *Journal of second language writing* Vol. 20, 1–5.

Taverniers, M. (2004) Grammatical metaphors in English. *Moderna Språk* Vol, 98 No. 1, 17–26.

Taylor, C., Wilkie, M. and Baser, J. (2006) *Doing action research: A guide for school support staff*. London: Paul Chapman Publishing Ltd.

Taylor, I. and Taylor, M. M. (2014) *Writing and literacy in Chinese, Korean and Japanese* (Revised edition). Amsterdam: John Benjamins.

The Design-based Research Collective (2003) Design-based research: An emerging paradigm for educational inquiry. *Educational Research* Vol. 32 No. 1 5–8. Available at: http://www.designbasedresearch.org

The Guildford Press Quintilian (2006) *Institutes of oratory*. (Edited by L. Honeycutt) (Trans by J. S. Watson), Available at: http://rhetoric.eserver.org/quintilian – accessed 28.3.2015 (Original work published 1856).

The Royal Society (2011) *Brain Waves Module 2: Neuroscience: Implications for education and lifelong learning*. London: The Royal Society.

Thomas, S. E. (Ed). (2007) *What is the new rhetoric?* Newcastle: Cambridge Scholars Publishing.

Thomas, T. K. (2002) Understanding objects. In E. Sears and T. K. Thomas (Eds). *Reading Medieval images: The art historian and the object*. Ann Arbor, MI: University of Michigan Press, pp. 9–15.

Thompson, G. (2014) *Introduction to functional grammar* (3rd edition). London: Hodder Education.

Thomson, E. A. (2012) *Effective academic writing: An essay-writing handbook for school and university*. Sydney: Phoenix Education.

Thomson, E. A., Sano, M. and de Silva Joyce, H. (in publication) *Mapping genres, mapping culture in Japanese*. Amsterdam: Walter de Gruyter.

Thorndike, R. L. (1968) Review of Rosenthal and Jacobson: *Pygmalion in the classroom. American Educational Research Journal* Vol. 5 No. 4 November 1968, 708–711.

Torr, J. (1997) *From child tongue to mother tongue: A case study of language development in the first two and a half years. Nottingham*: Department of English Studies, University of Nottingham. (*Monographs in Systemic Linguistics 9*).

Tracey, D. H. and Morrow, L. M. (2006) *Lenses on reading: An introduction to theories and models*. New York and London: The Guilford Press.

Trickett, S. and Trafton, J. G. (2009) A primer on verbal protocol analysis. In D. Schmorrow, J. Cohn and D. Nicholson (Eds). *The PSI Handbook of virtual environments for training and education* Vol. 1. Westport, CT: Praeger Security International, 332–346.

Trigger, B. G. (2004) Writing systems: A case study in cultural evolution. In S. D. Houston (Ed). *The first writing: Script invention as history and process*. Cambridge: Cambridge University Press, 39–68.

Trumpener, B. (1997) *Gimme shelter: A resource for literacy and homelessness project.* Ontario: National Literacy Secretariat.

Turbill, J. (2001) A researcher goes to school: The integration of technology into the early literacy curriculum. *Journal of Early Literacy* Vol. 1 No. 3, 255–279.

Uccelli, P. and Snow, C. (2008) A research agenda for educational linguistics. In B. Spolsky and F. M. Hult (Eds). *The handbook of educational linguistics.* Oxford: Blackwell Publishing, pp. 626–642.

UNESCO (2007) *Literacy Initiative for Empowerment (LIFE) 2006–2015: Vision and Strategy Paper* (3rd Edition). Hamburg: UNESCO Institute for Lifelong Learning.

UNESCO (2004) The Plurality of literacy and its implications for policies and programs.*UNESCO Education Sector Position Paper: 13.* 2004.

United Nations High Commission for Refugees (2013) *25 years of global forced displacement.* UNHCR Statistical Yearbook 2013. Available at: http://www.unhcr.org/54cf99109.html – accessed 26.3.2015.

Unsworth, L. (2010) Resourcing multimodal literacy pedagogy toward a description of the meaning-making resources of language–image interaction. In T. Locke (Ed). *Beyond the grammar wars: A resource for teachers and students on developing language knowledge in the English/literacy classroom.* New York and London: Routledge, 277–293.

Unsworth, L. (2001) *Teaching multiliteracies across the curriculum: Changing contexts of text and image on classroom practice.* Buckingham: Open University Press.

Unsworth, L. and Macken-Horarik, M. (2015) Interpretive responses to images in picture books by primary and secondary school students: Exploring curriculum expectations of a 'visual grammatics'. *English in Education* Vol. 49 No. 1, 56–79.

Ur, P. (2012) *A course in English language teaching.* Cambridge: Cambridge University Press.

van Leeuwen, T. (2008) *Discourse and practice: New tools for critical discourse analysis.* Oxford: Oxford University Press.

van Leeuwen, T. (2006) Word and image. In K. Brown (Ed). *Elsevier encyclopaedia of language and linguistics.* Amsterdam: Elsevier, 624–628.

van Leeuwen, T. (1999) *Speech, music, sound.* London: Macmillan.

Veel, R. (1999) Language, knowledge and authority in school mathematics. In F. Christie (Ed). *Pedagogy and the shaping of consciousness.* London and New York: Continuum.

Veel, R. (1997) Learning how to mean – scientifically speaking: Apprenticeship into science discourse in the secondary school. In F. Christie and J. R. Martin (1997) (Eds). *Genre and institutions: Social processes in the workplace and school.* London and Washington: Cassell.

Vellutino, F. and Schatschneider, C. (2004) Experimental and quasi-experimental design in literacy research. In N. K. Duke and M. H. Mallette (2004) *Literacy research methodologies.* New York and London: The Guildford Press.

Vincent, D. (1989) *Literacy and popular culture: England 1750–1914.* Cambridge: Cambridge University Press.

Vinson, T. (2010) The social context of literacy acquisition: Achieving good beginnings. In F. Christie and A. Simpson (Eds). *Literacy and social responsibility: Multiple perspectives.* London and Oakville, CT: Equinox, 71–86.

Vinson, T. (2007) The web of social disadvantage. *Developing Practice (online)* Vol. 19, 56–65.

von Randow, J. (2010) How much language do they need? The dilemma English-medium universities face when enrolling English as an additional language students. *VCELT colcetd esasy on learning and teaching* Vol. III. Available at: http://apps.medialab.uwindsor.ca/ctl/CELT/celtvol3.html – accesssed 30.4.2015.

Vygotsky, L. S. (1994/1929) The problem of the cultural development of the child. In R. Van Der Veer and J. Valsiner (Eds). *The Vygotsky reader*. Oxford and Cambridge: Blackwell, 57–72.

Vygotsky, L. S. (1987) *The collected works of L. S. Vygotsky*. New York: Plenum Press.

Vygotsky, L. S. (1978) *Mind in society: The development of higher psychological processes*. Cambridge, MA: Harvard University Press, (Edited by M. Cole, V. John-Steiner, S. Scribner and E. Souberman).

Vygotsky, L. and Luria, A. (1994/1930) Tool and symbol in child development. In R. van der Veer and J. Valsiner (Eds). *The Vygotsky Reader*. Oxford and Cambridge: Blackwell, 99–174.

Wagner, D. A. (2011) What happened to literacy? Historical and conceptual perspectives on literacy in UNESCO. *International journal of educational development* Vol. 31 No. 3, 319–323.

Walsh. M. (2010) *Multimodal literacy: Researching classroom practice*. Marrickville, NSW: Primary English Teaching Association Australia (PETAA).

Walshe, R. D. (1981) *Every child can write: Learning and teaching written expression in the 1980s*. Sydney: Primary English Teaching Association.

Watson, J. B. (1930) *Behaviourism* (Revised Edition). Chicago: University of Chicago Press.

Weaver, C. (2010) Scaffolding grammar instruction for writers and writing. In T. Locke (Ed). *Beyond the grammar wars: A resource for teachers and students on developing language knowledge in the English/literacy classroom*. New York and London: Routledge, 186–205.

Weekes, T. (2016). Mastering musical meaning: Images as interpretive resources in multimodal music texts. *Visual Communication*.

Weekes, T. (2014) Explaining the business world in HSC extended responses. *Journal of the Economics and Business Educators NSW* Vol. 2, 42–28.

Wells, G. (1994) The complementary contributions of Halliday and Vygotsky to a 'Language-Based Theory of Learning'. *Linguistics and Education* Vol. 6, 41–90.

Wheldall, K. and Beaman, R. (2011) Effective instruction for older low-progress readers: Meeting the needs of indigenous students. In C. Wyatt-Smith, J. Elkins and J. Gunn (Eds). *Multiple perspectives on difficulties in learning literacy and numeracy*. New York: Springer, 255–273.

White, D. (1956) *Books before 5*. New York: Oxford University Press.

Wickert, R. (1989) *No single measure: A survey of Australian adult literacy*. Canberra: Department of Education, Employment and Training.

Widdowson, H. (1990) *Aspects of language teaching*. Oxford: Oxford University Press.

Wignell, P. (n.d.) *Critical literacy: A linguistic perspective*. Melbourne: National Languages and Literacy Institute of Australia.

Williams, G. (2005a) Grammatics in schools. In J. Webster, C. Matthiessen and R. Hasan (Eds). *Continuing discourse on Language*. Volume 1. London: Equinox, pp. 281–310.

Williams, G. (2005b) Semantic variation. In R. Hasan, C. Matthiessen and J. Webster (Eds). *Continuing discourse on language: A functional perspective, Volume 1.* London: Equinox, 457–480.

Williams, G. (2004) Ontogenesis and grammatics: Functions of metalanguage in pedagogical discourse. In G. Williams and A. Lukin (Eds). *The development of language: Functional perspectives on species and individuals.* London and New York: Continuum, pp. 241–268.

Williams, G. (2001) Literacy pedagogy prior to schooling: Relations between social positioning and semantic variation. In A. Morais, I. Neves, B. Davies and H. Daniels (Eds). *Towards a sociology of pedagogy: The contribution of Basil Bernstein to research.* Oxford and New York: Peter Lang, 17–45.

Williams, G. (1999) Grammar as a metasemiotic tool in child literacy development. In C. Ward and W. Renandya (Eds). *Language teaching: New insights for the language teacher Series 40.* Singapore: Regional Language Centre, SEAMO, 89–124.

Williams, G. (1998) Children entering literate worlds: Perspectives from the study of textual practices. In F. Christie and R. Misson (Eds). *Literacy and schooling.* London: Routledge, 40–66.

Winkle-Wagner, R., Hunter, C. A. and Hunderliter Ortloff, D. (Eds). (2013) *Bridging the gap between theory and practice in educational research.* New York: Palgrave Macmillan.

Wood, D., Bruner, J. S. and Ross, G. (1976) The role of tutoring in problem solving. *Journal of Child Psychology and Psychiatry* Vol. 17, 89–100.

Wyatt-Smith, C., Elkins, J. and Gunn, S. (Eds). (2011) *Multiple perspectives on difficulties in literacy and numeracy learning.* Dordrecht, The Netherlands: Springer International.

Wyatt-Smith, C. and Gunn, S. (2007) *Evidence-based research for expert literacy teaching* – Paper No. 12 October 2007. Melbourne: Department of Education and Early Childhood Development.

Xue, Y. and Meisels, S. J. (2004) Early literacy instruction and learning in kindergarten: Evidence from the early childhood longitudinal study – kindergarten class of 1998–1999. *American Educational Research Journal* Vol. 41 No. 1, 191–229.

Yin, R. (1994) *Case study research: Design and methods* (2nd Edition). Thousand Oaks CA: Sage.

Yin, R. K. (1991) Advancing rigorous methodologies: A review of 'towards rigor in reviews of multivocal literatures'. *Review of Educational Research*, Vol. 61, No. 3 299-305

Zevenbergen, R. (2007) Digital natives come to preschool: Implications for early childhood practice. *Contemporary Issue Sin Early Childhood* Vol. 8 No. 1, 19–29.

Zhao, S. (2008) From her world to our world: Making history on a children's website. *Literacy Learning: The Middle Years* Vol. 16 No. 2, 44–52.

Index

CPI Antony Rowe
Chippenham, UK
2017-01-02 11:41